Rural and Regional Futures

I0891023

Agriculture, mining and related rural industries have been central to the development of Australia's economy. This book details the role that the Australian Government has played in the making of rural and regional Australia, particularly since World War II. The book reviews these policies and evaluates them with regards the commitments undertaken by the Government to contribute towards vibrant, rural communities.

Policy areas addressed include agriculture, water, education, welfare and population, natural resource management, resource extraction, Indigenous affairs, localism, rural research and regional innovation, youth affairs and the devolution of regional governance. Overall two distinct policy strategies can be observed: one wherein the government saw its role as part of the entrepreneurial state and a sector wherein government has increasingly taken itself out of industry development, leaving this role to the market. Having considered these strategies and their impacts, the book concludes that policy over the past 40 years has not in fact contributed to a more vibrant, prosperous rural and regional Australia.

Rural and Regional Futures concludes with several chapters looking to the future. One chapter explores what the role of the state can be within a social market economy while the final chapter gives consideration to the initial steps rural communities will need to take to begin the process of revitalisation. While these materials present as a case study of developments in Australia, the policy shift from the Government as entrepreneur to a focus on markets is an international one and as such, the insights offered by this book will have wide appeal.

Anthony Hogan is Chair, Regional Governance and Policy, Institute for Governance and Policy Analysis, at the University of Canberra, Australia.

Michelle Young is with the National Centre for Epidemiology and Public Health, at The Australian National University, Australia.

Routledge advances in regional economics, science and policy

1 **Territorial Patterns of Innovation**
An inquiry on the knowledge economy in European regions
Edited by Roberta Capello and Camilla Lenzi

2 **The Political Economy of City Branding**
Ari-Veikko Anttiroiko

3 **Structural Change, Competitiveness and Industrial Policy**
Painful lessons from the European periphery
Edited by Aurora A.C. Teixeira, Ester Silva and Ricardo Mamede

4 **Airports, Cities and Regions**
Edited by Sven Conventz and Alain Thierstein

5 **Rural and Regional Futures**
Edited by Anthony Hogan and Michelle Young

Rural and Regional Futures

Edited by
Anthony Hogan and
Michelle Young

Routledge
Taylor & Francis Group
LONDON AND NEW YORK

First published 2015 by Routledge

2 Park Square, Milton Park, Abingdon, Oxfordshire OX14 4RN
711 Third Avenue, New York, NY 10017

Routledge is an imprint of the Taylor & Francis Group, an informa business

First issued in paperback 2018

British Library Cataloguing in Publication Data
A catalogue record for this book is available from the British Library

Library of Congress Cataloging in Publication Data
Rural and regional futures / edited by Anthony Hogan and Michelle Young.
pages cm – (Routledge advances in regional economics, science and policy)
Includes bibliographical references and index.
1. Rural development–Australia. 2. Regional planning–Australia.
I. Hogan, Anthony.
HN850.Z9C658 2014
307.1′4120994–dc23 2014011790

ISBN: 978-1-138-02507-3 (hbk)
ISBN: 978-1-138-37926-8 (pbk)

Typeset in Times New Roman
by Wearset Ltd, Boldon, Tyne and Wear

Contents

Figures

Tables

Contributors

Margaret Alston PhD OAM is Professor and Head of Department of Social Work at Monash University where she has also established the Gender, Leadership and Social Sustainability (GLASS) research unit. Prior to commencing at Monash she was Professor of Social Work and Human Services and Director of the Centre for Rural Social Research at Charles Sturt University. She is an Honorary Professor at the University of Sydney and Charles Sturt University. She is a Foundation Fellow for the Australian College of Social Workers and is the current Chair of the Australian Council of Heads of Schools of Social Work. She has published widely in the field of rural gender and rural social issues. She has acted as a gender expert for UN–Habitat in Kenya, the Food and Agricultural Organization in Rome, UNESCO in the Pacific and UNEP in Geneva. She received her Medal of the Order of Australia in 2010 for services to social work and the advancement of women, particularly in rural areas.

Douglas Baker PhD is Professor of Property and Planning in the School of Civil Engineering and the Built Environment at the Queensland University of Technology, Brisbane, Australia. Dr Baker's areas of expertise include land use planning, performance-based measurement, airport management and regional governance. He has worked in the public and private sectors, and prior coming to Australia he was Acting Head of School of Environmental Planning at the University of Northern British Columbia.

Susan Brumby PhD, RN, RM, Dip. Farm M'ment, MHM is Founding Director of the National Centre for Farmer Health, Hamilton and leads five key strategies to improve the health, well-being and safety of farm men and women. She is a Clinical Associate Professor with Deakin University and course director for the Graduate Certificate in Agricultural Health and Medicine. Blending both a theoretical and practical understanding of agriculture her interests are in service delivery, workforce development, research on preventable disease, alcohol, climate adaptation and hearing loss in farmers. She is a member of the National Rural Advisory Council (NRAC), an independent advisory council to the Australian Government.

Lorelle Burton PhD is Professor of Psychology at the University of Southern Queensland. Lorelle has been an invited assessor for national teaching excellence awards and grants and has led numerous national collaborative research projects on student transition. She is an internationally-recognised psychology educator and her current research focus involves leading cross-community collaborations to promote community capacity building and well-being.

Laurie Buys PhD is a Professor in the School of Design, Faculty of Creative Industries at Queensland University of Technology and the Theme Leader for Secure and Resilient Infrastructure within QUT's Institute for Future Environments. She has numerous refereed publications and has led a range of national collaborative research projects focusing on her research interests including: community liveability, consumer energy use, social sustainability and active ageing.

Jen Cleary is the Senior Research Development Manager at the Centre for Regional Engagement (CRE) at the University of South Australia. Her role includes brokering research partnerships between CRE and community, industry and government to develop research projects of relevance to local, regional and national research priorities. Her research interests lie in human and cultural geography, with an emphasis on sustainable development in rural and remote communities. Jen co-chairs the International Rural Network, and most recently was elected Deputy Chair of Regional Development South Australia. Jen is also Chair of the Regional Development Australia Far North SA Board, and is a member of the Outback Communities Authority Board which administers the unincorporated areas of South Australia.

Geoff Cockfield PhD is Professor in Government and Economics at the University of Southern Queensland. His research interests include rural policy and natural resources management policy. He has received Federal government funding to research the socio-economics of expanding agricultural production in Northern Australia and the application of climate information in regional planning. He has jointly edited and contributed to books on Adam Smith, the Australian National Party and drought policy.

Paul Collits PhD is an Adjunct Professor in the School of Business at the University of the Sunshine Coast and an Economic Development Advisor at Gosford City Council in NSW. Previously he has been Director of Research for the Economic Development and Enterprise Collaboration at the University of Southern Queensland's Fraser Coast campus. He has also been a Senior Research Fellow at RMIT University's Hamilton Centre in rural Victoria. He is currently President of the Australian and New Zealand section of the Regional Science Association International (ANZRSAI). He has a 20-year track record in rural and regional development research and policy, including working as a senior government policy adviser, a teaching academic and a research fellow. He has presented and written extensively on such topics as the role of government in regional development, the drivers of regional development, small town decline and survival, community economic development, regional governance, regional planning, innovation and entrepreneurship in rural communities, economic development practice, the creative class and rural youth outmigration

Michael Cuthill PhD is Professor and Research Chair in Regional Community Development at the University of Southern Queensland. Prior to this he was Director of a community research centre at the University of Queensland.

Katherine Daniell PhD is a Research Fellow in the ANU's Centre for Policy Innovation. Her current research focuses on resolving the challenges associated with implementing multi-level participatory processes to bring about coordinated policy, adaptation strategies and local action for sustainable development. Her other research interests include public policy innovation processes, developing decision-aiding theory for 'multi-accountable' groups and encouraging effective inter-organisational collaborations. Katherine is the author of the Cambridge University Press book *Co-engineering and participatory water management: organisational challenges for water governance*, published in the UNESCO International Hydrology Series. She was also a guest editor for a special feature in the journal *Ecology and Society* on 'Implementing participatory water management: recent advances in theory, practice and evaluation', a compilation of papers that brings together policy, management and research lessons from the European Union's AquaStress and NeWater Integrated Projects.

Jo-Anne Everingham PhD is a Senior Research Fellow at the Centre for Social Responsibility in Mining at The University of Queensland, Australia. She holds a Master of Development Studies from Deakin University and a PhD in sociology from the University of Queensland. Since completing her PhD on regional planning in Central Queensland, her research and writing focuses on collaborative governance of policy challenges including the ageing population and more recently minerals and energy development. Jo-Anne's current projects relate to social impacts of resource development in mining-affected communities, primarily in Queensland and New South Wales.

Thomas Fell is a Research Assistant for Strategic Economic Solutions, a private economic consultancy based in Canberra, Australia. His work includes survey design and analysis, undertaking interviews and consultations, and preparing local and regional economic overviews. He has an Honours degree in natural resource management from the University of New England (Australia) and has worked in the areas of environmental policy and human resources with the Australian Government Department of Agriculture, Fisheries and Forestry. He has also completed a Bachelor of Music at the Australian National University.

Daniel M. Franks PhD is a Senior Research Fellow at the Centre for Social Responsibility in Mining at The University of Queensland, Australia. He has published widely on the topic of mining and sustainable development and has field experience at more than 40 mining and energy sites internationally. Daniel is the Co-Chair of the Social Impact Assessment Section of International Association for Impact Assessment, is an Adjunct Professor of the Mining Business School at the Universidad Católica del Norte, Chile, and is an Editorial Board Member of the *International Journal of Minerals Policy & Economics* (Resources Policy). He holds a PhD from Griffith University and a Bachelor of Science (Hons) from The University of Queensland.

Gordon Gregory OAM has been Executive Director of the National Rural Health Alliance (NRHA) since its establishment in 1993. The NRHA is Australia's peak NGO for rural and remote health, organiser of the biennial National Rural Health Conference, and owner-manager of the *Australian Journal of Rural Health.* Before 1993 Gordon worked at the Rural Development Centre at the University of New England, and then for nearly eight years in Canberra on the personal staff of a Federal Minister as an adviser on rural affairs, horticulture and fisheries. (His first task in the fisheries area was to address cranky fishermen from the South Coast of NSW – and their even crosser wives – about how the national interest was served by reductions in their annual quota.) He is a lapsed economist who has had a long-standing interest in policies and services for rural, regional and remote communities in Australia. He still makes regular use of his hockey stick and cricket bat, and is considering getting a mobile phone.

Catherine Gross PhD is a Visiting Fellow in the Fenner School, The Australian University. Catherine's research explores fairness, justice and injustice in natural resource management and societal issues relating to climate change adaptation. Catherine has researched several societal water conflicts in the Murray–Darling Basin, including water allocation cutbacks in the Murray irrigation area of NSW and the North South Pipeline project in Victoria. Catherine was principal investigator of a project funded by the National Climate Change Adaptation Research Facility which explored the limits to climate change adaptation in the Coorong and Lower Lakes area in South Australia.

Kirsten Henderson holds a PhD in sociology from La Trobe University. Her government and academic career has focused on the political, social and economic aspects of water policy, climate change and regional development. At the time of writing Dr Henderson worked for the Murray–Darling Basin Authority. The views expressed here are hers alone and do not necessarily represent the views of the Authority.

Anthony Hogan PhD is Professor and Chair of Regional Governance at ANZOG's Institute of Governance at the University of Canberra. He is also Adjunct Professor in Sociology at The Australian National University in Canberra. Anthony's main research interests are in the economic sociology, and in turn, subsequent governance of rural Australia, particularly country towns.

His most recent projects have included developing a methodology for use by rural communities to assist them in planning sustainable futures, a study of farmer suicide and a study on how farmers are adapting to drought and climate change in Australia.

Kim Houghton PhD established the specialist consultancy firm Strategic Economic Solutions in 1997 to help regional communities understand and prosper from economic changes happening around them. Under Kim's leadership the company has undertaken many practical and research projects on issues affecting regional economic growth. The company has also created innovative programmes to help small businesses directly – including the Springboard Business Development programme. Kim previously worked at the Australian National University in Pacific economic relations, and in the Department of the Prime Minister and Cabinet. Kim has a PhD in economics from the University of Tasmania and a BSc from the University of Tasmania.

Janet Hunt PhD is a Fellow at the Centre for Aboriginal Economic Policy Research (CAEPR) at the Australian National University where she teaches Australian Indigenous Development and has conducted research on the social benefits of Aboriginal involvement in natural resource management in regional NSW. She previously managed the Indigenous Community Governance Project, an ARC Linkage Project with Reconciliation Australia. Her background is in education and international development and she has lectured in International and Community Development at RMIT and Deakin Universities. She was Executive Director of the Australian Council for Overseas Aid, the peak body of international development NGOs, from 1995–2000 and prior to that was Executive Director of the International Women's Development Agency. Janet has lived most of her adult life in regional Australia and has a strong interest in regional Aboriginal communities, particularly in New South Wales.

Stewart Lockie PhD is Professor of Sociology and Director of The Cairns Institute at James Cook University. He is an environmental sociologist with expertise in environmental and natural resource management policy, social impact assessment and the sociology of food and agriculture. Professor Lockie's current research is primarily concerned with climate adaptation policy, biodiversity conservation, environmental and social standards for food production, sustainable consumption practices and food security.

Séan MacDermott PhD is a Research Fellow at RMIT's Regional and Rural Futures Research Group based in Hamilton in Western Victoria. Séan has lectured in Psychology and Management and has particular research interests in transition points such as from education to work. His current research covers the lifespan from working with disengaged youth, to regional workforce issues, and planning for an ageing community. Séan is lead researcher on the Landscapes for Young People (L4YP) project, which funded work on his chapter.

Rebecca Phillips PhD is a research consultant and a Visiting Fellow at the Institute for Governance and Policy Analysis at the University of Canberra. Rebecca's main research interests include the health and well-being of people, as well as the accessibility of health services. Her most recent projects have included the evaluation of a programme to improve the psychosocial outcomes of farmers with hearing loss, the social inclusion of children with hearing loss, and consumer and clinician perspectives of services available to self-manage chronic conditions.

Richard Price PhD balances his time as CEO of Kiri-ganai Research, Associate Professor at the Fenner School of Environment and Society (Australian National University), Adjunct Professor at the Australian Centre for Sustainable Catchments (University of Southern Queensland) and board director of Abundant Water. He was intimately involved in the reform of rural research arrangements under Federal Minister John Kerin, and helped pen the *Primary Industries and Energy Research and Development Act 1989*. Richard was a foundation manager at the Land and Water Resources R&D Corporation, where he established several national environmental and sustainable agriculture research programmes.

Bill Pritchard PhD is an Associate Professor in Human Geography at the University of Sydney. He has a long-standing interest in issues relating to rural and regional development in Australia, the food system and sustainability. Prior to his present appointment at the University of Sydney, Bill worked at Macquarie University and in the NSW Department of Premier and Cabinet.

Philip Roberts is Assistant Professor in Teacher Education (Curriculum and Pedagogy) at the University of Canberra, ACT. He has completed major national research projects on the staffing of rural and remote schools, equity, curriculum and pedagogy in rural and remote schools as well as having managed large-scale school based research projects.

Erin F. Smith is a Post-Doctoral Research Fellow in the Sustainability Research Centre at the University of the Sunshine Coast. Originally from a sheep and beef farm in New Zealand, her research interests include rural restructuring, the socio-economic organisation of farming, land and water ownership and vulnerability to climate change.

Susan Taylor has a Masters in Museum and Gallery Management. Working at Sovereign Hill as Manager of Learning and Visitor Programmes, Susan became interested in audience research which developed into an interest in social research. Prior to working for RMIT as a research assistant, Susan was employed in local government as a senior research officer. Currently Susan is completing a Graduate Diploma in Psychological Studies at Deakin University and lives on a cattle and sheep farm in the western district of Victoria.

Rebeka Tennent is a PhD candidate at the Australian National University. Her dissertation focuses on the relationships between private food standards, institutions and donor programmes in Vietnam. Her research interests include private food standards, food security, development and natural resource management.

Sharon Wheller Master of Arts (Hons) in Sociology is a social research consultant and a PhD candidate at the University of Queensland, Institute for Social Science Research and School of Political Science and International Studies. She has recently completed her thesis investigating the socio-spatial processes associated with employment disadvantage in Australia. This research examines labour market transitions and trajectories over space and time analysing information from the HILDA employment diary. Prior to this Sharon held senior positions in strategic planning and research within tertiary education and the public sector in New Zealand.

Bruce Wilson PhD is Professor and Director of the European Union Centre at RMIT University. He has worked with all levels of government on organisational and social change, and currently leads a major programme on comparative regional policy in Europe, Australia and Asia. He has co-authored and co-edited 11 books, and many more articles and book chapters.

Michelle Young is a research student at The Australian National University. Her dissertation focuses on the struggle to find value for kangaroo meat so that it can deliver the environmental benefits it potentially offers for rangeland grazing enterprises and the health benefits it offers citizens. Her research interests include the sociology of natural resource management, policy and planning relating to management of rural and regional change, and ethics in food production and consumption. Michelle is currently working at the Murray–Darling Basin Authority evaluating the impacts of the Basin water reforms on water dependent industries and communities.

Acknowledgements

This book would not have been possible without the support of a variety of people and organisations. Primarily resources to support the development of the book were provided by the Australian National University (The National Institute for Rural and Regional Australia (NIRRA) and the HC Coombs Forum) and more recently the Institute of Governance, at the University of Canberra. The support of these organisations, and in particular, Professor Stewart Lockie, Mr Mark Matthews and Professor Mark Evans, are gratefully acknowledged.

Thanks also go to NIRRA research assistants Harmony DenRonden, Pele Cannon, Sarah May and Melanie Glavimans for all their hard work in chasing up people and papers, organising workshops, and so on. Thanks go especially to Harmony DenRonden for her contribution in ensuring the quality of the written presentation of this book.

We would also like to acknowledge the input provided by of the National Institute for Rural and Regional Australia (NIRRA). NIRRA members nominated the names of leading experts in the field, whose advice we then sought with regards to both their assessment of the issues covered in many of the early chapters of the book as well as their views on policy challenges facing rural and regional Australia. These national experts included:

Prof. Margaret Alston
Dr Neill Barr
Prof. Linda Botterill
A. Prof. Ruth Beilin
Prof. Judith Brett
Prof. John Cary
Prof. Steve Dovers
Dr Quentin Farmer-Bowers
Prof. Vaughan Higgins
Prof. Geoff Lawrence
Prof. Stewart Lockie
Prof. John Martin
Dr Graham Marshall
Dr Alaric Maude
Prof. Lauren Rickard
Prof. Helen Ross
Dr Mark Stafford Smith
Prof. Daniela Stehlik
Prof. Frank Vanclay
Prof. John Warhurst

We thank them for the advice and support while noting that the views offered within the book do not necessarily reflect those of these advisers.

Abbreviations

AAA	Agriculture – Advancing Australia
ABS	Australian Bureau of Statistics
ACC	Area Consultative Committees
AHCA	Australian Health Care Agreements
AHMAC	Australian Health Ministers' Advisory Committee
AIHW	Australian Institute of Health and Welfare
ALRA	Aboriginal Land Rights Act
ATSIC	Aboriginal and Torres Straight Islander Commission
BRS	Bureau of Rural Sciences (now Australian Bureau of Agriculture and Resource Economics and Sciences)
CAP	Country Areas Programme
CDEP	Community Development Employment Projects
CEP	Community Employment Programme
CFOC	Caring For Our Country
CMA	Catchment Management Authority
COAG	Council of Australian Governments
CRAFT	Commonwealth Rebates for Employment of Apprentices on Full Time Training
CRANA	Council of Remote Area Nurses of Australia
DAFF	Department of Agriculture, Fisheries and Forestry
DEEWR	Department of Education, Employment and Workplace Relations
DFAT	Department of Foreign Affairs and Trade
DRALGAS	Department of Regional Australia, Regional Development and Local Government
DSEWPaC	Department of Sustainability, Environment, Water, Population and Communities
DURD	Department of Urban and Regional Development
EC	European Commission
EPBC	Environment Protection and Biodiversity Conservation Act 1999
EU	European Union
FIFO	Fly-in, fly-out
GDP	Gross domestic product
GFC	Global Financial Crisis

HREOC	Human Rights and Equal Opportunity Commission
ILC	Indigenous Land Corporation
ILUA	Indigenous Land Use Agreements
LCDC	Land Conservation District Committees
LCTW	Local Connections to Work
LEC	Local Employment Coordinators
MBI	Market based instruments
MCEETYA	Ministerial Council on Education Employment Training and Youth Affairs
MDB	Murray–Darling Basin
MDBA	Murray–Darling Basin Authority
MDBP	Murray–Darling Basin Plan
MLG	Multi-level governance
MoU	Memorandum of Understanding
MRRT	Mineral Resource Rent Tax
NAPLAN	National Assessment Programme – Literacy and Numeracy
NCP	National Competition Policy
NEAT	National Employment And Training
NGO	Non-governmental Organisation
NHMRC	National Health and Medical Research Council
NHT	Natural Heritage Trust
NIRRA	National Institute for Rural and Regional Australia
NRHA	National Rural Health Alliance
NRM	Natural Resource Management
NRMMC	Natural Resource Management Ministerial Council
NSCP	National Soil Conservation Programme
NURDA	National Urban and Regional Development Authority
NWC	National Water Commission
NWI	National Water Initiative
OECD	Organisation for Economic Co-operation and Development
PC	Productivity Commission
R&D	Research and development
RACGP	Royal Australian College of General Practitioners
RCIADIC	Royal Commission into Aboriginal Deaths in Custody
RCS	Regional Clinical Schools
RDA	Regional Development Australia
RDC	Research and Development Corporation
REDS	Regional Employment Development Scheme
RIRDC	Rural Industries Research and Development Corporation
RIRF	Rural Industry Research Funds
ROC	Regional Organisation of Councils
RPA	Regional Partnership Agreements
RaRA	Rural and Regional Australia
SDL	Sustainable diversion limits
SES	Socio-economic status

SLA	Statistical Local Area
SRA	Shared Responsibility Agreements
SSRM	State-Specific and Regional Migration
UDRH	University Departments of Rural Health
WTO	World Trade Organization

The making of rural and regional Australia

An introduction

Anthony Hogan and Michelle Young

Background

Significant change is occurring for people living in rural and regional Australia. Global economics, the resources boom, the declining economic significance of agriculture, climate change, drought and water policy, as well as population shift are just a few of the big issues on the agenda. Yet these issues are not new. Australia as a colony faced droughts in the mid-1800s. Agriculture as an export industry has had to compete on a world stage almost since its inception. Nonetheless, something has changed. Decline is evident across the Organisation for Economic Co-operation and Development (OECD) countries. Concerns are raised across the nation that the family farm, an entity which is so much at the heart of this nation's iconic settler culture, is becoming a thing of the past. Coupled with a changing understanding of the environment and natural resource management, serious questions are being raised about the economic viability of small family farms. Young people are leaving and not returning to their country areas, while the remaining population ages. While regional centres are growing, many smaller surrounding towns and villages are either shrinking or dying away. Critical policy assumptions, which have underpinned much of the early development of Australia, are either being revised or completely changed. Decisions which once seemed to be common sense, now appear to be highly questionable.

This book was born out of the need to help make sense of all this change. The HC Coombs Policy Forum at The Australian National University (ANU) was conducting a project on visioning Australia's future.[1] The Coombs Forum sought the assistance of the National Institute for Rural and Regional Australia (NIRRA; also at the ANU) to undertake a study to scope the development of Commonwealth Government public policy in the rural and regional space, seeking to learn from the past, to better understand the present, and to contribute to an enhanced evidence base for future public policy development. The project was framed with a view to producing a publication that would serve as a resource for new policy officers who come to work on policy issues from a Commonwealth perspective. While we wanted to challenge people to think about the Commonwealth's role with regard to rural and regional Australia, we did not seek to produce a work which was proscriptive in its findings. Rather, we saw this project as contributing towards a dialogue between policy researchers and policymakers in the rural and regional Australia space with each other, and in turn with rural communities and the industries upon which they rely for their livelihoods. Drawing on the material provided, and aware of the level of discontent which people living in rural and regional Australia report, we envisaged that this book, particularly the last chapter, may provide a call for action, and that it would open up and contribute to a new way of thinking about how we wish (or not as the case may be) to live and work in non-urban Australia.

Several strategies were utilised in scoping what would be covered within the book. First, following a call to NIRRA members, a range of experts volunteered their time to write specific chapters. Second, following initial peer review and community consultations, specific experts were sought out to write additional chapters so that the book provided a sufficient (although not exhaustive) coverage of key policy issues in rural and regional Australia. Given that almost every piece of national policy has implications for rural and regional Australia, it was beyond the scope of the book to address every one of them or to attend to each in great detail. In all, 19 chapters have been written providing an examination of policy initiatives relating to regional and economic policy, agriculture, water governance, health, education, youth, women's issues, Indigenous perspectives on regionalism, welfare and employment, population, natural resource management, resource extraction, rural research and regional innovation, youth affairs and the devolution of regional governance.

In inviting contributions to this book, we asked contributors to address three central questions:

1 What were the major policy initiatives that have shaped living and livelihoods in rural and regional Australia?
2 What have been the impacts of these policy decisions?
3 What are the critical issues for living and working in rural and regional Australia which need to be addressed going forward?

To keep the task manageable, we suggested that authors focus particularly on the period since the 1970s, but also, where resources permitted, on the period since World War II. Importantly, we wanted the authors to draw attention to the factors which have particularly shaped policy in rural and regional Australia over time. As a result some chapters reach back to the nineteenth century (for example, Gross on population (Chapter 6) and Henderson on water policy (Chapter 5)) for it is at this time that the author considered that the policy of interest today had its origins. Overall these contributions have resulted in a book which is structured into four main parts:

- Policy which has served to structure rural and regional Australia with regards to population, regional science and agriculture;
- An examination of a series of key policy issues, such as perspectives from Indigenous people, women and young people;

- Emerging issues including localism, rural aspirations, mining and economic issues;
- Moving forward, bringing together current issues and considering options for the future.

From the outset, it was not intended that we would produce a book that would be read in a sequential manner. Indeed, many of the issues which have served to shape life in rural and regional Australia did not arise within a neat, sequential fashion. Policy has been shaped by a collage of events, which have interacted with one another and in turn served to shape future events. The arrangement of the chapters represents the recognition that many of the policy issues of concern today had their origins in decisions taken in earlier times. There are nonetheless a number of overarching themes which cut across the book. These are:

- Early yet formative policy settings;
- Watershed moments;
- Specific policy issues and perspectives;
- The need for a new, overarching policy framework for rural Australia which is distinct from regional Australia.

In considering these themes, this introduction provides the reader with an overview of key insights arising within the book, leaving the substantiation of these insights to the details provided within the ensuing chapters.

Early yet formative policy settings

Early policy was underpinned by the goal to settle a nation, particularly by populating inland Australia and to develop industries there. The policy framework was based around a paradigm of state assistance, where governments co-invested in the development of rural industries and infrastructure. As this book makes evident, government was an innovator and a risk taker, investing in the development of industries at a time and in places where industry was not brave enough to venture alone. As with Canada, rural staples (Bunker 1989) such as ore, wheat and wool formed the basis of the rural economy. Governments based in colonial hubs sought to mobilise, and in turn draw in resources from the regions, to support colonial (and in turn urban) settlements and to exploit economic opportunities through exporting Australian products. To realise this vision, specific policy strategies were put in place. Following on from the success of America's inland strategy, Australian policy sought to 'let the deserts bloom' (Gross, Chapter 6) with people and productive rural enterprises. As Henderson (Chapter 5) points out, it was the era of the yeoman farmer 'who carried out honourable work by cropping a well-ordered garden landscape that not only overcame the aridity and unpredictability of the Australian environment but also sought to beautify the landscapes impoverished by the wool and wheat industries'. Various strategies were put in place (e.g. soldier settler blocks) which encouraged people to take up farming. Infrastructure development followed (e.g. inland telegraph and irrigation schemes) and workers followed the employment opportunities created by these initiatives. Towns emerged as service centres supporting a growing agricultural sector and resource booms. Government was active in the economy and the prosperity of the nation was central to policy goals.

A number of assumptions underpinned these policy settings including the development of agriculture as a state-assisted paradigm (Smith and Pritchard, Chapter 3) with support coming firstly from the states, and in turn the Commonwealth. From the early days of Australian settlement, agriculture significantly contributed to national policy goals and because of this, government could justify support to the industry because agriculture was important to Australia. Policy goals sought to expand agricultural product sales and in turn to increase the industry's efficiency and productivity – that is, to help it improve its profit margins. Later in the book, Price (Chapter 13) provides a detailed study of how governments yet again co-invested in agricultural industry development over many decades, noting the shift in this funding support to the Commonwealth. He tells us that research has been used in rural and regional Australia as a means of securing a preferred future, one that can be realised. Agricultural research and development policy, he notes, has had a strong and continued history of intervention, but this intervention has been focused on rural productivism rather than livelihoods per se. As Mazzucato (2013) points out, it was because of public sector investments like these that Australia, in this instance, could emerge in the 1950s and 1960s as an agricultural powerhouse.

Collits and Cockfield (Chapters 1 and 2 respectively) draw attention to the fact that rural and regional Australia was settled amidst conflicting beliefs as to what could be secured in this space, in terms of the capacity to support livelihoods. Cockfield (Chapter 2) draws our attention to the fact that there were debates even from our earliest days of European settlement about the environmental capacity of rural and regional Australia to support livelihoods.

In turn, policy initiatives ensured that support was available for rural industries in times of crisis and that rural people warranted equitable access to services for undertaking the difficulties of settling inland Australia. Australia was, as it were, a nation community (Wheller, Chapter 9). Indeed, underpinning the ideal of the yeoman famer was an implicit social contract between the city and the rural wherein farmers would supply the nation with food at reasonable prices while in turn society would support farmers financially, politically and socially. Alston (Chapter 11) points out that the policy vision was one which was concerned to maintain farming families within rural and regional settings. The social contract recognised the inherent difficulties in farming inland Australia and undertook to support farmers through hard times. Subsequent policies were used to enable industries to survive in changing environmental and economic circumstances (i.e. drought relief and structural adjustment). It is important to note that a social identity emerged around the yeoman farmers, the agrarian lifestyle, and the national role which farmers played. It is a vision of the rural which, as Gross (Chapter 17) observes, is still strongly held by the farming community today.

In many ways, these early policy settings put in place the foundation of the many issues we are facing in rural and regional Australia today. First and foremost people were governed in a top-down fashion, from state-based colonial hubs. From the outset, policy settings were metro-centric and industry-focused, in that they were developed from the populated hubs with a view to addressing needs as they were identified by policymakers. These early forms of governance were formalised in the Australian Constitution which, as Cockfield (Chapter 2) points out, provides the states with mechanisms of control over regional development and infrastructure, land use, health services and so on. The focus of policy strategy outside the major urban settlements then (and now) was a developmental one – the rural and regional was equated with the growth of agriculture as an industry and the exploitation of natural resources. Collits (Chapter 1) brings forward the important insight that policy has been more concerned with the impact of its initiatives on regions (e.g. questions of equity) rather than having policies that were about the regions per se (e.g. a clear articulation of the place of regions in Australian society).

Importantly, there was a policy vision for rural and regional Australia. Gross (Chapter 6) points out that following World War II the vision was to decentralise, regionalise and encourage the development of industry within those locations which had been settled. Over time, such initiatives were further supported by deploying military bases to rural and regional areas, building government office blocks and colleges of advanced education, and providing industry assistance funds, such that these localities could maintain an economic capacity to support population. Inherently though it was a population centred on the notion of the white, male breadwinner. As Hunt (Chapter 7), Alston (Chapter 11) and MacDermott and Taylor (Chapter 10) respectively observe, iconic notions of rural Australia were not about Indigenous people, women or young people. Indeed, these authors draw attention to the fact in many instances, legislative processes sought to extinguish the presence of these groups from the public record.

Watershed moments

While the Commonwealth Government became involved in rural and regional issues through a focus on productive issues, several watershed decisions cemented its role in rural and regional policy from a national perspective. These included a number of decisions from the High Court of Australia and the influence of neoliberalism on national economic policy. It is to these developments that we now turn.

Two key High Court decisions helped shape the parameters for the way that the Commonwealth would become involved in policy on matters which traditionally had been state responsibilities. Cockfield (Chapter 2) draws our attention to the decision on income tax which occurred in the early 1940s while Tennent and Lockie (Chapter 4) draw our attention to the Franklin Dam decision, which affirmed the Commonwealth's obligations under international treaties. The decision with regard to income tax gave the Commonwealth control over the major source of government income in Australia. And in keeping with the adage that 'those who have the gold, make the rules', control of these funds provided the Commonwealth with a specific capacity to influence policy in Australia. This influence was also nuanced by the implications of the Franklin Dam decision which saw the Commonwealth coordinating policy and resource allocation in natural resource management.

Wheller (Chapter 9) demonstrates that the Commonwealth also took on initial state programmes in welfare policy (e.g. aged pensions, maternity payments, wage decisions and social security generally) from quite early in the early 1900s, while the Commonwealth's national role in coordinating health (see for example Gregory, Chapter 12) is also evident. Taken together, a blurring has occurred along the lines of jurisdictional responsibilities; without resolution of these issues Cockfield concludes that persistent policy conflicts will continue to drag the Commonwealth Government back into issues which are essentially a state responsibility. Wheller observes that in the post-war period, the Commonwealth took the opportunity of having control of the tax base to put right many inequalities which were evident in Australia. The Commonwealth Government was increasingly able to set the policy agenda through a system of coordinated federalism in which the central government works with, and sometimes coerces, the state governments to develop and implement national policy frameworks.

The economic crises of the 1970s saw significant changes to Australia's economic policy strategy. In 1973 tariff protections were reduced by 25 per cent and in the ensuing decades Australia moved to deregulate its agricultural industries, commencing with dairy and continuing right through until recent years. To secure the exit of farmers who were deemed to be less efficient, the Commonwealth Government offered farmers from the targeted industries structural adjustment packages – that is, payments to leave the industry. Since under these policies less efficient operators needed to leave the market, Cockfield (Chapter 2) points out that the need for structural adjustment payments engaged the Commonwealth Government directly in rural and regional policy issues. In the 1980s, Smith and Pritchard (Chapter 3) report that economic policies took up what came to be known as the efficiency mantra, with a focus on hyper-productionism in agriculture, informed as they were by neoliberalist policies.

Cockfield observes that the convergence of these decisions, policies and practices resulted in a form of centralised federation, notably one that was underpinned by neoliberal policy values. The policy impact of neoliberalism was formative of Commonwealth Government approaches to rural and regional Australia. The policy paradigm shifted from one of state assistance to a discourse of self-sufficiency. Over time policy emerged which took the view that individuals were responsible for managing their own risks (e.g. drought policy and active employment/welfare policies) and communities were responsible for their own viability (e.g. localism). However, Smith and Pritchard point out that these kinds of policy strategies took no regard for the economic interrelationship between farmers and their local towns and specifically that the push for productivity gains and the need to achieve capacities of scale was often realised through mechanisation of the productive process. Improved productivity however came at the cost of rural employment opportunities and the loss of many small operators whose businesses lacked either scale or technological capacity to remain competitive.

And while policymakers focused on the capacity to progress productivity gains, attention was distracted from the ensuing costs of development and change. Environmental impacts were evident in terms of salinity, soil acidity, land degradation and over-irrigation. In keeping with the policy strategy of the day, market based instruments (MBIs) were in turn introduced to address the impacts of farming on the environment as a form of market failure. The development of MBIs as a policy instrument is significant because it embodies the policy value that markets are the most appropriate mechanism for resolving environmental problems. Henderson's study (Chapter 5) of water policy provides insight into how various approaches to policy manifested themselves in water management. Henderson identified four key phases in Commonwealth Government water policy: (i) coming to terms with the nature of Australia's hydrological environment; (ii) water as a tool for the development of the colony; (iii) stabilising water management during an era of closer settlement of inland Australia in order to grow communities and expand production; and (iv) the emergence of state-managed water resources. Henderson shows that the third phase ran from 1905 through to the 1980s. In the 1980s two new perceptions of water policy came into being: (i) water as a commodity, and (ii) water as a provider of ecological services. Henderson proposes that sustainability policy emerged in turn as a discourse to manage the conflicts between environmental and economic approaches to natural resource utilisation.

While natural resource management (NRM) saw the development of market approaches to managing scarce resources, regional and community policy reflected another face of neoliberalism in the desire to create small government. Localism promotes the view that local people know their needs best and that regions can and should invest in their own growth through the mobilisation of local assets and resources, so as to capitalise on their specific competitive advantages. Central to localism are the assumptions that regions are sustainable, that they have resources to develop which should be developed, and that they have the capacity to take development forward. Moreover, the development of such resources or assets will generate local economic flows which will underpin local livelihoods. While localist approaches are not new (Hogan and Lockie (2013) trace localism back to the tenth century), it serves as another watershed moment in rural and regional policy as it embodies the extension of neoliberalist values to the sustainability of rural and regional communities (see Hogan *et al.*, Chapter 15). In their chapter, Houghton and Fell (Chapter 14) also explore methods which local communities might use to assess their own socio-economic viability going forward.

Policy impacts

The environmental impacts of intensified agriculture have received significant attention in policy circles over recent decades. Henderson (as well as Tennent and Lockie, Chapter 4) draws attention to the fact that intensified agriculture has had a cumulative effect on flora, fauna, forests, wetlands, rivers and land. Tennent and Lockie remark that land degradation was evident during the times of early settlement when intensifying agriculture was a priority for both feeding the new colonies, as well as creating export products to ship overseas. Similarly Tennent and Lockie as well as Henderson draw our attention to the fact that a focus on productivism had very real environmental consequences in terms of the viability of river systems, soil quality and subsequent impacts on flora and fauna. That is, key policy concerns of today had their origins in unintended consequences of earlier policy decisions.

Another central theme running through most, if not all the chapters in this book is that the promises of neoliberalism have not realised more vibrant and prosperous communities, particularly in rural Australia. This body of insights raises the question that if the basic economic settings of a country are not resulting in the maintenance of livelihoods, then what is the purpose of economic policy? We return to this question shortly and in the closing chapters of this book.

In the face of challenge and change, resilience and transformation have become the new buzzwords in rural and regional policy – resilient individuals and resilient communities transforming the economic basis that underpins their livelihoods. A key problem with such a discourse is that it is inherently about the economic resilience of rural and regional communities. It echoes back to the staples thesis that has driven the development of much of rural and regional Australia that we noted earlier; where the rural and regional is considered in terms of how the outer areas contribute to central goals. Several of our contributing authors (e.g. Collits (Chapter 1), Alston (Chapter 11), Roberts (Chapter 8) and Gregory *et al.* (Chapter 12)) draw attention to the fact that rural and regional policy essentially means industry policy. Alston observes that the focus on industry, which she says is underscored by the rise of neoliberalism and its support for small government, has reduced attention to the community, health and social issues which exist in rural Australia. Alston argues that this policy strategy in turn has destabilised rural and regional families, fractured vibrant local economies and crippled their communities. Such policy, she suggests, is metro-centric in nature, as though one policy strategy could address the needs of all Australians.

Alston (and also Wheller, Chapter 9) specifically points out that by framing the rural and regional within an economic discourse, attention is firstly given (as we noted above) to iconic notions of white, male workers (once farmers and now more likely miners) and in consequence attention is drawn away the social nature of living in specific places at particular times.

In contrast to these stereotypical views (constructed as they were through policy initiatives), Alston points out that women make up more than a quarter

(28 per cent) of the farming workforce, contributing up to 48 per cent of farm income. At the same time, women are notably under-represented in rural and regional leadership. While specific attempts have been made to redress this situation, they have largely failed due to the absence of a long-term policy strategy which could be sustained across federal parliaments. For Alston, rural and regional Australia policy as a whole fails to support and sustain individuals and their communities, and as a result this has contributed to the demise of the viability of inland Australia. Overall, Alston also concludes that the rise of the neoliberal agenda in the 1970s negatively impacted on farming families and rural and regional communities.

Janet Hunt (Chapter 7) observes that the iconic construction of the rural and regional and iconic bush settings, with a pastoral and agricultural focus, similarly renders Aboriginal people almost invisible. Indeed, Indigenous peoples are not strongly featured in the literature of policies in relation to regional development. For Hunt, Indigenous Affairs policy has most strongly focused on social and economic disparities faced by Aboriginal people, while regional policy has focused on geographical disparities and uneven development. From the Indigenous perspective, regions reflect boundaries of particular tribal groupings and the social networks between them, providing a complex regional framework of a different type. Hunt proposes that if regional development is to address the disadvantage faced by individuals and their communities, there is a pressing need for Indigenous equality to become a prime focus for regional development strategies. Central to this issue though is the framing of Indigenous policy as problematic and marginal, rather than as being central to issues across the sector. Hunt suggests that a number of issues are of concern here. These include leadership, governance and policy coordination. Thematically these themes are resonant of Alston's issues of recognition, representation and rights for rural people.

The metro-centric nature of staples-based policy approaches to rural and regional Australia has manifested itself in a range of policy settings which in turn negatively impact people living in rural and regional Australia. This issue is taken up by Gregory *et al.* (Chapter 12), MacDermott and Taylor (Chapter 10), and Roberts (Chapter 8) respectively with regards to health, youth and education policy. As Gregory observes, health services in rural and regional areas have to operate in a different context to metropolitan-based services. Respectively they outline a situation where models for service delivery were developed on the basis of urban requirements with such models being applied to rural settings. As a policy framework, metro-centricity does not work. In rural and regional settings, distance alone can serve as a significant barrier to service delivery. Similarly the cost structures are different, as are the ways in which people gain access, if they do, to services. Collectively they contribute to the insight that a 'one size fits all policy' does not work well across urban and non-urban settings.

Interestingly, while resource extraction has the capacity to underwrite the viability of many rural and regional communities, Everingham and Franks (Chapter 16) draw attention to the fact that the Commonwealth Government is essentially sidelined with regards to policy concerning the mining industry.

In the post-war period there have been examples of the mining industry building communities which were needed to support their industries. When an industry has such a significant impact on our current and future well-being and national wealth, it is difficult to fathom why the Commonwealth Government would not have overall control over such a process. Hogan *et al.* (Chapter 15) note that while the Gillard Government (2010–2013) introduced a mineral resources rent tax (MRRT), this initiative is considered to have failed with the tax raising only about 10 per cent of projected revenues. This was especially problematic because the tax was raised with a view to funding significant infrastructure developments in rural and regional Australia.

The challenges to current policy settings

People living in rural and regional Australia, particularly those living in agri-dependent communities, have a clear view of what they want for their futures. As Gross reports (Chapter 17), this vision was seen to encompass the continuity and stability of family farming, including young people, and was situated within thriving local cultural and agricultural activities. Agriculture would continue to create wealth for the nation, feed the nation, and provide quality of life for rural, country and regional residents who will continue to manage the inevitable day-to-day challenges of living in rural and regional Australia. Food production would be sustainable, not breaking the rules of nature, and not simply be focused on gross domestic product for its own sake. Urban Australia would begin to listen to rural and regional Australia. They would appreciate the work which farmers do for them. Policy decisions would be made by people who understand the rural and regional, and in turn the existing urban–rural divide would be overcome. Government would be customer-focused. People living in rural and regional Australia would once again enjoy socio-economic well-being. Both they and their environment would be healthy, and society would be just, inclusive, fair and one where acceptance for difference was a given. Farmers would be recognised for being good environmental citizens and protectors of the animals they care for.

And while people living in rural and regional Australia have a vision for their futures, they are concerned that it is a vision that is not shared by policymakers. Gross reports that rural people are concerned about their future because a process of policy reform, which many regard as being ill-informed and which is being imposed on them, is overturning long-standing and well understood social and economic arrangements. The view is held that many policy officers have little practical knowledge about rural and regional Australia. Rural people feel disenfranchised and left out of critical decision-making processes which impact on the viability of their livelihoods. As one person aptly remarked, 'if you are not at the table you're probably on the menu!' Moreover, rural people found it difficult to participate in consultative processes which were inherently one-sided and where they had little power over the final decision which would be taken. The view was proposed that developing a vision for living in rural and regional Australia should be set by the people who actually live there.

Wheller (Chapter 9) points out that rural and regional Australia is no longer the 'bush' glorified in folklore. Rather, global corporations exist in the same space as family businesses. Rural and regional Australia is now multidimensional, working on multiple scales, simultaneously encompassing local, regional, national and international components. Moreover, each region is different with regard to its natural resources and amenity value, its labour capacity and infrastructure, and its industry mix and community. In the presence of such diversity, 'one size fits all' policies are likely to be ineffective. At the same time, competing policy agendas pose conflicting challenges for rural and regional Australia. Calls exist on the one hand for the development of collaborative, placed-based, self-initiated, localised business development strategies, envisaging family business and multinational partnerships utilising knowledge-based economies. On the other hand, market forces focus on competition, the need to produce actual products, the availability of a workforce which can learn and grow with the business, and achieving necessary economies of scale, but in an era where there is little or no state activity. The future under localism is one of innovation, of using smart technology to progress industry development in regional areas, albeit in a self-sufficient manner. Yet Edwards (2013, p. 161) points out that 'high-technology innovation needs economies of scale and will require active public sponsorship on a broader canvas'. Similarly Edwards remarks that 'national free trade orthodoxy is cosmopolitan in outlook – indifferent to the well-being of geographically-anchored producers (regions), and hostile to special incentives of the kind required to foster re-localisation' (Edwards 2013, p. 163). Moreover, Edwards argues that public investment and infrastructure are essential to the kinds of economic development required to make rural and regional Australia a viable setting for business and population.

Contributors to this volume including Collits (Chapter 1), Cockfield (Chapter 2) and Hogan *et al.* (Chapter 15), draw attention to the fact that localism highlights continuing tension in policy circles between centralised and localised approaches to governance. Cockfield in particular draws out the point that while Australia has pursued several decentralisation strategies, on balance, these strategies have not been successful, with Australia being one of the most urbanised countries in the world. Price (Chapter 13) also draws attention to the fact that Commonwealth Government attempts to support the development of rural industry research capacity has also been affected by shifts between centralised and decentralised approaches to policy. And just as NRM had raised the question of the extent to which the environment could sustain intensified forms of production, Hogan *et al.* draw attention to the fact that localism (managed as it has been from central Canberra) raises the Malthusian question as to the extent to which regional communities have the economic capacity to continue to provide livelihoods for people who live there. We return to these and other issues in the last chapters of this book where we will consider the potential scope for visioning a future for living in rural and regional Australia and the role, if any, that Commonwealth Government policy might play.

The need for a new, overarching policy framework for rural rather than regional Australia?

This book can be approached in two ways. This introduction and the concluding two chapters draw out what we consider to be the core issues facing the sustainability of living in rural and regional Australia. The core chapters provide the evidence base upon which these insights and conclusions are in turn drawn. Amidst the consultations and basic research that underpinned the development of this book (Hogan and Young 2012), many respondents bemoaned the absence of an adequate policy framework underpinning livelihoods in rural and regional Australia. But in contrast to such a view Stoker (2012) points out that in specific longer term policy settings, the absence of an articulated policy does not necessarily mean no policy at all. As the various chapters of this book illustrate, there are policy settings in place for rural and regional Australia and they have been in place for a long time. What this book also brings forward is a widespread concern about the narrow basis upon which these policies have been developed and executed. Many remain concerned that if policy settings are left as they are, then the continued decline of country towns and villages and the growth of regional service centres will be inevitable. However, if current trends are viewed from the perspective of the staples thesis which underpins them, the growth or decline of rural communities is not relevant to the policy agenda unless it impacts on industry's capacity to quickly and efficiently extract products from inland Australia. Indeed, for many policymakers, the script for the future of rural and regional Australia, like many westernised rural communities, is written. They take the view that the globalisation of agriculture (as well as mining) and its fuller integration within global markets is inevitable as are its consequences, which embody increasing mechanisation of labour processes, remote administration, mobile workforces (where required) and the concurrent decline of many country towns, villages and family farms. Within their visions, the inland countryside will be sparsely populated; key regional service centres will grow and provide for those needs which cannot be met online.

Building on the evidence brought forward within the core chapters, in the final chapters we raise an inconvenient yet important objection to this scenario. The above scenario may well be how global interests – the markets, as it were – see living in the rural space being played out, but it is not what many country people seek for their futures. Moreover, such a future may not be in the interests of country people, or their nation-states more generally. Far from delivering on the promise of more vibrant, prosperous rural communities, the neoliberalist strategy has created the opposite. The contributors to this text and the country people affected, have a view about the future of inland Australia which is bigger and more inclusive than turning it into one large extractive or amenity experience. This book provides an in-depth illustration of how changes in policy and practice have led to the demise of living in rural and regional spaces. In particular, in the context of neoliberalism and the push towards free trade and small government, the evidence presented in the core chapters leads to a discussion in Chapters 18 and 19 as to what the role of the state in advanced social market economies is. For sure, we do not argue for a more intensified role of the state than perhaps previously seen, but at the same time, we are strongly of the view that there is a role for the state. As Mazzucato (2013, location 468) observes, the state undertakes those roles which 'at present are not being done'. Mazzucato (2013, location 495) puts forward the perspective that the 'State is neither a "meddler" nor a simple "facilitator" of economic growth. It is a key partner of the private sector – often a more daring one, willing to take the risks that business won't.'

The Bureau of Rural Sciences (2008) makes it evident that rural livelihoods are primarily supported by agriculture, health and education services and retail. The conduct of each of these industries is undergoing significant change, especially in country Australia. Without a change in policy settings, agriculture will continue to be mechanised and intensified in both structure and practice, further reducing the need for locally-based, permanent employment. The building of freeways continues to see country towns bypassed. Motorcars are now so fuel efficient that they can travel 800 to 1,000 km on a single tank of petrol. This is a significant change to 100 years ago when towns emerged if only to service horses and people travelling on the Cobb and Co coach lines. Yet these changes have had significant implications for the economic viability of country towns because fewer and fewer people stop while travelling and when they do stop, it is now at roadside rest stops and highway service centres. And when people do not stop during their journey they do not spend.

If you are to walk up the main street of a country town today, try to imagine the impact of the internet on the remaining businesses. We have to wonder what businesses will remain in 20 years time? When we consider that, increasingly, transactional services (such as law, accounting, insurance), health monitoring and medications, media (newspapers and magazines), entertainment (videos, books and music), education and groceries can be purchased online and delivered to the home, we can similarly imagine that the need for such businesses will not exist at a local level. And when we recall that at least half of our family farms rely on the income women bring in through off-farm work, the circle of local viability closes further in on itself.

If business continues as usual in the rural and regional space, it will not just simply mean fewer people living in the country. As is evident in other countries, this change process is associated with a transfer of property ownership from small family farms and town-based businesses to globalised interests, resulting in a further intensification of the decoupling of economy from rural society discussed in Chapter 15. The agglomeration of farming as an industry has cascading effects on the viability of the livelihoods of those businesses and towns which were established to service them. Some forms of change also create stranded assets, such as the implementation of water policy as noted in Henderson's chapter. And this is where our text, albeit based as it is on the Australian experience, will be of particular interest to readers living outside Australia. These processes are playing out across OECD countries and the solutions are just as much of interest to the other member states as they are to Australian citizens.

Set against this scenario of change is the desire by some 10 per cent of the population to live in rural and remote settings and a further 20 per cent to live in regional settings. There is little doubt that Australia has a strong future as a producer and exporter of food and fibre. One can imagine that yet again agriculture will be central to the viability of our economy. What is less certain is who will own these productive processes and to what extent increasing agricultural productivity will realise improved standards of living for all Australians. How we as a nation envisage the future of rural and regional Australia will be central to that well-being. The people presently living in country Australia are arguing that the policy settings are not right, and that should we remain on our present course, it will be to the demise of the nation as a whole.

Chapter 18 outlines a process for managing change, through a multi-level approach to governance. The chapter highlights arguments that take the position that policymakers need to all recognise and acknowledge, in an open and honest fashion, the challenges which country Australia presently faces. Similarly such arguments propose that policymakers need to engage with the vision people have for living in country Australia and that in responding to the challenges faced and the futures envisioned, there needs to be an acceptance that the Commonwealth Government has policy responsibilities which it has to address; social issues cannot simply be left to the market to solve. The chapter also draws attention to the fact that a counter-argument also exists – a perspective which brings into question many of the aspirations noted above. What if it is the case that policymakers do not want to link up various aspects of policy which impact on country Australia? Or what if it is the case that they have in fact got their finger on the pulse of country Australia? What if the nature of the rural economy has changed and in turn society also must change? Or what if the policy settings in place are ones which, to some degree at least, seek to set in place a transition to a new future? If these latter perspectives are indeed what policymakers are working towards, what seems to be at stake is the question of mandate and the question of the extent to which the measures put in place are adequate to the task. The issue which seems to be on the table is a stand-off between trying to do business as usual versus doing this business in a different manner. At issue though are the livelihoods and aspirations of those who get caught up in such a change process, and such impacts cannot readily be resolved solely through a rational economic lens.

The final chapter opens up discussions for a practical agenda for recoupling economy with what we come to call country society. It brings forth the value position that rural decline is not inevitable, but that it results from specific economic and policy decisions which take price as the formative value of western society. This chapter sets aside the privileged place of price and seeks to recontextualise price within an economy, which is within a society, in a given place and at a given time. At the centre of this analysis is the principle that price alone is not a sufficient value upon which to build a society or social system. The chapter brings forth the need for thought, insight and strategy wherein we understand the economy within the context of the interface of society and markets;

that first and foremost the purpose of economy is that it is attached to place at a given time and that it provides the means through which citizens can secure their livelihoods. There is no questioning the fact that socio-economic change is omnipresent. However, such change can be addressed within a value framework centred on ensuring the continuity of the livelihoods of people living in the global village. The process of recoupling economy with local community will be a long and difficult one, commenced as it will be by a realistic assessment of where communities are at, and taking the initial steps that are involved in developing economic and governmental options for a country-based future.

Without a doubt, the state had a role in the making of rural and regional Australia through its role in both industry and community development. Similarly, and as is evidenced in Chapter 15, further industry and economic development is unlikely to occur in rural and regional Australia without the state embracing substantive risk and investing in infrastructure and innovation. The point of difference, however, in going forward, is that the place of community within the context of industry development can no longer be regarded as a non-core policy issue. Central to the notion of the public sector being a commander of risk, investment and innovation, is ensuring the ongoing coupling of economic and social development. As Mazzucato (2013) points out, the days of so-called 'useless government investment' are long gone, and the challenge ahead lies at the interface of public and private interests working together, grappling as they now must with what it means on the one hand to integrate macro and micro approaches to economic policy, while progressing towards the sustainability of rural and regional communities in an era of transformation.

Note

1 See http://publicpolicy.anu.edu.au/hc-coombs/ for further details.

References

Bureau of Rural Sciences 2008, *Country Matters. A social atlas of Country Australia – 2008*, Department of Agriculture, Fisheries, and Forestry, Canberra.

Edwards, G 2013, 'Regions and innovation: a reflection', in Kinnear, S, Charters, K and Vitartas, P (eds), *Regional advantage and innovation – achieving Australia's national outcomes*, Springer Verlag, Heidelberg, pp. 151–170.

Hogan, A and Lockie, S (in press), 'The coupling of rural communities with their economic base: agriculture, localism, and the discourse of self-sufficiency', *Policy Studies (Special Issue)*, vol. 34, no. 4, pp. 441–447.

Hogan, A, Young, M and Lockie, S (eds) 2012, *Visioning a future for rural and regional Australia*, National Institute for Rural and Regional Australia, The Australian National University, Canberra.

Mazzucato, M 2014, *The entrepreneurial state*, Anthem Press, United Kingdom.

Stoker, G 2012, 'Economic Recovery and the Politics of the Long-Term', SPERI Inaugural Conference: The British Growth Crisis–The Search for a New Model, Sheffield University, 16–18 July.

Part I

Background

Structuring policy

1 Regional policy in post-war Australia

Much ado about nothing?

Paul Collits

Introduction

The breadth of issues confronting regional Australia is enormous – economic, social, environmental, cultural and institutional – and their complexity growing, as other chapters in this volume readily attest. Government policy is an important part of the regional Australia story. On the one hand, the actions of governments at all levels have affected Australian regions in all kinds of ways, for good or bad. On the other hand, governments of all persuasions have recognised that regional Australia has its own set of issues, often the inevitable result of distance and the lack of critical mass. Hence they have crafted policies over time designed to ameliorate problems particular to regional Australia, through a range of initiatives and programmes.

Regional development itself means different things to different people. Moreover, the area of regional *policy* is problematic at many levels, in Australia as elsewhere. First, there is no broadly accepted definition and measure of 'success' with regional policy, nor agreement over its reach (Collits 2006); second, as is the case in many other areas of policy, there is no consensus as to which level of government should do what in relation to regional policy; third, there is no universally accepted explanatory theory of what drives regional growth and decline (Collits 2004); fourth, drivers of regional 'success' are known to vary and to be (largely) beyond the capacity of governments to control or even influence (Sorensen 2000); fifth, interventions occur over many time scales and their impact, in any case, is routinely questioned and remains largely unknown (Collits 2006; Grattan 2011); sixth, regional policy is overtly politicised and this is likely to continue (Collits 2002, 2006); and, finally, despite much talk about 'evidence based policy', there are few signs of the healthy interactions between theory, policy and practice that exist in other countries and inform the policies of central governments (Beer in Rowe 2009; Collits 2011a).

Of course, regional policy also operates in the territory of 'wicked problems' which defy easy answers due to their lack of easy definition, variability, complexity, continuity and shades of grey (Rittel and Webber 1973), as well as disagreements over even the definition of what 'regional' means and the core purposes of regional interventions (Stilwell 1992; Hudson and Brown 2004;

Beer, Maude and Pritchard 2003; Collits 2012a). Policy objectives are often unclear and multiple (Armstrong and Taylor 1993), and processes driving regional outcomes are complex, cross-cutting and ever-changing in their impacts (Sorensen 2000). It is not easy to untangle the impacts on regions of the many processes at work, and therefore, unsurprisingly, evaluations of regional policies in Australia have been done irregularly and poorly (Collits 2011a).

All this makes for a policy minefield (Sorensen 2000). Yet Australian Governments have, at most times, attempted to be seen to be addressing the concerns of 'regions', and on rare occasions have attempted quite bold interventions (Collits 2002, p. 377). This chapter seeks to address some of these long-running issues of regional development, and to examine the ways that Australian Governments have attempted to help people in regions overcome the challenges they face specifically as a result of their regionality. It outlines the nature of regional policies in general and the objectives of regional policies in Australia; sets out the key policy developments at the national level since World War II; attempts to draw out the main characteristics of Australian regional policy and the key patterns of policy change and evolution that have occurred over time; and, finally, makes some suggestions about what good regional policy might look like in Australia, drawing upon the critical questions of regional development, and how it might proceed in the coming years.

The nature of regional policies

The central problems that regional policy traditionally has tried to address are geographical disparities and uneven development on the one hand, and region-specific problems on the other. It is not always easy to differentiate 'regional policies' from 'policies that affect regions' in the Australian context. Arguably, all or many government policies affect regions differently, and some have very negative consequences for particular places. Indeed, in some cases (such as tariff reductions), governments have implemented policies to counter the negative impact on regions of their other policies. Most government policies are 'spatially blind', yet right across the range of government activity they affect regional development in many and often unforeseen and negative ways. It is probably the case that non-regional policies have far greater impacts on regions than regional policies (Collits 2006). That said, regional development might be defined as:

> The deliberate attempt by government (at any level) and/or regional actors to influence regional outcomes, either in relation to the economy, the community or the environment, or all three, with varying objectives that generally relate to some notion of "regional well being".
>
> (Collits 2006)

Regional policies in turn might be divided into those that are 'region specific' (or bespoke), that is, designed to address the problems of one region, and those more generally aimed at addressing the problems of a set of regions, say 'rural

Australia' or the north of the United Kingdom. As well, and following on from the definition above, regional policies are often conflated with regional economic development policies, that is, policies designed to influence the location of economic activity, though these policies might often also be aimed at growing the population in a region or set of regions. On the other hand, policies for regions are often aimed at increasing or maintaining a certain level of services, yet this might also have beneficial consequences for economic development. Kim Houghton and Thomas Fell have also discussed the importance of regional service delivery in detail in this volume (see Chapter 14).

Regional policies can focus on three kinds of regions – on persistently lagging regions; on regions that have declined as a result of some economic or social dysfunction or economic restructuring shock; on growing regions or regions with significant growth potential (or so-called 'bolters', as termed by Grattan 2011); or indeed, on all regions. The approach of the previous Labor Government is to support all regions in their efforts to contribute to national performance, and this is consistent with the OECD's recent policy approach (OECD 2009).

State and national governments in Australia have sought to address problem issues in regional development in four main ways – first, by providing services that aspire to replicate standards of services offered in the cities, for example in health and education, to support rural and regional lifestyles (notwithstanding the difficult realities of distance); second, by providing economic development support for regions to address the narrowness of their economies or the effects of economic shocks, through a range of programmes; third, by providing modest funding for a structure of local and regional institutions to help organise regional development (currently, the Regional Development Australia (RDA) Committees); and fourth, by compensating regions for the negative impacts of other government policies (Collits 2012b, p. 3).

Making things more complicated, however, is that increasingly governments have sought to bundle all the various policies they have for addressing regional issues as a way of showing their 'commitment' to the regions concerned, for example through regional budget statements and during election campaigns. Often regional policy has become a political contest to see who has the biggest (dollar) commitment to 'regional' Australia, or to address concerns among regions that 'they are missing out', for example in relation to infrastructure or services (Collits 2012b).

This tendency creates confusion and means that discussions about regional policy are often not actually about regional policy as it is understood here, but about something else, for example industry policy or natural resource management. There is a large grey area somewhere between what are clearly 'regional policies' on the one hand and 'policies that affect regions' on the other. A good example is the location of government offices or of university campuses (Grattan 2011). Locating services near customers is not really 'regional policy', though it might be motivated by the desire to improve regional conditions.

There is one final point on the nature of regional policy highly relevant to ongoing Australian debates (for example, the ongoing debates over the economic, cultural and political dominance of the cities). It is that policies can either encourage people to move to where the jobs are, or encourage the movement of jobs (industry, investment) to where the people are. Most regional economic policies try to move jobs to where the people are, that is, they are place-based. Regional policies are distinguished by their attempt to help 'regions', or, put another way, 'people-in-place'. These policies therefore reject the idea of encouraging people to leave places that are in difficulty, even if such people might be better off leaving. (The place prosperity versus people prosperity question is a long-recognised distinction in regional science, and a much debated issue (Hoover 1975; Bolton 1992).)

Such a policy focus on place over people is what makes regional policy so controversial. It raises many difficulties, not only due to the complexity of regional development processes, but because many factors affecting regional development are mobile and the intensity of these mobile factors changes constantly over time. Influencing the direction and location of these mobile factors, whether capital or labour, remains at the heart of regional policy. The approach favouring regional (or spatial or place) policies has been contested by neoclassical approaches to policy (Freebairn 2003; Grattan 2011; Collits 2012b).

Regional policy developments in Australia since World War II

What, then, have been the highlights of Australian regional development policy since World War II? Political attention to regional Australia in Canberra has been uneven over time, to say the least. It is generally accepted that it has been Labor governments that have intervened more, and more ambitiously, in regional development. This has not always been the case, however, and the strong tilt of regional policy towards a generically defined 'rural and regional Australia' and towards decentralisation has largely been the result of persistent lobbying by rurally based non-Labor parties, whether the Country Party (now Nationals), One Nation in the 1990s and, more recently, the rural independents who have made regional development one of the prices to be paid for minority government since 2010. It is fair to say that Labor, over time, has been much readier to include the cities in its regional policies. For the Coalition, certainly, 'regional' has meant 'outside the capitals' (Collits 2002).

In fact, regional policy in Australia has often meant decentralisation and the pursuit of what many have termed 'balanced development', especially up until the 1980s (Collits 2002). This persistent policy focus on the consequences of Australia's history of urbanisation and the dominance of its primate cities reflects the power of the old-but-lingering city versus country debates, and the culture of the urban–rural divide (Brett 2011). Policy has been seen by many in the regions as being essentially about redressing 'imbalances'. The grandness of the policy challenge to turn around entrenched economic and social processes and achieve major shifts in population and economic activity, and the relative incapacity of governments to deliver, have undermined regional policy to this day.

The history of regional development over the last nearly 70 years has been one of stop-start policy attention and funding; often incoherent, or at least ill-defined, policy objectives; the coming and going of fads and fashions (for example growth centres in the 1970s); a gradual shift away from central planning towards neoliberal or 'bottom up' approaches; a generally broad-brush rather than region-specific philosophy; and a lowest common denominator of helping regions by creating regional bodies. The phases of policy can usefully be summarised by reference to successive national governments, and to some sharp policy reversals as governments changed.

The Labor governments and post-war reconstruction 1945–1949: the grand decentralisation design

While debates over decentralisation date from the early twentieth century, and perhaps even earlier (Collits 2002), the focus on nation-building and decentralisation reached its first major peak during the 1940s, reflecting grand issues thrown up by the war experience and heightened national planning.

In the immediate post-war period, the Chifley Labor Government undertook various policy actions through the Department of Post-War Reconstruction, including the first division of Australian states into regions and the establishment of regional committees. These committees were the first of many experiments in regional governance overseen by state and Commonwealth governments attempting to deal with the relative weakness and parochialism of local councils and the absence of genuinely regional government. Decentralisation or 'dispersed development' had been placed firmly on the political agenda during the Premiers' Conference of 1944 and was championed after the War by ministers and by the prominent bureaucrat HC (Nugget) Coombs (Lloyd and Troy 1981; Collits 2002). While many arguments were advanced in support of decentralisation, and have been since, they included at this time the strategic and defence-related need for more dispersed population and industry.

The Industrial Development Division of the department created the first of many government efforts to implement a national policy of decentralisation of secondary industry, a pursuit that continued at all levels of government until the era of a largely post-manufacturing economy began in the 1980s. The department's Regional Planning Division also introduced into Australian debates for the first time the notion of 'selective decentralisation', or the concentration of dispersed population into a small number of regional centres. This was to become the pivotal regional policy argument of the 1960s, and an issue that has dogged government interventions ever since (Collits 2002).

The Coalition governments 1949–1972: regional policy in retreat

The coming of the Menzies Government in 1949 meant that regional policy largely reverted to the states, despite Menzies' own key role in driving perhaps the largest and most successful initiative in decentralisation in Australia's history – the development of a decentralised national capital. Canberra's creation was later to be described by a senior bureaucrat as an 'exemplar' for regional development (Lansdown 1971). Menzies himself very wisely noted in 1959 that decentralisation was 'extraordinarily difficult to implement' (quoted in Hurley 1989, p. 152).

It is, however, not the case that nothing happened in regional development prior to the Whitlam Government that came to power in 1972. From 1964, the workings of the Commonwealth/State Officials Committee on Decentralisation drove many of the debates over decentralisation, and in 1972 the McMahon Government created the National Urban and Regional Development Authority (NURDA), the precursor to the Cities Commission (Collits 2002). Hence, during the latter years of the Coalition's long reign, forces that had been building in Australia – in particular, continued and indeed accelerating urbanisation, a developing academic discipline of urban studies, an emerging policy community supporting balanced development, and attendant political pressures – compelled politicians to take notice. Gough Whitlam himself, very much a city-based leader, took up the issue of regional development in a big way, and set about to construct a considerable policy architecture to achieve his visions (Lloyd and Troy 1981).

The Whitlam Government 1972–1975: taking decentralisation seriously

In the 1970s, the Whitlam Government led a substantial effort (sometimes in collaboration with the states) to decentralise population and economic activity away from the capitals, especially Sydney and Melbourne. The most radical move was the creation of the legendary Department of Urban and Regional Development (DURD) and the Cities Commission. These bodies, especially DURD, were to set the scene for a dramatic shake up of bureaucratic politics in Canberra, greatly resisted by Treasury, that would introduce a focus on spatial issues at the heart of government. Treasury was particularly alarmed at the prospect of regional budgets (Lloyd and Troy 1981; Collits 2002).

Whitlam's Minister, Tom Uren, and the academic Patrick Troy, came together to simultaneously address the problems associated with urban growth and congestion, together with chronic underdevelopment and sparse population away from the capitals. There is considerable evidence that the Government's major concern was actually with the cities. Their efforts culminated in the development of a national settlement strategy, the general absence of which had been long lamented by many observers. DURD also introduced the notion of coordinating policies with regional consequences across departments (Lloyd and Troy 1981; Collits 2002). The Whitlam Government also formed (short-lived) alliances with conservative State Premiers to progress their own decentralisation agendas.

The main vehicle to achieve decentralisation (but by no means the only one) was the Growth Centres Programme, which implemented a strategy known at the time as 'selective decentralisation', an attempt to concentrate decentralisation efforts in medium-sized cities rather than to disperse regional assistance across many projects and towns. The principal centres chosen (and remembered) were Albury–Wodonga and Bathurst–Orange, though there were others including Holsworthy near Sydney and Monarto in South Australia. The interventions were substantial by today's standards, with the Government spending approximately $788.8 million (in 2013 dollars) on the growth centres (Collits 2002, p. 84). Other initiatives included the creation of regional organisations of councils (ROCs), the Australian Assistance Plan and the Area Improvement Programme. There is little doubt that the Whitlam Government provided the only serious attempt by an Australian Government to address what has been perceived historically as Australia's 'regional problem' of unbalanced development and the city–county divide.

The Fraser Government 1975–1983: another retreat from regional policy

After the fall of the Whitlam Government in 1975, the pattern of 1949 was somewhat repeated, with the incoming Fraser Coalition Government largely rolling back the DURD empire and turning its back on big-ticket decentralisation policies. The rollback, however, was not as rapid or as all-embracing as is often thought, and a number of the Whitlam initiatives survived in various forms for several years. A change in government in 1976 in New South Wales (ironically to Labor) also helped to signal the end of the growth centres initiatives, and decentralisation (selective or otherwise) largely, if gradually, vanished from Australian politics as a serious regional policy objective (Collits 2002).

The Hawke Government 1983–1991: beginning the shift to 'DIY' regional policy

There have been two notable exceptions to the general pattern of greater interventions by Labor governments. The first was the relative absence of policy interest in regional development by the Hawke Government in the 1980s, and the second, detailed below, was the (periodic) policy activism of the Howard Government.

The Hawke Government had a far greater focus on recovery from the severe recession of the early 1980s (though this indeed had severe regional consequences), on industry policy and on macro and microeconomic reform. Some regional policies were enacted to counter the negative regional impacts of macro policies, but the earlier, highly-charged focus of the Whitlam Government on the causes and consequences of urbanisation and the urban rural divide was totally gone (despite the presence in the Government of the former Whitlam Government DURD architect Tom Uren). Observers of the scene in the 1980s found, in general, virtually no interest in Canberra in regional development or urban affairs (Collits 2002). Regional development was largely dormant in Canberra during this period, except for the important (though apparently minor) development of local employment initiatives and of the Country Centres Strategy in the late 1980s. This was one of the earliest attempts by an Australian Government to focus on 'bottom up', community-centred self-help regional policy, which was followed in due course by most state governments and which has remained the usual vehicle for regional policy interventions to this day, currently embodied in the much touted 'localism' approach (Collits 2002, pp. 108–109).

The Country Centres Project in effect predicted the way regional policy would shift in Australia, and is noteworthy for this reason. It portended a more nuanced approach to regional development, emphasising local efforts and local 'ownership', and by definition, scaling back from the earlier, more ambitious policy agendas. Gone by now was the attempt to remake settlement patterns and to effect a reversal of demographic and economic forces, and in its place was a greater focus on practical attempts at improving life in regional communities. It suited the times and the emergent ideologies which placed more emphasis on market forces and globalisation, and which accepted the primacy of Australian cities as our natural condition.

The Keating Government 1991–1996: regional competitive advantage

In the 1990s, the Keating Government more than made up for the absence of regional policy under Labor in the 1980s, by establishing a number of inquiries (the Kelty Report 1993; the Industry Commission 1993; the Bureau of Industry Economics 1994) and commissioning a report by McKinsey and Company in 1994. On the advice of these inquiries, the Government then introduced a new Regional Development programme which, while modest as an intervention, ushered in a new emphasis on 'regional competitive advantage' driven by local leadership, embodied in the creation and resourcing of around 50 Regional Development Organisations (RDOs) (Collits 2002). Part of the Keating Government's motivation was to address the regional consequences of another severe recession, which, perhaps for the first time, saw highly regionalised unemployment patterns both in the cities and in non-metropolitan regions. The emphasis on labour markets in the Government's regional development thinking was reflected in its *Working Nation* initiative of 1994 (Keating 1994) and in the creation of Area Consultative Committees (ACCs) alongside the RDOs.

The upswing in interest in regions coincided with important analytical work being undertaken in government on regions (the most substantial to that time outside the Whitlam period in office), and with the publication of the highly influential work by Michael Porter, *The Competitive Advantage of Nations* (Porter 1990). The emerging regional realities of the 1990s also coincided with new ideas in regional policy and a heightened focus on competitiveness, and a number of the elements of modern Australian regional policy took clearer shape at this time:

- The aim became not to redistribute economic activity but to lift productivity in all regions to achieve better national productivity.

- The emphasis was now on 'bottom up' rather than 'top down' approaches with 'empowerment' the new buzz phrase (or what Sorensen (2002) has termed 'DIY regional development').
- The theme was now 'local solutions to local problems', or a more region-specific approach to problem solving.

Again, the relatively modest nature of the 1990s interventions and the focus on specific regional concerns rather than on grand schemes provided a contrast with the 1970s and signalled a seemingly permanent shift in the style of regional policies pursued in Australia.

The Howard Government 1996–2007: addressing 'two Australias'

The second exception to the 'rule' that Labor governments did most to drive regional policy was the substantial interventionism of the Howard Conservative Coalition government in the period after 1998, driven by the Nationals under John Anderson. In 1999 Anderson convened a Regional Australia Summit and then introduced a number of new programmes including the highly controversial Regional Partnerships Programme. John Anderson spoke with great passion about 'two Australias' and the need to restore services outside the cities, and this drove much of the focus within the Government (Anderson 1999; Collits 2008). Anderson's approach resuscitated old themes but with a new concentration on the delivery of services rather than the old style decentralisation approach.

The interventionism of the later Howard Government contrasts sharply with its initial reaction against regional policy upon coming to office in 1996, and reflected (to many observers) a response to a rise in rural disaffection seen in the emergence of country independents and the One Nation Party (Collits 2008). Despite its early termination of funding for RDOs, the Howard Government did continue to support regional organisations in the form of ACCs. These bodies, while provided with little core funding and little independence, were important regional actors in their role of identifying and supporting regional spending programmes such as the highly controversial Regional Partnerships programme. This was the subject of a number of inquiries which found that some of the programme's initiatives were either politically motivated or ineffective. Neither of these conclusions should be a surprise to students of regional policy, since the target areas of regional policy interventions have often been found to coincide with the electoral interests of the governing party of the day, and since many regional policy initiatives do not deliver on their promise, for reasons outlined earlier in the chapter (Australian National Audit Office 2007; Collits 2008).

One of the Howard Government's main policy interventions was the Sustainable Regions programme, aimed at assisting what in the UK might have been known as 'depressed' or lagging regions. Twelve regions were identified and supported through a range of initiatives. The significance of this programme was that it underscored the shift away from earlier decentralisation objectives to a much greater focus on specific 'regions in difficulty', and an emphasis on tailoring approaches to the needs of regions, with considerable local input into strategic directions (Collits 2008).

The Rudd and Gillard Governments 2007–2013: a new paradigm for regional Australia?

In the 2000s, the Rudd and Gillard Governments established RDA Committees through formal agreements with the states and territories, and more significantly, following the 2010 election established an agreement with the independent members of parliament to significantly ramp up the focus within government on regional Australia and to increase infrastructure spending on regional Australia (Australian Labor Party 2010). This is said by its supporters to have initiated a 'new paradigm' in regional development for Australia, and by sceptics to simply signify another peak in policy interest in regional Australia, to be followed by further inevitable troughs in the future.

The RDA Committees have replaced the former ACCs, which in turn had superseded the RDOs. There are a number of regional funding programmes, with the focus very much on hard infrastructure spending. There are now additional machinery of government measures to embed regional development as a permanent focus of Canberra policy-making. The current Government's approach is on 'localism', an approach that is neither unique nor new (Collits 2008).

The significance of these developments is uncertain. On many occasions in the past, governments have elevated regional development to a higher level of consciousness without actually improving the quality of the interventions. Certainly, between 2010 and 2013, the electorates of the two rural Independents have fared well. And an important advance has been the creation of the Regional Australia Institute, supported by government funding but promising political independence and a more evidence based approach to regional policy. On the other hand, the Department of Regional Australia's contribution has been, to date, largely hidden from view. The continued focus on regional infrastructure has, seemingly, been at the expense of building strategic regional policy collaborations and well-resourced networks of innovation. The continued chronic underfunding of RDA Committees has diluted their effectiveness and mission. The Government's contribution has seemed more 'localism lite' than 'localism', and many regional policy questions remain unresolved.

All in all, this falls well short of a fundamentally new paradigm. The regional policy directions of the newly elected Abbott Government remain unclear, save for an increased emphasis on infrastructure.

So what has really happened? Patterns of regional policy interventions in Australia and core themes

What to make of all this?

The history of regional policy since World War II is not just the sum of all the various policy interventions and programmes, and some overall conclusions can be drawn from an examination of all the interventions, government by government. There have been regional policy problems that have come and gone, to be replaced by new problems, shifts in ideology, swings in political attention to regions and in policy fashions, and some policy learning has occurred along the way, driven both by the world of ideas as well as by changing circumstances (Collits 2002).

Regional development policy's long history in Australia has often been accompanied by the perception by many observers that it has not really 'worked' and that its promise has not been fulfilled, and by some that it has not really been tried properly. Following an early focus on decentralisation, more recently regional policy has clearly shifted toward the support of regional competitive advantage and community driven development strategies. There is a shared commitment by governments to assisting (still mainly) rural places to diversify their economies. As well, in the last decade, there has been a shift away from productivity focused policies towards 'sustainability' and 'liveability' (Collits 2012a). Policies are now more region-specific in the sense that regional strategies are generally developed locally or regionally rather than by central governments.

It is important to note that regional development interventions in Australia have been the province of all three levels of government, and the subject of ongoing political dispute and debate. For example, local government has long had an interest in economic development and industry attraction, now formalised in most councils through the employment of economic development officials. At the state level, since World War II all governments have pursued investment attraction strategies, in an increasingly competitive way, as well as attempting through various means to steer as much development as is economically and politically possible and feasible towards non-metropolitan regions. For example, during the Whitlam Government's highly-focused efforts at regional policy, the New South Wales and Victorian Governments were active partners in the decentralisation efforts of the day (Collits 2002). And, at various times, the states have been in conflict with Canberra over the arrangements related to regional bodies.

Interventions have been uneven in intensity and varying in purpose, with substantial swings between periods of heightened policy interest and periods of negligible interest in regional matters. Despite the peaks and troughs of policy interest, the policy reversals that have accompanied changes of government and the coming and going of policy fashions, it is possible to detect patterns of regional policy intervention in Australia and to make sense of these.

First, there has been a broad focus on non-metropolitan regions in policy interventions, reflecting a long-standing historical emphasis on the country-city divide and a sense that in Australia, the 'regional problem' is the over-concentration of population and economic activity in the capital cities. This is analogous to the long running regional problem in the UK of the so-called 'north-south divide'. While Australia has escaped some of the more extreme disparities of other countries, there has been persistent and growing urbanisation as well as the much discussed cultural unease (noted earlier) among many inhabitants outside the cities that 'there is something wrong' with the 'unbalanced' distribution of people, economic activity and political power between city and country (Collits 2002, 2012c). This has been described colourfully by the rural Independent member of parliament Tony Windsor as the 'feedlot' approach to the economy and settlement pattern (quoted in Brett 2011). In other words, there is something wrong and artificial about crowding our people into a few very large cities. This is, for Windsor and for many other (mainly) rural Australians both inefficient and inequitable (Collits 2002).

This view – that Australia's highly concentrated patterns of settlement and economic activity are somehow unnatural – is disputed by many urban and regional economists and economic geographers. These critics have argued persuasively that market-driven urbanisation processes (not only in Australia) are both inevitable and desirable for national economic performance, especially in a globalised world, and that cities now largely drive innovation and economic development (Polese 2008; Glaeser 2011; McCann and Acs 2011). Moreover, it is also the case that Australia's settlement pattern has evolved the way it has for very good reasons that may well make countervailing policies impossible (Collits 2011b).

The focus on non-metropolitan Australia as the place to concentrate regional policy efforts reached its high point(s) in the various attempts at 'decentralisation'. Before World War II, these included soldier settlement schemes, the creation of Canberra as the capital city, the establishment of the Commonwealth Grants Commission, various large infrastructure projects, and irrigation schemes in the dry interior (Collits 2002). Despite these efforts, one academic observer in the 1960s, the economist Max Neutze, famously described decentralisation in Australia as 'everyone's policy but no one's programme' (Neutze 1965, p. v). Another described the efforts at decentralisation as 'puny' (Hurley 1989, p. 363).

Second, while many policies and programmes have, from time to time, sought to stimulate economic activity and population decentralisation, there has also been an ongoing policy theme of providing adequate services in non-metropolitan regions, to support a reasonable lifestyle for those living away from the cities and access to services taken for granted in the cities.

Third, each of the main political parties has sought to take ownership of concern for non-metropolitan Australia. This often has meant that regional policy debates and political practice often descend into arguments over the size of one's commitment rather than the quality or impacts of the policies under discussion (Brett 2011; Collits 2012b). This is typically reflected in the perception among many people outside the capitals of an inequality of resources. It also has led, over the last decade or so, to the annual budgetary practice of governments releasing information on budget night on regional (non metropolitan) government spending across the whole range of portfolios.

Fourth, in contrast to other countries, in particular the European Union, the overall preference of Australian Governments has been for relatively limited interventions (often described as neoliberalism or economic rationalism). This has partly reflected the relative absence of serious regional disparities, and an unwillingness to embrace the level of intervention routinely accepted by the Europeans.

Fifth, there has been a notable evolution in policy approaches over time that has resulted in a broad consensus among the major political parties now about the possibilities of regional policy and its core concerns (Collits 2006). This has consisted in two broad policy developments – the abandonment (since the late 1970s) of any serious attempts to decentralise population and economic activity away from the cities; and, not unrelated, a move away from top down approaches and towards 'bottom up', region-specific approaches (Collits 2002, 2012c).

Sixth, regional policy in Australia has suffered (like many other areas of policy) from constitutional uncertainty over ultimate responsibilities, and therefore debates over policy have often deteriorated into arguments between Canberra and the states, generally where one side of politics is in power in Canberra and the other side in the state(s) or territories (Hudson and Brown 2004). Often, the arguments concern the establishment and operations of regional bodies set up by one level of government or the other (Collits and Brown 2004; Collits 2012a).

Finally, regional policy has often focused on regional governance arrangements. In the absence of regional government, and in view of the general unwillingness of central governments (either state or commonwealth) to devolve real responsibility for regional development to regions themselves (or to local government), regional governance has remained informal, complex and problematic, and its impacts on regions uncertain. Different roles have been assigned to the various bodies created over time, including the development of projects, strategic planning and the provision of advice to Canberra, without the Commonwealth ever providing the resources for these bodies to effect major change, or indeed ever settling the argument as to what their primary role should be (Collits and Brown 2004; Collits 2012a).

Where to from here for regional policy? Summary, conclusions and policy recommendations

Overall, Australian governments have intervened in regional development in many ways since World War II, with a range of often unstated and complex objectives and using a range of policy instruments, all the while generally focused on supporting development and lifestyles beyond the cities. These interventions have generally been poorly evaluated and heavily influenced by the electoral cycle and political considerations. This has meant that, on many occasions, policies commenced are discontinued before they have had time to work, there has been duplication across jurisdictions, and there has been a general disconnect between theory, policy and practice that continues to this day.

Regional policy in Australia will always be shaped by political realities, such as:

- Federalism is recognised by all as a constraint on policy development.
- Blame shifting between levels of government occurs routinely.

- Regional policy is largely about solving visible (hence political) problems and creating visible solutions (like infrastructure).
- New policy often emerges through a process of 'pragmatic incrementalism' (see Lindblom 1959 for a discussion of incrementalism).
- Governments are increasingly averse to picking 'place winners', and have been since the days of the growth centres era when selective decentralisation dominated the policy thinking. They now have a preference for 'covering all bases' in relation to where and how they intervene, both in terms of place interventions and policy instruments, and this means also that governments do not see their role as only helping declining or lagging regions, or, for that matter, 'bolters'.
- Central governments want local communities to solve their own problems, but do not fund them and their regional institutions to implement the strategies they are funded to draw up.
- Local government suffers from its lack of capacity to raise taxes.
- Governments have come to recognise their regional policy limitations and the complexity of the drivers of regional growth and decline.
- Regional development is not always a priority of governments – this is a critical constraint on policy, far greater than ideology, for example.
- Regional policy can take a long time to work, and as the fictional Sir Humphrey Appleby once said, government is about surviving until Friday afternoon (Collits 2002, 2006).

Remarkably, no Australian government has come to office with a plan for regional development that addresses what might be termed the 'prior questions'. The core questions of regional development might reasonably be said to include the following:

- What are we trying to achieve (or, put another way, what is the 'regional problem')?
- Whose responsibility is regional well-being and regional development? (i.e. which level of government is responsible, or should local communities and industries be responsible?)
- What really drives regional growth and decline?
- Critically, what can government policies do about these drivers?
- What has actually worked in terms of strategies and programmes, and at what cost?
- When should governments intervene (what triggers intervention)?
- Where (that is, in which regions) should governments intervene?
- And, how much should governments intervene?

The answers to these questions are complex and contested by scholars, policy-makers and practitioners alike. However, good regional policy would include a considered position on these fundamental questions, and would appeal to empirical evidence where this would help clarify answers to the questions.

More importantly, there is little evidence that Australian governments, when framing regional policies, have attempted to consider, let alone resolve, them. Of course, there are many reasons why these core questions are ignored, or not even asked. One might have something to do with the words of JM Keynes:

> There is nothing a politician likes so little as to be well informed; it makes decision making so complex and difficult.
>
> (quoted in Sanderson 2002, p. 5)

Another reason relates to the notions of wicked problems and complexity referred to earlier, which seem to have particular resonance for regional policy formulation and implementation.

Answering these questions has very practical and not merely academic consequences, for resources are finite, there are opportunity costs in pursuing some interventions while ignoring others, and people's expectations are high. For example, knowing something about what drives regional growth and decline has explicit consequences for strategy and policy – interventions invariably seek to find what drives growth and to push it harder or further. And clarifying objectives is at the core of all good policy, despite the notorious tendency in regional policy (which the most cursory reading of policy statements and strategies confirms) to blur or generalise objectives and to reduce the conversation to clichés and motherhood statements. And while selecting which regions to support is largely a political question rather than one in which an evidence base can help, decisions in this area nevertheless deserve some kind of consideration of guiding principles. Otherwise regional policy will inevitably be diminished and be destined to be seen always and everywhere as merely 'political', something long concluded by its chief critics.

The absence of an ongoing dialogue among those interested in good regional policy outcomes is disappointing for many with an interest in the area. There is a sense, which continues despite the coming of the so-called 'new paradigm' of Australian politics in 2010, that regional policy is not done very well in Australia. The Australian way of doing regional policy also contrasts dramatically with the position in Europe where, whatever one might think of the effectiveness of the massive regional policy interventions there, there is an informed and ongoing three-way dialogue between governments and their advisers, academics working in the field, and practitioners. This has led to what might be regarded as an 'evaluation culture' in regional policy, where a real policy community exists and there are opportunities for policy innovation. This probably stems from a shared agreement on the importance and purposes of regional policy, something that has been conspicuously lacking in Australia since World War II.

So, what would good regional policy look like? Here are some suggestions. Regional policy should be based on evidence where that is available. It should have clearly defined objectives, and policy evaluation, while difficult, must be a routine part of the policy cycle, with appropriate and agreed metrics. Governments should offer to help all regions, not just those defined somehow as lagging or declining regions. Cities should be recognised as regions. There should be substantial (and more than at present) devolution of responsibility for funding decisions to local authorities and regional bodies. Regional bodies (currently RDAs) should be better funded and given clear and important tasks. Regions should have a say in determining their boundaries. Ministers should not micro-manage regional development. There should be greater opportunities for conversations between those who operate in the realms of theory, policy and practice. Mechanisms for collaboration between jurisdictions should be reactivated. Policies should be measured for their effectiveness rather than for the size of the spend. Professional development for practitioners and regional leaders should be a government priority. Overall, there needs to be an advance from the 'localism-lite' that we have now.

There are three particular matters that an incoming government needs to resolve as part of the 'prior questions' exercise. First, there needs to be an early consideration and a reassessment of regionalism and what it now means in our age of more mobile labour and capital, more casualised and project-driven work, highly porous regional boundaries and increased long distance travel for work and relationships. Regions need to be redefined to recognise functional economic areas, and be defined by regional people as a basis for regional policy. We now have fundamentally different types of regions from those we used to have. Regional policy must become place-based in new and innovative ways to match the innovative new business and mobility models that are emerging. Not only should regional policy operate at different scales, but also in different modes.

Second, regional institutions should be encouraged to self-govern and should be rewarded for collaboration. RDAs, while varying in quality, in general are floundering and are unsure of their mission. They lack resources and they lack incentives to collaborate. A Memorandum of Understanding (MoU) across regional bodies should be a first point for any funding.

Third, regional development research needs urgent attention and, in particular, boosting. This is particularly the case for regionally engaged research. The silos between research and innovation policy on the one hand and regional policy on the other must be broken down. Governments should not set national research priorities. Universities should. And regional universities must be incentivised to create new opportunities for working collaboratively with regional development institutions and industries to deliver effective and implementable local and regional strategies. EU-style interactions must be encouraged. New methodologies for collaboration should be investigated and models developed. Regional universities must be unleashed from the red tape in which they currently drown.

In view of the comments above about what good regional policy might look like, and considering the three urgent questions, what are the basic first steps to a better policy approach? Some very specific actions might improve the process of regional policy in order to get us from the current impasse to a better honed regional policy approach, and these should be considered up front by an incoming government:

- A Regional Policy Futures Commission should be set up as a statutory authority with some distance from ministers, to oversee the work of voluntary regional institutions established to implement regionally agreed strategies, to determine funding and to evaluate regionally-driven programmes and initiatives.
- These institutions should be driven by collaboration (as noted previously) and funded to build 'collaborative capital'.
- The Board of the Commission should bring together scholars, practitioners, civic entrepreneurs and policymakers.

While regional policy is, indeed, highly problematic, and while governments cannot control all, or perhaps even many, of the complex processes and drivers of regional development, there is considerable room for improvement in the ways governments attempt to assist regions and their communities to be more sustainable. We urgently need a period of creative, locally-driven and centrally-funded regional development.

References

Anderson, J 1999, *One Nation or Two? Securing a Future for Rural and Regional Australia*, Address to the National Press Club, 17 February, Canberra.

Armstrong, H and Taylor, J 1993, *Regional Economics and Policy*, Harvester Wheatsheaf, Hemel Hempstead, UK.

Australian Labor Party 2010, *The Australian Labor Party and the Independent Members Agreement*. Available at: www.scribd.com/doc/37069401/Agreement-With-the-Independents. Accessed: 29 March 2012.

Australian National Audit Office 2007, *Performance Audit of the Regional Partnerships Programme*, vols. 1–3, Commonwealth of Australia, Canberra.

Beer, A 2009, 'The Theory and Practice of Developing Locally', in Rowe, J (ed.), *Theories of Local Economic Development: Linking Theory to Practice*, Ashgate, Farnham.

Beer, A, Maude, A and Pritchard, B 2003, *Developing Australia's Regions: Theory and Practice*, University of New South Wales Press, Sydney.

Bolton, R 1992, '"Place Prosperity vs People Prosperity" Revisited: An Old Issue with a New Angle', *Urban Studies*, vol. 29, no. 2, pp. 185–203.

Brett, J 2011, 'Fair Share: Country and City in Australia', *Quarterly Essay*, no. 42.

Bureau of Industry Economics 1994, 'Regional Development: Patterns and Policy Implications', *Research Report No. 56*, Bureau of Industry Economics, Canberra.

Collits, P 2002, 'A Question of Balance? The Fate of Balanced Development as a Regional Policy Objective in New South Wales', PhD thesis, University of New England, NSW.

Collits, P 2004, 'Successful Cities and Regions: the Search for the Regional Development Holy Grail', paper presented at the 28th Annual Conference of the Australian and New Zealand section of the Regional Science Association International, Wollongong, September.

Collits, P 2006, 'Great Expectations: What Regional Policy Can Realistically Achieve in Australia', *Australian Farm Policy Journal*, August, based on a paper presented at the National Regional Research Colloquium, Bureau of Transport and Regional Economics, Canberra, February 2004.

Collits, P 2008, 'The Howard Government and Regional Development', *Australasian Journal of Regional Studies*, vol. 14, no. 3, pp. 287–312.

Collits, P 2011a, 'Towards a Theory of Regional Development', presentation to the Institute of Australian Geographers conference, Wollongong, July.

Collits, P 2011b, 'Country Towns in A Big Australia: the Decentralisation Debate Revisited', in Martin, J and Budge, T (eds), *The Sustainability of Australia's Country Towns: Renewal, Renaissance, Resilience*, VURRN Press Inc., Bendigo.

Collits, P 2012a, 'Planning for Regions', in Thompson, S and Maginn, P (eds), *Planning Australia: An Overview of Urban and Regional Planning*, 2nd edn, Cambridge University Press, Melbourne.

Collits, P 2012b, 'Big Spending on Regional Australia is Not Regional Policy: But Are Either Worth Having?', unpublished paper.

Collits, P and Brown, AJ 2004, 'When the Wicked Meet the Vicious: Addressing Long-Term Problems of Capacity and Legitimacy in Australian Local and Regional Governance', unpublished paper presented to the RMIT University/ASSA Workshop on Participation and Governance for Regional Development, Hamilton, Victoria, July.

Freebairn, J 2003, 'Economic Policy for Rural and Regional Australia', *Australian Journal of Agricultural and Resource Economics*, vol. 47, pp. 389–414.

Glaeser, E 2011, *Triumph of the City: How Our Greatest Invention Makes Us Richer, Smarter, Greener, Healthier and Happier*, Penguin Press, New York.

Grattan Institute 2011, *Investing in Regions: Making a Difference*, Grattan Institute, Melbourne.

Hoover, EM 1975, *An Introduction to Regional Economics*, Knopf, New York.

Hudson, W and Brown, AJ (eds) 2004, *Restructuring Australia: Regionalism, Republicanism and the Reform of the Nation-State*, The Federation Press, Sydney.

Hurley, F 1989, 'An Event that Never Happened: The History and Politics of Decentralisation in Victoria and New South Wales 1885–1985', PhD Thesis, Deakin University, Melbourne.

Industry Commission 1993, 'Impediments to Regional Industry Adjustment', *Report No. 35*, Industry Commission, Canberra.

Keating, P, 1994, *Working Nation: Policies and Programs*, Australian Government Publishing Service, Canberra.

Kelty, W 1993, *Developing Australia: A Regional Perspective*, vol. 1–3, Australian Government Publishing Service, Canberra.

Lansdown, R 1971, 'Canberra: An Exemplar for Many Decentralised Australian Cities', *Australian Quarterly*, vol. 43, no. 3, pp. 71–85.

Lindblom, C 1959, 'The Science of Muddling Through', *Public Administration Review*, vol. 19, no. 2, pp. 79–88.

Lloyd, C and Troy, P 1981, *Innovation and Reaction: The Life and Death of the Federal Department of Urban and Regional Development*, Allen & Unwin, Sydney.

McCann, P and Acs, Z 2011, 'Globalisation: Countries, Cities and Multinationals', *Regional Studies*, vol. 45, no. 1, pp. 17–32.

McKinsey 1994, *Lead Local Compete Global: Unlocking the Growth Potential of Australia's Regions*, Final Report of the Study for the Department of Housing and Regional Development, McKinsey and Company, Sydney.

Neutze, GM 1965, *Economic Policy and the Size of Cities*, ANU Press, Canberra.

OECD 2009, *How Regions Grow: Trends and Analysis*, OECD, Paris.

Polese, M 2009, *The Wealth and Poverty of Regions: Why Cities Matter*, University of Chicago Press, Chicago.

Porter, ME 1990, *The Competitive Advantage of Nations*, Free Press, London.

Rittel, H and Webber, M 1973, 'Dilemmas in a General Theory of Planning', *Policy Sciences*, vol. 4, pp. 155–169.

Sanderson, I 2002, 'Evaluation, Policy Learning and Evidence-Based Policy Making', *Public Administration*, vol. 80, no. 1, pp. 1–22.

Sorensen, AD 2000, 'Regional Development: Some Issues for Policy Makers', *Australian Parliamentary Library Research Paper No. 26*, Australian Parliamentary Library, Canberra.

Sorensen, AD 2002, 'Regional Economic Governance: States, Markets and DIY', in Bell, S (ed.), *Economic Governance & Institutional Dynamics*, Oxford University Press, Melbourne.

Stilwell, F 1992, *Understanding Cities and Regions: Spatial Political Economy*, Pluto Press, Sydney.

2 From state direction to community self-efficacy

The devolution of responsibility for regional development in Australia

Geoff Cockfield

The main purpose of this chapter is to examine the general movement from direct and centralised government efforts to promote regional development in Australia to a situation where greater responsibility for that development falls on local government, communities and individuals. Given differential settlement and development patterns across the country and a federal system in which power and responsibilities cross three tiers of government, there are no easily identifiable steps or periods in this transition. The approach here is to think in terms of policy layers, with periodic changes in emphasis that add to, but do not entirely extinguish previous approaches. The 'layers' described in this discussion, in order of their initial significant manifestation, are classified as: producer settlement and retention; services equity; decentralisation; and self-sufficiency and adjustment. The pre-European layer of social and economic activity, in which indigenous groups were spread throughout the country and engaged in varying forms of resource use, is not considered here as decision-making was highly devolved and this discussion focuses on national approaches.

From this discussion, several contentions are developed. First, Australian governments have generally moved away from direct support for regional development, such as providing subsidies for producers to 'settle' in regional areas, in favour of enabling industries and communities to help themselves. There are however, remnants of direct support in ad hoc responses to political circumstances and in some state and local government programmes. Second, regional development policies have largely been an extension of industry policy, especially agricultural and manufacturing industry policy, but there are two exceptions to this. There is some notion of equity of communication, transport, health and social services no matter where people live, and there is a largely ineffectual but recurring interest in decentralisation as an extension of urban policy. I also argue that a form of post-productivist industry policy is emerging whereby governments resume certain rights to the use of selected natural resources, which will have a significant impact on regional development in Australia. This discussion will describe some manifestations of the policy layers and then consider the evidence for overarching directions in regional development policy. To start the discussion though, some features of the policy context are described.

The policy context

Regional development is shaped, and constrained, by Australian geography. There is a concentration of population in an 'archipelago' of settlements, running from Cairns in the far north east, down through the major population centres of Brisbane, Sydney and Melbourne, around to Adelaide, with relatively isolated settlements in other parts of the coast and further inland than 200 km of the eastern and southern coasts. That is, we mainly live on some edges of a vast continent. This in contrast to the US where both the east and west coasts have population concentrations and there are more substantial infrastructure connections across the country. Australia has however one of the most concentrated populations in the world, and that concentration is in or near several major cities, and in or near some selected coastal areas. There is some 'inner regional' population growth in areas that have 'natural' amenity, not too far from major centres, with some interest in a somewhat idealised and softened rural lifestyle (Tonts and Greive 2002, p. 60).

Inland areas that are still relatively dependent on rural industries are generally depopulating (Argent and Walmsley 2008, p. 142). The number of farm businesses decreased from a peak of approximately 220,000 in the mid-1950s to about 135,000 by 2011 and there is extensive and relentless adoption of labour saving technologies in agriculture and mining. This contributes to relatively high outmigration rates amongst young people and women in rural areas (Argent and Walmsley 2008, pp. 143–145). There is, however, also a net loss of young people from coastal areas that otherwise have growing populations (Argent and Walmsley 2008, p. 144). Apart from the social attractions, the majority of Australia's universities are in the state capital cities and jobs in the services sector, which is a growing part of the Australian economy, are disproportionately located in metropolitan areas (Birrell and O'Connor 2000). Given Australia's large area and five major metropolitan centres spread around the population archipelago, a move to the city usually means a move far from regional origins, which weakens ongoing social and cultural connections to those regions (Argent and Walmsley 2008, p. 148).

There are three exceptions to the depopulation of the rural inland, with growth in some regional service and administrative centres, some remote Indigenous peoples' communities and mining services towns. While there are cultural and traditional pull factors to the remote Indigenous communities, social problems, lack of employment opportunities and the social attractions of urban areas are push factors for outmigration just as they are for non-Indigenous people in remote areas. Mining towns are also subject to fluctuations in commodity demand and many rely on a 'fly-in fly-out' workforce, which limits some of the regional economic benefits from having a large labour force. This also affects the social structures of those communities, with the 'original' town and then outlying camps of transient workers.

In relation to political institutions, as with the US and Canada, Australia is a federation with a layer of local governments covering most of the country, so responsibility for regional development is distributed between three tiers. Constitutionally, states have control of the conventional mechanisms of regional development in infrastructure, land use regulation, health and education services and the direct regulation of business operations. From that, states (colonies prior to 1901) have a considerable history of competing for investment, using a variety of incentives and protection measures to attract businesses (Linge 1967, p. 47), with this patchwork of policies and internal competition being reasons for national governments having sought to coordinate economic, industry and regional development policy. Local governments also have some powers over land use regulation, local infrastructure and business operation but they remain subservient to the states, being created under state legislations. So, states are in some ways the central tier in regional development. However Australia is also a centralising federation due to particular constitutional judgements in relation to taxation powers, so that the national governments are increasingly able to set and lead the policy agenda through a system of coordinate federalism, in which the central government works with, and sometimes financially coerces, the state governments to develop national frameworks.

Regionalism, that is the defining and administration of regions that are more than local government areas but less than states, has some institutional manifestations but as yet is not a major component of Australian federalism. Institutional arrangements have included voluntary aggregations of local governments into regional organisations of councils (ROCs), which can engage in as little as information sharing and as much as sharing resources and jointly managing regional development organisations. Some of these organisations, along with business groups, also promote a regional identity to attract business and tourists, emphasising particular features, such the 'surf coast', 'alpine country' or the 'green triangle'. Then there are also local government amalgamations, most notably the ones forced by state governments in Victoria in the late 1990s and Queensland in 2008 that created some regional-scale councils. Another regional-scale arrangement is the set of natural resources management (NRM) organisations that cover most of the country, which are state-defined but jointly (state and Commonwealth) funded. The strongest regional institutional arrangements are in Western Australia, where the state government has defined regions with a government minister responsible for each one, and there is routine reporting of expenditure in those regions.

Finally, Australian economic policy has undergone a major change since the 1960s and early 1970s, under the influence of neoliberalism, which is really a revival of the principles of classical liberalism, of limited state intervention (for further explanation see Argent 2005; Beer *et al.* 2005). This is in contrast to a long policy history of intervention in areas such as land ownership and use, commodity pricing and industry protection. Such intervention was not only tolerated by citizens but expected, and explanations for this tendency have variously included: the authoritarianism of the original penal settlements that were the foundation of the current states; the sparse settlement and harsh climate of the continent; and the influence of British social liberalism and to some extent emerging social democracy, at the time of the formation of the nation. The widely accepted narrative, by both critics (Bell 1997; Carroll and Manne 1992; Schott 1991; Pusey 1991) and supporters (James *et al.* 1993; Kelly 1992) is that the revival of classical liberal ideas in the UK and the US spread to New Zealand and Australia in the late 1970s, becoming the dominant policy paradigm in the 1980s.

The dominance part of this story is evident in policy changes of the 1980s, which included a significant decrease in levels of industry protection (Productivity Commission 2008 summarised in Figure 2.1), the floating of the Australian currency, campaigning to reduce international trade 'distortions' (Hawke and Kerin 1986, pp. 70–72) and a raft of microeconomic 'reform' policies. But there are three qualifications to this. First, while the contemporary neoliberal story is of 70 years of insularity, followed by economic enlightenment, the Australian economy has long been subject to international economic forces and pressures for change and innovation (Jones 2002, p. 313). Second, there were home-grown and vocal critics of agricultural protectionism in the 1960s (see for example Campbell 1964; McKay 1965; Anon. 1967; Gruen 1986), and moves to reduce protection to manufacturing industries started in the late 1960s were evident during the time of the Whitlam Labor Government (1972–1975) (see Figure 2.1). Third, as will be shown in this discussion, governments have not eschewed intervention, though they are more reluctant to commit to direct and/or ongoing support for industries and communities. This reluctance is partly due to a belief in the limits of state intervention and also because in contemporary political discourse, a balanced or surplus budget has become the mark of good government (Argent and Walmsley 2008, p. 71).

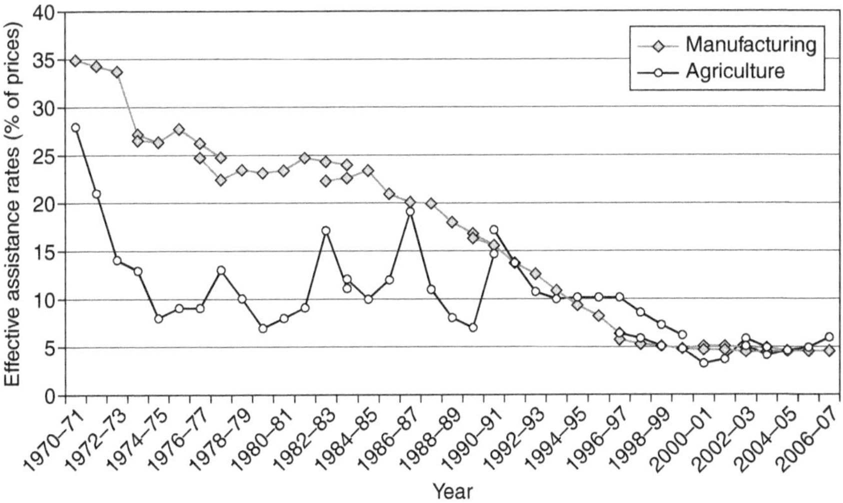

Figure 2.1 Trends in effective assistant rates (source: Productivity Commission 2008).

The development of approaches to regional policy

Producer settlement and retention

This sub-section is a review of government efforts to settle 'producers' in non-metropolitan areas and then to keep them there. The overwhelmingly dominant regional development 'strategy' in Australia from European settlement until at least the 1920s and far beyond that time for some of the northern and western areas was to encourage the establishment of agricultural producers, in what became known as 'closer settlement', or the process of encouraging an increase in population in agricultural areas. This form of industry policy was not just about economic growth, since other goals included: the reform of emancipated convicts through agricultural labour (Connors 1970; Ward 1975); promoting desirable (agrarian) characteristics in the populace (Davison 2005, p. 01.4); counterbalancing the power of the squattocracy (class of large-scale livestock producers) (Roberts 1924); the 'civilisation' of the frontier (Waterson 1968; Pike 1962; Johnston 1988); offsetting the effects of an economic depression (Connors 1970); supplying resources to the industrial hub of the British Empire (Schedvin 1988); and managing social unrest after the gold rushes and World War I (Callaghan and Millington 1956; Connors 1970; Lake 1987; Ward 1975). Though the reasons for promoting settlement varied, the closer settlement dream of farms and communities spread across the 'countryside', perhaps even reminiscent of European landscapes, was strongly supported in political and popular discourses (Davison 2005, p. 01.2).

Initially the main policy instruments were the assumption, resumption and allocation of property and property rights and the provision of direct and indirect subsidies. All colonial governments assumed control of land, initially from the Indigenous peoples and later from the 'squatters' who had occupied large holdings for grazing purposes, and then they redistributed that, often with subsidised financial arrangements for purchasing and development. Usually the allocation of land required that people clear and cultivate it and even grow particular crops (Shaw 1990; Roberts 1924; Bromby 1986; Lines 1991). There were major closer settlement schemes from the 1860s through to the 1920s, with some later activity after World War II and again in the 1960s in Queensland and Western Australia. From early in the twentieth century, state governments, recognising the limits of dryland agriculture, started to build major irrigation infrastructure to support further intensification, with the last of these major developments in the 1980s.

Closer settlement is however a remarkably persistent idea and concerns about climate change leading to a reduction in output in the southern agricultural areas resulted in yet another discussion of developing 'the north' (*The Sydney Morning Herald* 2007; Shanahan 2007), which has loomed large in post-settlement 'dreaming'. Under climate change projections, some northern areas may get higher rainfall, while there are expected decreases in the south (Bureau of Meteorology 2008). The Labor Government agreed to a modest expansion of the Ord

River irrigation scheme in the north of Western Australia (ABC News 2008), while the Coalition developed a much more ambitious discussion paper (ABC 2013). Such dreaming is somewhat constrained by historical experiences, with earlier grand settlement schemes being cautionary tales for policymakers (see for example Davidson 1966, 1981; Graham-Taylor 1982), but nation-building generates its own enthusiasm. The problems of closer settlement schemes, such as uneconomic farm sizes, inappropriate crops and a lack of understanding of the environment were known in government circles at least as early as the 1920s and were identified in: a 1929 inquiry into the soldier settlement schemes that followed World War I (Royal Commission on Soldier Settlement 1929); a 1933–1935 inquiry into the state of the wheat industry (Royal Commission into the Wheat Flour and Bread Industries 1935); and the 1944 Rural Reconstruction Commission (Rural Reconstruction Commission 1944b). The Queensland and Western Australian Governments had land distribution schemes into the 1960s, with some even in the 1980s, but in the post-war era governments generally turned from producer settlement to supporting those who survived.

Support measures started in the colonial era with governments developing scientific and education facilities devoted to the primary industries. Governments also provided the infrastructure to support production, with rail lines, grain handling facilities and roads, as well as social infrastructure to support farm families and farm workers, such as country schools and hospitals. The post-war era to the early 1970s was the high point of industry and farm business 'stabilisation'. In this period, state and federal governments developed a network of commodity boards that included minimum pricing schemes, government underwriting and regulated central marketing arrangements, including export monopolies, as well as interest rate, machinery and fertiliser subsidies (Wilkinson 2005; Malcolm 1989; Martin 1990; Watson 1979). Thus, farmers could concentrate on production while specialists could take care of the marketing, with compulsory collectivism increasing the market power of the particular industry, in an environment where other countries had even more significant industry protection (Coleman 1998).

While support for agriculture helped develop major export industries, such as the wheat industry, and closer settlement did increase populations in particular areas, relentless technical innovation in Australian agriculture meant that fewer and fewer people were needed to deliver an increasing volume of commodity exports. Larger farms, mechanisation and lean supply chains meant that rural towns became increasingly economically decoupled from agriculture. This was recognised as early as 1944 when the Rural Reconstruction Commission broadly defined 'the rural economy of a country' as covering 'every aspect of its rural life as well as the economics of those industries which are the mainspring of the existence of its countryside' (Rural Reconstruction Commission 1944a, p. 5). In 1973, another Labor Government commissioned an inquiry that was to 'consider rural policy that serves the interests not only of those directly involved in farming, but of the rural community as a whole' (Harris *et al.* 1974, p. 3). This recognition of the non-agricultural aspects of regional development led to support measures for other industries, some based on local business attraction and others growing out of secondary industry policy which also tended to be interventionist.

Following a period of free trade (1850–1865) the Victorian colonial Government started to impose manufacturing tariffs which, with the inflow of surplus labour from the goldfields, enabled an expansion in secondary industry (Logan 1966, p. 144). With federation, the national government increasingly engaged in industry policy, accelerated by central planning during two World Wars, and took over tariff setting, with the states moving to other forms of inducement to attract business investment. The southern states (NSW, Victoria and SA) started to press for industrialisation in the 1930s, though there was little in the way of explicit efforts at regional distribution of industry (Linge 1967). In the post-war period, some state governments had decentralisation funds, and there was some initial growth in major regional coastal cities, such as Geelong, Newcastle and Wollongong, but little activity elsewhere (Linge 1967, p. 55).

In 1944 state and Commonwealth governments established regional development committees, following a structure used for planning during the War, but little industrial devolution came from that (Beer 2000, p. 173; Stilwell 1974, p. 154), with this first attempt at regionalism fading after the election of a Coalition Government in 1949 (Stilwell 1974, p. 154). A Commonwealth Secondary Industries Division (Later Division of Industrial Development), set up during the War, did oversee the allocation of land in some regional centres for manufacturing (Jones 2002, p. 324). Some state governments provided money so that local governments could reduce services costs to businesses and engaged in individual negotiations with firms (Stilwell 1974, p. 154). By the early 1970s, all states had some establishment and retention incentives, usually to offset start-up costs, with some having ongoing measures (summarised in Wilson 1978, p. 182). The most interest in regional industry development was in NSW and Victoria, whereas the less populated states were more concerned about competition from the big two states (Wilson 1978, p. 182).

So, by the early 1970s, there was an array of support measures for agriculture and some secondary industries, as well as some incentives for regional businesses. As noted above, successive Federal governments then started to wind back industry assistance and to concentrate on national economic policy settings (see below). This tended to leave programmes to support the establishment and retention of businesses in regional areas with individual states and, increasingly, with local governments or regional development bodies. A review in the early 1990s identified some typical forms of assistance available at state and local levels, including:

- provision of administrative and informational services;
- relocation of government departments;
- cheap land and buildings;
- subsidised infrastructure and/or services;
- tax (and rates) concessions; and

- grants, loans and other forms of financial assistance (to lower the cost of labour, capital, relocation, etc.).

(Industry Commission 1993, p. 330)

Many of these policy instruments are still in use but state governments have increasingly moved towards supporting community and business self-help. The problem for many regions though, is that they have struggled to attract non-agricultural businesses and as argued here, there has been almost no national policy to support the decentralisation of capital.

Services equity

Initially, rural communities and the social services therein were seen as extensions of, and support for, agricultural producers and industries. However, by the 1920s the idea of services as a means of making rural life more bearable started to take hold (Davison 2005, p. 01.8). The Rural Reconstruction Commissioners (of the 1940s) thought that rural industries and towns could only be viable if living conditions were satisfactory and so housing, electricity, education and health services needed to be supplied, including where necessary, through some degree of implicit subsidy (Rural Reconstruction Commission 1944a). By the late 1960s services such as telecommunications, mail and electricity had three forms of cross-subsidisation: the cost of the infrastructure for the service; the price of the service; and the staffing of the services, which also contributed to the local economies (Tonts 2000, p. 61) and this assistance was by then seen as partly about social equity (Tonts 2000, p. 60). Australia had long had a fiscal mechanism with a geographical services equity component. Since 1934, the Grants Commission redistributed money to the states as part of 'horizontal fiscal equalisation' (Gerritsen 2000, p. 135; Walmsley 1993). In addition, since 1974, there has been a requirement that states pass on money as general purpose grants to local governments, which was an effort to prevent funds from pooling in the state capitals and surrounds.

The increasing influence of neoliberalism undercut arguments for cross-subsidisation, which was considered economically inefficient (see below), but programmes with a component of geographical equity remained, with governments particularly highlighting them in periods of political unrest in non-metropolitan regions. In 1989, the Federal Labor Government released a statement in the wake of anti-government protests in rural areas, pointing to the 'special' programmes for health services and decentralised social services agencies and services (Hawke 1989, pp. 18–33). That one of these programmes was for Rural Counselling might have highlighted the protestors' concerns. The Prime Minister, Bob Hawke, also pointed to the continuation of 'subsidised' postal, telephone and, for some areas, air services (Hawke 1989, pp. 38–39). The return of the Federal Coalition (Liberal and National[1] Parties) to government in 1996, with most Liberals having rediscovered Classical Liberalism, led to cuts in many regional programmes and public sector agencies, just as some states were also cutting service delivery areas.

Once again though, the Commonwealth was drawn back into regional development policy following the sudden rise of a populist party, One Nation (McGrath-Champ and Searle 2005, p. 7). In 1998, 11 One Nation members were elected to the Queensland Parliament, further damaging a once dominant state National (formerly Country) Party. In that same year, the Federal National Party also lost ground to One Nation in the national election, being widely seen to have failed to protect rural and regional Australia. As a further lesson, the Victorian State Government, known for its attachment to neoliberalism, unexpectedly lost the 1999 election, with unfavourable results in regional areas. The Federal Government held a Regional Australia Summit and enacted a range of 'regional' programmes, such as Rural Transaction Centres and Networking the Nation, to directly address what was seen as a services deficit (Gerritsen 2000, p. 132). There followed specific, though financially limited regional development programmes and regional adjustment packages for dairy and sugar producing areas, which were feeling the cold winds of international competition. Over time though and with the decline of One Nation, regional disadvantage faded from the political agenda until 2010, when neither major political party managed to secure a majority and the balance of power was in the hands of two 'rural' independents. The independents supported the Labor Party on the conditions that,

> governing for Australia means ensuring regional Australia:
>
> a Had its voice heard in the Federal Parliament and in the Federal Government;
> b Had its needs and special circumstances considered diligently;
> c Benefited from economic development; and
> d Had fair access to services.
>
> (The Australian Labor Party and The Independent Members 2010)

This led to some initial expansion of the Regional Affairs Department (under various titles and agglomerations) and its programmes, which were then later cut back in the wake of the Global Financial Crisis (GFC) and the increasing focus on managing the national budget.

It is, however, notable that the Labor Party did not agree to undo the major market-based 'reforms' enacted in the previous 30 years, despite the efforts of a third rural independent (Bob Katter) to bring such ideas to the negotiating table. The contemporary attitude to the supposed rural/urban services deficit is one of qualified sympathy, and caution in making promises. In a statement prior to the Regional Australia Summit, the then-leader of the Nationals and the Deputy Prime Minister, John Anderson, displayed this caution. The Government recognises the urgent need to address a growing sense of alienation in many parts of regional Australia and to bridge the increasing gulf between metropolitan areas and the bush' (Anderson and McDonald 1999, p. 1). Notably, the Government did not so much 'recognise' the problems of 'the bush', but the discontent therein. Nonetheless, there are special rural health and education programmes, such as assistance for remote area students, and there has been some commitment to 'whole of government' approaches to the provision of services (Anderson and McDonald 1999).

Decentralisation

Decentralisation as a theme was evident from at least the 1920s, when there were inquiries into the problem of the 'townward tendency' (Davison 2005, p. 01.3). This was initially about the possible effects on the sustainability of communities and the impact that depopulation would have on the quality of services (Harris *et al.* 1974, p. 262). This remains a theme in contemporary discussions of rural depopulation, especially in relation to small towns. The Federal Labor Government's 1974 rural policy discussion paper noted that decentralisation of population was becoming an extension of urban policy, especially to alleviate pressure on infrastructure and services (Harris *et al.* 1974, p. 262). Decentralisation came back on the Federal Labor Party platform in the 1960s, and the long-reigning Coalition Government had formed a National Urban and Regional Development authority in 1972 (Beer 2000, p. 174). The Labor Government, elected in 1972, formed the Department of Urban and Regional Development (DURD) which proposed decentralisation as an urban strategy that would have regional development benefits (Beer 2000, p. 174). The Government opted for a more targeted approach, identifying regional 'growth centres', some of which were to be virtually new towns and some of which were to be enhanced regional centres. Little progress was made with these centres and once again a change of government led to the programmes being wound up, replaced by a small Regional Development Programme.

The Labor Government of 1972–1975 also changed legislation to allow the Grants Commission to allocate money to regional organisations of councils, in what Stilwell describes as 'back door regionalism' (Stilwell 1974, p. 185). The aim was to enable the ROCs to undertake regional planning and to develop strategies to attract and retain businesses and people. In the 1980s ROCs were supported to some extent through the Commonwealth Local Government Development programme, to enable them to take a greater role in regional development, but there were very uneven performances in these organisations and resistance from local governments (Marshall *et al.* 2003, pp. 171–172). Some local governments have tried well-publicised land and house giveaways, while the Queensland Labor Government (to 2012) even offered housing subsidies for people who built away from the crowded south east of the state. The Victorian Coalition Government (from 2010) also claimed to want to develop existing regional centres to take the pressure off Melbourne. Generally though, decentralisation policies have been limited and appear to have had little effect. Almost 24 per cent of the population live in Sydney or Melbourne and both continue to grow and sprawl outwards, with metropolitan infrastructure pressure issues being routine features of Victorian and NSW state elections. Outside of the major cities, the growth appears to be more related to minerals and energy, beaches, mild climates and certain types of landscapes rather than to any decentralisation policies.

Self-sufficiency and structural adjustment

The final, most recent and still most dominant policy approach to regional development is the drive for businesses and communities to be self-sufficient, with governments helping with structural adjustment to ease the transition to these states. The new paradigm was evident in a 1986 rural policy paper, where the focus was on the benefits that would flow to rural industries from internationally focused macroeconomic policies (Hawke and Kerin 1986, pp. 24–25) and reduced export costs (Hawke and Kerin 1986, pp. 54–55). It also highlighted the need to continue to reduce protection to other industries in order to reduce input costs (Hawke and Kerin 1986, p. 27), implying that to be consistent there could be no additional assistance for agriculture, other than delaying progress on deregulation. There would continue to be programmes to help structural 'adjustment' and to support 'technical progress and innovation' through industry research funds (Hawke and Kerin 1986, pp. 27–45). This focus on national economic policies and assistance with adjustment were again evident in a 1989 rural and regional statement, highlighting programmes to support businesses, especially for export industries and Indigenous peoples' enterprises (Hawke 1989).

There was a restatement of the various market reforms as a 'series of changes which would further lower costs faced by farmers, thereby contributing to improved living standards in country and regional Australia' (Hawke 1989, p. 8) and reference to the benefits of 'economic self-help' which 'requires a local commitment to change' (Hawke 1989, p. 10). Generally there was an implicit effort to 'wean' industries and communities away from assistance, with industry and regionally specific programmes seen to distort the efficiency of cumulative individual choices (Freebairn 2003). There was also a focus on 'small government', or rather minimising the direct involvement of governments in economic production and service delivery (Beer *et al.* 2005; Gerritsen 2000). While the manifestations of neoliberalism were most apparent from the 1980s on, state directed development had its early critics. The 'rural romantics' who wanted farms spread across the countryside were criticised by the 'environmental determinists', who were sceptical about the economics of closer settlement in a harsh climate (Davison 2005, p. 01.2).

The Rural Reconstruction Commission of 1944–1946 thought that price support mechanisms were 'both politically troublesome and financially awkward to the governments concerned' and they discouraged 'efforts to improve efficiency and remedy faults in the cost structure' (Rural Reconstruction Commission 1944a, p. 30). The Commissioners were also cautious about efforts to attract industries to the regions, noting potential problems with transport costs and water (Rural Reconstruction Commission 1944a, p. 53). They also noted the importance of the 'general spirit which pervades the district' that 'can do much to overcome difficulties' (Rural Reconstruction Commission 1944a, p. 46). The

1974 rural policy paper, though commissioned by a party nominally of the left, also noted that 'the market is generally the most effective method of allocating productive resources' though there was still some attachment to intervention in that,

> government will not accept the full implications of the free working of the market mechanism in the agricultural sector and recognises the need for it to intervene to improve the manner in which the market operates or to compensate for its consequences.
>
> (Harris *et al.* 1974, p. 48)

It was concern about the consequences of, and political fallout from, structural adjustment that kept the Federal Government involved in regional policy.

With a general economic downturn in the early 1980s and differential unemployment rates across regions, the Federal Labor Government introduced a Regional Development Programme (RDP) that was to focus on infrastructure that would: enhance competitiveness; facilitate local initiatives; and establish Regional Development Organisations (RDOs) with a broader development focus (Beer 2000, p. 177). The RDOs would also support some of the burgeoning labour market programmes, developed in the face of persistent unemployment in some regions (Beer *et al.* 2005, p. 53). Nonetheless, there the major national policy focus remained on macroeconomic management. The Labor Government commissioned a report in 1993 that noted many regions were growing faster than the metropolitan areas (McKinsey and Company 1994, p. 14) and recommended that the regions 'experiencing decline' should not be 'propped up' because it would be inefficient to do so (McKinsey and Company 1994, p. 15). These vulnerable mining communities and small rural towns were subject to the big external forces and the role of government was to facilitate adjustment. The consultants argued, from their review of regions, that 70 per cent of investment in regions was endogenous, and they also emphasised the importance of 'local leadership' (McKinsey and Company 1994, p. 25). They then went on to instruct prospective regional leaders on how to encourage growth, citing examples, far from the Australian rural town experience, such as Glasgow.

This was followed by the Working Nation initiative in which 'industry policy and regional strategy were positioned as central and complementary elements in national economic development' (McGrath-Champ and Searle 2005, p. 2). This was the culmination of several reports on the state of the regions and although the orthodoxy of microeconomic reform remained, there was some attention to spatial disparities (McGrath-Champ and Searle 2005, p. 4). The components of the strategy were: 'improving finance options, facilitating infrastructure investment, encouraging best practice, promoting export activity, and better programme delivery' (McGrath-Champ and Searle 2005, p. 4). There was also some support for industry clustering (Enright and Roberts 2001, p. 71). With the 1996 election of the Federal Coalition Government, the RDP was abolished, as were the RDOs, with arguments that regional development was the responsibility of the state and local governments (Beer 2000, p. 177; McGrath-Champ and Searle 2005, p. 7).

Once again though, political unrest dragged the Federal Government back into this policy arena. A particular area of contention was National Competition Policy (NCP), set up by the previous government to pursue microeconomic policies that would enhance economic competition and efficiency. This included ensuring that government entities charged competitive prices for external work, which was often a source of revenue for local governments. NCP, an institutional expression of neoliberalism, enjoyed little support in the bush. It was seen as hastening the withdrawal of services, especially from smaller towns (Tonts 2000, p. 63) and contributing to a loss of jobs (Gerritsen 2000, p. 126). Competition policy was described by one notable National Party Senator as acting 'like a giant vacuum sucking people out of the bush and putting them on the shores of the seaboard' (Boswell cited in Productivity Commission 1999, p. XXIII). In 1997, the Productivity Commission, another institution steeped in neoliberalism that had evolved from the Industries Commission, which in turn had evolved from the Tariff Board, was set the task of examining the impact of competition policy 'reforms' on rural and regional communities.

From its public hearings, the Commission found considerable concern about the withdrawal of services, the centralisation of management functions and the threshold effects of losing services (Productivity Commission 1999, p. 10). The Commission concluded though that the impacts between rural areas were more variable than those between metropolitan regions. That is, some regional areas gained more than most metro areas, while some fared worse; but in the end, the Commission concluded that the greater threats to communities came from the major external forces (Productivity Commission 1999, p. XXXIX; Banks 2000). Where there were regional disadvantages, then the best approach was to use existing 'assistance measures', such as welfare payments and job placement services to facilitate 'adjustment' (Productivity Commission 1999, p. XLI), rather than designated regional development programmes.

With the political backlash of the late 1990s however, the Government re-entered the policy field. It had already set up Area Consultative Committees (ACCs), though these were restricted to labour market issues and providing advice to the government (Beer 2000, p. 177). Following the Regional Australia Summit of 1999, several regional development programmes were provided to support local projects to improve services, which later shifted to business support and some support for clustering initiatives (Enright and Roberts 2001, p. 72). This then set the pattern for the next decade and beyond. There were programmes to support communities that show initiative with levels of funding and policy interest varying according to the political situation. This broad approach continued across yet more changes in the regional advisory/delivery structure, most notably the replacement of ACCs with Regional Development Australia, following the election of the Labor Government in 2007. There has been a developing consensus between the states and the Federal Government for devolution to regional and local levels (McGrath-Champ and Searle 2005, p. 6), with state programmes also now tending to focus on education, leadership and clustering (McGrath-Champ and Searle 2005, p. 8). The intention is to 'build capacity' (Martin 2006, p. 218) so that businesses and communities are resilient and able to make their own adjustments.

There is also an increasing focus on environmental issues (McGrath-Champ and Searle 2005, p. 11) and this has ramifications for regional development. On the positive side, many renewable or low-carbon emission energy enterprises such as solar farms, geo-thermal sites, wind farms, biofuel plants and natural gas extraction, will potentially be located in regional areas, though with current technologies, none of these are likely to generate high levels of employment. On the negative side, governments are withdrawing or reducing access to some natural resources, such as native forests, mineral sands and water for irrigation. Both timber and sand mining regions have received regional adjustment packages, just as dairy farming areas did. The most dramatic example of this trend however is the plan to buy back water entitlements in the Murray–Darling Basin, the inland region that runs from South Australia, through northern Victoria to southern Queensland, where most irrigated crop production takes place. In 2004 the National Water Commission (NWC), another manifestation of coordinate federalism, was formed, with the aim of addressing 'over-allocation' and of securing sufficient environmental flows to create 'sustainable' river systems. In 2008, the Murray–Darling Basin Authority (MDBA) took over from the Murray–Darling Basin Commission (MDBC) and it is required by the Commonwealth *2007 Water Act*, amongst other things, to '...protect, restore and provide for the ecological values and ecosystem services of the Basin' (Murray–Darling Basin Authority 2010, p. xii).

The Federal Government will buy water on behalf of the environment from willing sellers, based on proposed regional targets (Murray–Darling Basin Authority 2010, p. xxv). The argument is that nation-building through agricultural intensification resulted in over-allocations of water which resulted in the decline of natural capital. The Murray–Darling Basin Authority proposed the acquisition of 20–49 per cent of current diversions, depending on the region (Murray–Darling Basin Authority 2010, p. xix) and this would again necessitate structural adjustment, with some irrigation areas having little in the way of alternative industry.

Reviewing Australian regional development policy

From this review, I argue that the dominant approach to regional development policy has been industry policy that is expected to produce beneficial spillover effects in the regions. The initial focus was on producer establishment, then later on producer retention and business attraction which remain major foci of local governments and regional development bodies. As Beer *et al.* (2005, p. 55) argue however,

> Australia does not have a strong national policy on regional development, or strong industry policies (apart from a few exceptions, such as the motor vehicle industry) which, in turn, constrains the ability of regional development organisations to promote regional development.

This is true unless the definition of industry policy is extended beyond the conventional thinking on direct intervention, for there has been a second 'stage' of industry policy whereby governments try to create an environment favourable to business no matter the location of that business. The problem with the macroeconomic approach is that capital overwhelmingly concentrates in major cities, with even mining companies having their headquarters there. The 'third' stage of industry policy, in which environmental costs are considered, will further affect resources-based communities that are disproportionately in regional areas. The use of regional and industry adjustment strategies will continue, but these are generally time limited and project driven (Beer *et al.* 2005, p. 55). Governments must be seen to be doing something but they are constrained by an attachment to neoliberalism (Stilwell 2000), or as Beer (2005, p. 54) argues, 'the practice of regional development in Australia has been subject to both ideological pressures for less intervention in regional economies and local demands for more assistance for regions'.

Other than industry policy, attempts at planned decentralisation have been occasional, limited and have had little institutional or geographic impact. Services equity is an idea that has some currency in the community and government, but attention to this tends to vary according to the political influence of regional voters and it too is subject to neoliberal constraints. The 'small government' aspect of neoliberalism has seen governments move away from direct delivery of services to become coordinators (Beer *et al.* 2005; Gerritsen 2000), which particularly affects regional programme delivery with the networks distributed across three layers of government and business and community organisations (Beer *et al.* 2005). Argent (2005) argues that devolved networks have undermined the capacity of central government agencies to deliver outcomes (Argent 2005). Similarly Gerritsen (2000, pp. 126–127) argues that the privatisation of services allows for a strong centre and cutting at the 'periphery' that gives the appearance of small government. The retreat of the state, at least in many regions is, however, well entrenched and Argent (2005, p. 30) argues that the model of the 'entrepreneurial, self-reliant community' has been adopted so widely and readily across Australia (and in other countries) that large-scale, central state-initiated intervention in regional affairs has generally come to be seen as unwelcome, wasteful and/or inappropriate.

The problem remains that there are limits to the self-reliant community. Just because the 'locals know best' (Tonts 2000, p. 65) does not mean they can manage the large economic forces to which they are subject. This approach still relies on generating funding and having local leadership capacity (Tonts 2000, p. 67). For some, this apparent devolution is just 'regulatory dumping' with responsibility passed to communities (Argent 2005, p. 37), or as Gerritsen sees it, there is 'jurisdiction shifting' with responsibilities passed to the states and increasingly local governments (Gerritsen 2000, p. 123). The problem with this is that local government is based on an infrastructure culture, not social services and economic development and may not have the people with the necessary skills (Martin 2006, p. 233) or the funding.

Conclusions

In Australia, governments have moved away from directly supporting producer establishment. This is partly a function of the rise of neoliberalism but there is also a history of producer establishment schemes generating considerable economic, social and even environmental costs, eventually making governments understandably wary. Then too, the seemingly relentless growth of the major metropolitan areas, common to almost all countries, must seem a social and economic phenomenon that is hard to influence. On the other hand, there is little policy continuity. The federal system is part of the problem, but so too is the tendency to tear apart the works of previous governments and then seemingly rebuild similar regional structures, as is the flurry of 'regional' programmes that appear during political crises.

Perhaps though, the approach to industry policy in Australia has created a degree of path dependency. The forms of assistance to agriculture, for example, were largely indirect, as opposed to the direct payments to US and EU farmers. Australian governments could therefore dismantle these without obviously stopping direct income. In the EU and to some extent in the US, there was greater political pressure for commodity support money to be redirected into regional development and agri-environment programmes. Perhaps though, the scale of those economies also enables more money to be set aside for regional development. Then too, Australia is still a vast country with an inhospitable interior and landscapes that hardly conform to modern notions of attractiveness, while many country towns show little more than their functional origins. Regional development in Australia is difficult, but there has hardly been much of a coordinated effort to achieve it.

Given that the period of post-GFC 'austerity' measures is likely to be fairly long, there will be little appetite for interventionist regional policy. The Federal Coalition, with the support of the Queensland and WA non-Labor governments, has disinterred northern development, foreshadowing new dams, but it is hard to see where the infrastructure investment will come from. The resource-rich states could adapt the WA Royalties for Regions programme which aims to retain mining income through regional expenditure, but states have many calls on their limited income and the mining boom may be deflating. Decentralisation is likely to remain a discussion point, but again, a serious approach to that requires expenditure – for example, on high-speed rail connections to the relevant major cities, and on the water supply system – but the problem of shallow labour markets in regional areas remains. One cost-saving and perhaps even equitable, but politically difficult (impossible) strategy, would be to reduce real expenditure on urban infrastructure, which is in itself a considerable cross-subsidy, making living conditions more difficult and thereby encouraging autonomous decentralisation in accord with 'market' principles.

Also politically unlikely, given the centralist tendencies in Australian politics, but perhaps the best approach within the current political economy, would be some serious devolution of finances and responsibilities. This could start with the recognition of local government in the national constitution, followed by more serious alignments of regional bodies, including the natural resource management organisations and regional organisations of councils, and direct funding of regions to include infrastructure and business programmes. The role of RDAs, or whatever follows them, could then evolve into true coordinating agencies. The history of regional development and Australian federalism would seem to mitigate against true devolution, with Federal and state governments nominally supporting the notion that communities know best while supporting funding and policy models based on central control.

Note

1 The National Party was formerly the Country Party and remains a largely agrarian party, with some recent efforts at developing a more regional identity. It usually attracts 6–8 per cent of the popular vote and holds about 8–10 per cent of Federal House of Representative seats.

References

ABC News 2008, *Rudd touts Ord River expansion as 'new food basket'*, ABC, Sydney, broadcast 16 December 2008. Available at: www.abc.net.au/news/2008–12–16/rudd-touts-ord-river-expansion-as-new-food-basket/241702. Accessed: 22 December 2010.

ABC News 2013, *Coalition water plan leak makes splash in the north*, ABC, Sydney, broadcast 15 February 2013. Available at: www.abc.net.au/news/2013–02–14/northern-food-bowl-dam-report-leak-coalition-plan/4518818. Accessed: 13 March 2013.

Anderson, J and McDonald, I 1999, *Regional Australia: Meeting the Challenges*, Commonwealth of Australia: Department of Transport, Territories and Local Government, Canberra.

Anon. 1967, 'Milking the Australian economy', *Current Affairs Bulletin*, vol. 39, no. 13, pp. 195–207.

Argent, N 2005, 'The Neoliberal Seduction: Governing-at-a-Distance, Community Development and the Battle over Financial Services Provision in Australia', *Geographical Research*, vol. 43, no. 1, pp. 29–39.

Argent, N and Walmsley, J 2008, 'Rural Youth Migration Trends in Australia: an Overview of Recent Trends and Two Inland Case Studies', *Geographical Research*, vol. 46, no. 2, pp. 139–151.

Banks, G 2000, 'Meeting the challenge of change in regional Australia', an address to *Renaissance of the Regions* symposium, Institute of Public Administration Australia, Melbourne Exhibition Centre, Victoria, 9 November.

Beer, A 2000, 'Regional policy and development in Australia: Running out of solutions?', in McManus, P and Pritchard, B (eds), *Land of Discontent: The Dynamics of Change in Rural and Regional Australia*, UNSW Press, Sydney, pp. 167–194.

Beer, A, Clower, T, Haughtow, G and Maude, A 2005, 'Neoliberalism and the Institutions for Regional Development in Australia', *Geographical Research*, vol. 43, no. 1, pp. 49–58.
Bell, S 1997, *Ungoverning the Economy*, Oxford University Press, Australia.
Birrell, B and O'Connor, K 2000, Regional Australia and the 'new economy', *People and Place*, vol. 8, no. 4, pp. 52–62.
Bromby, R 1986, *Unlocking the Land: the saga of Farming in Australia*, Lothian Publishing, Melbourne.
Bureau of Meteorology 2008, 'Trends in annual total rainfall 1970–2008', in *Trend maps – Australian Climate Variability and Change*, Bureau of Meteorology, Melbourne.
Callaghan, A and Millington, TA 1956, *The Wheat Industry in Australia*, Angus and Robertson, Melbourne.
Campbell, K 1964, 'Agricultural Adjustment in a Changing Economy', *The Journal of the Institute of Agricultural Science*, vol. 30, no. 3, pp. 159–165.
Carroll, J and Manne, R (eds) 1992, *Shutdown: The Failure of Economic Rationalism and How to Rescue Australia*, Text Publishing Company, Melbourne.
Coleman, W 1998, 'From protected development to market liberalism: paradigm change in agriculture', *Journal of European Public Policy*, vol. 5, no. 4, pp. 632–651.
Connors, T 1970, 'Closer settlement schemes', *Australian Quarterly*, vol. 42, no. 1, pp. 72–85.
Davidson, B 1966, *The Northern Myth*, Melbourne University Press, Melbourne.
Davidson, B 1981, *European Farming in Australia: An economic history of Australian Farming*, Elsevier Scientific Publishing Company, Amsterdam.
Davison, G 2005, 'Country Life: The rise and decline of an Australian ideal', in Davison, G and Brodie, M (eds), *Struggle Country: The Rural ideal in twentieth century Australia*, Monash University ePress, Clayton, pp. 01.01–01.15.
Department of Environment, Water, Heritage and the Arts 2010, *Securing our Water Future*, Australian Government, Canberra.
Enright, M and Roberts, B 2001, 'Regional Clustering in Australia', *Australian Journal of Management*, vol. 26, pp. 66–85.
Freebairn, J 2003, 'Economic policy for rural and regional Australia', *The Australian Journal of Agricultural and Resource Economics*, vol. 47, pp. 389–414.
Gerritsen, R 2000, 'The management of government and its consequences for service delivery in regional Australia', in McManus, P and Pritchard, B (eds), *Land of Discontent: The Dynamics of Change in Rural and Regional Australia*, UNSW Press, Sydney, pp. 123–139.
Graham-Taylor, S 1982, 'A critical history of the Ord River Project', *Lessons from the Ord*, Centre for Independent Studies, Sydney, pp. 23–53.
Gruen, F 1986, *A quarter of a century of Australian agricultural economics: Some personal reflections*, Centre for Economic Policy Research, Australian National University, Canberra.
Harris, S, Crawford, J, Gruen, F and Honan, N 1974, *The Principles of Rural Policy: A Discussion Paper*, Commonwealth of Australia, Canberra.
Hawke, R 1989, *Rural and Regional Australia: A statement on Federal Government policy for rural and regional communities by Bob Hawke, Prime Minister*, Commonwealth of Australia, Canberra.
Hawke, R and Kerin, J 1986, *Economic and Rural Policy*, Australian Government Publishing Service, Canberra.
Industry Commission 1993, *Impediments to Regional Industry Adjustment Volume 1 Report*, Industry Commission, Canberra.

James, C, Jones, C and Norton, A (eds) 1993, *A Defence of Economic Rationalism*, Allen & Unwin, Sydney.

Johnston, W 1988, *A Documentary History of Queensland*, University of Queensland Press, St Lucia.

Jones, E 2002, 'Post-World War Two industry policy: Opportunities and Constraints', *Australian Economic History Review*, vol. 42, no. 3, pp. 312–333.

Kellow, A 1992, *Saline solutions: Policy dynamics in the Murray Darling Basin*, Centre for Applied Social Research, Deakin University, Geelong.

Kelly, P 1992, *The End of Certainty*, Allen & Unwin, Sydney.

Lake, M 1987, *The Limits of Hope: Soldier Settlement in Victoria 1915–1938*, Oxford University Press, Melbourne.

Lines, WJ 1991, *Taming the Great South Land*, Allen & Unwin, North Sydney.

Linge, GJR 1967, 'Governments and the location of secondary industry in Australia', *Economic Geography*, vol. 43, no. 1, pp. 43–63.

Logan, MI 1966, 'Capital City Manufacturing in Australia', *Economic Geography*, vol. 42, no. 2, pp. 139–151.

Malcolm, LR 1989, 'Rural Industry Policies', in Head, BW and Patience, A (eds), *From Fraser to Hawke*, Longman Cheshire, Melbourne, pp. 132–158.

Marshall, N, Dollery, B and Witherby, A 2003, 'Regional organisations of councils (ROCs): The emergence of network governance in metropolitan and rural Australia', *Australasian Journal of Regional Studies*, vol. 9, no. 2, pp. 169–188.

Martin, J 2006, 'Local Government in the Australian Country Town: New Challenges in the 21st Century', in Rogers, M and Jones, D (eds), *The Changing Nature of Australia's Country Towns*, VURRN Press, Ballarat, pp. 217–235.

Martin, W 1990, 'Rural Policy', in Jennett, C and Stewart, R (eds), *Hawke and Australian Public Policy*, Macmillan Education Australia, South Melbourne, pp. 155–179.

McGrath-Champ, S and Searle, G 2005, 'Regional Policies over the Last Decade: Imprinting Working Nation', *Journal of Economic and Social Policy*, vol. 9, no. 2 pp. 89–109.

McKay, D 1965, 'Stabilization in Agriculture: A Review of Objectives', *Australian Journal of Agricultural Economics*, vol. 9, no. 1, pp. 33–52.

McKinsey and Company 1994, *Lead Local Compete Global*, McKinsey and Company, Sydney.

Murray–Darling Basin Authority 2010, *Guide to the proposed Basin Plan*, Murray–Darling Basin Authority, Canberra.

Pike, D 1962, 'The smallholder's place in the Australian tradition', *Tasmanian Historical Research Association, Papers and Proceedings*, vol. 10, pp. 28–33.

Productivity Commission 1999, *Impact of Competition Policy Reforms on Rural and Regional Australia*, Productivity Commission, Canberra.

Productivity Commission 2008, 'Trade & Assistance Review 2006–07', *Productivity Commission Annual Report Series*, Productivity Commission, Melbourne.

Pusey, M 1991, *Economic Rationalism in Canberra*, Cambridge University Press, Sydney.

Roberts, S 1924, *History of Australian Land Settlement (1788–1920)*, Macmillan and Co., Melbourne.

Royal Commission into the Wheat Flour and Bread Industries 1935, *Second Report*, Commonwealth Government, Canberra.

Royal Commission on Soldier Settlement 1929, 'Report on the Losses Due to Soldier Settlement By Mr Justice Pike', in Commonwealth Parliamentary Paper (ed.), *Australian Cultural History*, Commonwealth of Australia, Canberra.

Rural Reconstruction Commission 1944a, *A General Rural Survey*, Rural Reconstruction Commission, Canberra.

Rural Reconstruction Commission 1944b, *Land Utilisation and Farm Settlement*, Government Printer, Canberra.

Schedvin, CB 1988, *Australia and the Great Depression*, Sydney University Press, South Melbourne.

Schott, K 1991, 'Economic Rationalism in Canberra', *Current Affairs Bulletin*, vol. 68, pp. 30–31.

Shanahan, D 2007, 'Taskforce looks to clear path for foodbowl's shift north', *The Australian*, Sydney.

Shaw, A 1990, 'Colonial settlement 1788–1945', in Williams, D (ed.), *Agriculture in the Australian Economy*, Sydney University Press, Sydney, pp. 1–18.

Stilwell, F 1974, *Australian urban and regional development*, Australia & New Zealand Book Company, Sydney.

Stilwell, F 2000, *Changing Track: a New Political Economic Direction for Australia*, Sydney: Pluto Press.

The Australian Labor Party and The Independent Members 2010, *Agreement*. Available at: http://greens.org.au/sites/greens.org.au/files/Final%20Agreement%20_ALP_GRNS.pdf. Accessed: 29 May 2013.

The Sydney Morning Herald 2007, 'The great desert dream', *Sydney Morning Herald*, Sydney.

Tonts, M 2000, 'The Restructuring of Australia's Rural Communities', in McManus, P and Pritchard, B (eds), *Land of Discontent: The Dynamics of Change in Rural and Regional Australia*, UNSW Press, Sydney, pp. 52–72.

Tonts, M and Greive, S 2002, 'Commodification and Creative Destruction in the Australian Rural Landscape: The Case of Bridgetown, Western Australia', *Geographical Studies*, vol. 40, no. 1, pp. 58–70.

Walker, K 1994, *The political economy of environmental policy: An Australian introduction*, University of New South Wales Press, Sydney.

Walmsley, D 1993, 'The Policy Environment', in Sorensen, T and Epps, R (eds), *Prospects and policies for rural Australia*, Longman Cheshire, Melbourne, pp. 32–56.

Ward, R 1975, *Australia: A Short History*, Ure Smith, Sydney.

Waterson, D 1968, *Squatter, Selector and Storekeeper*, Sydney University, Sydney.

Watson, A 1979, 'Rural Policies', in Patience, A and Head, B (eds), *From Whitlam to Fraser*, Oxford University Press, Melbourne, pp. 157–172.

Wilkinson, J 2005, *Rural Assistance Schemes and Programs*. NSW Parliament Library Research Service. Briefing Paper 8/05.

Wilson, R 1978, 'Urban and regional policy', in Scotton, R and Ferber, H (eds), *Public Expenditures and Social Policy Volume 1 The Whitlam Years, 1972–75*, Longman Cheshire, Melbourne, pp. 179–211.

3 Australian agricultural policy

The pursuit of agricultural efficiency

Erin F. Smith and Bill Pritchard

Introduction

Australian agricultural policy has undergone a fundamental transition in the nearly 70 years since the end of World War II. For most of the first half of the twentieth century, the Australian agricultural sector was one of the most protected in the developed world: an approach that was consistent with the 'state-assisted paradigm' in which agriculture warranted special consideration because it contributed towards national policy goals (Coleman, Skogstad and Atkinson 1997, p. 275). In Australia, a philosophical attachment to agrarian ideals for the nation, dubbed by Aitkin (1985) as 'countrymindedness', provided a central pillar of government policies. The post-1945 regional development agenda of the Chifley Government, orchestrated by the Director-General of Postwar Reconstruction, HC 'Nugget' Coombs, envisioned a decentralised Australia populated by farming communities who would tend their flocks and harvest their fields in line with the heavy hand of government regulation (Brown 2006). Within half a century, these ideologies had been turned on their heads, challenged by the 'market liberal paradigm' in which 'market allocation takes precedence over state intervention and efficiency over equity' (Coleman *et al.* 1997, p. 275). This process took place step-wise, through a series of (at the time, highly contested) Inquiries and Reviews, including the 1974 Green Paper on Rural Policy (Harris *et al.* 1974; see also Tothill 1975), and various reviews during the Hawke Government of the 1980s, generally associated with the reformist Primary Industries Minister of the day, John Kerin (as discussed in further detail below). Seen in historical context, however, the transformation from 'one kind' of Australian agriculture to another occurred remarkably quickly. Now, at the beginning of the twenty-first century, Australian agriculture is one of the most deregulated in the world. This chapter focuses on this process of change and what it has implied for how we assess the efficiency of the rural economy.

The starting point for this discussion is the framing structure for rural policy developed by Geoffrey Lawrence in his 1987 book, *Capitalism and the Countryside*. Lawrence identified seven rural policy goals, of which the first three are highly pertinent to the issues at hand in this chapter: to expand agricultural output, to expand sales of agricultural products, and to increase efficiency/productivity of farmers. Frequently, though, there is no clear line demarcating these policy arenas. There is an inevitable overlap between these policy aspirations. Hence, policies to expand agricultural output are entwined with those to improve the productivity of farmers and/or to secure valuable export markets.[1] Thus, rather than focusing on the specific policy instruments and legislation that were generated to help achieve these policy goals, this chapter considers more broadly the way in which agricultural policy, pertaining to the productive and marketing aspects of the industry, has developed since World War II. Specifically, it synthesises a body of literature that provides a more nuanced account of agricultural policy transitions and the resultant impact on Australian agriculture and agriculturally-dependent regions. The common thread throughout this literature is that despite the widespread discourse of a liberal, market-orientated agricultural sector being the best mechanism to achieve well-being for regional Australia and the nation more generally, the tangible outcomes of this policy stance are experienced differently throughout Australia, with commercial benefits from production and exports bypassing some participants and regions, and being counterposed, moreover, by a new set of social and environmental stresses.

In doing so, we do not suggest that the government has withdrawn all support from rural and regional Australia, but that this support has moved away from directly targeting production and the marketing of agricultural products. Indeed, other chapters contained herein address policy transitions that might be considered more social in nature and which might be seen as attempts to redress negative externalities of the neoliberal approach (see, for example, Wheller; and Tennent and Lockie, this volume). Thus, our argument is that the way in which agricultural production specifically is encouraged has undergone a fundamental transition towards a market-orientated approach.

This chapter is organised into three key sections. First, the origins of the ideological currents underpinning the transition from 'state paternalism to neoliberalism in Australian rural policy' (Tonts and Jones 1997, p. 171) are presented. In the second section, the impact of Australia's adherence to the 'efficiency mantra' is discussed. In the final section of the paper, rural adjustment schemes – the dominant policy mechanism used by successive governments to achieve efficiency for the agricultural sector – are discussed. First, though, an overview is provided of the key policy events and transitions that took place during the 1970s and 1980s.

Development of Australian agricultural policy

The 1970s and 1980s heralded a marked change in the overall ideology and rationale for Australian agricultural policy. These changes can be understood as being both part of a broader ideological transition in the Australian economy, and a changed conception of agriculture's social and economic manifestations. With regards to the former, this period witnessed a shift in the ideology of economic management favouring markets. In terms of the latter, notions of farmers as a distinctive social and political category (and thereby justifying government support) were steadily transformed to a more hard-edged conception of 'farmers as business-people', whose fate rested on their ability to survive within the market economy (Brett 2007; Pritchard 2005a).

These transitions flowed into agriculture in accordance with national and international political events. A vital instigator of change was Britain's decision in 1973 to join the (then) European Economic Community (now, European Union). This heralded a demise in Australia's (and indeed, New Zealand's) status as privileged supplier of agricultural products to a captive market. Henceforward, Australian agricultural exporters would be required to face the (fair and unfair) winds of global competition when securing export sales and, as a consequence, future efforts to increase sales of Australia's agricultural produce would need to focus upon the more emergent export markets at the time. Also around this period, the Whitlam Government took the initial steps of dismantling protectionism in the Australian economy through a 25 per cent across-the-board tariff cut. For agriculture, this step towards a more market-driven economy was reinforced by the decision to abolish the superphosphate bounty, a 'sacred cow' in terms of government support for the farming sector.

The subsequent Liberal-National Party Government of Malcolm Fraser (1975–1983) did little to transform the overall agricultural policy settings it inherited from Whitlam. However, upon the election of the Hawke Government, dramatic change occurred. Primary Industries Ministers John Kerin (1983–1991) and Simon Crean (1991–1993) implemented a raft of reforms that deregulated industry arrangements in key agricultural sectors of the Australian economy. These microeconomic reforms dovetailed with shifts in Australia's trade policy regime during the 1980s. A focus on bilateral trade agreements (orchestrated through single market desks and statutory marketing authorities) was replaced by a clearer focus on multilateral trade within market settings (Pritchard 2005a).

Acceleration of market-driven microeconomic reforms in the 1990s further entrenched these directions. Crucially for agriculture, the decision by the Council of Australian Governments in 1994 to embark on National Competition Policy reforms (recommendations from Hilmer, Rayner and Taperell 1993) led to the systematic review of all legislation which potentially impinged on free markets.[2] This enacted the final curtain for the last vestiges of state-driven agricultural production (Pritchard 1999). In the late 1990s, a review of state-based drinking milk regulations in Victoria resulted in the Victorian government having to remove price support in order to conform to National Competition Policy. Other milk producing states recognised that they would need to deregulate as well to remain competitive with Victorian milk producers. Then, in 2008, the export monopoly for wheat was removed which provided the last withdrawal of a major area of state intervention in agricultural markets.

Despite the relatively recent removal of the wheat export monopoly and the farm gate milk price, the trajectories for these changes were established much earlier. In the case of the wheat industry, for example, the enactment of the *Wheat Marketing Act 1989* dismantled price protection for wheat growers and ended the Australian Wheat Board's monopoly over the domestic wheat market

(Botterill 2011). However, there were even earlier precursors to these policy (and legislative) changes, evident in the recommendations from the Industries Assistance Commission. In 1979, 1983 and 1988, the Commission called for the removal of protective wheat pricing and marketing arrangements.

Often these moves towards greater liberalisation of agricultural production have been accompanied by adjustment packages designed to assist farmers in adapting to new terms of production. In the case of the dairy industry, the largest adjustment package in Australia's history (A$1.92 billion) was provided following the removal of the farm gate milk price outlined above. However, while monetary support was provided, the adjustment package was time bound, thus the point here is that the intended outcome of these measures was to create a considerably different set of market conditions in which agricultural producers would be required to operate into the future. The events described above were the tangible outcomes of a fundamental ideological shift in Australian politics. Yet, 'to ascribe policy formulation to the rationale metrics of evidence-based analysis is to give insufficient credence to the dynamic connectivity between institutions, interests and agency in the mobilisation of particular worldviews and their application to government action' (Pritchard 2005a, p. 9). Consequently, the next section explores the less obvious origins of Australia's neoliberal agriculture.

The emergence of the neoliberal agenda: evidence-based analysis or ideological insistence?

The 30-year history of policy change in agriculture (from the highly regulated farm economy of the early 1970s to the market-driven economy of the early 2000s) demonstrates the ways in which ideology and policy are connected, often in messy and coincidental ways. First, a key point to make is that these transformations were inaugurated through a 'policy window' created by the influx of neoliberal ('Chicago School') ideas among Australian agricultural economists from the late 1960s (see Pritchard 2005a for a detailed discussion of this point). Programmes and administrative reforms were hatched in the 'economic heartlands' of Treasury and the Productivity Commission, not the 'rural heartlands' of farming.

Second, Australia's continued adherence to multilateral agricultural reform (see further on) was aided and abetted by structural changes to the Department of Trade in 1987 (Pritchard 2005a). Trade as a standalone Department was disestablished and amalgamated with the Department of Foreign Affairs, creating the Department of Foreign Affairs and Trade (DFAT). The only division to remain unchanged was the Multilateral Division which came to dictate much of Australia's trade policy (Jones 1994).

Third, despite the imposed nature of these changes, they elicited remarkably little sustained dissention within farming. Australia's peak agricultural organisation, the National Farmers' Federation, was an early advocate of the shift to market-driven agriculture. Its position was sporadically challenged by state divisions and individual farmers, but the overall commitment to market reforms within the Australian farming sector prevailed throughout (Halpin and Martin 1999). As argued by Coleman *et al.* (1997), these specialist groups representing farmers of a given industry were key agents of control in negotiating and managing policy formulation and implementation. That is, a series of smaller shifts over time, culminated in a larger shift from the state – assisted paradigm to the market-driven paradigm.

In sum, then, 'neoliberal agriculture was a policy choice driven by the ideological insistence within influential policy communities' (Pritchard 2005a, p. 5). With this general overview provided, attention turns now to a more specific discussion of Australia's continued adherence to agricultural efficiency over the intervening years since the inception of neoliberal ideology, before considering the key policy mechanism used to create an efficient agricultural sector – i.e. rural adjustment.

Efficiency – the dominant policy objective

Australian agricultural systems typically have always been quite efficient. Farmers who were settled on the land via closer settlement and soldier settlement schemes implemented in the late nineteenth and early twentieth centuries had to aspire to some degree of efficiency in order to meet their contractual obligations. Similarly, it has been argued that the agricultural efficiency achieved by Australian farmers enabled the high levels of protection afforded to the manufacturing sector for much of the twentieth century (Galligan and Capling 1992, cited in Brett 2007, p. 6). The changes that took place in Australian politics in the 1980s, however, created the context in which the 'efficiency mantra' began to more directly dictate the nature of Australian rural policy. Prior to this, the Commonwealth and state governments had provided financial assistance to farmers in a myriad of ways. The economic losses incurred through government sponsored infrastructure developments, input subsidies and tariff protection were justifiable because of the importance of country Australia to the nation's society and economy[3] (see Cockfield, this volume). At the same time, societal changes more generally were beginning to erode the privileged status of country Australia as a key contributor to Australia's economic prosperity and cultural distinctiveness (Brett 2007). Against this backdrop the neoliberal agenda was 'rolled-out'. With regard to agriculture, Brett (2007, p. 8) described the impact of the neoliberal turn with the following: 'Neoliberalism, with its hostility to special claims of any sort, and its priority on economic measures of national contribution, has taken to ... [country Australia] ... with a sledge hammer.' Thus, greater economic rationalisation compounded the difficulties many rural areas were already experiencing from the changed social and cultural position of agriculture (Brett 2007; Tonts and Jones 1997).

The fundamental policy change bought about then, was that agricultural productivity and commodity sales would be increased through improved levels of agricultural efficiency which farmers would achieve by being exposed to the open market. With this policy stance having been in effect for almost three decades, the Australian agricultural sector is now one of the least government-supported agricultural sectors in the developed world, second only to New Zealand (OECD 2010). The Australian Government, along with other nations (e.g. New Zealand, Uruguay, Argentina, Malaysia, Canada and others) continues to advocate strongly for the liberalisation of global trade. On a domestic level then, the pursuit of an efficient agricultural sector is justified by the assumed economic benefits that will accrue once the liberalisation of the agricultural sectors in other economies occurs (e.g. United States, European Union and Japan) (Pritchard and Tonts 2011).

Social researchers have critiqued the rationale underlying this adherence to market efficiency (see, for example, Gray and Lawrence 2001; Pritchard 2005a, 2005b; McManus and Pritchard 2000; and Pritchard and Tonts 2011) and questioned the degree to which the assumed benefits are realised in country Australia. Pritchard and Tonts (2011, p. 30) raised the question '...does reliance on market efficiency alone provide the optimal policy framework to secure the economic, social and environmental interests of Australia's agricultural regions?' The importance of this question emerges when the global context is considered. Despite several decades of advocacy for global trade liberalisation on the part of Australia and others, key agricultural producers and potential markets for Australian products remain heavily protected by their nation states (e.g. United States, European Union and Japan) and, at present, World Trade Organization negotiations (the Doha Round) are deadlocked. In this context, the claimed benefits of agricultural efficiency do not manifest to the extent anticipated (Pritchard and Tonts 2011).

The international reputation of Australia as a staunch proponent of the disestablishment of all agricultural subsidies results in the need to uphold the efficiency mantra in domestic policy (Dibden, Potter and Cocklin 2009). This unwavering commitment to the neoliberal agenda has resulted in some costs, primarily social and environmental. That is, the demands placed on farmers of achieving agricultural efficiency within the context of liberalised trade generates 'hyper-productivism' (Dibden *et al.* 2009, p. 302) and undermines broader social and environmental objectives. Interestingly, it is the potential manifestation of these detrimental impacts that the European Union uses to support its position to maintain protective measures for farmers (Dibden *et al.* 2009).

The social and environmental impacts of an agricultural sector operating within a free-market regime are now well documented (see, for example, Bourke 2001). For the most part, this literature reports the many social disadvantages rural people experience compared with their metropolitan counterparts. These include higher suicide rates (Caldwell, Jorm and Dear 2004), higher rates of domestic violence, fewer opportunities for higher education, and fewer health services and medical professionals (Bureau of Transport and Regional Economics 2006).

Many of these impacts can be attributed to the pursuit of efficiency, both at the farm and government levels. For example, farmers continue to modernise their operations, incorporating better technologies to increase productivity. Many of these technologies reduce labour requirements and displace farm workers who are forced to migrate from rural areas for employment (Brett 2007). Similarly, the efficiency imperative pursued by individual government departments obscures the social costs caused by cumulative withdrawal of services in rural areas (Gerritsen 2000). In a somewhat perverse way, then, the preoccupation with an efficient agricultural sector undermines populous, vibrant communities. In a study of the Western Australian wheatbelt, Tonts and Jones (1997, p. 183) concluded that

> …the 'economically rational policies' which were designed to improve competitiveness and efficiency, and to reduce government spending, actually contributed to inefficiencies through the need for higher levels of spending on welfare, public housing, infrastructure and other social services in depressed areas.

Some of these inefficiencies, the negative social and economic implications of neoliberalism, are masked by ongoing processes of rationalisation within the farm sector. One of the vital tenets of market-driven agriculture is that efficiency and productivity is associated with an increase in the average size of farm establishments. Hence, there is little place within the contemporary Australian farming sector for small-sized farms (except, of course, if this smallness is connected to niche, high-value production). Correspondingly, the past 30 years has witnessed a steady decline in the number of farm establishments, and an even starker shift in economic concentration towards large farm establishments. (Routinely in Australian agriculture, the largest 10 per cent of producers contribute upwards of 50 per cent of industry output.) Clearly, this raises the question of what has happened to all those farmers who have exited agriculture during recent decades? Yet unlike (say) manufacturing, where industry demise is marked by (highly visible) stories of worker redundancies, processes of farmer exit are often entwined with life-cycle circumstances attached to retirement and succession. Moreover, declining opportunities to sustain households through on-farm income encourage a diversification of livelihood strategies based around increased off-farm work (especially by females). And in those cases where farm exit is inevitable, burdens are softened by the provision of financial counselling services and exit grants through programmes like the Rural Adjustment Scheme (see below).

Similarly, achieving agricultural productivity and efficiency via market forces has potentially exacerbated environmental damage (Broderick 2005) such as salinisation, soil acidification, wind and water erosion, and the spread of agricultural pests. Somewhat ironically, these (potentially) unintended consequences from the retraction of the State in agricultural production have resulted in the re-involvement of State forces through regulations and the creation of market-based instruments (e.g. the water market, payments for ecosystem services) to allocate and protect scarce environmental assets (Dibden and Cocklin 2005). These developments materialised from acknowledgement of the contradiction between the expectation that farmers will be self-sufficient and the expectation that they will voluntarily remediate environmental problems for the social good (Dibden and Cocklin 2005). Consequently, there has been an increase in rural policy targeted at addressing some of these 'unforeseen' consequences, though largely with respect to environmental degradation. Researchers have argued that rural policy targeting environmental issues allows the Australian government to provide a type of agricultural subsidy that is technically not directed at production, and hence contravenes neither Australia's World Trade Organization obligations nor its international reputation for being a leading advocate of trade liberalisation (Dibden *et al.* 2009, p. 307).

Australia's adoption of neoliberal economic and agricultural policy has not meant a complete withdrawal of government assistance for agriculture, but rather that assistance is provided in particular ways. Thus, the final section of this chapter considers the use of adjustment schemes for rural reconstruction when pursuing efficiency and productivity.

Agricultural efficiency via 'rural reconstruction'

Since the 1970s, improving the efficiency of the agricultural sector as a whole has been the dominant policy objective which has been operationalised via rural reconstruction (or adjustment) schemes.[4] The first of these schemes – the Marginal Dairy Farms Reconstruction Scheme – came into effect in 1971; its purpose was to facilitate the exit from the industry of 'dairy farmers whose farms [had] insufficient potential to become viable economic units while based on the sale of milk or cream for manufacturing purposes' (*Marginal Dairy Farms (Agreement) Act 1971*, the schedule, part b). This legislative change was the precursor to all subsequent reconstruction schemes that transformed the role of the State in Australian agriculture from actively protecting farmers, to actively supporting farmers to adapt to the realities of a market regime of regulation. In most cases, 'agricultural adjustment' meant providing incentives to farmers owning non-viable (inefficient) farms to leave the industry. Each successive scheme differed only slightly from its predecessor and, in general, the provisions of rural reconstruction legislation have not been enough of an incentive for the anticipated numbers of non-viable farmers to exit the industry. Consequently, the success of these programmes, on both welfare and efficiency grounds, has been questioned largely because the schemes have failed to take into consideration the high value many farmers place on non-economic considerations for remaining in agriculture (Botterill 2000, 2001).

The key rural adjustment scheme throughout the 1990s included support for farmers to leave farming and was enacted by the *Rural Adjustment Act 1992*. Similar support has continued to be provided into the twenty-first century under a range of different schemes including the 'Farm Help Re-establishment Grant', the 'Climate Change Adjustment Programme Re-establishment Grant' and, more recently, farm exit support was included in a pilot programme of drought reform measures developed between the Commonwealth and Western Australian Governments (Department of Agriculture, Fisheries and Forestry 2013). However, it has been suggested by Barr (1999) and Bjornlund (2002) that rather than assisting the exit of non-viable farmers, policy would be better targeted at supporting viable farmers who intend to remain in the industry. If adequately supported, these farmers will then be in a better position to purchase the properties of farmers who leave the industry either through retirement (with no identified successor) or death. In addition, within formalised adjustment schemes, there are also provisions that align with the policy stance that farmers are business managers, thus other aspects of these schemes target capacity building, risk management and self-reliance through the provision of funds for up-skilling.

Conclusion

Since the early 1980s, the key theme of Australian agricultural policy has been the liberalisation of the market contexts in which farmers are situated. The aim of this agenda has been to use the market as a spur for farmers to engage in cycles of efficiency improvement. These aspirations have been in lock-step with the nation's agricultural trade policy stance, which has been to advocate for global free trade of agricultural products so as to increase sales of surplus produce that cannot be consumed domestically. As noted by Pritchard though (2005b, p. 11), this relatively unsophisticated policy framework was brought about by a '*particular kind* of agricultural politics' (emphasis in original), resulting in a unique set of arrangements between the State, Australian society and agriculture. These new arrangements have impacted differently upon rural areas, benefiting those areas which tend to attract flows of capital while disadvantaging other areas. Correspondingly, the adjustment opportunities available to farmers differ between localities, affecting the quality of life for Australians living in rural areas.

During much of this reform period, the overarching critique of these policies has been to emphasise their implicit prioritisation of national-scale efficiency concerns, over and above the social costs of farmers in transition, and the uncertainties for regional economies. For many observers, it appeared as though the economic rationalism of Canberra-centric policymaking had usurped the grounded concerns of the real world. Writing ten years ago, Alston (2004 p. 44) concluded,

> If Australia is to provide viable rural communities that give support to farm families and for agricultural production, then a reappraisal of its policy commitment in line with EU commitments may be in order.... A move away from neoliberal mantra appears necessary to ensure a viable future for rural people and rural communities.

At the present moment, there is a need and opportunity to move forward from the oppositional narrative of what might be labelled 'economic rationalism versus the regions'. While market liberalism still remains ascendant within the Australian rural policy imagination, there is an emergent need to frame this philosophy within a more robust appreciation of social and environmental externalities associated with markets. To date, this reframing of the efficiency concept is most visibly apparent in the case of water policy. Water as a resource is no longer considered the privileged domain of agriculture. Now, other uses for water such as recreation and the environment are considered legitimate for which water provision must be made (Smith and Pritchard, 2014). Water for environmental purposes has been secured through two main approaches. The first is through government purchases of water access entitlements from willing agricultural sellers. The second approach focuses on achieving greater water use efficiencies through upgrades of irrigation infrastructure.

This reworking of the efficiency agenda might have two specific outcomes that should be considered in future agricultural policy. First, spatial unevenness in rural and regional Australia is potentially further exacerbated as irrigated areas receive substantial capital investment on the part of governments, while dry land areas remain outside these policy intents. The creation of such regional disparities needs to be continually recognised as particular areas and/or agricultural industries enter and exit the policy spotlight. Second, the interaction between different policy spheres and their cumulative impact upon Australian farm businesses requires greater attention, as demonstrated by current shifts in water policy in which the primary objective is greater water efficiencies. As farmers respond to these changes, indirect consequences will become clear in terms of how they manage production, land use and business expansion.

Notes

1 See Lawrence (1987, p. 184) for recognition of the way in which agricultural policy goals overlap.

2 While the National Competition Policy brought about significant reforms across the Australian economy, including agriculture, earlier reports made recommendations that aligned with National Competition Policy (see, for example, 'Australia. Department of Primary Industry' 1986; and Industry Commission, 1991).

3 Brett (2007) provides a convincing discussion for the inclusion of country Australia as the sixth, additional pillar of the Australian Settlement as proposed by Kelly (1992) in *The end of certainty: The story of the 1980s*. Kelly argued that these pillars of the Australian Settlement were dismantled with the political changes that occurred during the 1980s that brought about the end of protective statism in Australia.

4 For example, the *States Grants (Rural Reconstruction) Act 1971*; *States Grants (Rural Adjustment) Act 1976*; *States and Northern Territory Grants (Rural Adjustment) Act 1985*; *States and Northern Territory Grants (Rural Adjustment) Act 1988*; *Rural Adjustment Act 1992*; and the Agriculture – Advancing Australia 1997 package.

References

Aitkin, D 1985, 'Countrymindedness: The spread of an idea', *Australian Cultural History*, vol. 4, pp. 34–40.

Alston, M 2004, 'Suicide and mental health in rural, remote and metropolitan areas in Australia', *Agriculture and Human Values*, vol. 21, no. 1, pp. 37–46.

Australian Department of Primary Industry 1986, *Reform of Commonwealth Primary Industry Statutory Marketing Authorities. A Government Policy Statement*, Australian Government Publishing Service, Canberra.

Barr, N 1999, 'Salinity control, water reform and structural adjustment: The Tragowel Plains Irrigation District', PhD thesis, The University of Melbourne, Melbourne.

Bjornlund, H 2002, 'The socio-economic structure of irrigation communities: Water markets and the structural adjustment process', *Rural Society*, vol. 12, no. 2, pp. 123–147.

Botterill, L 2000, *Policy approaches to farm exit: Some factors influencing the efficacy of Commonwealth programs*, Bureau of Rural Sciences, Canberra.

Botterill, L 2001, 'Rural policy assumptions and policy failure: The case of the re-establishment grant', *Australian Journal of Public Administration*, vol. 60, no. 4, pp. 9–16.

Botterill, LC 2011, 'Life and death of an institution: The case of the collective wheat marketing in Australia', *Public Administration*, vol. 89, no. 2, pp. 629–643.

Bourke, L 2001, 'One big happy family?: Social problems in rural communities', in Lockie, S and Bourke, L (eds), *Rurality bites: The social and environmental transformation of rural Australia*, Pluto Press Australia, Altona, pp. 89–102.

Brett, J 2007, 'The country, the city and the state in the Australian settlement', *Australian Journal of Political Science*, vol. 42, no. 1, pp. 1–17.

Broderick, K 2005, 'Sustainability and rivers: A case study of communities in the Collie Catchment, Western Australia', PhD thesis, The University of Western Australia, Perth.

Brown, AJ 2006, *Reform of Australia's Federal System: Identifying the Benefits*, A Discussion Paper, Griffith University and NSW Farmers' Association. Available at: www.griffith.edu.au/__data/assets/pdf_file/0003/206562/fedreform-discussionpaper0506.pdf. Accessed: 2 October 2012.

Bureau of Transport and Regional Economics 2006, *About Australia's regions*, Department of Transport and Regional Economics, Canberra.

Caldwell, TM, Jorm, AF and Dear, KBG 2004, 'Suicide and mental health in rural, remote and metropolitan areas in Australia', *Medical Journal of Australia*, vol. 18, no. 7, pp. S10–S14.

Coleman, WD, Skogstad, GD and Atkinson, MM 1997, 'Paradigm shifts and policy networks: Cumulative change in agriculture', *Journal of Public Policy*, vol. 16, no. 3, pp. 272–301.

Cockfield, G 2015, 'From state direction to community self-efficacy: The devolution of responsibility for regional development in Australia', this volume.

Department of Agriculture, Fisheries and Forestry 2013, Pilot of Drought Reform Measures in Western Australia. Available at: www.daff.gov.au/agriculture-food/drought/drought-program-reform/drought-pilot. Accessed: 1 August 2013.

Dibden, J and Cocklin, C 2005, 'Sustainability and agri-environmental governance', in Higgins, V and Lawrence, G (eds), *Agricultural governance: Globalization and the new politics of regulation*, Routledge, London, pp. 135–152.

Dibden, J, Potter, C and Cocklin, C 2009, 'Contesting the neoliberal project for agriculture: Productivist and multifunctional trajectories in the European Union and Australia', *Journal of Rural Studies*, vol. 25, no. 3, pp. 299–308.

Gerritsen, R 2000, 'The management of government and its consequences for service delivery in regional Australia', in Pritchard, B and McManus, P (eds), *Land of discontent*, UNSW Press, Sydney, pp. 123–139.

Gray, I and Lawrence, G 2001, *A future for regional Australia: Escaping global misfortune*, Cambridge University Press, Cambridge, UK.

Halpin, D and Martin, P 1999, 'Representing and managing farmers' interests in Australia', *Sociologia Ruralis*, vol. 39, no. 1, pp. 78–99.

Harris, SF, Crawford, JG, Gruen, FH and Honan, ND 1974, *The principles of rural policy in Australia: A discussion paper, Report to the Prime Minister by a Working Group*, Australian Government Publishing Service, Canberra.

Hilmer, FG, Rayner, MR and Taperell, GQ 1993, *National Competition Policy. Report by the Independent Committee of Inquiry*, Australian Government Publishing Service, Canberra.

Industry Commission 1991, *Statutory marketing arrangements for primary products*, Report No. 10, Australian Government Publishing Service, Canberra.

Jones, E 1994, *Bureaucratic politics and economic policy: The evolution of trade policy in the 1970s and 1980s*, Working Papers in Economics (no. 212), The University of Sydney, Sydney.

Kelly, P 1992, *The end of certainty: The story of the 1980s*, Allen & Unwin, St Leonards.

Lawrence, G 1987, *Capitalism and the countryside: The rural crisis in Australia*, Pluto Press, Sydney.

Marginal Dairy Farms (Agreement) Act 1971, Government of South Australia,. Available at: www.legislation.sa.gov.au/LZ/C/A/MARGINAL%20DAIRY%20FARMS%20%28AGREEMENT%29%20ACT%201971/2001.02.21_%281971.04.22%29/1971.33.PDF. Accessed: 2 February 2012.

OECD 2010, *Producer support estimates database 2010*. Available at: www.oecd.org/agriculture/pse. Accessed: 27 August 2011.

Pritchard, B 1999, 'National Competition Policy in action: The politics of agricultural deregulation and the Murrumbidgee Irrigation Area Wine Grapes Marketing Board', *Rural Society*, vol. 9, no. 2, pp. 421–443.

Pritchard, B 2005a, 'Implementing and maintaining neoliberal agriculture in Australia: Part I: Constructing neoliberalism as a vision for agricultural policy', *International Journal of Sociology of Agriculture and Food*, vol. 13, no. 1, pp. 1–12.

Pritchard, B 2005b, 'Implementing and maintaining neoliberal agriculture in Australia: Part II: Strategies for securing neoliberalism', *International Journal of Sociology of Agriculture and Food*, vol. 13, no. 2, pp. 1–14.

Pritchard, B and McManus, P (eds) 2000, *Land of discontent: The dynamics of change in rural and regional Australia*, University of New South Wales Press Ltd, Sydney, Australia.

Pritchard, B and Tonts, M 2011, 'Market efficiency, agriculture and prosperity in rural Australia', in Tonts, M and Siddique, MAB (eds), *Globalisation, agriculture and development: Perspectives from the Asia-Pacific*, Edward Elgar Publishing Ltd, UK, pp. 29–53.

Rural Adjustment Act 1992 (Commonwealth), Commonwealth of Australia. Available at: www.comlaw.gov.au/Details/C2004C06518. Accessed: 2 October 2010.

Smith, EF and Pritchard, B 2014, 'Water reform in the 21st century: The changed status of Australian agriculture', in Dufty-Jones, R and Connell, J (eds), *Rural change in Australia: Population, economy and environment*, Ashgate Publishing, UK, pp. 169–186.

Tennent, R and Lockie, S 2015, 'Natural resource management in Australia: A historical summary', this volume.

Tonts, M and Jones, R 1997, 'From state paternalism to neoliberalism in Australian rural policy: Perspectives from the Western Australian wheatbelt', *State and Polity*, vol. 1, no. 2, pp. 171–190.

Tothill, JC 1975, 'Tropical grassland agriculture and the Green Paper on Rural Policy in Australia – A resume', *Tropical Grasslands*, vol. 9, no. 1, pp. 1–8.

Wheat Marketing Act 1989, Commonwealth of Australia. Available at: http://www.comlaw.gov.au/Series/C2004A03806. Accessed: 2 February 2012.

Wheller, S 2015, 'Commonwealth employment and welfare policies in post-war regional Australia', this volume.

4 Natural resource management in Australia

A historical summary

Rebeka Tennent and Stewart Lockie

With agriculture occupying more than 60 per cent of the Australian landmass (Beeton *et al.* 2006), and the nation one of just 17 megadiverse countries that together harbour the majority of the Earth's species, a key challenge for policy-makers lies in establishing an appropriate balance between protection of natural resources and the maintenance of viable agricultural industries. In excess of A$6.5 billion in public funding consequently was directed at natural resource management (NRM) between 1990 and 2008 (Hajkowicz 2009), and a further A$2 billion up to 2013 (Department of the Environment, Water, Heritage and the Arts 2008). Historically, NRM policy has tended to preserve individual property rights, achieved to a varying extent through diverse and often competing policy approaches, and coupled with a coordinating (arm's length) role for government. However, the underlying assumption – that well-informed land managers will deliver favourable environmental outcomes – belies the pressure on land managers to innovate and intensify production in the face of declining terms of trade and the deregulation of marketing arrangements for agricultural commodities. Financial constraints have slowly eroded opportunities to manage land degradation, while the nature of Australian soils puts them at particular risk of degradation (Watson 1992). More recent policy initiatives conceptualise and respond to environmental degradation as a form of market failure. The Commonwealth government, in partnership with the states and territories, has moved towards a business approach for investing in NRM, using market based instruments (MBIs) and stewardship payments to landholders to incentivise delivery of favourable environmental outcomes. The use of these instruments is premised on the argument that, as a form of market failure, environmental degradation should be resolved through market means. The outcomes of this programme logic, and the wider implementing programme, Caring for Our Country (CFOC), are yet to be comprehensively assessed. Nonetheless, a recent review found cautious support for the ability of CFOC to deliver targeted, economically efficient NRM deliverables (Caring for Our Country Review Team 2011). As well, concerns were raised about the reduction in guaranteed base level funding available to regional bodies, whose key goal is to deliver tangible NRM outcomes. This chapter examines the history of NRM policy in Australia. While the focus is on policies and programmes from World War II onwards, initiatives predating this period provide relevant context for today's policies and will be briefly described.

NRM in Australia: the formative years

In the century following European settlement of Australia, exploration and expansion was sponsored by the new government in attempts to increase production and ease hunger in the new colonies (Dovers 1992). Policy at this time focused on intensifying agricultural production by establishing research capacity, distributing land to family farmers and constructing infrastructure to support agriculture (Bolton 1992). Land degradation was evident, though agricultural scientists highlighting this were largely ignored while budding conservation groups focused on the preservation of bushlands and native flora and fauna (Bolton 1992). By the 1930s, however, media attention over the American dustbowl combined with similar dust storms affecting Australian cities contributed to a more open recognition of rural land degradation. Following, as it did, the declaration of the Australian Federation in 1901, any response based on this recognition was dependent on the negotiation of appropriate Commonwealth and state powers. Although calls were made for Commonwealth action due to the magnitude of the problem, this was resisted and responsibility was left with the various state and territory governments, while the Commonwealth reserved for itself a coordinative role (Bradsen 1988), which became the pattern for NRM governance more generally. The state and territory governments formed a Standing Committee on Soil Conservation in 1946, the aim of which was to coordinate soil conservation measures nationally and make recommendations on relevant legislation. The focus at this time was on the provision of education and advisory services in support of voluntary conservation activity (Vanclay and Lawrence 1995). Underlying this approach was an assumption that the provision of education to farmers would lead to behavioural change. A few regulatory provisions were legislated, though they were rarely enforced due to the conflicting roles this engendered for field extension officers and a belief in the primacy of individual property rights (Bradsen 1988).

As a political issue, NRM slipped from prominence through the post-war economic boom years of the 1950s and 1960s. The mechanisation of agriculture and other technological developments led to substantial productivity gains and contributed towards the amelioration of the more obvious degradation problems. Nonetheless, key natural resources were subject to an accelerating and widespread threat from agricultural activities supported by the various governments. Land-clearing technologies developed by government agencies, coupled with continued financial support for clearing, which, for example, resulted in substantial biodiversity loss from the removal of woody vegetation. In the early 1970s, major studies were undertaken that found serious water and wind erosion, salinity and vegetation damage across the country (Hajkowicz 2009). This prompted the re-emergence of rural land degradation as an issue of political and social importance (Department of Environment, Housing and Community Development 1978), though when it appeared on the Australian political agenda in the 1980s, it was framed as a global problem affecting international economic and social development.

Domestically and internationally, a series of cultural and political shifts were underway that became the precursors for a more active Commonwealth role in NRM policy. Within Australia, this is perhaps best illustrated by the dispute over the proposed Gordon-below-Franklin Dam (Bonyhady 1993, p. 50), a significant feature of which was the legal process that the state and Commonwealth governments underwent in determining relevant powers. The Tasmanian government argued that the Commonwealth had no constitutional power to legislate or regulate for the environment, while the Commonwealth justified its legal rights by reference to its external affairs powers in relation to international treaties. The High Court upheld the rights of the Commonwealth, giving the Commonwealth power to legislate on any issue necessary to enforce an international treaty.

Internationally, the emerging discourse of sustainability also marked the landscape for future Commonwealth NRM policy. The influential World Commission on Environment and Development convened to determine how best to manage natural resources to prevent the loss of native species and ecosystems. Its report, *Our Common Future* (World Commission on Environment and Development 1987), played a key role in shifting the focus of Australian NRM policy from 'land degradation' to 'sustainability'. Subsequent to this, an agriculture sectoral working group, tasked with developing plans that were based on *Our Common Future*, endorsed an approach to sustainability in agriculture that emphasised responsible land management through the incorporation of economic and environmental principles, the formation of community-based self-help groups, and integrated farm planning (Commonwealth of Australia 1991b). The emphasis, again, was ostensibly on preserving individual property rights though, in reality, landholders had long been subjected to a 'duty of care' that imposed some constraint on their ability to do as they pleased on private property (Reeve 2002). Nonetheless, this reinforced the importance of community-based action towards sustainable land management, and underscored the important role Landcare was to play into the future.

In response to increasing threats to natural resources, and in an effort to invigorate greater NRM activity by the states, the Commonwealth established the National Soil Conservation Programme (NSCP) which inter alia funded state agencies to boost their activities and assist them to implement high priority NRM projects. Funding was also provided to organisations to undertake projects of 'special significance or broad application across Australia'. Overall funding levels were low, but apparently useful for the states in expanding existing programmes. In the latter years of the NSCP, funding was directed from the Commonwealth through the NSCP to community projects. As community Landcare groups developed in the late 1980s, they too were entitled to funding through the NSCP. Integrated catchment management, which asserted that localised, catchment-based groups were better equipped to establish and coordinate environmental outcomes, was also gaining momentum within government, though nothing was formalised at this stage. This was mirrored at the community level, in particular in Western Australia and Victoria where Land Conservation District Committees (LCDCs) and Landcare groups respectively provided frameworks for pastoral and farming communities to address land degradation issues at the catchment or neighbourhood level (Cary and Webb 2000).

NRM policy initiatives from this point onwards can be characterised in three distinct phases (Hajkowicz 2009). These include: (Phase One) raising awareness and changing attitudes; (Phase Two) building new institutional capacity; and (Phase Three) more recently, experimentation with direct payments. While these phases generally indicate a shift in policy approach, they are not discrete phases.

Phase One: raising awareness and changing attitudes

The key motivation for the development of a nationwide Landcare programme came in the form of a submission to the Commonwealth in 1989 by the National Farmers' Federation and the Australian Conservation Foundation. Heavily influenced by the growth of community LCDCs and Landcare groups in Western Australia and Victoria, the submission suggested that a programme be established based on a self-help approach to NRM that relied 'heavily upon local community groups, within a framework which recognises the responsibilities of Local, State and Federal Governments' (Toyne and Farley 1989, p. 6). A secondary motivation was a review of NRM programmes that recommended Commonwealth funding draw on Commonwealth, state and private sector resources according to their degree of responsibility. Framed by a strong belief in preserving individual property rights, and leveraging off the early success of community Landcare groups, in 1992 the Commonwealth announced the establishment of the National Landcare Programme (NLP) which, at the time, was the single largest standalone programme in the country's history (Hajkowicz 2009). The NLP subsumed the NSCP and placed greater emphasis on integrated management, combining government land and water programmes and targeting catchment scale management.

The principal goal of the NLP was to promote the development and implementation of management practices that would improve natural resource conditions, and that were sustainable and consistent with the philosophy of sustainable development. The specific objectives of the NLP were to encourage the community to learn about and take ownership of land degradation problems, create new partnerships within communities, establish an improved NRM policy environment and contribute to sustainable agriculture (Agriculture, Fisheries and Forestry Australia 1997). The underlying principle was that building a greater recognition among landholders of the harmful effects of poor natural resource management for sustainable agriculture would establish enhanced stewardship ethics, leading to increased private investment in improved practices and thence on-ground outcomes. Framed in a language of partnerships, cooperation and community (Lockie 2000), the success of the NLP depended to a large extent on its ability to educate and mobilise various stakeholders to action – usually through project funding. While ostensibly community initiated and controlled, the availability of government support for specific activities heavily influenced what the majority of community Landcare groups actually did. Assistance was available from non-government sources, though government remained the largest funding source for community Landcare groups, and the partnership between community and government was, at least in rhetoric, a fundamental element of Landcare (Curtis and De Lacy 1997).

At a community level, the NLP translated into establishment of, and support for, community Landcare groups, that could apply for funding for group coordinators and for education, conservation and demonstration purposes. NLP funding for Landcare contributed to the achievement of impressive outcomes with some 4,500 community Landcare groups mobilised nationwide (Department of Agriculture Fisheries and Forestry 2011). Landcare group members were more likely to be aware of and report land degradation issues and more likely to adopt sustainable management practices (Hodges and Goesch 2006). Furthermore, over 90 per cent of Landcare group members made changes to their land management as a result of Landcare (Department of Agriculture Fisheries and Forestry 2011). At the property and local level, changes in management resulted in noticeably improved resource conditions, including less erosion, and better water quality and soil condition (Commonwealth Scientific and Industrial Research Organisation 2003). Evidence demonstrated that active participation in Landcare was linked to undertaking on-ground works (Australian Bureau of Agricultural and Resource Economics 2003; Curtis and De Lacy 1996a, 1996b; Lockie and Rockloff 2004; Lockie *et al.* 2002; Mues *et al.* 1998) and participation in the educational aspects of Landcare was related to the adoption of more sustainable farming practices, such as property planning and tree planting (Curtis and De Lacy 1996; Curtis 1999; Mues *et al.* 1998). Furthermore, Landcare was deemed a coup for public policy practice, demonstrating the results to be achieved through partnerships between community and government. Yet questions remain about the extent to which Landcare functioned as a community-based movement, with notions of partnerships between government and community nonexistent among many landholders and the focus on building partnerships and cooperation as much about securing these among state agencies as encouraging public participation (Lockie 1999).

Phase Two: establishing new institutional capacity

As catchment-wide approaches appeared to be the answer to the landscape scale degradation issues facing Australia, it was suggested that more responsibility be devolved to catchment-based groups in line with moves towards a more regionalised management model. Based on this, as well as concerns regarding the insufficient funding available to move landholders beyond awareness raising, the Commonwealth entered a phase of institution building. Thus, the Natural Heritage Trust (NHT) was implemented in 1996. The objectives of the NHT were to stimulate environmental investment; balance environmental protection, NRM and sustainable agricultural outcomes; and provide a framework for partnership between stakeholders. Through the NHT, greater provision was made for the funding of on-ground conservation works where catchment planning processes had determined these to be of high priority at an integrated regional level. The role of the regional catchment groups in determining funding outcomes was cemented, and this ostensibly removed the influence of politics on funding allocations for Landcare (Dann *et al.* 2009).

The main shift on the ground in the early years of the NHT was in the funding mechanisms to community groups. The NLP, along with another 16 environment and primary industries programmes were brought together under a single banner, though they remained standalone programmes and the objectives of each remained stable. An influential 1999 Commonwealth discussion paper recommended that the educative aspects of Landcare be complemented with resources devolved to the regional level for investment in NRM. It was proposed that decisions should be made at the regional level regarding the appropriate mix of projects, regulations and so on (National Natural Resource Management Task Force 1999). A major strategy in this process was the establishment of the National Action Plan for Salinity and Water Quality (NAP), launched in late 2000, which formalised the role of the burgeoning regional catchment groups in catchment management and coordination. While the statutory and administrative arrangements of these groups varied between the states, from institutional models with high levels of community engagement, to those where state government agencies retained responsibility for all legislative functions, in all states and territories, regional catchment groups began to play an important role in moderating catchment-scale programmes and outcomes, and working in close partnership with Landcare groups. A key outcome of the scaling up of NRM activity from the level of community Landcare groups was that, while these groups had tended to encourage planning for the intentional management of native biodiversity through farm planning, the institutionalised approach tended to have a more overt focus on native biodiversity, while farmed biodiversity was of less importance.

In 2000, in response to increasing institutional complexity at the regional level, the Commonwealth House of Representatives Standing Committee on the Environment and Heritage tabled its report *Coordinating Catchment Management*. Its recommendations included that the Commonwealth adopt a lead role in facilitating and implementing NRM principles, priorities, programmes and institutional arrangements; that a National Catchment Management Authority be established through COAG to coordinate and assist in the development of catchment, regional and local plans; that national catchment management legislation be implemented, and that there be consolidation of inconsistent laws and programmes by multiple layers of government in Australia. To this end, the Natural Resource Management Ministerial Council (NRMMC) was established in 2000, superseding the Australian Agricultural Council. The aim of the NRMMC remains to facilitate the implementation of plans and proposals that otherwise may not have been possible due to the division of constitutional powers between Australian, state and territory governments.

If institutional complexity was perceived at the government level, institutional crowding was certainly occurring at the community level. In NSW, for example,

127 NRM and catchment groups existed. This, in some areas, contributed to the undermining of both community Landcare groups and regional Landcare networks and contributed to decline in participation rates (Tennent and Lockie 2012; Simpson and Clifton 2010). In addition, the NAP and NHT had established regional NRM groups that were either in competition with, or unsympathetic to, the needs of community Landcare groups. A culture was found within these groups that assumed they should replace rather than support community engagement mechanisms, as well as a poor understanding of NRM models and funding regimes that were unsupportive of Landcare groups (Curtis and Cooke 2006; Forge-Zirkler and Prior 2006). Further, there were inequities in resource allocation (Robins and Dovers 2007), and challenges in implementation of catchment-scale projects stemming from limited funding, restrictive timelines, insufficient guidelines, poor communication and limited community participation (Farrelly 2005). While the large regional organisations were said to be instilled with the capacity to decide for themselves the appropriate mix of regulations, MBIs and other projects, in reality, they had no power to compel any change in management practices. Despite the high cost of building institutional capacity questions remain as to whether the desired outcomes were likely to be delivered. Nonetheless, in 2000, a second phase of the NHT was announced and was funded to $1.2 billion, and a third NHT phase was announced in 2007, and funded to $2 billion. The outcomes of this institutional approach remain to be seen, yet what is certain is that the regional approach taken through this phase will shape NRM in the coming years (Hajkowicz 2009).

Phase Three: NRM 'through the market'

In the early 2000s, following international leads, Australian governments began to experiment with MBIs. Domestically, it was argued that regulation alone was too blunt an instrument to achieve a balance of protection of industry and of natural resources, while previous policy approaches appeared to be costly for the benefits achieved. In an NRM context, MBIs involve the provision of incentives – usually direct payments – to landholders in exchange for the provision of environmental and social services in agricultural landscapes. A market-like approach is applied to the allocation of incentives to secure the most cost-effective or most desirable outcomes. These schemes, under a different name, are of course similar in many ways to previous policy projects, such as competitive tendering run by the NHT, though the mechanisms through which on-the-ground benefits are measured have changed (Hajkowicz 2009) and a more centralised approach to determining targets has been adopted. A key goal in utilising MBIs to deliver NRM outcomes is to allow land managers flexibility in deciding how to approach conservation activities (Commonwealth Treasury no date). This was of particular relevance in rural Australia, given long-term financial pressure that limited landholder engagement in NRM projects that did not directly maintain or improve short-term profitability (Lockie 1999, 2006; Campbell 1994). MBIs are also said to be the best mechanism for addressing market failures and/or creating markets for environmental services because they stimulate behavioural change and innovation (Commonwealth Treasury no date); deliver more targeted outcomes than regulation (Hajkowicz 2009; National Market Based Instruments Working Group 2005); and are more cost effective than traditional instruments (National Market Based Instruments Working Group 2005; Commonwealth Treasury no date). As noted above, MBIs were thus endorsed by the NAP, firstly, to achieve water and salinity goals. This was followed closely by the Department of the Environment and Heritage which, in conjunction with the Ministers for Environment from each state and territory, developed conservation agreements with outcomes to be met through the use of MBIs. The Australian Commonwealth, state and territory governments then funded 11 pilot MBI projects between 2003 and 2006. Early reporting suggested that MBIs were able to deliver cost effective natural resource outcomes, and delivered more targeted outcomes than regulation and provided flexibility for landholders in choosing whether and how to engage in conservation activities (National Market Based Instruments Working Group 2005).

In mid-2008, the Commonwealth announced a new five year, $2 billion environmental management plan, Caring for Our Country, jointly administered by the Department of Agriculture, Fisheries and Forestry (DAFF) and the Department of Sustainability, Environment, Water, Population and Communities (DSEWPaC). The initiative integrated the NHT, NAP and other relevant programmes to streamline the previously separate regional planning processes required for each programme. Also brought together under a single banner were monitoring and evaluation processes, communications strategies, capacity-building strategies, the development of market-based instruments and the development of environmental management systems. Caring for Our Country was claimed to have 'one clear goal, a business approach to investment, clearly articulated outcomes and priorities and improved accountability' (see www.nrm.gov.au). National priorities were determined at the Commonwealth level, and the application of MBIs to environmental preservation and protection was cemented in the programme's objectives. The businesslike approach within Caring for Our Country that included contracting for NRM outcomes certainly appears to represent a step away from resource condition monitoring towards programme and project monitoring. Moreover, this is repeated in the 2012–2013 budget that reaffirmed a further five year commitment to the programme, with outcomes measured through, for example, greater numbers of businesses adopting innovative practices, increased community engagement and clearer frameworks and action plans. From 2013, the programme has been delivered through two 'separate but complementary' streams, sustainable agriculture and sustainable environment (Burke, budget announcement). The agriculture stream is overseen by DAFF, and the environment stream, by DSEWPaC. The goal of separating streams was to place greater emphasis on land stewardship projects for farming communities, though whether this occurs remains to be seen. Certainly it seems at odds with the government's general principle of linking agriculture and environment. Funding for

Landcare continued under the agriculture stream and will be directed through regional NRM agencies, reaffirming the institutional complexity developed in Phase Two.

The way forward?

The existing suite of legislation, programmes and policies – including MBIs, which are relevant to NRM in Australia – has not yet been subjected to the same degree of systematic public evaluation that characterised the NLP. While it is certainly clear that previous approaches, including raising awareness, changing attitudes and building institutional capacity, will be insufficient alone to bring about significant change in the conservation of natural resources (Curtis and De Lacy 1996; Hajkowicz 2009; Lockie 1999, 2006), assumptions around MBIs are not unchallenged. Claims that MBIs are not prescriptive, for example, are at odds with the design of such projects, which involve 'unique, tailor-made arrangements with products tailored to the buyer's needs, characterised by large requirements of highly specific information' (Kroeger and Casey 2007, p. 325). The cost-effectiveness of MBIs for government also remains to be seen. An inability on the part of government to apply typical economic evaluation methods to MBIs has caused economic evaluations to be 'often only partial, rudimentary and of variable reliability' (Ward *et al.* 2005, p. 4). Other concerns include that suboptimal outcomes may be achieved through an inability to adequately model the complexity of interactions within ecosystems. The efficiency and cost-effectiveness of MBIs has also been called into question when insufficient sellers, or service providers, exist to participate in a genuine market mechanism or where they have a poor understanding of the relative public and private benefits of conservation activities (Lockie 2012). Mechanisms have been proposed to deal with this complexity (Scherr *et al.* 2010), although this has tended to lead to trade-offs between ecological accuracy and socio-economic reality, with compromises towards practical metrics (Hartig and Drechsler 2009). There is a general consensus that more research is needed to determine how best to manage these trade-offs (Ring *et al.* 2010). However, the persistent issues of modelling, targeting and outcome evaluation had not been adequately addressed prior to 2010 (Hajkowicz 2009). It is notable that for all the assessment, planning and institutional development that accompanied the devolution of funding to regional groups and the establishment of new NRM project types, the kinds of on-ground activities that have been promoted, to date, have not differed substantially from those activities promoted under the NLP and through community Landcare groups. Certainly it seems that a key assumption within each NRM policy initiative is that environmental degradation would cease if markets adequately recognised the interrelationships between agriculture and functional environmental landscapes. What has changed is the delivery mechanism and the potential to target specific NRM goals and groups of landholders. This may be reflective of the inherent complexity of translating the economic rationale behind MBIs into workable, on-the-ground solutions.

The outcomes of Caring for Our Country have yet to be assessed, although the top-down approach to priority setting implemented under the programme is at odds with earlier attempts to establish community ownership over NRM issues, and may not necessarily align with priorities identified by catchment-based groups. Indeed, a key finding from a 2012 review into Caring for Our Country was the need for broader stakeholder consultation in establishing desired outcomes and targets for the programme, and the need for these to more adequately reflect stakeholder experiences. A different approach, and perhaps one more consistent with earlier NRM policies, could be to leverage off the work of the catchment-based groups it spent substantial amounts of money establishing and the work they have done at a regional level to develop relevant priorities. Caring for Our Country may also have contradictory impacts on the level of reporting undertaken by regional groups. While considerable emphasis is placed on a 'businesslike' approach to investment, this new programme requires that regional groups apply for more of their funding on a competitive basis. In the absence of guaranteed base level funding, the capacity of regional groups to undertake detailed and continuing monitoring may, in fact, be diminished.

Reflections

There is a growing recognition in Australia that creating awareness and educating landholders, while an important first step, is likely to be insufficient to adequately protect and conserve the nation's natural resources (Curtis and De Lacy 1996). In light of international experimentation with market mechanisms, therefore, the gradual transition from the early days of Landcare towards contract-based systems based on payment for service may seem like a natural step. It would, of course, be a stretch to describe the NLP as a purely community driven programme, yet the programmes, policies and legislative approaches to NRM implemented through the mid-to-late 1990s were overtly more top-down responses to a range of national and international political pressures. This was clear, first, in the regionalisation of NRM through the NHT and NAP which placed greater control at the regional level via the formation of ostensibly apolitical, community friendly regional groups (rather than government bureaucracies) even though goals, objectives and performance metrics were still decided at the Commonwealth and state and territory levels. Second, this was clear in the application of technical expertise and MBIs to allocate resources. Nonetheless, governments are not retreating from active involvement in NRM, the 'market' turn coinciding both with increased Commonwealth involvement and experimentation in direct regulation. The most obvious example of the latter are land clearing regulations that have been implemented at the state level across much of Australia. These examples are, however, the exception rather than the rule; the overall trend is for policies, legislative frameworks and programmes that treat natural resource degradation as a form of market failure and which seek to address that failure through primarily market means.

This is currently played out in a complex governance environment, with four levels of government acting on NRM policy – Commonwealth, state or territory, regional and local, each creating its own policies and projects. National coordination is managed by the Cabinet Productivity Committee, while COAG provides inter-jurisdictional coordination on higher level national issues and the Department of Environment, Water, Heritage and the Arts heads interdepartmental coordination. Each state manages structural arrangements for NRM policy integration independently, and this may include policy and programmes, budget sustainability and monitoring, and evaluation integration. As commentators have pointed out, however, attempting to decipher what and where activities have been funded is, in itself, a complex task (Hajkowicz 2009). What is clear is that the latest NRM policy approaches represent a particular worldview with regard to the primary role of government – the increase and stability of economic stock – and the mechanisms through which natural resource protection and agri-environmental policy is best achieved: a businesslike approach to financial management combined with incentive mechanisms.

References

ABARE 2003, *Natural Resources Management on Australian farms*, ABARE, Canberra.

AFFA 1997, *Evaluation Report on the Decade of Landcare Plan—National Overview*, Australian Government, Department of Agriculture, Fisheries and Forestry, Canberra.

Bolton, GC 1992, *Spoils and Spoilers: Australians make their Environment*, George Allen & Unwin, Sydney.

Bonyhady, T 1993, *Places worth keeping: conservationists, politics, and law*, Allen & Unwin, St Leonards, Sydney.

Campbell, A 1994, *Landcare: Communities shaping the land and the future*, Allen & Unwin, Sydney.

Caring for Our Country Review Team 2011, *Report on the review of the Caring for Our Country Initiative*, Australian Government, Land and Coasts, Canberra.

Cary, J and Webb, T 2000, *Community Landcare, the National Landcare Program and the Landcare Movement: The Social Dimensions of Landcare*, Bureau of Rural Sciences, Canberra.

Commonwealth of Australia 1991b, *Ecologically Sustainable Development Working Groups: Final Report – Agriculture*, Australian Government Publishing Service, Canberra.

Commonwealth Treasury no date, *Public Good: Conservation and the Impact of Environmental Measures Imposed on Landholders*, Commonwealth of Australia, Canberra.

Curtis, A 1999, 'Landcare: beyond onground work', *Natural Resources Management*, vol. 2, no. 2, pp. 4–9.

Curtis, A and Cooke, P 2006, *Landcare in Victoria: after twenty years. Report to the Department of Agriculture, Fisheries and Forestry*, Report #20, Institute for Land, Water and Society, Albury, NSW.

Curtis, A and De Lacy, T 1996a, 'Landcare in Australia: Beyond the expert farmer', *Agriculture and Human Values*, vol. 13, no. 1, pp. 20–31.

Curtis, A and De Lacy, T 1996b, 'Landcare in Australia: Does it make a difference?', *Journal of Environmental Management* vol. 46, no. 2, pp. 119–137.

Curtis, A and De Lacy, T 1997, 'Examining the assumptions underlying Landcare', in Lockie, L and Vanclay, F (eds), *Critical Landcare*, Centre for Rural Social Research, Charles Sturt University, Wagga Wagga, pp. 185–199.

Dann, CS, Lockie, S and Tennent, R 2009, *Australian policy for the protection of on-farm biodiversity*, CQ University, Rockhampton.

DEHCD 1978, *Basis for Soil Conservation Policy in Australia, Report No. 1*, Department of Environment, Housing and Community Development, Canberra.

Department of Agriculture Fisheries and Forestry 2011, *National Landcare Program*, Australian Government, viewed 6 April 2011, www.daff.gov.au/naturalresources/landcare/national_landcare_program

Dovers, S 1992, 'The history of natural resource use in rural Australia: practicalities and ideologies', in Lawrence, G, Vanclay, F and Furze, B (eds), *Agriculture, environment and society: contemporary issues for Australia*, Macmillan, Melbourne.

Farrelly, M 2005, 'Regionalisation of environmental management: A case study of the natural heritage trust, South Australia', *Geographical Research*, vol. 43, no. 4, pp. 393–405.

Forge-Zirkler, K and Prior, J 2006, 'Community Landcare and the CMA: a question of survival', paper presented to International Landcare Conference, Melbourne, 8–11 October.

Hajkowicz, S 2009, 'The evolution of Australia's natural resource management programs: Towards improved targeting and evaluation of investments', *Land Use Policy*, vol. 26, no. 2, pp. 471–478.

Hartig, F and Drechsler, M 2009, 'Smart spatial incentives for market-based conservation', *Biological Conservation*, vol. 142, no. 4, pp. 779–788.

Hodges, A and Goesch, T 2006, *Australian Farm: Natural Resource Management 2004–05*, ABARE, Canberra.

Kroeger, T and Casey, F 2007, 'An assessment of market-based approaches to providing ecosystem services on agricultural lands', *Ecological Economics*, vol. 64, no. 2, pp. 321–332.

Lockie, S 1999, 'The state, rural environments, and globalisation: 'Action at a distance' via the Australian Landcare program', *Environment and Planning A*, vol. 31, no. 4, pp. 597–611.

Lockie, S 2000, 'Environmental governance and legitimation: state-community interactions and agricultural land degradation in Australia', *Capitalism, Nature, Socialism*, vol. 11, no. 2, pp. 41–58.

Lockie, S 2006, 'Networks of agri-environmental action: Temporality, spatiality and identity in agricultural environments', *Sociologia Ruralis*, vol. 46, no. 1, pp. 22–39.

Lockie, S 2012, 'Market Instruments, ecosystem services, and property rights: Assumptions and conditions for sustained social and ecological benefits', *Land Use Policy*, vol. 31, pp. 90–98.

Lockie, S, Dale, A, Taylor, B and Lawrence, G 2002, 'Capacity for Change: Testing a Model for the Inclusion of Social Indicators in Australia's National Land and Water Resources Audit', *Journal of Environmental Planning and Management*, vol. 45, no. 6, pp. 813–826.

Lockie, S and Rockloff, S 2004, *Landowner Attitudes to Wetlands and Wetland Conservation Programs and Incentives: Report to the Commonwealth Department of Environment and Heritage*, Cooperative Research Centre for Coastal Zone, Estuary and Waterway Management, Brisbane.

Mues, C, Chapman, L and Van Hilst, R 1998, *Landcare: Promoting Improved Land Management Practices on Australian Farms: A Survey of Landcare and Land Management Related Programs*, ABARE, Canberra.

NMBIWG 2005, *An Interim Report. Interim Report on the National Market Based Instrument Pilot Program Round One*, National Market Based Instruments Working Group, Canberra.

NNRMTF 1999, *Managing Natural Resources in Rural Australia for a Sustainable Future: A Discussion Paper for Developing a National Policy*, National Natural Resource Management Task Force, Department of Agriculture, Fisheries and Forestry Australia, Canberra.

Reeve, I 2002, *Property rights and natural resource management*, Institute for Rural Futures, University of New England, Armidale.

Ring, I, Hansjürgens, B, Elmqvist, T, Wittmer, H and Sukhdev, P 2010, 'Challenges in framing the economics of ecosystems and biodiversity: the TEEB initiative', *Current Opinion in Environmental Sustainability*, vol. 2, no. 1–2, pp. 15–26.

Robins, L and Dovers, S 2007, 'NRM regions in Australia: The "haves" and the "have nots"', *Geographical Research*, vol. 45, no. 3, pp. 273–290.

Scherr, S, Milder, J and Shames, S 2010, 'Paying for biodiversity conservation in agricultural landscapes', in Lockie, S and Carpenter, D (eds), *Agriculture, Biodiversity and Markets: Livelihoods and agroecology in comparative perspective*, Earthscan, London.

Toyne, P and Farley, R 1989, 'A national land management program', *Australian Journal of Soil and Water Conservation*, vol. 2, no. 2, pp. 6–9.

Ward, J, Bryan, B, Gale, G and Hobbs, T 2005, 'Market-Based Instrument approaches to implementing priority revegetation in the South Australian Murray–Darling Basin', CSIRO Land and Water, Canberra.

World Commission on Environment and Development 1987, *Our Common Future*, Oxford University Press, Oxford.

5 Dams, pumps, pipes and dreams

Water and the making of regional Australia

Kirsten Henderson[1]

Introduction

Water management policy has been shaping rural and regional Australia ever since Alfred Deakin introduced the *Irrigation Act* in Victoria in 1886. The Act helped establish the irrigation colony of Mildura and subsequent horticultural industries that still support the community there today. Many jurisdictions followed Deakin's lead so that irrigated agriculture now contributes around $12 billion a year to Australian agricultural production and vibrant communities have been established across much of regional Australia.

However, there is much evidence to suggest that such development has had unintended ecological consequences. Water resources development and regulation has changed the natural conditions of many of the nation's rivers, especially those in the Murray–Darling Basin. Alteration of riverine ecosystems has resulted in the decline of species diversity among native fish, birds and invertebrates. It has also resulted in the loss of ecological condition of many wetlands and riparian forests and caused toxic algal blooms. This situation has been the catalyst for much water policy reform undertaken by both state and Commonwealth governments in the past 30 years. Moreover, in order to maintain productive capacity from Australia's rivers, reassessment of the current policy settings is required.

This chapter first provides some of the historical context of water resources development in Australia and explains some of the objectives of Deakin's policies – many of which remain evident in contemporary water policy reform. The chapter then outlines four 'policy regimes' or phases of Australian water management, describing some of the institutions, instruments, and governing ideas that dominated for extended periods of time. Finally it discusses contemporary water reforms and their implications for rural and regional Australia.

Setting the scene

Water policy has been shaping rural and regional Australia ever since Alfred Deakin (then the Attorney-General of Victoria) introduced the *Irrigation Act* to that colony's Parliament in 1886. Deakin had visited California and Colorado in the United States on a study tour of irrigation colonies on behalf of the Victorian Royal Commission on Water Supply and had published a report on his tour: *Irrigation in Western America* (1885). In this report Deakin was enthusiastic about what irrigation could achieve for Victoria, especially in terms of the development of regional communities, and he recommended the administrative arrangements that he thought would help achieve this goal.

The recommendations were based on three beliefs about water management policy that Deakin had formed during his tour. He argued that the responsibility, care and custody of water should be invested in the state only; that the state's right to water must not be compromised by riparian rights to anyone else; and that the rights of the state and the rights of individuals they applied to in terms of water resource access needed to be clearly defined in order to avoid lengthy and costly litigation (Deakin 1885; Harris 2007; Ingle-Smith 1998; Powell 1989). The resulting *Irrigation Act* was an innovative piece of legislation and understanding this early water management policy instrument is important for understanding the development of the subsequent phases of Australian water management policy (outlined in the following section) and the implications they have for rural and regional Australia. Some of the key characteristics of the Act are outlined below.

The *Irrigation Act* was the first statute in Australia to abolish riparian rights on any future claims to water by declaring state ownership of water. Riparian rights give a landowner the right to use water that is on and/or flowing past their land as long as such use does not substantially affect water quality or another individual's economic use of their land (see Fisher 2000 and Godden 2003). This doctrine was inherited by the Australian colonies from British law. A key feature of the doctrine is the assumption of an abundance of water and a scarcity of land – with the implicit priority being to protect the apparently scarcer resource. In Australia, of course, the situation is reversed: there is an abundance of land and scarcity of water (compared to the volume of water available for European methods of agricultural production). The *Irrigation Act* was the first statute to formally recognise this situation (Fisher 2000; Godden 2003).

The *Irrigation Act* also rejected another commonly used doctrine of water use and management called 'prior appropriation', often used in the regions that Deakin had visited on his study tour. Prior appropriation states that the person who first claims access to a water source has the right to use it as they see fit. It is a 'first come, first served' doctrine that not only completely ignores any Indigenous claims to water, but also enshrines in law an individual rather than collective 'water ethic'. Unlike the riparian rights doctrine, it contains no consideration for any other individual's or group's use of the available water. As a consequence, within those jurisdictions that rely it, there can be a tendency towards litigation when parties disagree as to who had first claim to the water source. Deakin regarded the prior appropriation doctrine as the major cause of the many disputes over water rights in the USA, and this was a problem he aimed to avoid with his legislation (Powell 1989).

Deakin implemented a solution to this problem by devising legislation that recognised water as a public resource. Under the *Irrigation Act*, the state would manage Victoria's rivers and streams for the collective good. However, Deakin's legislation retained the autonomy of local irrigation trusts to establish the direction of water management within their own jurisdiction. This was significant because Deakin was determined that the 'individual energy and joint action of farmers' (in Powell 1989) would counter any tendency towards state authoritarianism that the *Irrigation Act* might be seen to encourage. Deakin's vision was of a hybrid scheme of water management that would allow for 'state aid, (but) not state initiative' in the development of the water resources of Victoria, a scheme that would allow for the 'dynamic forces of individualism' to enable 'men to invest their capital and their labour in order that they obtain a better return for their efforts' (in Powell 1989).

Finally, understanding the *Irrigation Act* is important because it unlocked the potential for the accumulation of wealth and power that control of the water in an arid region represents. The riparian rights doctrine, with its definition of water as common property, has a perceived tendency to hold back development. Allowing for another individual's economic use of their land means not interfering with the natural flow of a river in a significant way. The innovation of the *Irrigation Act* was to preserve the common ownership of water (through the state) but allow for the provision of individual benefit from its development. Members of the irrigation trusts received autonomy in decision-making about water management *and* the freedom to accumulate profits resulting from that development. The *Irrigation Act* enshrined in statute law the concept of water in an arid continent as a *public* resource, the use of which needs to be balanced between the requirements of individuals and those of society as a whole. And with other states and territories subsequently following Victoria's lead, the Act ensured that water policy in Australia became solely a public policy and administrative matter (see also Connell 2007).

Of course, Deakin was not undertaking his reform in a political or cultural vacuum. There were a number of very influential ideas prevalent at the time that drove the support for water resources development in the colonies. These are also important for understanding the development of the subsequent phases of Australian water management policy. The major objective of water resource management at the time was the development of a society of yeoman farmers, carrying out honourable work by cropping a well-ordered garden landscape that not only overcame the aridity and unpredictability of the Australian environment but also sought to beautify the landscapes 'impoverished' by the wool and wheat industries (Ingle-Smith 1998; Tyrrell 1999). Irrigation was regarded as insurance against drought and a variable climate, and it was to allow for the 'conservation' (meaning the planned and efficient use) of Victoria's water resources. The use of water for irrigation also had religious connotations. Irrigation was regarded as a strategy to overcome the emerging tensions between scientific rationality and religious faith. It provided a scientific basis for controlling the environment but at the same time allowed for 'creation of an earthly paradise by finishing off

God's work in arid regions through allowing the land to become productive' (Bellanta 2002; Ingle-Smith 1998; Sinclair 1994; Tyrrell 1999). As will be discussed later in the chapter, many of these are policy objectives that remain a priority for Australian water management policy today.

Phases of Australian water resources development[2]

Bearing in mind the above outlined historical context, the history of water management in Australia from settlement to the present day can be usefully organised into four phases or 'policy regimes',[3] each characterised in terms of the actors, institutions, instruments, and governing ideas that dominated for extended periods. Four Australian water policy regimes or phases can be identified corresponding to the timeframes: settlement to 1886, 1886 to 1905, 1905 to 1980, and 1980 to the present day.[4]

The first phase lasting from settlement to 1886 was a period of coming to terms with an hydrological environment that was very different to European conditions and expectations. Water was not subject to great control and despite improving knowledge of the continent's hydrological characteristics and increasing indication that a riparian rights doctrine was an inappropriate policy instrument when applied to an arid climate, no attempt was made to adjust the policy settings. Water was used for survival, and it was locally controlled with minimal technological intervention. This was a stable period of water resource management in Australia and no attempt was made to adjust the regime for approximately 100 years.

By contrast, with Deakin's *Irrigation Act* as a catalyst, the next policy phase, from 1886 to 1905, was short-lived but encompassed rapid and significant change in water management strategy (as outlined previously). Water became a tool to be used in the development of the Australian colonies, first in Victoria, and then in the other colonies. Control of water became a fundamental policy issue and along with it grew the political and state power that control of water can bring. Nevertheless, within this regime, water was conceptualised as a public good to be managed for the benefit of all citizens. This necessitated significant alteration of the management regime from one based on common law to one based on statutory legislation, coupled with considerable physical engineering works built to control water delivery.

The third phase of Australian water management policy represents a return to a long-lasting stable configuration of water management. It persisted for 75 years, from 1905 to 1980. However, unlike the previous instance of long-term stability (from settlement to 1886), this period is defined by intervention into rivers and control of water resources. This era is characterised by centralised, state-run enterprises such as the Victorian State Rivers and Water Supply Commission (SRWSC) and the Water Conservation and Irrigation Board (WC&IB) in NSW. The objective of water management policy in this period was closer settlement of the land, the establishment of white, hard-working communities and the expansion of economic production.

It was during this period that the 13 locks and 16 weirs were constructed along the length of the River Murray, and the very large storages of the Hume and Dartmouth Dams were completed. These allowed for total management of the river so that water can be delivered at the times required by irrigators. However, although they benefited directly from this regime, irrigators themselves retained very little control over the resource and consequently held little political agency. This era was the provenance of the engineer. They held and controlled the knowledge about water flow, volumes, pressures, and evaporation rates and they combined this knowledge with bureaucratic skills to play an integral role in realising water benefits through the actions of the state (Henderson 2008).

However, the engineers were not acting in isolation. During this period, despite the occasional dissenting voice (see Davidson 1969), there was a widespread societal consensus that the technological transformation of rivers and use of water for population and economic growth was a worthwhile exercise. When compared to the level of change that was occurring in other aspects of Australian life during this timeframe – from post-war immigration and the baby boom to the expansion of the welfare state, from dramatic increases in agricultural productivity, increasing wealth and consequent consumer demand to the expansion of the suburbs, the second wave feminist movement and the rise of the civil rights movement – the level of change in water policy during this time was negligible (Henderson 2008).

There are three reasons for this situation. First, as mentioned, powerful cultural ideas continued to drive the development policy. European-derived ideals about the productive use of land, aesthetic beauty and the place of nature within human culture were combined with religious imperatives to make the desert bloom. Second, the water policy regime during this era consolidated the power and control of the state over water resources. It was congruent with the state's interests to maintain the status quo. Third, while irrigators lost some of their political autonomy in the change from one regime to the other (i.e. from the decentralised trusts during Deakin's time to the centralised water management by institutions like the SRWSC) they gained a low-cost and relatively reliable supply of water to use in a variable climate. This was a trade-off irrigators were willing to make for the best part of 75 years (Henderson 2008).

This phase of water resource management policy came to a close in the 1980s as its certainties and securities were challenged by two new perceptions of water and the appropriate methods for its management. The result has been rapid change in the objectives and character of the water policy regime. No longer is water appreciated solely for the value it can impart to land, that is, by enabling the use of that land for production of agricultural commodities destined for national and international marketplaces. Water under the current policy regime is now valued as a commodity in its own right. Water has also gained an intrinsic value in another way. It is valued for the ecological services it provides in maintaining healthy wetlands and riverine ecosystems. Scientists and economists are now the authoritative voices of water management, while major agriculturalists, government bureaucrats and environmentalists compete and combine to exert a control over water that is 'unprecedentedly thorough' (Worster 1985).

Contemporary water policy

Past water policy regimes resulted in the establishment of vibrant communities and allowed for closer settlement within Australia's inland regions. They also underpinned the growth of many important industries such as the historically significant table grape, dried fruit, citrus, rice and dairy industries, as well as the more recently established wine grape, almond, olive and cotton industries. However, there have been unintended ecological consequences as a result of this economic success. River regulation and intervention has altered riverine ecosystems and resulted in the decline of species diversity of native fish, birds and invertebrates, the loss of wetlands and riparian forests, and caused toxic algal blooms (Australian Bureau of Statistics 2003; National Land and Water Resources Audit 2001; Schofield, Burt and Connell 2003; MDBA 2011). While the implementation of water management policies has been profitable, in order to maintain the productive capacity from Australia's rivers at all, reassessment of the policy settings is required.

It is this realisation that led to the agreement by all members of the Council of Australian Governments (COAG) in 2004 to a new guiding framework for nationwide water reform, known as the National Water Initiative (NWI). The aim of the NWI is 'a nationally-compatible, market, regulatory, and planning based system of managing surface and groundwater resources for rural and urban use that optimises economic, social and environmental outcomes' (Council of Australian Governments 2004), while one of its explicit provisions is the statutory recognition of the use of water to meet environmental objectives. Alongside the NWI sits the Murray–Darling Basin Agreement (initially signed by Victoria, New South Wales, South Australia and the Commonwealth in 1987, but which now includes Queensland and the Australian Capital Territory as well) that recognises management of the Basin requires integrated responses to issues of land *and* water management, as well as coordination across jurisdictions. Even more recently we have the *Water Act 2007* which created the Murray–Darling Basin Authority; led to the development of a proposed Basin Plan that sets a limit on the amount of water that can be extracted for consumptive use from the Basin; created a Commonwealth Environmental Water Holder; and expanded the roles of the Australian Competition and Consumer Commission and the Bureau of Meteorology in water regulation and provision of water information. At the state government level, water reforms have taken place to align their respective water policies with the provisions of the NWI. (See Department of Prime Minister and Cabinet 2003; Victorian Department of Sustainability and Environment 2004; Department of Environment, Water, Heritage and the Arts 2008; Connell and Grafton 2011; Murray–Darling Basin Authority 2012).

The trajectory of water policy reform in Australia since the 1980s can be seen as a response to the tension between the prevailing concepts of economic rationalism and sustainable development. To explain these a little further, ecologically sustainable development is defined as using, conserving and enhancing the community's resources so that the ecological processes on which life depends are maintained, and the total quality of life now and in the future can be increased. The sustainability discourse attempts to remove the division between economic development and the environment. Balance is the key here, but while some redefinition of the concepts of growth and development is recognised, for example that economic growth depends on environmental protection, no reorientation of the values of industrialist society is expected. Economic growth remains the objective of society, even within the sustainability discourse (Commonwealth Government 1990; Dryzek 1997). Economic rationalism is about more than purely economics. It contains ideas about the role of the state in the political economy. Rather than being actively involved in markets via government instrumentalities (for instance water utilities and or telecommunications bodies), the government's role is to set the parameters for the efficient operation of the market. The guiding principle is of 'steering not rowing' the economy. Hence there is emphasis on deregulation of industries, privatisation or corporatisation of government businesses, the removal of cross-subsidies in prices and the separation of the service and regulatory roles of institutions.

According to these two philosophies, water can no longer be regarded as a free good that is unlimited in supply. Its use in a manner that is unheeding of the potential environmental impacts has also become increasingly untenable. The water reforms of the past ten to 15 years have resulted in a shift from state-directed centralised management and guarantee of water supply to the more flexible but less secure (for individual irrigators) agency of market-based allocation of water to users. In concert with calls for consideration of the long-term environmental consequences of water use, the reforms have also seen statute law recognise the challenges to the sustainability of the Australian continent that over 200 years of European agricultural practices has caused. Unlike the perception of water in the past, where there was a general societal consensus on the appropriate role and use of water within society, water in the contemporary policy regime is understood to have two competing forms: it is regarded as 'private property', a commercial commodity in its own right valuable for wealth creation, and it is also understood as a collectively and inter-generationally valued entity with a value that is distinct from its economic worth. Water in this policy context is regarded as a vital constituent of a healthy ecosystem that provides services quite apart from its potential to create wealth, including the facilitation of many recreational activities (e.g. swimming, fishing, boating and skiing) and aesthetic appreciation.

The consequences of contemporary water reform for rural and regional Australia

For many decades, for rural and regional Australia the provision of water for irrigation was part of a broader social contract between the 'city and the country' (Brett 2011). This social contract valued the rural way of life and accepted that farmers would supply the nation with food at reasonable prices, while in return society would support them in financial, political, and, most crucially, social terms. This engendered a sense of equity and certainty for irrigators. This situation was part of a broader political and economic settlement known as the 'Australia Settlement' which included a range of policies designed to achieve as much certainty as possible for Australian businesses and workers. These included the White Australia policy, protection of industry (through tariffs, etc.), centralised wage fixing, 'state paternalism' and imperial benevolence (Kelly 1992). A defining feature of the settlement was the active role of government in the economy.

As part of the settlement governments in Australia developed and applied a 'corporatist' model in their dealings with farmers, and their communities. That is, they adopted policies and programmes that treated farmers and their organisations as partners in a development project for agriculture. Governments saw their role in that partnership as involving market intervention to create optimal conditions for the development of agricultural production (Gray and Lawrence 2001). The development of irrigation schemes was part of this philosophy.

Despite having some flaws, the Australia settlement delivered prosperity to a great many people. However, by the 1980s this prosperity was under serious threat. The combination of the globalisation of capital, communications and services with a domestic economy heavily reliant on primary products meant that Australia's net foreign debt rose sharply throughout the 1980s and early 1990s. Australia's credit rating was downgraded and per capita income relative to other OECD countries began to fall. Unemployment rose and so did inflation (see Hughes 1998; Kelly 1992; Melleuish 1997). As a result the Commonwealth Labor government of the time chose to radically restructure the Australian economy. From 1983–1996 a comprehensive programme of economic and monetary policy reform encompassing the removal of trade barriers, the floating of the Australian dollar, privatisation of public utilities and the creation of markets for water and power, and deregulation of the banking sector resulted in a vastly different social and economic landscape than before (Tonts 2000).

These changes, combined with the changing objectives of water management policy have had dramatic effects on rural and regional communities, and on agricultural producers in particular. Some changes have been positive: improvements in communications technology and transport, together with changes in the organisation of production have meant that sectors such as tourism and services have been able to relocate or grow in regional areas. There has also been increased access to credit for farmers to expand their operations, and increased access for their produce to be sold on international markets (Tonts 2000).

However, economic restructuring has also had negative consequences for regional communities and people. While the opening of international markets has been advantageous for many farmers, including irrigation farmers, in the global market for commodities farmers are generally regarded as price takers – that is, they are forced to accept the internationally set price for their produce and cannot directly influence that price. Over several decades the real prices of agricultural products have been in decline, while the cost of inputs to the production process have either increased, or not fallen at the same rate as prices. This phenomenon is known as the 'cost-price squeeze'. As they have limited ability to pass on cost increases to end consumers in this environment, irrigators and other agriculturalists have been forced to increase productivity and manage input costs to remain competitive (Frontier Economics 2010).

To achieve increased productivity, farmers can seek to minimise costs though such actions as delaying spending on maintenance of farm equipment, but in the longer term this will not solve the problem as it ultimately means more expenditure in the future. For most farming enterprises the only way to increase productivity and keep the business performing at a socially sustainable level (i.e. keeping pace with the general standard of living) is to expand the farm and, of course, larger farms means fewer farms, with consequent impacts on farming communities (Barr 2009).

Regional and rural communities suffer 'collateral damage' from these economic and demographic forces. They lose population, businesses, services, and social outlets. Once these attributes are lost, it is very difficult for such places to regenerate (Barr 2009). Irrigation towns have been shielded from these impacts to a certain extent, especially those that rely on high-value horticultural industries (i.e. fruit and vegetable production). However, due to technological changes (which make it cheaper to invest in greater amounts of more efficient infrastructure) and the need to increase efficiency in water use (both to increase productivity and to deal with reduced water availability), pressure remains for irrigation enterprises to increase in size.

In many older irrigation districts which were developed under the philosophy of closer settlement (and consequently consist of generally small blocks), expanding or amalgamating the many small blocks is difficult and expensive. Many of these areas are located on the edges of expanding towns and are attractive to what Barr calls 'amenity buyers' (generally people from larger cities attracted to areas close to urban centres, that have good views, are close to water and have a benign climate) (Barr 2009). As a result, farmers wishing to expand their operations often have to compete for land with those who value it from quite a different perspective (i.e. for the pleasure of living on a rural block rather than the business return it might make) and are willing to pay higher prices. Conversely, of course, for those wishing to exit farming this can be an advantage as they are likely to receive higher prices for their land, but such sales still contribute to the changing demographics and culture of previously agriculture-based towns.

People who live in regional Australia have been willing to overcome all the above challenges because they understood farming and the rural way of life to be valued by Australian society. However, increasing urbanisation has meant that fewer Australian families have personal contact with agriculture either through work or through relatives, while increasing affluence has meant that many people now have enough income to satisfy their basic needs for food and shelter (with very little physical effort on their part) and so tend to turn their energies to satisfying more esoteric needs for 'beauty, justice, goodness and environmental richness' (Barr 2009). In contemporary Australia, this has often meant an increasing focus on environmental issues. A corresponding development has been a decline in farming's iconic status in Australian society. The small farmer, 150 years ago, was a symbol of the 'common man' seeking freedom from the repression of a class-bound Europe. Through the 1960s agriculture was seen as the engine that drove Australia's economy: we 'rode on the sheep's back'. But as agriculture's share of the national economy has decreased over time, and as environmental issues have come to the forefront of the public mind challenging previously accepted notions of how natural resources should be shared and used, so too has farming's status in society declined (Barr 2009; Brett 2011).

In many senses farmers and their communities are caught at the intersection between these political, economic and cultural shifts. Farmers and farming families are often forced to make a number of difficult decisions about their businesses in response to circumstances that are beyond their control. The choice tends to be 'get big or get out'. But getting big involves significant and ongoing investment under conditions of declining terms of trade and is much easier if the business is already big. Getting out often means changing occupation, moving house, moving to a new community, and crucially, changing identity. For many people, especially those who are older, less well educated and who may already have significant debts, the challenges of those two options are just too great. Stress is induced because people see no way out of their situation combined with the perceived uncertainty of their future. This leads to the development and exacerbation of social issues around stress and depression and family breakdown. Meanwhile, agriculture's political influence is also waning and along with it, the ability of rural and regional Australians to have their issues heard by those in power. To many people in rural and regional Australia it seems that their way of life is no longer understood, nor valued by the rest of Australian society.

It was into this dynamic context that the Murray–Darling Basin Authority introduced the Proposed Basin Plan. Reaction in rural and regional Australia has been well covered elsewhere (for instance, see Connell and Grafton 2011) but for many people who see themselves as directly affected by the Plan's proposals, with its emphasis on protecting and restoring environmental assets, it symbolises a shift away from the societal support that agriculture used to enjoy in Australia towards outright opposition. The reaction to the Basin Plan is as much a reflection of the contested understandings of the use and meaning of water as it is a political battle over scarce resources.

The challenge of the changes in Australian water policy objectives since the 1980s for rural and regional Australia is that adjustment is likely to have uneven consequences with the greatest burden falling on smaller, more remote towns that rely heavily on irrigated agriculture and have less diversified economies. Individuals, communities, and businesses with the greatest adaptive capacity are those most likely to be able to make the change and thrive. But as with many of the other processes causing change in regional areas, such as declining terms of trade for agriculture and demographic shifts, those with the greatest adaptive capacity is likely to mean individuals who already have better income, and/or better education, or communities with an already broad economic base, or farm businesses that are already large and more efficient. The risk here is that the diversity of Australia's regional and rural communities will be reduced. If change is not managed appropriately, it is possible that the result could be a few very large farms producing a restricted range of foodstuffs, via industrialised methods as part of a vertically integrated supply chain for large companies. This may make economic sense, but it will mean a very different social landscape to that which exists in many parts of regional Australia today (Henderson 2012).

Further political manoeuvring will also come into play. Those with vested interests in such businesses (supermarket chains, peak stakeholders and investors) are likely to work towards this outcome and are more likely to be able to obtain the political support to do so. Smaller farms and the communities that rely on them are less likely to be able to mobilise such support. Australia's established political parties seemingly have difficulty articulating a vision for regional Australia, beyond maintaining that it should be 'sustainable'. This may explain the current popularity of independent candidates in regional electorates. The question that needs to be asked and answered is what do we, as a nation, want for and from our regional communities? The lesson that can be drawn from this brief outline of Australian water policy history is that in this 'driest inhabited continent', the management of water, as much as the management of any other policy issue, must be considered a priority when answering that question.

Notes

1 **Please note:** While Kirsten Henderson currently works for the Murray–Darling Basin Authority, the views expressed here are hers alone and do not represent the views of the Authority.

2 For alternative characterisations of the phases of Australian water policy development see Connell 2007; Blackmore 2002; and Ingle-Smith 1998.

3 Howlett and Ramesh (2003) present a useful overview of understanding policy change in terms of policy regimes. As they go on to explain (p. 234), policy regimes describe long-term patterns found in both the substance and process of public policy-making in a particular sector. They describe how policy-making can tend to develop in such a way that the same actors, institutions, instruments and governing ideas dominate for extended periods of time, infusing a policy sector with both consistent content and a set of typical policy processes or procedures. Such a pattern will become clear in the analysis of the history of Australian water management presented here.

4 Although this chapter focuses on the water management policies of settler Australians, it is recognised that Indigenous people have been managing water resources in Australia in a variety of ways born from understandings that are the direct consequence of thousands of years of coming to terms with the environmental conditions of the continent. Water forms an integral part of the Aboriginal peoples' cosmology as a sacred, elemental symbol and a source of life, while direct action to care for and manipulate water resources is evident in discoveries of extensive fish and eel traps in inland Victoria, fishing stations in the Barwon River in Brewarrina and mikiri wells of the southeast Simpson Desert. For more details see Rose 1997; Strang 2005; Toussaint, Sullivan and Yu 2005; and Langton 2006).

References

Barr, N 2009, *The House on the Hill. The Transformation of Australia's Farming Communities*, Land and Water Australia in association with Halstead Press, Canberra.

Bellanta, M 2002, *Irrigation Millennium: Science, Religion and the New Garden of Eden*. Available at: www.arts.monash.edu.au/eras. Accessed: 27 April 2005.

Blackmore, D 2002, 'Protecting the Future' in Connell, D (ed.), *Uncharted Waters*, Murray–Darling Basin Commission, Canberra.

Brett, J 2011, 'Fair Share: Country and City in Australia', *Quarterly Essay*, no. 42.

Commonwealth Government 1990, *Ecologically Sustainable Development: A Commonwealth Discussion Paper*, Commonwealth Government, Australian Government Printing Service, Canberra.

Connell, D 2001, 'The River Murray and Writing the Constitution', *Proceedings of the 'Water History – Lessons for the Future' conference*, 28 September, Hydrological Society of South Australia, Goolwa, South Australia, pp. 31–35.

Connell, D 2007, *Water Politics in the Murray–Darling Basin*, The Federation Press, Sydney.

Connell, D and Grafton, RQ (eds) 2011, *Basin Futures: Water Reform in the Murray–Darling Basin*, ANU E Press, Canberra.

Davidson, BR 1969, *Australia Wet or Dry?*, Melbourne University Press, Victoria.

Deakin, A 1885, *First Progress Report: Irrigation in Western America*, John Ferres, Government Printer, Melbourne.

Department of Conservation and Environment 1991, *Water Victoria. The Next 100 Years*, Department of Conservation and Environment, Victoria.

Department of Environment, Water, Heritage and the Arts 2008, *Water for the Future*. Available at: www.environment.gov.au/water/index.html. Accessed: 5 May 2008.

Department of Prime Minister and Cabinet 2003, *National Water Initiative*. Available at: www.dpmc.gov.au/docs/national_water_initiative_progress.cfm. Accessed: 26 February 2004.

Doyle, T and Kellow, A 1995, *Environmental Politics and Policy Making in Australia*, Macmillan, Australia.

Dryzek, J 1997, *The Politics of the Earth*, Oxford University Press, Oxford.

Fisher, DE 2000, *Water Law*, LBC Information Services, North Ryde, NSW.

Frontier Economics 2010, *Structural Adjustment Pressures in the Irrigated Agriculture Sector in the Murray–Darling Basin. A Report Prepared for the Murray–Darling Basin Authority*, unpublished report, Frontier Economics Pty. Ltd., Australia.

Griffin, G 2003, 'Selling the Snowy: The Snowy Mountains Scheme and National Mythmaking', *Journal of Australian Studies*, vol. 79, pp. 39–49.

Groom, LE 1920, 'President's Address' in *Harnessing Australia's Greatest River*, The Industrial Australian and Mining Standard, Melbourne.

Harris, E 2007, 'Institutional Change And Economic Growth: The Evolution Of Water Rights in Victoria, Australia 1850–1886', *Economic Papers: A journal of applied economics and policy*, vol. 26, pp. 118–127.

Henderson, K 2007, 'Water Myths and Water Reforms' in Ensor, J, Polak, I and Van Der Merwe, P (eds), *Other Contact Zones. New Talents 21C*, Network Books, Perth, pp. 149–157.

Henderson, K 2008, 'Rethinking the Political of Water in Australia: Water Paradigms and Water Policy Regimes 1788–2008', PhD Thesis, La Trobe University, Australia.

Henderson, K 2012, 'The Murray Darling Basin', in Beilharz, P and Hogan, T (eds) *Sociology: Antipodean Perspectives*, 2nd edn, Oxford University Press, South Melbourne.

Howlett, M and Ramesh M 2003, *Studying Public Policy. Policy Cycles and Policy Sub-systems*, 2nd edn, Oxford University Press, Oxford.

Hughes, OE 1998, *Australian Politics*, Macmillan, Melbourne.

Independent Committee of Inquiry into Competition Policy in Australia 1993, *National Competition Policy*, Australian Government Publishing Service, Canberra.

Ingle-Smith, D 1998, *Water in Australia. Resources and Management*, Oxford University Press, Oxford.

Kelly, P 1992, *The End of Certainty*, Allen & Unwin, Sydney.

Langton, M 2006, 'Earth, wind, fire, and water: the social and spiritual construction of water in Aboriginal societies', in David, B, Barker, B and McNiven, I (eds), *The Social Archaeology of Australian Indigenous Landscapes*, Aboriginal Studies Press, Canberra, pp. 139–160.

Mead, E 1920, *Helping Men Own Farms*, The Macmillan Company, New York.

Melleuish, G 1997, 'Living in an age of Packages: "Economic Rationalism" and "The Clever Country" in Australian Political Thought', *Australian Journal of Politics and History*, vol. 43, no. 2, pp. 200–215.

Murray–Darling Basin Authority 2011, *Socioeconomic analysis and the draft Basin Plan: Part A – Overview and analysis*. Murray–Darling Basin Authority, Canberra.

Murray–Darling Basin Authority 2012, *About the Murray–Darling Basin Authority*. Available at: www.mdba.gov.au/about. Accessed: 2 September 2012.

Murray–Darling Basin Commission 2005, *A Brief History of the Murray–Darling Basin Agreement*. Available at: www.mdbc.gov.au. Accessed: 28 April 2005.

National Water Commission 2011, *National Water Initiative*. Available at: www.nwc.gov.au. Accessed: 30 July 2011.

Powell, JM 1989, *Watering the Garden State. Water, Land and Community in Victoria 1834–1988*, Allen & Unwin, Sydney.

Powell, JM 1993, *The Emergence Of Bioregionalism in the Murray–Darling Basin*, Murray–Darling Basin Commission, Canberra.

Powell, JM 2000, 'Snakes and Cannons: Water Management and the Geographical Imagination in Australia', in Dovers, S (ed.), *Environmental History and Policy. Still Settling Australia*, Oxford University Press, Oxford, pp. 47–72.

Rose, D 1997, 'When the Rainbow Walks', in Webb, E (ed.), *Windows on Meteorology*, CSIRO, Australia.

Schofield, N, Burt, A and Connell, D 2003, *Environmental water allocation: principles, policies and practices*, Land and Water Australia, Canberra

Sinclair, P 1994, *Making the Deserts Bloom: Attitudes Towards Water and Nature in the Victorian Irrigation Debate 1880–1890*, Masters Thesis, University of Melbourne.

Strang, V 2005, 'Common Senses: Water, Sensory Experience and the Generation of Meaning', *Journal of Material Culture*, vol. 10, no. 1, pp. 92–120.

Tonts, M 2000, 'The Restructuring of Australia's Rural Communities' in Pritchard, B and McManus, P (eds), *Land of Discontent. The Dynamics of Change in Rural and Regional Australia*, UNSW Press, Sydney.

Toussaint, S, Sullivan, P, and Yu, S 2005, 'Water Ways in Aboriginal Australia: An Interconnected Analysis', *Anthropological Forum*, vol. 15, no. 1, pp. 61–73.

Tyrrell, IR 1999, *True Gardens Of The Gods: Californian-Australian Environmental Reform, 1860–1930*, University of California Press, Berkeley, California.

Victorian Department of Sustainability and Environment 2004, *Our Water, Our Future*, Vega Press, Melbourne.

Worster, D 1985, *Rivers Of Empire. Water, Aridity and the Growth of the American West*, Pantheon Books, New York.

Wright, DI 1975, 'River Murray: A Continuing Debate', *Journal of the Royal Australian Historical Society*, vol. 61, no. 3, pp. 165–182.

Part II

Policy-specific issues

6 Perspectives on population policy in Australia

Catherine Gross

Introduction

Population is a key policy issue for rural and regional Australia. Since the time of European settlement, where and how people should live has been a frequent and often controversial topic. Government policies across a range of sectors have contributed directly and indirectly to settlement patterns in rural and regional Australia. Some were specifically-targeted population policies whereas others were more broadly concerned with nation-building and infrastructure. Whether specific or implied, deliberations on many aspects of population have long been embedded in the political and policy context. These include population numbers, for example the 'Populate or Perish' slogan used by the Australian Government after World War II (Barr 2009); the population profile and immigration, for example the post-Federation White Australia policy; and matters of equity and quality of life between different sections of the population, such as between rural and urban Australia (Brett 2011). And yet, even as a nation of immigrants, Australians are considered to be ill-informed about many aspects of population – such as immigration and its impact on the nation – and have been described as '…confused, bemused or misled on what is a key public policy issue' (Productivity Commission 2010, p. iii).

In the last few years the population issue has moved higher on the political agenda. This complex topic is discussed widely by politicians, activists, non-governmental organisations (NGOs), academics and the media. The humanitarian and refugee aspect of immigration became a focus of debate after the number of refugees and asylum-seekers arriving by boat increased sharply in the late 1990s and early 2000s (Phillips and Spinks 2011). Another controversial issue is the hiring of temporary migrant workers as a response to perceived shortages of labour in some areas. Many publications seek to clarify the facts about different aspects of population, and answer questions such as whether Australia needs more immigrants to support the ageing population (Hugo 1999; McDonald and Kippen 1999; Productivity Commission 2010). There is no shortage of opinion or academic literature on population in relation to growth, economics, sustainability or the well-being of the nation as a whole. As McDonald argues in a March 2011 Productivity Commission Roundtable proceedings:

> The scope, strength and dimensions of the debate about population growth, and its potentially divisive character, justify an explicit statement of population strategy by the Australian government.
>
> (McDonald 2011, p. 21)

Subsequent to this Roundtable, the Australian Government issued 'the nation's first ever dedicated sustainable population strategy' (Burke 2011, p. 1). Tony Burke, the Minister for Sustainability, Population and Communities, launched the strategy as a framework for a sustainable Australia, with a focus on population change and growth in regional areas rather than specifying particular population targets (Department of Sustainability, Environment, Water, Population and Communities 2011). In this strategy the population question is framed in sustainability terms, not in purely economic terms.

This chapter presents a contextual analysis to show how historical events and government policies and programmes have influenced the location and make-up of the Australian population, culminating in this Australian government policy. It outlines problem areas or opportunities that these government programmes sought to address. This analysis did not set out to consider the overall Australian population question per se, being more focused on population issues and associated initiatives that relate to regional, rural and 'country' Australia. However, as this chapter shows, the population question must be considered in its entirety: the issue of population is complex and there are misconceptions that need to be addressed. A historical perspective is necessary if we, as citizens, are to understand the make-up of our society, and how different perspectives about settlement in Australia have arisen and persist. Thus, unlike many of the chapters in this book that focus on the period after World War II, I provide perspectives that go back to early European settlement. Following this historical review the chapter outlines some viewpoints from commentators who offer alternative scenarios to guide Australia's population policy. The chapter concludes with a reflection on current population questions facing rural and regional Australia and how these might be addressed. The issues of population and population policy are highly topical and will remain so well into the future.

A historical perspective

Since the early days of European settlement differences of culture and geographic location have defined the nation's population. Indigenous nations saw crimes committed against their culture and land by the white occupiers (Ngarrindjeri Nation 2007). Many injustices remain unresolved. For example, the first white settlers in South Australia ignored orders from the British Crown to grant the indigenous people of the Ngarrindjeri Nation rights to the land and resources on which they lived. Despite these orders being clearly documented in the *Letters Patent* of 1836, all South Australian governments since that time have failed to recognise the rights of this nation of traditional owners (Ngarrindjeri Nation 2007). Arguably, culture and geography are twin descriptive themes in

Australian history. Geographic distances divide city and regional populations, and there is also a cultural tension between country and city, rural and urban. The densely settled coastal fringe of Australia is separated from the dry and sparsely populated inland by the mountains and hills of the Great Dividing Range that extends the full length of eastern Australia. From the early days of European colonisation of this large continent, culture, geography and climate have been major influencers of where people live at different stages of their lives, initially in setting out to develop their livelihoods and in later years to live out their retirement.

The history and distribution of population in Australia has followed the demands of agriculture, jobs and economic development. Australian population distribution has been shaped by opportunity rather than direct policy. Although convicts (approximately 160,000) were the first immigrants from Europe, it was not long before free immigrants realised they could escape poverty or unemployment in their countries of origin by making the long trip south to Australia. The wool industry in the 1820s and the Gold Rush in the 1850s saw major influxes of Britons and Chinese. Large numbers of Irish came to escape famine in the 1840s. In the second half of the century people from Melanesia came to work on plantations in Queensland and camel-handlers came from Afghanistan, Pakistan and Turkey to develop transport services in the dry interior. Migration has also been a result of localised and global events such as war and persecution. Increasing numbers of refugees have migrated from the 1950s onwards and large numbers of people in countries suffering internal conflict aspire to migrate (Department of Immigration and Citizenship 2011a).

Since the early days of settlement the availability of water for towns, agriculture and industry has been a predominant concern. Maintaining water security in a dry and arid country known for its searing droughts became a political and policy concern after a series of major droughts in Victoria toward the end of the nineteenth century (see also Henderson, this volume). Droughts and economic development became the drivers of large-scale infrastructure works to build water storage dams and irrigation infrastructure. As irrigation expanded in New South Wales and Victoria, governments sought to settle the rural regions more closely under an agrarian philosophy in which people would own the land on which they farmed (Reeve *et al.* 2002). Intrinsic within this notion of 'closer settlement' was the idea that as a nation Australia needed to populate the country and 'defend its claim to the continent' (Brett 2011, p. 26).

Agrarianism is an important notion in the history of Australian settlement and in understanding tensions between large cities and regional areas (Botterill 2006). A key idea behind agrarianism is that farming is not only a necessary occupation on which other economic activity depends, but also represents a virtuous way of making a living based on hard work and a wholesome lifestyle. This is in comparison to work in cities where it is easier to make a consistent living and lifestyles are perceived as being more artificial, less fulfilling and more likely to lead to the vices and stresses of the under-occupied (Botterill 2006). The differences that make up this notion of agrarianism create divisive tensions between urban and rural communities (Curran *et al.* 2000). People in rural communities frequently feel a general lack of awareness of rural issues on the part of city folk. This includes a lack of understanding, lack of support, lack of infrastructure, lack of essential services and less opportunity for country people's voices to be heard.

Brett (2011, p. 26) traces the history of a 'country-city compact' and sketches three clear phases of development. In outlining these phases Brett (2011) develops an argument as to why country Australia deserves 'special treatment'. First, Australia became wealthy as a result of agricultural endeavour and export of wool; second, the post-Federation settlement of country areas in which settlers either prospered or failed were direct government initiatives and thus within the authority of the government to fix; and third, 'special treatment' is justified in light of the greater contribution by the people of the country to the development and character of the nation.

It is worth exploring this history to understand the relationship and tensions between country and city when considering population shifts and the reasons for these. The first phase of Australia's prosperity, described by Brett as riding on 'the sheep's back' (Brett 2011, p. 26) resulted in the development of Australian cities as transport hubs for the export of Australian rural produce. Nation-building then took over as the predominant strategy: to develop the nation, the population and society. The irrigation schemes in Victoria and NSW, roads and railways, and schools and hospitals were products of this post-Federation worldview. Increasing the population was a major preoccupation. This heralded in the White Australia policy, which had its roots in the 1850s clashes between white miners and Chinese diggers. The *Immigration Restriction Act* of 1901 gave effect to this policy, which was again reinforced during World War II after the outbreak of hostilities with Japan. This policy remained in force until the 1950s when non-Europeans were allowed to become Australian citizens. Although first steps to remove the White Australia policy took place in 1966 when non-Europeans with qualifications useful to Australia were welcomed as immigrants, it took many more years for the policy to be fully removed (Department of Immigration and Citizenship 2011b).

In the first half of the twentieth century governments encouraged people to take up land across the country, in the soldier settlement and closer settlement schemes designed to increase the number of small farms. Increasing the rural population was seen to benefit the nation overall in terms of rural production (Reeve *et al.* 2002). But there were many failures, for a range of reasons including land parcels being too small, lack of skills and capital, and variability of water supply. Land degradation and environmental problems followed, frequently caused by the mismatch of agricultural practice and land type. Despite these failures the allure of grand nation-building continued to drive government investment. The Snowy Mountains Scheme of hydroelectricity is a poignant example, which added life to the 'make the deserts bloom' slogan used by those in favour of irrigation schemes (Lloyd 1988). The scheme contributed to the expansion of irrigation settlements in dry areas of Victoria and NSW with the diversion of water from the Snowy River into the Murrumbidgee and Murray rivers. A technological triumph, the Snowy Mountains Hydro Scheme was built by a workforce made up of 70 per cent immigrants from over 30 countries in Europe. Around 100,000 people came to Australia to work on this 25-year project. The scheme became a symbol for the post-war migration programme (Lloyd 1988; Snowy Hydro 2011). One of the major motivations for the scheme was that it would allow the establishment of inland towns with a population of the order of one million people (Lawrence 1987).

Another population slogan was the post-World War II 'populate or perish' imperative that linked the safety of larger numbers with the perceived threat of the more populous nations to the north (Lawrence 1987; Brett 2011). In 1945 the Department of Immigration and Citizenship was established. The shortage of labour in Australia and the desire for population growth combined with the post-war displacement of many Europeans resulted in a large-scale migration programme. Many were given government-assisted passages. Australia's population increased from seven million at the end of World War II, 90 per cent of whom were born in Australia to 22 million in 2009 of whom 25 per cent were born overseas (Department of Immigration and Citizenship 2011a).

The spatial distribution of population throughout Australia has been largely influenced by employment prospects: population settlement and movement has varied from region to region, depending on opportunities in each location. For example, in 1933 one in three Australians lived in rural areas. By 1976 a gradual process of urbanisation resulted in only one in seven Australians living in rural areas (Gray and Lawrence 2001). Since that time there have been further changes in population characteristics, with various terms used to describe the types and reasons for these migrations, including tree-changers, sea-changers, repopulation, rural dilution and counter-urbanisation (Gray and Lawrence 2001; Murphy 2002; Smailes 2002). Counter-urbanisation has been observed from the 1970s, in which some metropolitan areas were seen to have a decreasing share of the total population. However, trends vary depending on the region. For example coastal growth in NSW took place at the expense of inland NSW, which was largely unanticipated by demographers (Gray and Lawrence 2001). Following this gradual shifting of population throughout the twentieth century it has been suggested that there are now three main areas outside the major towns and cities, 'a sparsely settled interior, an agricultural zone suffering a downward population spiral, and a metropolitan hinterland which is experiencing growth through counter-urbanisation' (Gray and Lawrence 2001, p. 96).

Reasons given for the general decline in rural area population are two-fold. One is the expansion of the agricultural sector in the 1950s through the provision of capital which increased the mechanisation of farming. As a result, the agricultural workforce reduced in numbers from the 1950s through to the 1970s (Argent 2002). Second, the trend to larger agricultural holdings, the advent of corporate agriculture and private cooperatives resulted in the notion of closer settlement being abandoned in the early 1970s (Lloyd 1988).

This same period saw the growth of regional centres which expanded at the expense of small rural towns. Lawrence (1987, p. 183) outlines post-World War II rural policy goals for state intervention in Australian agriculture and rural society. These included specific objectives of decentralising the population, regionalising government administration and encouraging industrial development in rural areas. The policy instruments to carry these out included the irrigation schemes and settlement schemes described above, as well as establishing military bases, government offices and assistance in setting up industries. Despite these objectives and programmes, the goal of decentralisation was not achieved and even though population levels in some regional centres increased there was still an overall rural decline (Lawrence 1987). The notion of decentralisation, with its aim of achieving some sort of balance of population between rural and urban areas, has been a constant theme for over 100 years (Hugo 2011). In the 1970s there was a renewed push towards decentralisation with the establishment of the Commonwealth Department of Urban and Regional Development and the development of the National Growth Centre Policy (Productivity Commission 2011; Hugo 2011). Investment under these policies was initiated in several regional centres including the twin towns of Albury-Wodonga. However, support for this initiative declined with a change in government (Hugo 2011) and these programmes are seen to have been generally unsuccessful in achieving their objectives (Productivity Commission 2011). Nevertheless, despite this ebb and flow, the question of decentralisation is still central to the population debate, as the title of Hugo's paper indicates: 'Is decentralisation the answer?' (Hugo 2011).

By the 1990s it was perceived that Australian agriculture was in crisis (Vanclay and Lawrence 1995). Environmental problems, declining terms of trade, structural adjustment, and drought were taking their toll on the social structure of rural communities. The rise of the neoliberal agenda in the 1980s had seen changes in attitude towards farmers and agriculture, away from nation-building initiatives towards markets and competition (see Cockfield, this volume). Farmers now had to become entrepreneurs and manage their enterprises according to market forces (Brett 2011). It was not only agriculture in rural areas that was forced to change: government bureaucracies were also rationalised. The changes to rural towns hit communities hard. The closure of post offices, banks and government buildings resulted in the loss of jobs, and consequently in contracting towns and villages (Gray and Lawrence 2001). This 'global misfortune of regional Australia' cut across entire populations which saw a withdrawal of state support, loss of jobs and loss of essential services, such as health and aged care (Gray and Lawrence 2001, p. 1). This has reignited the discussion about 'the consequences of living in a big country with a sparse population' and how we share the benefits and burdens of the country's settlement pattern. For example, Brett (2011, p. 53) has used the theme 'we all live in a big country and we should all share the cost' for her essay 'Fair Share: Country and City in Australia'. While fairness concerns are not a focus of this analysis, a discussion of population should note that disparities in benefits (such as access to health care) between metropolitan areas and regional areas do have some influence on settlement patterns.

Australia at the beginning of the twenty-first century

Population in Australia: a complex and moving picture

In mid-2011 the population of Australia was just over 22 million people, having increased by nearly three million people or 15 per cent since 2001 (Australian Bureau of Statistics 2011). The majority of Australia's population is concentrated in the coastal cities of Brisbane, Sydney, Melbourne, Adelaide and Perth, with 64 per cent of the population living in capital cities, 81 per cent living within 50 km of the coast, and 87 per cent living in urban areas (Hugo 2011). Although this settlement pattern has been in place for the last 150 years, there is still substantial 'mobility' between areas. As Hugo describes it, 'this pattern of stability within the Australian settlement system belies a great deal of dynamism and change' (2011, p. 135). International migration, internal migration and temporary relocation contribute to population movement and changing trends. As a result some areas rise in population at the expense of others, for example coastal areas have seen substantial growth whereas inland areas have suffered population loss. Examples of recent trends in population movement include long-distance commuting such as the fly-in, fly-out workforce to remote mining locations, 'grey nomads' and others who migrate seasonally (Hugo 2011).

Three other trends are notable: the fertility rate of Australia's population is now at half what it was in the 1960s; younger people have been increasingly attracted to settle in capital cities; and life expectancy has increased substantially resulting in larger numbers of older people. The Australian Bureau of Statistics reports that people aged between 20 and 44 years make up 38 per cent of the overall capital city population, compared with 31 per cent of the population in the rest of Australia (ABS 2011). This movement has resulted in a 'structural ageing' of the farm population, with older farmers and subsequent problems with succession in farming families (Barr 2009, p. 33). Across Australia the number of people aged 65 years and over has increased from 13 per cent of the total population in 2001 to 14 per cent in 2011 (ABS 2011). However, the distribution of people in this age group varies substantially, with higher proportions in the Mid North Coast, Southern Highlands and Shoalhaven areas of NSW and lower proportions in Darwin and outback areas of the Northern Territory and Western Australia (ABS 2011).

There are a set of key components that determine how a population changes over time. These include the current age structure, births, deaths, emigration and immigration (McDonald 2011). It is generally understood that little can be done to influence the number of births and deaths or the numbers of people that emigrate, thus population discussion and policy has tended to focus on immigration. As explored in the section above, immigration has been a constant and important aspect of Australian settlement. There are many lessons to be learned from this history. Net overseas migration (the difference between immigration and emigration) has increased since the 1980s and 1990s where it was relatively stable at about 100,000 per year, reaching a peak of 300,000 in 2008–2009.

Migrant populations have tended to settle in major urban areas, with the result that the migrant population has a greater degree of urbanisation than the Australian-born population. For example, in 2006 83 per cent of migrants lived in major urban areas with 53 per cent living in Sydney and Melbourne (Massey and Parr 2012). To counterbalance this settlement pattern, the Commonwealth government embarked on a series of migration incentive schemes in the mid-1990s, in part to respond to labour shortages in country areas. These State-Specific and Regional Migration (SSRM) schemes were designed to promote regional development and respond to ageing of the rural population and movement of younger people from country areas to regional centres and cities. Requirements of the schemes included that migrants had to live in specified areas for a period of time and had to have certain skills, as well as meeting health and language requirements (Massey and Parr 2012). Analysis of these schemes indicates 'apparent success' in that those migrants settling in regional and rural areas have become integrated into the local economy (Massey and Parr 2012, p. 17). In his summary of these schemes Hugo notes that some local communities have been more welcoming towards migrants and deployed more support services to the newcomers than other communities which have conservative mindsets to newcomers and 'even racist attitudes' (2008, p. 568). Hugo (2008) recounts a range of issues that need to be addressed for this targeted migration settlement to be seen as successful. These include availability of housing, understanding of the local labour market, determining what type of skills are needed in what area, and how to retain migrants once they have completed their specified time in the area.

Since the 1980s, net overseas migration has contributed more to Australia's population growth than natural increase (Productivity Commission 2010). Immigration accounted for 60 per cent of Australia's population growth in the late 2000s (Banks 2011). The components of immigration as it relates to the overall population are complex. Population concepts, statistics and projections tend to be obscure and difficult to understand, which is one reason the Productivity Commission (2010) published a research paper *Population and Migration: Understanding the Numbers*, followed by its *Submission to the Task Force on the Sustainable Population Strategy for Australia* report in 2011. Demographers have written about this topic from a variety of angles in the last decade or so to shed light on the population debate, demystify some of the concepts and generally inform the public as to why some proposals about population are not feasible (for example, McDonald and Kippen 1999; Hugo 1999, 2011; McDonald 2011). This analysis now highlights some of these areas relevant to the Australian population and the future of regional and rural communities.

The population debate: hotspots and perspectives

Much of the population debate in Australia is concerned with future population numbers and it is here that there is confusion about what factors influence population changes (McDonald 2011). There are disparities between the target numbers that people perceive as a desirable population for Australia. One school of thought proposes a 'big Australia' anywhere between 35 million and 100 million, whereas others advocate a smaller population of the order of 6 to 15 million (McDonald and Kippen 1999; Banks 2011; Sustainable Population Australia 2011). The Intergenerational Report of 2010 outlined the challenges facing Australia with an ageing population (Commonwealth of Australia 2010). The report describes how the percentage of people 65 years and over will increase from 13 per cent in 2010 to 23 per cent in 2050. This creates a problem because there will be fewer people in employment able to support the elderly. One solution is to continue with a policy of net overseas migration at the rate of 0.6 per cent of the total population. However, this would result in a population of 35.9 million in 2050. This would place considerable stress on infrastructure, services and the environment.

Some argue in favour of a growing population to develop the economy in regional areas whereas others fear that immigrants will take jobs away from people seeking work. Some propose a national population policy that stabilises the population to reduce environmental degradation and resource use, whereas others see immigrants as essential for economic development and to fund improved infrastructure (Productivity Commission 2011, p. 7). Immigration is seen by some as a cause of problems and by others as a solution to problems.

In a report comparing some of the widely disparate population alternative positions put forward by well-known public figures, McDonald and Kippen (1999, p. 1) summarise some 'populist statements' as 'sheer demographic nonsense'. They argue that the notion of an 'optimum population for Australia' does not make good policy sense because of the continually changing economic, environmental and political circumstances. The report outlines the importance of careful analysis in which projected fertility and mortality rates are combined with differing immigration scenarios. It advocates a set of demographic criteria which includes avoiding excessively high or low numbers of immigrants.

McDonald (2011) also reminds us of the lessons of history, in that migration was primarily driven by jobs and in periods of economic downturn migration levels fell. Thus future demand for labour should be the main reason for planned immigration numbers and this should operate on a multiple year time period rather than a number in any one year. McDonald (2011) advocates a balance between labour demand and supply, and a well-managed immigration programme.

Another area of population debate is the number of people seeking to enter Australia, either as refugees or asylum-seekers. Steketee (2011) points out that the proportion of people entering the country as asylum-seekers by boat is less than 1.5 per cent of Australia's total immigration – a very small percentage. In terms of the overall debate about migrants and asylum-seekers, Steketee (2011, p. 2) argues that refugee policy is based on 'political perceptions rather than realities' and describes the 'contortions' of refugee policy developed by a government that 'has given up trying to educate and lead on the issue'. The implications are that people appear to have little knowledge about the overall picture of immigration, and that the government is failing in its obligation to educate the public.

Another misconception is that increased immigration is seen as an antidote to the ageing population problem. This is debunked as a 'fallacy' because as each intake of immigrants becomes older they also add to the number of elderly people, thus requiring ever more immigrants to fill the gap (Banks 2011, p. 5). Demonstrating this erroneous hypothesis the Productivity Commission estimated that to maintain the current age profile of the population the overall Australian population would reach 100 million by 2050 (Banks 2011). Clearly a population policy is needed in which the broader context of employment, the economy, social concerns and the environment are considered.

Implications for policymakers

The previous sections have shown that there are lessons to be learned from an understanding of how Australia has been settled and how policies and programmes have had different impacts throughout the history of the nation. The discussion has shown the complexity of the population issue and a range of different perspectives. This analysis now considers what can be done by planners and policymakers.

A first implication is that it is worthwhile considering what a population policy is intended to do, and at what level: national or regional. Fincher (1998, p. 32) proposes that population policy 'aims to enhance the well-being of the population in its diversity…'. Along the same lines the Productivity Commission (2011, p. 6) describes well-being as a 'multi-dimensional concept' including social, cultural and environmental aspects of life. Banks (2011) extends this to maximising well-being for future generations and thus encounters the idea of sustainability.

Shifting to a 'sustainability paradigm' requires a reframing of the population problem from estimated target numbers to a rate of change at any one time (Banks 2011, p. 2). This is in line with an earlier proposal by Fincher (1998) who calls for a broad framework in which to consider both populations and environments, but with less emphasis on the causal relationship between these two. She advocates that changing economic, political and international parameters need to be included in this framework. The relationships between economic development, environmental degradation, environmental resources (such as water availability) and population should also be considered (Fincher 1998, p. 34). As this analysis has shown, people move to where they see opportunities for jobs and lifestyle. Frameworks that consider the broader context offer an alternative and less controversial strategy for population planners. Policymakers involved in regional development need to consider how their initiatives on infrastructure (Hugo 2011) and support services fit in with their population goals of retaining the current population and attracting newcomers.

The Australian Government's May 2011 *Sustainable Australia – Sustainable Communities: a Sustainable Population Strategy for Australia* introduced earlier does go some way to setting out this type of broad framework. The Strategy outlines economic prosperity, liveable communities and environmental sustainability.

Reform objectives include the promotion of regional living and the facilitation of funding support for regions. The government also initiated a 'Suburban Jobs' programme to provide for increased employment in regional areas, as well as a *Sustainable Regional Development* programme for environmental assessment in regions. The Strategy outlines changes to Australia's migration programme in order to target skills needs to regional migration. However, it is worthwhile noting Hugo's caution on employment and regional growth:

> Failed early efforts at decentralisation have clearly demonstrated that the jobs cannot be created artificially. Any effort at regional development must be focused on regional communities where there is demonstrated evidence that the local economy provides the basis for sustained demand for workers.
>
> (2011, p. 144)

A second implication is that Australia needs a more sophisticated and well-informed bipartisan debate over what kind of future the current population aspires to. For example, the practice of discussing population in terms of future targets should be recognised as essentially futile (Banks 2011). Continually changing social, economic, environmental and international circumstances render targets an unhelpful part of the population debate. A population debate should consider economic development, resource extraction, food production, manufacturing, and regional development, as well as Australia's place in the global context of increasing refugees due to climate change, natural disasters and conflict. The processes by which this debate takes place and by which policies and programmes are developed should be based on sound consultation methods that are based on facts and well-informed perspectives. Banks proposes:

> [H]aving a 'policy' is unavoidable. The only real choice is between one that effectively emerges by default – conceived in *ad hoc*ery or stealth – and one that is explicit and has been properly thought through, and therefore is acceptable to the electorate.
>
> (2011, p. 3)

As this chapter has shown, there is no lack of information about this topic. What is required, however, is continued open debate facilitated by those responsible for continuing to develop regional and national population policies.

Reflections on the future

This analysis has explored the history of settlement in Australia, government policies and a range of issues relating to population. This final section now draws some of these themes together in reflecting on the future. Areas to consider include the continuing question of the balance between country and city, and what can or should be done to maintain what can be perceived as a fair approach between the two. Further questions concern where people live, what they do and how many can be supported in different regions of the country. As Hugo (2011, p. 133) points out, '[t]here are no simple "single bullet" solutions to achieving a sustainable population in Australia', so these reflections should be considered part of an ongoing debate.

The cultural, environmental, employment, climatic and social challenges faced by Australians in their working lives revolve around employment and the social fabric of the community they live in. It is the responsibility of government to consider these larger issues in the context of the well-being of current and future populations. However, to what degree is the government responsible for ensuring equality of access to services or opportunities between people living in different areas of the country? This is a question that needs to be debated. As McDonald argues:

> The critical nexus between regional job availability and population growth must be recognised as fundamental in any policy to support growth in regional Australia. Provision of quality infrastructure and services in regional centres will be a vital element of any such strategy.
>
> (2011, p. 20)

The lessons of history have shown that people feel that governments (and corporations) have an obligation to support them if they have encouraged them to settle and work in a particular area. This means a sustained level of support, not support that is temporary. For example, there are many opportunities for regional development and employment within the mining industry, but history has also shown that mining is not a good basis for permanent settlement (Hugo 2011). Thus decentralisation initiatives must consider these perceived obligations prior to being implemented. As Hugo (2011) sums up, we do not know whether decentralisation is an answer to achieving a sustainable population, but we do know that future regional development requires careful consideration of many environmental, economic and social factors.

Finally, the future sustainability of Australia's regions may arise from the benefits rural and regional areas provide to the nation as a whole (Brett 2011). The list of benefits is long and includes: food and fibre production; recreation and enjoyment of the forests, coasts and inland country areas; retirement settlement areas; temporary employment for overseas visitors and nomadic retirees; maintenance of biodiversity and biological processes to sustain life; conservation of natural resources such as rangelands and their flora and fauna; extraction of resources for economic development; maintenance of heritage areas and an ongoing source of national identity and pride (Brett 2011). Research from current initiatives, such as 'Caring for Our Country' in remote Aboriginal communities, shows that there are mutual benefits in projects where local communities are actively involved in a range of landscape conservation projects. There are many co-benefits from these types of arrangements including better health for participants as well as biodiversity and sustainability benefits for ecosystems and the broader population (Berry *et al.* 2010).

Thus the future of regional Australia should be considered not only in terms of places for people to live, but also for the vast range of benefits that the regions supply to the nation as a whole that have not been adequately counted or valued in the country-city conversation.

References

Argent, N 2002, 'From pillar to post? In search of the post-productivist countryside in Australia', *Australian Geographer*, vol. 33, pp. 97–114.

Australian Bureau of Statistics (ABS) 2011, *Population by Age and Sex, Regions of Australia*, Australian Bureau of Statistics, Canberra. Available at: www.abs.gov.au/ausstats/abs@.nsf/mf/3235.0. Accessed: 25 October 2012.

Banks, G 2011, 'Introduction. A "Sustainable" Population? – Key Policy Issues', Roundtable Proceedings, Productivity Commission, Canberra.

Barr, N 2009, *The House on the Hill: The Transformation of Australia's Farming Communities*, Land and Water Australia, Canberra.

Berry, HL, Butler, JRA, Burgess, CP, King, UG, Tsey, K, Cadet-James, YL, Rigby, CW and Raphael, B 2010, 'Mind, body, spirit: co-benefits for mental health from climate change adaptation and caring for country in remote Aboriginal Australian communities', *New South Wales Public Health Bulletin*, vol. 21, pp. 139–145.

Botterill, LC 2006, 'Soap operas, cenotaphs and sacred cows: country mindedness and rural policy debate in Australia', *Public Policy*, vol. 1, pp. 23–36.

Brett, J 2011, 'Fair Share: Country and City in Australia', *Quarterly Essay*, no. 42, pp. 1–67.

Burke, T 2011, *Gillard government delivers first sustainable population strategy*, media release, 13 May, Department of Sustainability, Environment, Water, Population and Communities, Canberra.

Cockfield, G 2015, 'From state direction to community self-efficacy: The devolution of responsibility for regional development in Australia', this volume.

Commonwealth of Australia 2010, *The 2010 Intergenerational Report. Australia to 2050: future challenges*, Commonwealth of Australia, Canberra.

Curran, B, Garnaut, J, Lindsay, R and Connell, P 2000, 'Country Australia: Influences on population and employment', *Outlook 2000*, Australian Bureau of Agricultural and Resource Economics, Canberra.

Department of Immigration and Citizenship 2011a, *Fact Sheet 4 — More than 60 Years of Post-War Migration*, Department of Immigration and Citizenship. Available at: www.immi.gov.au/media/fact-sheets/04fifty.htm. Accessed: 2 August 2011.

Department of Immigration and Citizenship 2011b, *Fact Sheet 8 — Abolition of the 'White Australia' Policy*, Department of Immigration and Citizenship. Available at: www.immi.gov.au/media/fact-sheets/08abolition.htm. Accessed: 2 August 2011.

Department of Sustainability, Environment, Water, Population and Communities 2011, *Sustainable Australia Sustainable Communities: A Sustainable Population Strategy for Australia*, Department of Sustainability, Environment, Water, Population and Communities, Canberra.

Fincher, R 1998, 'Population Questions for Australian Cities: reframing our narratives', *Australian Geographer*, vol. 29, pp. 31–47.

Gray, I and Lawrence, G 2001, *A Future for Regional Australia: Escaping Global Misfortune*, Cambridge University Press, Cambridge.

Hugo, G 1999, *Regional Development through Immigration? The Reality behind the Rhetoric*, Department of the Parliamentary Library, Canberra.

Hugo, G 2008, 'Immigrant settlement outside of Australia's capital cities', *Population, Space and Place*, vol. 14, pp. 553–571.

Hugo, G 2011, 'Is decentralisation the answer? A "Sustainable" Population? – Key Policy Issues', Roundtable Proceedings, Productivity Commission, Canberra.

Lawrence, G 1987, *Capitalism and the Countryside: The Rural Crisis in Australia*, Pluto, Sydney.

Lloyd, CJ 1988, *Either Drought or Plenty: Water Development and Management in New South Wales*, Department of Water Resources New South Wales, Parramatta, NSW.

Massey, SL and Parr, N 2012, 'The socio-economic status of migrant populations in regional and rural Australia and its implications for future population policy', *Journal of Population Research*, vol. 29, pp. 1–21.

McDonald, P 2011, 'The determinants of Australia's future demography. A "Sustainable" Population? – Key Policy Issues', Roundtable Proceedings, Productivity Commission, Canberra.

McDonald, P and Kippen, R 1999, *Population Futures for Australia: the Policy Alternatives*', Department of the Parliamentary Library, Canberra.

Murphy, P 2002, 'Sea Change: Re-Inventing Rural and Regional Australia', *Transformations*, vol. 2. Available at: www.transformationsjournal.org/journal/issue_02/pdf/murphy.pdf. Accessed: 22 May 2013.

Ngarrindjeri Nation 2007, *Ngarrindjeri Nation Sea Country Plan: Caring for Ngarrindjeri Country and Culture*, Ngarrindjeri Nation, Meningie, SA.

Phillips, J and Spinks, H 2011, *Boat arrivals in Australia since 1976*, background note, Department of the Parliamentary Library, Canberra.

Productivity Commission 2010, *Population and Migration: Understanding the Numbers*, Australian Government Productivity Commission, Canberra.

Productivity Commission 2011, *Submission to the Task Force on the Sustainable Population Strategy for Australia*, Australian Government Productivity Commission, Canberra.

Reeve, I, Frost, L, Musgrave, W and Stayner, R 2002, *Agriculture and Natural Resource Management in the Murray–Darling Basin: A Policy History and Analysis*, Institute for Rural Futures, University of New England, Armidale, NSW.

Smailes, PJ 2002, 'From Rural Dilution to Multifunctional Countryside: some pointers to the future from South Australia', *Australian Geographer*, vol. 33, pp. 79–95.

Snowy Hydro 2011, *Snowy Mountains Scheme: The People*. Available at: www.snowyhydro.com.au/energy/hydro/the-people. Accessed: 25 October 2012.

Steketee, M 2011, 'Misapprehensions, not facts, drive our dysfunctional asylum-seeker debate', *The Weekend Australian*, 13 August, News Limited.

Sustainable Population Australia 2011, *Half intake enough to service resource boom*, newsletter no. 99, Sustainable Population Australia Inc.

Vanclay, F and Lawrence, G 1995, *The Environmental Imperative: Eco-Social Concerns for Australian Agriculture*, Central Queensland University Press, Rockhampton, Queensland.

7 The Commonwealth's policies and Aboriginal people in regional Australia

Janet Hunt

Indigenous peoples have not featured strongly in the literature or policies relating to regional development; nor has regional, rather than remote, development been a strong theme in the literature on Indigenous Australia. Collits observes that the key problems regional development has tried to deal with are 'geographical disparities and uneven development', as well as the problems specific to particular regions (Collits 2011, p. 19). Indigenous Affairs policy has focused strongly on social and economic disparities and uneven development, most recently articulated as the national Closing the Gap policy, yet the two areas rarely meet in theory or practice.

The concept of a 'region' in relation to Indigenous Australia is itself problematic. For statistical purposes, the Australian Bureau of Statistics (ABS) defines 37 Indigenous Regions across the nation, which were originally similar to the former Aboriginal and Torres Strait Islander Commission's regions, although subsequently modified (Biddle, Taylor and Yap 2008). From an Indigenous perspective the boundaries of particular tribal groupings, and the social networks between them, provide a complex regional framework of a different type. Taylor (forthcoming) highlights the confusing discourses surrounding rural and regional terminologies as they apply to Indigenous Australia. Indeed, rural and regional terminology suggests iconic colonial bush images, with a pastoral and agricultural focus, but with Aborigines almost invisible.

Yet almost 200,000 Indigenous Australians live in what the ABS defines as regional areas of Australia, comprising 44 per cent of the total Indigenous population. A further 24 per cent live in remote and very remote locations (see Figure 7.1). This chapter will focus predominantly on what the ABS refers to as 'regional' Australia, rather than 'remote' parts of the country, although these artificial constructs have no resonance with Indigenous regionalisms. However, remote Australia, with its high proportion of Indigenous people, has not generally been the focus of regional development attention (although the current focus on Pilbara development is an exception). Remote Australia is where Indigenous policy, and minerals and resources policy, tend to dominate.

In light of their socio-economic situation relative to other Australians, the need for regional development to benefit Indigenous people is very clear. This point was made a decade ago:

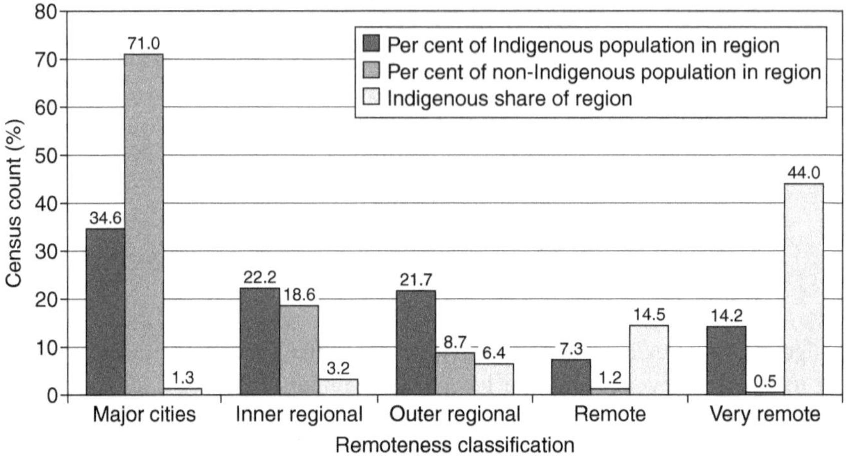

Figure 7.1 Proportion of Indigenous and non-Indigenous people by remoteness classification, 2011[1] (source: 2011 Census of Population and Housing).

> If regional development is to address the disadvantage of individuals and communities, there would seem to be pressing reasons for Indigenous inequality to be a prime focus for regional development strategies.
>
> (Beer, Maude and Pritchard, 2003, p. 171)

Yet, as these authors point out, the separation of responsibilities between the various government agencies responsible for Indigenous Affairs and Regional Development has perpetuated the lack of dialogue which would bring the two areas together for policy development and programme implementation. The need to bring them together remains, as that inequality still persists.

Table 7.1 compares selected socio-economic outcomes for Indigenous and non-Indigenous people living in inner and outer regional areas of the two most populous states which are home to the largest numbers of Aboriginal people. They show that Aboriginal people are more likely than other Australians living in regional areas to be unemployed or not in the labour force, to be on low incomes, and to have low levels of education. Their health is also likely to be considerably poorer than that of other Australians.

Collits also distinguishes between 'regional policies' and 'policies that affect regions' (Collits 2011, p. 21). This chapter necessarily takes the latter as its focus, exploring how Commonwealth policies since the 1960s have impacted on Indigenous people living in regional areas of Australia and their experience of regional development. I will first briefly describe the period before Commonwealth involvement in Indigenous policy, and then outline how the Commonwealth became involved in Indigenous policy in the 1960s. I will trace the role that Commonwealth policies played in Indigenous employment in particular,

Table 7.1 Selected socio-economic indicators for Indigenous Australians compared to non-Indigenous Australians in regional New South Wales and Queensland (18–64 year olds) (%) (source: 2011 Census of Population and Housing)

	Regional NSW – Indigenous	*Regional NSW – non-Indigenous*	*Regional QLD – Indigenous*	*Regional QLD – non-Indigenous*
Education: Completed Year 12 or equivalent	24.13	43.59	36.27	48.55
Highest level of education is a degree or higher	4.54	15.01	4.22	14.00
Income per week less than $400	49.67	32.83	44.51	29.51
Unemployed	10.90	4.14	12.11	3.94
Employed (incl. CDEP)	45.43	71.81	48.82	74.33
Not in labour force	43.67	24.05	39.07	21.73

through the 1970s until the end of the twentieth century. Then I will discuss developments since 1990, particularly the establishment of the Aboriginal and Torres Strait Islander Commission (ATSIC) and its Regional Councils, followed by their subsequent abolition in 2004/2005. I will finish with discussion of the most recent policy phase of so-called 'mainstreaming' of Indigenous policy and the setting of national targets for Indigenous policy through the Council Of Australian Governments (COAG). I will argue that Commonwealth policies have had mixed impacts on the development of Indigenous people in regional Australia, at times providing opportunities, at other times creating constraints. They have focused, with mixed success, on income security and provision of services. The chapter will focus largely on New South Wales as a case study, although these policies obviously applied across the nation in interaction with diverse state and territory contexts and policies. I will conclude that Indigenous people should be seen as central to regional development, both due to their socio-economic situation and because of their growing asset-base, arising from land rights and native title legislation. There are important regional development opportunities to be harnessed through cooperation.

Early colonisation and 'missionisation'

'*Terra nullius*' (empty land) was the accepted wisdom in Australia until 1992, when the 'Mabo' decision of the High Court overturned this legal fiction. Indeed, at colonisation, the entire Australian land mass was populated by diverse Aboriginal peoples, many of whose descendants now live on or near their ancestors' original 'country' (lands and waters to which they had strong cultural attachments). Yet colonial incursion caused major, sometimes violent, displacement of Aboriginal peoples from their lands and livelihoods, as squatters and pastoralists spread across the country. In New South Wales this rapid expansion of pastoralism occurred between 1830 and 1850, and the plight of Aboriginal people thereafter eventually led to the establishment of the Aborigines Protection Board (APB) in 1883 (Castle and Hagan 1984, pp. 82–83). Protectionist policies led to the settlement of Aboriginal people into reserves and missions, which in NSW were often on the fringes of country towns. Aboriginal lives became almost totally controlled by mission managers, and soon boys and girls were being apprenticed for employment on properties and in domestic service respectively. From that time, and to varying degrees in different parts of the state, Aboriginal people provided essential labour in the developing white economy into the early decades of the twentieth century (Lloyd 2010; White 2010). Some Aboriginal people ran small businesses and even their own farms until the latter was disallowed by the APB in the 1930s (Castle and Hagan 1984, pp. 88–89). By the 1940s, increased Aboriginal involvement in the labour-starved wartime economy was followed by the official policy position of 'assimilation'; yet Aboriginal people still largely survived through seasonal or casual employment in primary industries.

Commonwealth involvement in Indigenous affairs until that time (with the exception of its administration of the Northern Territory from 1911), simply involved child endowment payments, though these frequently went directly to mission and reserve managers, rather than to the Indigenous families who were entitled to them. But at the end of the 1950s, child endowments started to be paid to parents, and some Indigenous people deemed of good character also became eligible for unemployment benefits (Altman and Sanders 1991; Castle and Hagan 1984). This was in contrast to the earlier 1908 Commonwealth social security legislation, which provided for aged and invalid pensions, as well as the 1912 maternity allowance legislation, each of which explicitly excluded Aboriginal 'natives' from their provisions (Kewley 1972). While the Commonwealth's role in social security legislation expanded in the 1940s, by the late 1950s the sense grew that many of the provisions relating to Indigenous people were discriminatory. By 1966 all discriminatory provisions in Commonwealth social security legislation were removed and Aboriginal people gained equal entitlements to social security with other Australians, providing at least a minimum income to everyone.

Strengthening the Commonwealth's role

Significant changes came in the late 1960s, following the 1962 extension of the Commonwealth franchise to Indigenous people (on a voluntary, rather than compulsory basis), and the 1967 referendum which gave the Commonwealth power to make laws relating to Indigenous Australians (which would of course override state laws). State 'protection era' institutions were being dismantled, and Commonwealth programmes started to address the combined effects of casual or no employment, lack of adequate housing, poor health and low educational outcomes among Aboriginal people. But the 1960s also brought technological change and mechanisation in many primary industries, which had a disproportionate effect on Aboriginal workers, pushing them out of agricultural and primary industries that had been substantially built on their labour. The 1965 decision by the Commonwealth Conciliation and Arbitration Commission to award equal wages to Aboriginal pastoral workers, while responding to largely northern Australian Aboriginal demands for equality, coincided with these technological changes and contributed to the exclusion of Aboriginal workers from an industry which had kept them connected to their country and provided a livelihood. Some moved into public sector jobs, but Aboriginal unemployment became a major concern, reaching 50 per cent of the Indigenous labour force in NSW by the early 1980s (Castle and Hagan 1984, p. 92).

Following these national changes, by the 1970s, a large proportion of remote Aboriginal people were unemployed, and concern was mounting, so the Fraser Government devised the Community Development Employment Projects (CDEP) scheme, to be administered by the Commonwealth Department of Aboriginal Affairs. This involved paying Indigenous community-controlled organisations to employ Indigenous people for 16 hours a week, instead of them receiving unemployment benefits. While originally designed to solve what was perceived as a problem largely evident in remote Australia, by the mid-1980s, under the Hawke Government, the CDEP scheme expanded to many other parts of Australia, so that by the mid-1990s 35,000 Aboriginal people, about one-third of the total Aboriginal labour force, were participating in the scheme. 'Top up' provisions enabled participants to boost their hours and receive a higher wage if the CDEP organisation had additional funds to employ them, either through grants or contracts gained. The programme was grasped by Aboriginal people throughout regional Australia. It was particularly useful on the old New South Wales missions and reserves which had been transferred to Aboriginal freehold title and hence were not serviced by local governments. CDEP programmes fulfilled at least some of the services which were provided to other Australians by local government.

In 1997 concerns were raised about racially discriminatory aspects of the CDEP programme in comparison to unemployment benefits. While these were resolved with some minor changes, business leader Ian Spicer was tasked to undertake a major review of CDEP, which by then was being managed by the Aboriginal and Torres Strait Islander Commission that had been established from 1990. Apart from the employment CDEP provided, Spicer's report 'confirmed that the CDEP Scheme has enormous social and cultural benefits for those indigenous communities that participate in the Scheme', referring to improved self-esteem, better health, less alcohol and drug abuse, and reduced anti-social behaviour in communities with CDEP programmes (Spicer 1997, pp. 112–123). Spicer raised two major criticisms: that in remote areas Aboriginal people were not really working, and that in areas with existing labour markets (i.e. in regional and urban areas) more should be done to move Aboriginal people into regular employment. It was the latter agenda that became more central in regional Australia, and to some degree is occurring, with levels of Indigenous employment increasing. Yet Aboriginal unemployment rates remain high across most regions, although there is considerable variation across the nation, with some regions needing at least 3,000 or more Indigenous people to be employed in the next few years if the gap in employment between Indigenous and non-Indigenous people is to be halved by 2016 (Biddle, Taylor and Yap 2008).

ATSIC had been established by the Commonwealth Government in a policy environment which since the 1970s had shifted from assimilation to self-determination. The Royal Commission into Aboriginal Deaths in Custody, another Commonwealth initiative, believed however that the policy of self-determination overlooked the economic limitations facing Indigenous people, and 'the process by which the principle of self-determination may be exercised' by them (RCIADIC 1991 (vol. 2), p. 20.2.15). Nevertheless it strongly argued that the ability of Indigenous people to exercise self-determination was essential to overcoming the parlous state in which they found themselves. How self-determination could occur without an adequate asset-base and with the marginality of Aboriginal people in the nation's economy was the problem.

ATSIC's objectives were to ensure maximum participation of Aboriginal and Torres Strait Islander people in government policy formulation and implementation;

promote Indigenous self-management and self-sufficiency; further Indigenous economic, social and cultural development; and ensure coordination of Commonwealth, State, Territory and local government policies affecting Indigenous people (Davis 2008, p. 75). It had a national board, but its important regional impact arose through its Regional Councils (initially 60, though reduced to 35 by 1993), elected by regional Aboriginal and Torres Strait Islander people (Sanders 2004). These Councils were required to develop regional plans for Indigenous development but such plans tended to be broad in scope and governments were not often involved in the process of developing them, nor did they feel particular responsibility to help implement them, leaving the Regional Councils with largely aspirational documents (Hannaford, Huggins and Collins 2003, pp. 32–35). Self-determination had become separate 'do-it-yourself' development. However, some Regional Councils actively engaged with a range of government departments to address specific priorities until their mandate ended in 2005 (ATSI Social Justice Commissioner 2005, p. 123). The Regional Councils also provided a valuable two-way communication mechanism between the national Commission and Aboriginal people in the regions. Whilst the effectiveness of these regional councils clearly varied, those that performed well, such as the Murdi Paaki Regional Council in north-western New South Wales, tried hard to make a significant contribution to regional development for Aboriginal people, although they were less attentive to Aboriginal women's needs than men's concerns (Davis 2008).

The period from 1990 to 2000 was also the decade of Reconciliation. The Keating Government established the Council for Aboriginal Reconciliation with bipartisan support, with a view to gaining widespread community support for Reconciliation between Indigenous and other Australians. The process was intended to lead to a negotiated agreement between Indigenous and other Australians by the year 2000. This process saw some important engagements between farmers, miners and other regional Australians and Indigenous people, and in many regional towns local voluntary reconciliation groups began working to improve relationships. Fear and prejudice had escalated following the High Court's Mabo decision in 1992, and the Keating Government's decision to enact the *Native Title Act* in 1993, which enabled Indigenous people to claim their rights and interests in non-freehold land. Pastoralists and miners operating on leasehold land were particularly vocal, and the Reconciliation Council stepped in to try to negotiate more constructive relationships between them and Indigenous people (Brown and Boden 2012, pp. 219–221; Davies 2003, p. 30). When the Human Rights and Equal Opportunity Commission's (HREOC) *Bringing Them Home Report* (HREOC 1997) about the traumatic consequences of earlier policies involving separation of children from Aboriginal families was released in 1996, and the Prime Minister refused to apologise to them, further activity began across the country. Many groups in urban and regional areas mobilised to say 'sorry' to Indigenous people for past policies. Local governments, churches and community groups were particularly active, and relationships between Aboriginal people and sections of settler society strengthened, while others fractured further. Some private landholders negotiated access agreements for Aboriginal people to access culturally important sites.

Meanwhile, the Howard Government, utilising a rhetoric of 'failure' in Aboriginal affairs, began dismantling ATSIC in 2004, laying much of the blame for the continuing sorry state of Aboriginal affairs on ATSIC, which in fact had a very restricted mandate (confined largely to managing CDEP, a major housing and infrastructure programme, and a range of cultural programmes). It has been argued, however, that the administrative separation of Aboriginal housing from mainstream housing programmes was indeed a major reason for the continuing problems of inadequate housing for Indigenous people (Dillon and Westbury 2007). The Howard Government intended to 'mainstream' government services and programmes for Indigenous people into the appropriate departments, which would work in direct partnership with Indigenous communities (Vanstone 2004).

As a precursor to this, in 2002 the Council of Australian Governments had established some whole-of-government community trials. These trials were intended to build Indigenous community capacity to negotiate with governments and enable various levels of government in Australia (federal, state/territory and local) to work in coordinated, innovative and flexible ways in partnership with Indigenous communities (ATSI Social Justice Commissioner 2003, 2004). One trial was held in each state or territory, mainly in regional or remote areas of the jurisdiction. Responsibility for leadership in each was allocated to the head of a federal government department, working in concert with a lead department from the state/territory jurisdiction. Coordination arrangements were developed on the Indigenous side, appropriate to the specific location. The New South Wales trial built on the successful work which had been undertaken by the ATSIC Murdi Paaki Regional Council. It transformed itself into a Murdi Paaki Regional Assembly, a non-government body with which the governments partnered in the New South Wales COAG trial. Progress in these trials was reportedly slow, although the Murdi Paaki trial was deemed the most successful and the Regional Assembly continues its programmes with the support of a Regional Partnership Agreement (see further on). Subsequent evaluations of the COAG trials revealed many of the challenges they faced, but in mid-2004 the Australian Government announced a set of 'new arrangements' in Indigenous affairs which appeared to draw from this approach and were to apply nationally (Office of Indigenous Policy Coordination (OIPC) 2005).

These arrangements were based on five principles:

- Collaboration within and among national and State or Territory governments.
- Responding to regional need.
- Flexibility, particularly in relation to funding.
- Improved accountability with a focus on outcomes.
- Leadership – within government and through representative Indigenous networks at local and regional level (OIPC 2005; Shergold 2005).

The dismantling of ATSIC signalled the end of the era of self-determination, although implementation of this policy had always been more a matter of rhetoric than reality. The new 'whole-of-government mainstreaming' approach included the establishment of Indigenous Coordination Centres in 30 locations around Australia, most of them in major regional towns, designed to coordinate among the various levels of government and departments within them to better serve Aboriginal communities. High-level bilateral agreements were negotiated between the Commonwealth and state/territory governments on matters relating to particular sectoral services such as housing, employment or education. At the same time, sometimes involving more than one level of government and occasionally the private sector, Shared Responsibility Agreements (SRAs) and Regional Partnership Agreements (RPAs) became the new mechanisms for governments to partner with Indigenous communities and regions. However, by 2007, mainstreaming had paradoxically resulted in an increase in the number of departmental relationships many Indigenous community organisations had to maintain, rather than the reverse, since, despite the efforts of Indigenous Coordination Centres (ICCs), individual government departments frequently retained their autonomy to deal directly with communities (Hunt 2007).

After an initial flurry of Shared Responsibility Agreements, these soon faded away as policy mechanisms, while Regional Partnership Agreements, though far fewer in number, have been more long-lasting. Most were larger, multi-year agreements with a clear Indigenous regional development focus. Yet, the original idea of developing Indigenous regional and local networks was never consistently implemented. States and territories were left to make their own arrangements. The New South Wales Government, for example, invested its energies into 40 'partnership communities'. These were generally regional or smaller towns in which the government endeavoured to establish improved governance arrangements for interaction and planning service delivery between the state government and the Indigenous community organisations within that location. The NSW Land Council network with its 119 Local Aboriginal Land Councils, established under the *New South Wales Land Rights Act 1983*, provided another mechanism for policy interaction, both locally and at statewide level, although such engagement was usually more in the realm of the state rather than the Commonwealth Government.

Although the *New South Wales Land Rights Act 1983* had been visionary legislation at the time, the slow process of dealing with and granting land claims under the Act means that Aboriginal people's land asset base in New South Wales is particularly small, less than 1 per cent of the state, with 26,000 claims still outstanding. However, the Commonwealth's *Native Title Act*, which has delivered most to Aboriginal people in remote parts of Australia, particularly Western Australia, has also begun to have its effect in regional areas of south-eastern Australia. Aboriginal people who succeed in gaining legal recognition of their native title rights and interests in non-freehold land are able to exercise those rights or negotiate agreements with landowners, public or private, using their rights and interests as leverage. While initially it seemed that Aboriginal people in south-eastern Australia were going to have enormous difficulty proving unbroken connection to their land and continuity of their cultural traditions, particularly following the unsuccessful Yorta Yorta case in regional Victoria in 2002, in fact, increasingly native title claimants are managing to establish their native title rights and negotiate valuable Indigenous Land Use Agreements (ILUA) which are contributing to Aboriginal development. In New South Wales for example, the Bunjalung people of Byron Bay and the Githabul people in northern New South Wales have each negotiated significant ILUAs which are contributing to Aboriginal employment as well as other cultural benefits (Hunt, Altman and May 2009).

At the time the *Native Title Act* was passed, an Indigenous Land Corporation (ILC) was also established with the mandate to purchase land for Aboriginal people. This was in recognition of the fact that some Aboriginal groups would find it impossible to assert their native title over freehold land, and this mechanism provided them some land justice. The ILC has now purchased many properties in remote and regional Australia – a total of 238 nationwide, of which 51 were in New South Wales, most of the latter in regional areas. These may be former pastoral properties or other lands which are purchased for commercial or cultural reasons. If the land purchased is of high conservation value and represents an ecosystem which is under-represented in the national conservation reserve system, such land may be eligible to be declared an Indigenous Protected Area (IPA) and hence attract funding from the Commonwealth's Indigenous Protected Area Programme for its continued management. This is providing a valuable basis for Aboriginal development in a number of regional as well as more remote locations (Hunt 2010).

However, the almost nationwide abolition of the CDEP scheme in 2007 has affected Aboriginal programmes in many regional areas. Some groups used CDEP funding to maintain the employment of Aboriginal people through periods when contracts for services were unavailable. For example, in many areas there were small 'Green Teams' or Aboriginal Ranger groups who carried out cultural heritage and environmental work on contract to various government agencies such as national parks or catchment management authorities. The abolition of CDEP has made it difficult for many of these groups to sustain their programmes. Aboriginal people now transferred from CDEP to Centrelink benefits have to be exceptionally careful that by taking intermittent short-term contract work they don't jeopardise their social welfare payments and end up worse off. This makes sustaining a Green Team or a Ranger Group extremely difficult, as in most cases there is insufficient local work to support a team in reliable full-time employment. People have often, in fact, moved from work to welfare as a result of the abolition of the CDEP. This is not contributing to regional development; rather it is a movement in the wrong direction.

It is in the area of land and natural resource management that opportunities for regional development to engage with Aboriginal people is most evident today. The Commonwealth has expanded its role in the environment and natural resource sector over the past 25–30 years (Lane, Robinson and Taylor 2009), and in doing so has from time to time opened up more space for Aboriginal participation in these areas. In the late 1990s Aboriginal native title claimants in Eden, NSW, uniquely took advantage of the joint Commonwealth and States Regional Forest Agreement processes to negotiate greater access and use rights for themselves in relation to forests, including transfer of some lands to their ownership, although their aspirations for greater employment in forest industries have not materialised. A regional architecture for community-based natural resource management that was built from 2002 onwards, and most recently framed as the Caring for Our Country Policy framework, has provided opportunities for Aboriginal engagement in Natural Resource Management (NRM) activities within the regions, usually at a very local scale. In NSW, regional Catchment Management Authorities (now Local Land Services) have recognised the social as well as environmental value of engaging with Aboriginal peoples, and are often contributing to Aboriginal development through their partnerships. The Indigenous Protected Area Programme (with 50 IPAs representing almost a quarter of the National Reserve System) and the Working on Country Programme provide further Commonwealth resources to support Aboriginal employment in management of country. Such activities have clear socio-economic and reconciliation benefits, building on Aboriginal strengths and aspirations (Hunt 2010). Other opportunities arise from the Commonwealth Government's carbon farming initiative (*Koori Mail* 2 May 2012).

The challenge of governance

If regional development is to seriously engage with Indigenous Australia in a more deliberate and effective way, then governance arrangements to facilitate that are required. Within regional development literature, the focus is on the interaction of Commonwealth, state and local governments, and most recently Regional Development Australia, as one mechanism to facilitate that interaction.

Indigenous governance is complex and includes customary governance arrangements of kin and clan networks, nested within identified 'peoples' or 'nations' (such as the *Wiradjuri* or *Yuin* peoples). Moreover, identities are also framed by statutory arrangements such as recognised native title claimant groups or native title holders and their Prescribed Bodies Corporate, or, in NSW identified Aboriginal 'owners' in selected areas, under the *New South Wales Land Rights Act 1983*. Layered over that are other bodies formed under land rights legislation – for example, in NSW there are 119 Local Aboriginal Land Councils whose membership qualification is residential and whose boundaries may or may not coincide with the customary governance boundaries of Aboriginal peoples. The Local Aboriginal Land Councils in NSW have a statutory responsibility to manage their Aboriginal land assets, to develop a 'community, land and business plan' and to 'facilitate business enterprises' consistent with it (ALRA 1983, Division 1A, s52, 5). Thus in working for the improvement of Aboriginal communities, Local Aboriginal Land Councils in NSW clearly have economic development responsibilities which need to connect to wider regional economic development planning. Furthermore, outside the statutory land rights systems there are other incorporated Aboriginal organisations striving for Aboriginal development; in the past these have included CDEP organisations, some of which have transformed into Aboriginal employment or training organisations, as well as a host of other local initiatives in a variety of sectors, from human services to natural resource management.

Clearly, for Aboriginal people to participate in, contribute to and benefit from regional development there needs to be strengthened relationships between these diverse governance arrangements, which often do not intersect well with non-Indigenous systems. Such connections must be strategic and purposeful, through collaborations developed through trusted relationships and shared aspirations. There is a weight of history to overcome, but a continuation of the separate spheres of regional development and Indigenous affairs would see important opportunities missed, particularly in those regions where Aboriginal land assets and interests are growing, and where Aboriginal people are becoming a significant proportion of the regional population.

Already, significantly more than half of Australia's land area is within the native title system, either with native title rights recognised or in the process of determination. As more native title determinations are made, and more land rights claims settled, Aboriginal people across regional Australia will have assets and interests which may contribute to their own and wider regional development. As Davies points out, a native title claim 'is not an end in itself but a step towards the recognition by others of the claimant group's native title and its authority as part of the governance in its traditional territory' (Davies 2003, p. 37). As she argues, to overcome Aboriginal marginalisation, and secure sustainability in regional areas, it will be critical to 'rebuild Indigenous institutions for governance of country' so that Aboriginal people can collaborate with others to manage their traditional lands and waters (Davies 2003, p. 1). Support will be important to strengthen these currently relatively weak and poorly-funded (and often unfunded) Aboriginal institutions, to enable them to work in effective collaboration with other regional players to leverage appropriate development from 'country'. Through building such institutions and relationships, other potentials will emerge. Regional development which fails to deal with the uneven development between Indigenous and other Australians will otherwise perpetuate inequality and exclusion rather than ensure that Aboriginal people are at the heart of the endeavour. In many parts of regional Australia, where Aboriginal populations are growing rapidly in contrast to declining numbers of other Australians, this coming together of regional and Indigenous policy and the formation or strengthening of the necessary relationships to achieve it, is all the more urgent and important.

Acknowledgement

I am grateful for assistance with Figure 7.1 and Table 7.1 from my Centre for Aboriginal Economic Policy Research colleagues, Nicholas Biddle and Mandy Yap respectively.

Note

1 Data in this figure are based on the ABS population count released on 28 March 2011, rather than population estimates which factor in an undercount. As remote Australian population counts frequently underestimate the population, these figures are likely to be somewhat conservative for the Indigenous population in remote Australia.

References

Aboriginal and Torres Strait Islander Social Justice Commissioner 2003, *Social Justice Report 2003*, Human Rights and Equal Opportunity Commission, Sydney.

Aboriginal and Torres Strait Islander Social Justice Commissioner 2004, *Native Title Report 2003*, Report No. 2/2004, Human Rights and Equal Opportunity Commission, Sydney.

Aboriginal and Torres Strait Islander Social Justice Commissioner 2005, *Social Justice Report 2005*, Report No. 3/2005, Human Rights and Equal Opportunity Commission, Sydney.

Altman, JC and Sanders, W 1991, 'From exclusion to dependence: Aborigines and the Welfare State in Australia', *CAEPR Discussion Paper No. 1*, ANU, Canberra.

Beer, A, Maude, A and Pritchard, B 2003, *Developing Australia's Regions: Theory and Practice*, UNSW Press, Sydney.

Biddle, N, Taylor, J and Yap, M 2008, 'Indigenous participation in regional labour markets', *CAEPR Discussion Paper No. 288*, CAEPR, ANU, Canberra.

Brown, N and Boden, S 2012, *A Way Through: The life of Rick Farley*, NewSouth Publishing, Sydney.

Castle, R and Hagan, J 1984, 'Aboriginal unemployment in rural NSW', in Castle, R and Mangan, J (eds), *Unemployment in the Eighties*, Longman Cheshire, Melbourne.

Collits, P 2011, 'Regional Policy in Australia since World War Two', in National Institute for Rural and Regional Australia (ed.), *Scoping a Vision for the future of rural and regional Australia: Collection of Papers*, Australian National University, Canberra, pp. 19–34.

Davies, J 2010, 'Contemporary geographies of Indigenous rights and interests in rural Australia', *Australian Geographer*, vol. 34, no. 1, pp. 19–45.

Davis, M 2008, 'ATSIC and Indigenous Women: Lessons for the future', *Balayi: Culture, Law and Colonialism* , vol. 10, pp. 73–86.

Dillon, M and Westbury, N 2007, *Beyond Humbug: Transforming Government Engagement with Indigenous Australia*, Seaview Press, West Lakes, South Australia.

Hannaford, J, Huggins, J and Collins, B 2003, *In the hands of the Regions – A new ATSIC. Report of the Review of the Aboriginal and Torres Strait Islander Commission*, Aboriginal and Torres Strait Islander Commission, Canberra.

Human Rights and Equal Opportunity Commission (HREOC) 1997, *Report of the National Inquiry into the Separation of Aboriginal and Torres Strait Islander Children from Their Families*, HREOC, Sydney.

Hunt, J, Altman, JC and May, K 2009, 'Social benefits of Aboriginal engagement in natural resource management', CAEPR Working Paper No. 60, CAEPR, ANU, Canberra.

Hunt, J 2007, 'The whole-of-government experiment in Indigenous Affairs: a question of governance capacity', Public Policy, vol. 2, no. 2, pp. 155–174.

Hunt, J 2010, 'Looking After Country in New South Wales: Two Case Studies of Socio-economic Benefits for Aboriginal People', CAEPR Working Paper No. 75, CAEPR, ANU, Canberra.

Kewley, TH 1973, *Social security in Australia, 1900–72* (Vol. 6) Sydney University Press, Sydney.

Koori Mail 2012, *Carbon farming scheme targeted*, 2 May, p. 34.

Lane, M, Robinson, C and Taylor, B 2009, *Contested Country: Local and regional resources management in Australia*, CSIRO Publishing, Collingwood.

McKenna, M 2002, *Looking for Blackfella's Point: An Australian history of place*, UNSW Press, Sydney.

Office of Indigenous Policy Coordination (OIPC) 2005, *New Arrangements in Indigenous Affairs*, DIMIA, Australian Government, Canberra.

Royal Commission into Aboriginal Deaths in Custody (RCIADIC) 1991, *National Report*, vol. 4. Available at: www.austlii.edu.au/au/other/IndigLRes/rciadic/national/vol.4/5.html. Accessed: 14 May 2013.

Sanders, W 2004, 'ATSIC's achievements and strengths: implications for Institutional Reform', *Journal of Australian Indigenous Issues*, vol. 7, no. 3, pp. 14–21.

Shergold, P 2005, 'Delivering services to Indigenous Australians—a whole-of-government approach', *presentation to the Australian Government Indigenous Affairs Forum for the Northern Territory*, 17 February.

Spicer, I 2007, *Independent review of the Community Development Employment Projects (CDEP) Scheme*, ATSIC, Canberra.

Vanstone, A 2004, *Opening Speech to Bennelong Society Conference*, September, Sydney. Available at: www.bennelong.com.au/conferences/conference2004/conference2004.php. Accessed: 2 October 2006.

White, J 2010, 'Peas, beans and riverbanks: seasonal picking and dependence in the Tuross Valley', in Keen, I (ed.), *Indigenous Participation in Australian economies: historical and anthropological perspectives*, ANU E Press, Canberra, pp. 109–126.

8 Education *for* rural Australia

Philip Roberts

The education of rural communities has been a concern for all levels of government since the arrival of Europeans. Primarily these concerns have been in relation to issues of achievement and access, particularly school achievement and access to post-compulsory schooling. As education remains a state or territory responsibility in the Australian Federation, there has been no single coherent approach to education in rural regions. When the Federal Government has intervened into education policy over the preceding 60 years, it has focused on the primary Federal concerns of national economic growth. Education policy has been positioned as a branch of economic policy, subsequently resulting in tension with the broader philosophy and purpose of schooling that is often conceived on social grounds. As the importance of the rural economy to the nation's prosperity has changed over the last 60 years, there has been an increasing disjuncture between the education provided to, and the education needed in, rural regions. This disjuncture has seen education conceived in terms of the values and priorities of the increasingly powerful metropolitan communities that dominate the nation's economy. Cosmopolitan values and economic concerns have taken precedence over the educational needs and desires of the rural communities whose interests Federal policy is meant to serve.

Rural education and the state

Since the second half of the nineteenth century, the local public school has been the symbolic representative of the state in most rural communities. Along with the main roads, the local public school has endured and become a key symbol of what the state provides, as well as a practical site for other activities of the state such as itinerant clinics and community meetings. While the numbers of such schools peaked in the late 1960s (Campbell and Sherington 2006), today public primary schools are still in far more locations than any other state or federal agency. It is surprising then to note that there is no coherent national policy in relation to rural, regional and remote education. It has, however, been the subject of numerous reports and inquiries in the second half of the twentieth century (HREOC 2000). Policies and programmes that do exist for rural education equate rurality with poverty and regard education as a crucial component of economic growth and development. In this way, education is an economic commodity and inequity an economic problem. Against this backdrop of neglect and marginalisation, rural education is increasingly gaining recognition in the research community as a productive site for understanding the impact of globalisation and neoliberal economic policies. In a social environment where standardisation is a marker of quality, the rural stands alone as something recognisably different from cosmopolitan society due to its 'location' and distinct cultures. This recognisable difference enables researchers to clearly observe the incursions of global economic and social ideologies as they transform rural understandings and lifestyles.

Much of the interest in rural education has focused on the comparatively poor educational outcomes and the limited access to education in rural communities (HREOC 2000). The NSW Education Minister, representing a rural electorate, summed up the situation of rural education in early 2011 when he successfully placed the issue of closing the gap between rural and urban students on the national reform agenda. In so doing, he cited statistics indicating that: one in seven students from remote areas falls below minimum national standards for literacy compared with one in 20 for urban areas; in international data, rural students are one and a half years behind city students; in the National Assessment Programme – Literacy and Numeracy (NAPLAN) 2009, an average of 47 per cent of students in very remote areas fell behind the national minimum benchmark in literacy and 40 per cent below on numeracy; and that rural students face higher costs in accessing education.[1] While this is an important focus, it fails to recognise that this has been the situation in rural schools since the beginning of universal education, and that the poor educational outcomes are mirrored in poor participation in post-compulsory education (Dalley-Trim and Alloway 2010). To date, no policy intervention has had a significant impact on changing the outcomes in education for rural communities. Highlighting this lack of consideration is that rural education has slipped from the explicit considerations of the National Goals for Schooling (MCEETYA 2008) over the last decade, and with this slide the potential of the National Framework for Rural and Remote Education (developed in 2001) has been lost and the Ministerial Council for Employment, Education, Training and Youth Affairs (MCEETYA) Taskforce on Rural and Remote Education disbanded.

The causes of continued rural educational underachievement comparative to non-rural regions are much debated, but explanations generally relate to the average lower socio-economic status (SES) of rural communities, location or distance, economic decline of regions, and rurality (Commonwealth of Australia 2010; Welch *et al.* 2007; Creswell and Underwood 2004; HREOC 2000). Consequently, approaches to overcoming education problems in rural communities focus on equity and overcoming distance, with little attention on the affordances of rurality or understanding of its relationship to educational achievement or the different achievement levels between rural places. Between one quarter and one-third of school-age students attend schools in rural and remote areas; however, as rural schools are generally much smaller they make up approximately half the total number of school sites (HREOC 2000). As the 2000 Human Rights and Equal Opportunity Inquiry into Rural and Remote Education noted, the social and educational achievement of these communities is a fundamental human rights issue, especially in a developed nation. This report noted that education needs to take into account the particular needs of these communities, however all policy and public rhetoric constructs interventions in economic terms and judges the rural against the social and cultural traditions of the urban (HREOC 2000). Similarly, the many state and Federal inquiries that have looked at the issue of rural education consistently point out the difference of the rural context and the need for rural-specific approaches (Vinson 2002; HREOC 2000). The singular focus that the rural should model the urban is increasingly being recognised as the cause of continued inequity (Roberts and Green 2013), and is an assumption that needs to be challenged in future policy. While this is at odds with the prevailing social and political attitudes, what is evident is that these approaches have not succeeded in the past 60 years and have arguably made matters worse (Thomson 2011).

The development of Federal policy

The increasing Federal government involvement in education policy has coincided with a repositioning of education as primarily an economic concern, and the marginalisation of social considerations. Education is constitutionally a state responsibility in Australia and is the second largest expenditure in each state after health. Prior to Federation, the states each had legislation setting up their respective education systems. It was not until the establishment of the Commonwealth Education Office in 1945, and the establishment of the Commonwealth Department of Education and Science in 1966, that the Federal Government started to show an interest in the field. These moves were however linked with the primary discourse of federal involvement in education – namely, the skills and innovation requirements of the economy. A second discourse of choice, based on the economic principle that competition results in greater quality and efficiency of service delivery, has also been important throughout this period (Wilkinson *et al.* 2006). Consequently the social imperative of education and its related programmes and approaches in schools has been of secondary importance. By placing the economic values of the urban centres of capital at the centre the goal of education has been redefined, and any rural specific focus or non-urban related economic concerns have been shifted to the fringes.

The economic role of education was an important reframing of the humanitarian principles under which state-based education systems developed. Initially the moral imperative saw education as a state responsibility to develop the character of the colonies, and partly, as revisionist histories suggest, to control the disparate fringes of settlement (Green and Letts 2007). The logic of control is important to the evolution of education policy as each state subsequently developed a centre vs periphery (i.e. urban–capital vs rural/regional) approach to education. Curriculum, staffing and accountability were all managed by the centre to ensure quality, as defined by the centre. Furthermore, the moral imperative behind the development of state-based education rested upon the state controlling education in order to ensure the transmission of 'appropriate' social attitudes and moral character. For this reason there was a consensus that non-government schools should not be supported by state funds as they were beyond the moral control of the state (Wilkinson *et al.* 2006).

The initial shift to an economic imperative from a moral one can be seen in the initial development of the Office of Schools to assist in post-war growth, and was all but complete when, faced with the need to develop a skilled workforce, the Menzies Government passed legislation in 1964 using the state grants provision of the Constitution to fund science facilities in all Australian schools (Campbell and Sherington 2006). This initiative represents the Federal Government's first substantial involvement in education, and also changed the previous state consensus on schools funding by applying the science funding to both government and non-government schools. It was subsequently followed in 1968 by a scheme to fund libraries, using the same provisions (Wilkinson *et al.* 2006). While these schemes were addressing longer-term economic needs, they also opened a political divide around school funding. These state aid debates, as they became known, soon became an accepted component of federal spending in education, such that education is now the third largest federal expenditure after welfare and health. While not specific to rural areas, the Federal Government had opened a mechanism to fund education programmes. Since the 1960s, the Federal Government has increasingly used these provisions to enter into arrangements with states in relation to education priorities, often linking funding to meeting certain federal targets.

The newfound federal concern about education in the 1960s was also partly based on a concern that existing educational facilities in Australia were not of appropriate quality for the country's future needs (Wilkinson *et al.* 2006). Here the concern for quality is a loosely masked economic concern. It also coincided with the expansion of secondary schooling internationally and in Australia, and the debates about the appropriate support for schools. To resolve these issues, the Commonwealth Schools Commission was established in 1974 to examine the needs of schooling in Australia and propose directions to meet these needs. Arising from these was recognition that the provision and quality of education across the nation was not uniform, and that there were particular issues in rural areas. This echoed previous state-based inquiries, such as the 1969 Karmel Inquiry in South Australia that singled out problems associated with rural education. Unfortunately the problems identified in the 1969 report, the 2000 Human Rights and Equal Opportunity Commission report into Rural and Remote Education, and many reports in between and since, all came to the same conclusion: that rural schools significantly underperform compared with their metropolitan counterparts, and that rural students are therefore disadvantaged. This disadvantage is consistently attributed to a restricted and/or inappropriate curricula and teaching strategies; lack of support services; inadequate teacher preparation for teaching in rural and isolated areas; limited curriculum options; high staff turnover rates; and a lack of social and cultural facilities in the local community. These disadvantages then flow into concerns in relation to lower rates of post-compulsory participation, where poor school achievement compounds other accessibility issues.

The Country Areas Programme

The main policy developed over the past 30 years to address the poor educational outcomes of rural, remote and isolated communities is the Country Areas Programme (CAP). This is a special programme funded by the Commonwealth Government that provides additional funding to education authorities in each state and territory to assist schools in rural and isolated areas. It developed from the Disadvantaged Schools Programme, itself proposed by the Schools Commission to address inequity in education, but was separated from it in 1976 in recognition that the criteria applied in urban areas were unsuitable for rural areas (Country Areas Programme 1997). This reflected a change in rationale from one that addressed both rural and socio-economic disadvantage, to one that addressed rural disadvantage specifically. The Country Areas Programme is therefore founded upon the view that students in geographically isolated areas can be educationally disadvantaged by geographic isolation, and aims to help schools and school communities to improve the educational outcomes and opportunities of students who are educationally disadvantaged precisely because of their geographical isolation.

The goal of the Country Areas Programme is to ensure that the learning outcomes of the 5 per cent of school-age students who attend schools receiving Country Areas Programme funding match those of students in metropolitan areas (Country Areas Programme 1997). Problematically, as with all equity programmes in rural schools, the benchmarks are metropolitan in nature and do not recognise the particularities of rural places. The programme aims to achieve its objective by providing additional funds, under the schools assistance acts, to supplement the education provided by schools by supporting curriculum resources, professional development for staff, and access to extra-curricula activities that are otherwise too expensive due to distance. Underpinning all this is an assumption of a deficit in the rural that can only be overcome by supplementing it with more metropolitan-type culture and material. The Country Areas Programme remained the primary 'policy' in relation to rural and remote schools until the national partnerships agreements in 2009; however, the outcomes in these schools remain well below national averages. Since the abolition of federal Country Areas Programme funding, and its replacement with a generic focus on low SES schools, there is no equity scheme that addresses rural educational achievement as a distinct issue. Instead educational disadvantage has been reconstituted as an issue of literacy, numeracy or lack of principal autonomy, all defined in terms of an imagined metropolitan cultural norm.

The persistence of rural school inequity (Thomson 2011) brings into question the appropriateness of approaches that implicitly have a rural deficit assumption, which may in fact further entrench the attitude of deficit in relation to the accepted curriculum and culture in rural communities. The recent move towards a national curriculum potentially only furthers this disconnect, in that it represents just another form of high-cultural knowledge determined by people far removed from the rural, and inevitably measured against criteria with no consideration of rural needs. To underline this potential is the fact that the school-developed options in initial drafts were removed – which would have allowed rural schools to use local knowledge – as they were not seen as being proscriptive enough.

Choice

The dominance of economic ideologies has had a significant impact in rural education. The funding of non-government schools, partly intended to give choice and drive improvements, does not apply in rural areas where there are often no alternatives other than boarding schools. This 'choice' is only accessible for a relative few, given the generally lower SES of many rural communities (Commonwealth of Australia 2010). Leaving, as an extreme form of choice, is actively encouraged by federal assistance to isolated parents since 1973, and is reinforced as an important programme for the most isolated 1 per cent of the school age population by the Human Rights and Equal Opportunity Commission (HREOC 2000). However, the encouragement to leave rural communities is at odds with the large investment in distance education and the technology it uses, and potentially undermines this important site of educational technology innovation. The loss of many students to the city, especially many with arguably greater social capital, compounds the lower SES of rural communities. In addition to undermining the connection with rural place and knowledges, notions of 'choice' ensure that communities are educationally segregated along economic lines, with those likely to lead such communities having greater affinity with metropolitan knowledges.

In addition to ideas of school choice, many have argued that national competition policy and economic rationalism are having a significant influence on education in rural areas. While the Productivity Commission may discount national competition policy as having an impact, it does not take into account the connection between town size, student enrolment and school resourcing. It is difficult to attribute the issues faced by rural communities to this particular approach, as the poor achievement has been perennial for these areas. However the factors contributing to comparatively lower educational achievement, such as parental unemployment or income, have not been helped by this approach, and may very well have been exacerbated by it. While the Productivity Commission has noted the impact of competition policy on rural areas, albeit within the context of global economic forces, and the importance of education in growing economic capacity (Smith 2001), it has done so based on a narrow economic framing of education. That is, the purpose of education, and the economic opportunities it creates, have privileged the opportunities afforded by global capital that ultimately encourage students to leave rural regions.

The problems caused by national competition policy are intertwined with subsequent rural decline and the removal of services. These combine to make rural communities less attractive places for staff, and also reduce the local population as people move to larger centres such as Dubbo, Ballarat and Toowoomba. As economic models also apply to the staffing and resourcing of schools, any rural decline results in a number of additional disadvantages for those serving rural communities (Roberts 2005). Foremost amongst these is that schools are staffed and resourced on a per-student basis, meaning that a reduction in the student population due to community downsizing such as that outlined above, reduces the school's staffing entitlement and resources. This acts as a multiplier effect in further reducing the breadth of what the school can offer (HREOC 2000) and reduces their competitiveness with schools in larger regional centres with a broader curriculum and greater resources. The formulas upon which staffing and resourcing decisions are made are applied on a procedural basis by central bureaucracies with scant regard for local conditions and concerns. When they existed, the equity provisions that were central to improving rural educational outcomes such as the Country Areas Programme entrenched this economic modeling, as they were merely additional formulas with little recognition of the issue of the appropriateness of what schools teach and are measured against. They had no impact on the nature of the schooling provided and merely reinforced the psychology of disadvantage by providing additional resources based on values that reinforced rural difference.

Through the myth of 'choice' the cycle develops, so that as a community shrinks due to changes in the rural economy the local school also shrinks, which further encourages families with school-aged children to move to larger centres resulting in further community shrinkage. This cycle is not unique to schools however, as it can also be seen in relation to the provision of vocational education, and the economics of higher education in these communities (Dalley-Trim and Alloway 2010). The eternal embrace between rural schools, economy and community also sees any economic reduction limiting the social capital and community resilience beyond the school. The local school is often also the site of many governments service visits, including health clinics, and the staff are often an important social capital in the community, coaching sport teams, running cultural events, and adding to the cultural capital of the community.

Staffing

The staffing of rural and remote schools is perhaps the most critical issue facing education in rural areas, with the difficulty in attracting and retaining staff consistently noted over the last 150 years. The nature of the problem was productively linked to the issue of rural difference in the 1987 report 'Schooling in Rural Australia' for the Schools Commission, which began with the observation that attracting staff and maintaining reasonable staffing continuity can be difficult in schools in remote areas. While going on to reiterate the familiar issues, the report also noted the different space occupied by rural schools when it observed that teachers in rural schools face special challenges and conditions not necessarily experienced by other teachers (Roberts 2005). To date, no approach has really addressed this difference. Instead, staff are allocated to schools in each state and territory through a centralised system of placement. To encourage staff to take up positions and increase retention, an array of incentives are used throughout the country. However these incentives are invariably linked to the difficulty of these locations and their undesirability, compared with metropolitan or coastal locations. As such, they reward staff for working in these schools by encouraging their transfer out, after a set period, and focus on the deficits of rural areas (Roberts 2005).

The provision of staff is crucial for all other interventions to improve rural education outcomes, as without appropriately trained staff nothing else is possible. Unfortunately rural schools experience a persistent turnover of staff, staff shortages, an inappropriate number of newly-qualified staff, fewer experienced staff to act as mentors, and a lack of staff in specialist subjects. Furthermore, the lack of staff and casual relief, combined with the resourcing levels of schools, inevitably means that staff miss out on professional development and ongoing training. This is compounded by funding systems that see central bureaucracies charging schools for services and consequently further reducing their capacity for ongoing training and support (Roberts 2005; HREOC 2000). Notions like online training and support have limited impact in these communities, as staff are not able to get away to take part, due to these staff shortages. Similarly, evening training is not appropriate as many staff in these schools are in the early years of their career where preparation for teaching takes up much of their time.

There is no uniform national policy in relation to the staffing of rural and remote schools due to the state-based nature of education. While there is considerable ongoing demand for teachers in rural areas, Australia's population spread and the cultural gravity of the metropolitan and coastal areas means that rural areas cannot sustain their own staffing requirements. Magnifying this problem is that there are proportionally a large number of rural schools, albeit mostly smaller than their non-rural counterparts, and that each secondary school needs a range of curriculum experts. Consequently, the unmet demand for teachers in rural areas is significantly higher than any other public service workforce and will conceivably remain a perennial issue without significant reform. Such reform should not however seek to set up a separate rural teaching service as such an approach would lock these teachers out of seeking a similar lifestyle to the other 90 per cent of the Australian population not living in rural and remote areas. This style of approach was introduced in Western Australia in 1996 in the form of the Remote Teaching Service; however it soon collapsed as it could not overcome the need to ensure staff could transfer and essentially separated them from the professionally, and culturally, important needs of a system built on metropolitan knowledge. Teachers soon found they were locked out of transfer and promotion precisely because of their rural expertise – this experience was seen as not relevant to the schooling approaches valued in the urban area, or they were seen to be 'behind' other metropolitan teachers due to having limited access to professional learning or having only taught small classes and were therefore likely to struggle with large classes (Roberts 2005).

Aboriginal education

The increasing proportion of the Aboriginal and Torres Strait Islander populations in rural areas, and the subsequent increasing proportion of these students in rural schools, highlights that rural education is intertwined with Aboriginal education. This creates certain challenges and opportunities for talking about rural schools, in that while separating Aboriginal education is important to highlight the unique challenges, it also risks separating the needs of Aboriginal communities from the broader rural community. This is problematic as the history of Aboriginal education cannot be separated from prevailing attitudes in the wider community towards the Aboriginal community and culture. This history has seen Aboriginal students initially excluded from local schools or confined to separate schools often run by missions. While these approaches were officially abolished in the mid twentieth century, Aboriginal students could still be practically excluded from mainstream schools based on the 'clean, clad and courteous' rule up until the first Aboriginal Education policies of the early 1980s. As a result Aboriginal students received a poor quality education, with many not completing the compulsory years, and consequently had their employment and economic opportunities limited. This history needs to remain at the forefront of thinking about rural education as these policies set up the social conditions of many Aboriginal communities and influences the attitudes of some Aboriginal parents to their children's schooling today.

In an attempt to improve the education, employment and economic outcomes of Aboriginal Australians, the 1989 Hobart Declaration of the national goals of schooling for the first time recognised the need for equity among all groups in Australia and the need to include Aboriginal culture and history in the school curriculum. This is significant as it was the first policy action to include, rather than systematically marginalise, a significant proportion of the rural population from one of the main functions of the state – education. The Hobart Declaration resulted in the first national Aboriginal and Torres Strait Islander Education policy, implemented in 1993 (Craven 2011). It was shortly followed by the report of the Royal Commission into Aboriginal Deaths in Custody that highlighted the systematic marginalisation of Aboriginal people from education and recommended that Aboriginal views and perspectives be included in the curriculum, that Aboriginal communities be involved in education, and teachers be better prepared for teaching Aboriginal students (Craven 2011). These inquiries and policies all recognised that a connection between education, knowledge and place is important; however, by doing so in a context of deficit, they effectively positioned such approaches as also deficit relative to the metropolitan knowledge in the 'mainstream' curriculum.

Subsequent to the 1993 policy, there have been various other reports and inquiries into a range of Aboriginal-related issues, all of which position inclusion in education as an essential component of improving the social and economic outcomes of Aboriginal Australians. Flowing from this have been a number of federal programmes to add funding to Aboriginal education initiatives, provide support staff in schools, and assist students' access to education, variously administered by Departments of Education, Aboriginal Affairs, Communities and Social Services. Importantly, the various state and federal policies all mandate consultation with communities and the involvement of communities in education.

Vocational and higher education

The issues impacting upon vocational and tertiary education mirror the same access, location, staffing and economic issues of school education. This is particularly the case in relation to vocational education as it is generally managed by the same state bureaucracy as school education, and increasingly integrated into the school curriculum. It may appear on paper that an institute of vocational education has a large course offering and many satellite campuses; however in reality they cover large areas with courses and staff allocated by demand and size similar to schools. The availability of appropriately certified staff to deliver vocational courses and the availability apprenticeships for students to develop their skills is also limited, and more so since the economic restructuring policies of the early 1990s (HREOC 2000), with the exception of areas experiencing a mining boom. The promotion of vocational education may be argued to be a success as rural areas account for a third of vocational education in schools, 40 per cent of school-based apprenticeships and a similarly large proportion of all vocational training (MacDermott and Taylor, this volume). However, the restructuring of the rural economy has also resulted in a significant gender division in vocational training, with a third of female vocational students concentrated in three service industries (Dalley-Trim and Alloway 2010) whose jobs and most apprenticeships are concentrated in larger centres such as Cairns, Albury-Wodonga and Alice Spings. The strength of vocational training in rural education does raise concerns about whether rural communities, and therefore rural schooling, are being socially constructed as relative to trades rather than more formal and academic educational and career pathways.

The relatively high rates of vocational education in rural areas may however mask a greater social problem, as students are not accessing other post-school options such as higher education. Students from rural areas make up only 18.1 per cent of the participation rate in higher education, compared to a national average of 25 per cent, and this is decreasing (Commonwealth of Australia 2010). Recent studies highlight access to courses due to poor school outcomes, the cost of relocating, course fees, employment, and a general culture shock of moving from their rural community to the city as significant in limiting this participation rate (Dalley-Trim and Alloway 2010). It remains to be seen if recent policies of funding universities for increasing their intake of rural students will have a marked effect, especially as previously rural subsidies have not overcome the higher costs to institutions of delivering courses in these areas and providing a reasonable range of course offerings. This does not however address the issue of cultural conflict for students in needing to move out of rural areas into largely urban areas. To assist with scale, the notion of a rural university amalgamating existing providers has been suggested; however such an approach would need to be aware of the school-based experience in Western Australia of providing an attractive career prospect for staff. The focus on higher education access may, by association, lead to a renewed focus on rural school education in order to raise participation rates in post-compulsory education.

Online and distance learning

While advances in technology have improved online and distance learning for students from crackly two-way radio to sophisticated online systems, it is questionable if this approach will see significant improvements. There is little evidence to date to suggest that it is an effective means of overcoming educational disadvantage, with the potential exception of higher education. Online learning often simply reinforces the lack of access that it is aiming to overcome, with students still not being able to discuss their studies or ask a teacher for assistance, while also needing high intrinsic motivation and time management skills. Very little is known about the educative processes involved in school distance education from the perspective of the child or the family member who facilitates the student's learning (Downes 2013). This is a critical oversight as, particularly in the early years of 'schooling', the child's parent effectively fulfils the role of the teacher but is poorly supported and receives little training in their critical role (Downes 2013). Furthermore, as a professional development approach for teachers, online learning has not been successful, and is often resented as teachers get minimal release and cannot be away from the school to focus on the training (Roberts 2005). Vocational online learning is not a substitute for trades training that requires physical involvement with materials. There have however been successful higher education providers for a number of years, using a model of blended learning where online work is combined with residential periods of study. The success of this model, and the ambivalent results of online only material, needs to be the focus of discussion as the National Broadband Network is rolled out, with its associated rhetoric of transforming education in rural areas.

Future challenges

Looking at rural education policy from the second half of the last decade reveals that there is in fact little formal policy to speak of; instead, most is in the grey literature and embedded in other policies and conflated with economic rationales and philosophies. Furthermore, while the issues of rural education have been ongoing they remain persistent, along with approaches that continue to position the rural as deficit against metropolitan measures. The challenge for future policymakers is to imagine how the rural can be conceived differently and on its own terms so that what it affords can be utilised. Regardless, there needs to be greater coordination across agencies and with the various states and territories, so that a situation such as that in 2008 can be avoided – when the Federal Government announced $300 million on local infrastructure projects, while at the same time teachers in one state had impending industrial action in support of incentives for hard-to-staff schools (Reid *et al.* 2010). This example also highlights the relative importance of educational issues compared to those of economic development.

The needs of rural schools and communities need to be clearly on the national policy agenda, and not left to exist in a growing series of reports and recommendations alone. However, to achieve this requires a refocusing of priorities onto people and communities and away from economics alone. There was hope that this may be achieved when the 1999 Adelaide Declaration on the National Goals for Schooling in the Twenty-First Century positioned the provision of education as an issue of social justice and raised the particular issue of locational disadvantage. However, consistent with evolving national discourse, the subsequent Melbourne Declaration of 2008 (MCEETYA 2008) modified the social justice agenda to an 'equity and excellence' agenda, and removed any reference to location. It would appear, as evidenced by the focus of the national partnerships agreements in education, that the rural has instead become invisible and been consumed by either concerns for Aboriginal communities and/or low socio-economic communities.

Defining the rural

One area requiring the attention of future policy may be the definition of rural and its assorted synonyms and degrees. Presently there is considerable diversity in how state and federal agencies and national and international research defines the rural, with definitions ranging from not including capital cities and their satellites, to distance from a centre of a certain size of population. There are also state cultures that influence these definitions within certain spheres, such as that in the state-based centralised world of education. For example, schools in Tweed Heads in far northern NSW are less than 100 km from Brisbane, yet are rather remote from their head office in Sydney. In education, the issues associated with rural and remote are generally seen to magnify towards schools that qualify for Country Areas Programme funding (i.e. over 110 km from a regional service town). However it is only a matter of degree as many schools in large regional centers also underperform compared with their metropolitan counterparts, with the exception of communities with a regional university. Complicating this however is that many coastal regional communities experience the same issues of access and poor educational achievement that remote inland schools experience, but are however not difficult to staff; here distance and community socio-economic status may be stronger factors. None of these definitions based on distance or location takes into account the social construction of the rural, and how this social construction mediates the relationship with education and the various indicators of educational achievement.

Repositioning the rural in policy

The challenges facing education in rural Australia require at least two semantic shifts: firstly from the rural as quasi-urban to a recognition of the particularity of places, and secondly from education as primarily an economic concern to a broader concern for the sustainability of regions. Achieving this requires a sustained effort to disrupt the dominant discourses, such as those powerfully summarised in Judith Brett's *Quarterly Essay* 'Fair Share: Country and City in Australia' (2011). In this essay Brett gives a comprehensive account of the issues impacting on rural areas in Australia and the challenges rural areas face. Using Paul Kelly's five pillars of the Australian Settlement (White Australia, industry protection, wage arbitration, state paternalism, and imperial benevolence), Brett (2011) proposes a sixth pillar, namely the trade-off between country and city. This trade-off involved an acceptance that the state compensated people for the costs of remoteness and sparse settlement in return for the contribution of agriculture to the national economy. This broad acceptance that rural residents should be given a fair share of Australia's resources has been undermined by the neoliberal economic policies of the last 20 years and the relative decline of agriculture in the national economy (Gross, this volume). Consequently, 'regions' have needed to pull their own weight, something the rural has generally been unable to do. To counter this Brett argues for a renewed understanding of the benefits the city gets from the country through agriculture, pleasure and recreation, national identity and stewardship of the land (Brett 2011). These 'benefits' however tend to position the rural as serving the broader interests of the city and are not necessarily rural interests empowered on their own terms.

Notably missing from Brett's essay is any reference to, or consideration of, education.[2] This should not be surprising however as rural policy, sociology and economic commentary rarely consider the issues pertaining to education. This omission is perhaps symptomatic of the prevalence of economic considerations that the essay, and much social policy, ironically criticises. It would appear that there still exists a bias towards viewing these regions within a subtle economic frame, perhaps because this is the dominant discourse of our times. Regardless, the social institution of the local school is a microcosm of exactly all the concerns much of the literature canvases. To use one example from Brett's essay, writing about the decline of services in rural areas Brett makes the case of the significance of the loss of the local bank manager in rural towns and the loss of social capital of their wives and children who assist in community organisations and add to local sports teams and the like. In every town with a bank there is at least a public school, and for each town with a bank there are many smaller localities that have a public school and not a bank, as well as towns large enough to have schools with secondary departments or separate secondary schools. Each of these employs a number of teachers, many more than the bank manager. While some of the remaining staff may be local like the bank staff, the fact that these schools find it hard to attract and retain staff indicates that many are not staffed by locals.[3]

From another perspective Brett's addition of a sixth pillar of a trade-off between the country and the city recognises a historical commitment to spatial (regional) equality. This is significant as the example of the Country Areas Programme cited above illustrates how such notions of equality have been overshadowed by economic equality. Looking at this issue from an alternative perspective we could also argue that educational, and rural, policy is geographically blind (Green and Letts 2007) and unable to either conceptualise rurality or consider it as a factor separate from economics. This results in ongoing social disadvantage, such as average lower SES and higher unemployment in rural regions (Commonwealth of Australia 2010), which then results in a form of educational disadvantage. However this approach does not take into account complex social factors that in the most basic terms can be highlighted by the fact that many rural students do not succeed at university due to the social factors of fitting in, and subsequent loneliness, rather than academic achievement (Commonwealth of Australia 2010). Instead of considering such factors of difference, the focus remains upon initiatives that redistribute resources rather than challenge the broad causes of disadvantage.

When the causes of rural disadvantage are not considered, policy becomes complicit in the continuation of this disadvantage through implicitly constructing all the rural as the same and as a mere extension of urban centres; in essence a policy construction of the rural as either deficit or quasi-urban. In relation to education this has seen rural schools constructed in the image of metropolitan schools rather than in relation to the communities they serve, supported by a centralised system to ensure adherence to this model. To counter this, a new visioning of the rural in policy is necessary. Moreover, to counter this spatial hegemony in policy work, rural meanings need to be advocated and included (Howley, Theobald and Howley 2005). This necessitates a definition of the rural that does not predetermine all the rural as one, but recognises the particularities and differences of rural places.

A difficulty in recognising the rural in policy is that there are many competing definitions of the rural, many of which differ on the geographic determinations, economic basis or cultural definitions (Cloke 2006). Donehower, Hogg and Schell (2007) however transcend these concerns to arrive at a definition that combines quantitative measures, including statistics, with geographic and cultural ideas to allow the rural to be identified as a distinct entity with distinct characteristics. This use of objective statistics and the physical certainties of geography, as well as a recognition that culture also exists and is related to both of these, conceivably satisfies the concerns of the various policy interest groups. Taking this approach further, Reid *et al.* (2010) propose a model of rural social space that links demography, economy and geography as key considerations for policy. In so doing, the connection between the local industry, be it pastoral or irrigated crops, the geography that enables or constrains it and the subsequent impact on the population make up are all interlinked. Thus, sparsely populated grazing land is clearly seen as having different needs to more densely populated irrigation regions. As a result of geography and economy some areas are more densely populated and more affluent affording greater social and economic opportunities. This in turn not only influences students' understandings of the world through their experiences, but also mediates their expectations and aspirations (Dalley-Trim and Alloway 2010).

In terms of education policy, an approach that puts the rural at the centre would necessitate a decoupling of schools from central urban-based bureaucracies, and allow greater scope for the local interpretation and implementation of broad policy objectives. This would challenge policymakers to rethink the measures upon which the rural is determined to be disadvantaged, as well as rethinking the standard policy responses of the last 30 years. Furthermore, it would ask serious questions about the appropriateness of the centralised and mandated curriculum and its associated high-stakes examination and assessment regimes, which all too often value knowledges and skills that are not reflective of the rural lifeworld. Importantly, careful implementation and vigilance on behalf of rural communities would be needed to ensure that such an approach did not descend into relativism, lower expectations or lower standards. Instead, such an approach requires the highest of expectations and standards and a complex skill set to both recognise the particularities of rural places, whilst also opening opportunities in the cosmopolitan global world.

While it remains a policy extension of cosmopolitan values, rural education will remain the subject of continuing negative comparison and subsequent inquiry and policy adjustment. The inability to separate rural education policy speaks to our general inability to conceive of society as anything other than a vessel of national economic growth and our general unwillingness to engage with complex double meanings. In popular culture there is little debate that rural communities are seen as distinct, comprising particular social values, lifestyles and interests that are clearly different from their urban counterparts. However, we are unable to allow these to be valued in education policy. Consequently, achievement is measured against inappropriate cultural values, and decisions such as staffing, resources and post-compulsory institutions are funded and physically located according to economic principles of efficient resource distribution. For as long as such simple policy approaches remain dominant, rural educational disadvantage will remain a salient feature of the Australian social landscape. Instead we need the courage, and the vision, to decouple rural education policy from pure economic concerns.

Decoupling rural education

Decoupling rural education and focusing upon rural meanings inherently challenges the metro-centric assumptions of 'efficiency and effectiveness' as the dominant criteria for policy. In terms of education, 'efficiency and effectiveness' implies a scientistic-technical view of education that ignores the situated enactment of all effective learning. That is, an approach used in one school in a metropolitan centre, or a highly effective teacher in a metropolitan centre, are not necessarily applicable in another context, such as a rural or remote school (Roberts 2005). Consequently a policy structure, such as localism, that allows local flexibility and reinterpretation is an important avenue for further thinking in education. As Hogan and colleagues (Hogan *et al.*, this volume) point out, localism implies an inevitable tension when centralised policy or higher-scale policy goals are involved. Arguably education is one of these centralised higher-scale policy areas, evidenced by the attention given to it and its funding in federal politics and moves towards the first Australian Curriculum, National Professional Standards for teachers and national benchmarks for achievement. Echoing the tension of localism, such approaches, and the accompanying rhetoric of a crisis in Australian education, place national concerns ahead of the concerns of communities. These national concerns, and localism generally, have an economic focus that is ambivalent to the nature of education whilst positioning education at the service of local economic goals.

Broadening the concept of localism to include the nature of education, as well as its outcomes, may well assist rural communities to reconstitute their relationship with education. Such an approach would move away from the purely redistributive assumptions that dominate the discourse of educational disadvantage. The Gonski Review and funding debates are, after all, confined to discussions about funding and achievement within the existing system, and do not consider alternative systems. Similarly, an Australian curriculum is an amalgam of knowledge deemed important by dominant cultural and economic groups, and presents as a fait accompli to rural areas what is, and should be, important to them. Such an education becomes about 'learning to leave' (Corbett 2007), as students need to value other ways of being to succeed in education, rather than learning for rural communities. However, as Cuervo and Wyn (2012) illustrate, some rural youth use education in a particular and nuanced fashion to achieve their goals of remaining with land, family and place. Herein lies the insight for rural education policy and an enlarged version of localism: curriculum and achievement structures need to be driven by the needs of the communities, defined in their own terms, rather than in the interests of staff or placeless national goals.

Such a localism would imply a new professionalism based on genuine decentralisation as opposed to the facade of decentralisation evident in recent policy reforms. For example, principal autonomy limited to only the financial side of schools and accompanied by strict guidelines and reporting mechanisms, curriculum implementation accompanied by the public reporting of results against a predetermined criteria, and teacher professionalism regulated by detailed standards and performance pay all ultimately shift authority to the organisations setting and monitoring the benchmarks, and in practice result in far greater governmental control than in any previous era (Roberts and Green 2013). Through the scale of their application such approaches cannot be responsive to local conditions, whilst concerns for transparency and accountability in public funding impose practices without reference to context. Should we be able to decouple a national curriculum from high-stakes testing and reporting, decouple professional standards from discussions of performance pay, and give principals genuine autonomy over things that matter like the implementation of curriculum, then we may well be moving towards a genuinely place-conscious education.

With the earlier point about genuine decentralisation in mind, there would be value in considering a national staffing system, not necessarily as an industrial structure but perhaps through the cooperation of registration authorities. At the moment there are different systems with different incentive mechanisms in each educational jurisdiction. The jurisdictional confines of transferring, promotions and reward for service constrain teachers' abilities to move within rural regions and ultimately positions most careers to finish in large metropolitan areas. Considering the perennial problem of staffing for many rural and remote schools (Roberts 2005) from the perspective of localism would also result in a recalibration of existing policies. At present most policies are focused upon the teacher and their needs, with equity for the community positioned as a reason to provide for these needs. However, this does not necessarily mean the best person is attracted to the job. Such a concern is at the heart of discussions around rewarding high performing teachers to work in rural schools with greater pay, however this approach is problematic due to the contextual nature of effective teaching. Shifting the emphasis to the needs of the community may be risky by initially exacerbating unmet demand for positions, but ultimately may result in increased pay as an incentive, and subsequently increased competition for places that the community would have a role in judging. Potentially the cost may be equal to paying more for teachers deemed of a high enough quality, however, importantly, the community controls the selection and criteria. Such an approach, within a national system, would encourage the development of a degree of rural specialisation in teachers' careers, however it would need commensurate national career pathways to avoid the limitations experienced in the Western Australia trial outlined earlier in this chapter.

Technology has been touted as the panacea for rural education for some time now, and while it has made a significant positive impact for access to information, whether it has actually improved education remains debatable. Educationally, the benefit of technology in education is its role in facilitating the joint construction of knowledge, both between students and with their teachers. This is how technology and social media are used in popular culture, not as an input mechanism but as a democratising tool. However, when it comes to education for rural areas the rhetoric markedly shifts to knowledge transmission and overlooks the benefits discussed in other areas of society, geographically located away from rural areas. While there are plenty of examples of schools in rural regions essentially sharing a teacher via technology, the approach overlooks the important interpersonal and social aspects of teaching and learning. So called 'flying squads' of subject-specific teachers who work across a range of schools in a region may overcome this interpersonal limitation of technology, but would also result in fractured relationships with students and communities and therefore are not likely to achieve the benefit commensurate with the required investment. Often overlooked in such approaches is that effective teaching requires the teacher to implement the official curriculum with their knowledge of their students and their community at the forefront of their planning and ongoing assessment of learning. A shift in emphasis to the student and the site of delivery, rather than access to school subjects, may enable some of the touted benefits of technology. However, to do so needs a deep consideration of new situated approaches of teaching with technology. Ironically, the rhetoric around the National Broadband Network and its important role in rural and remote education, as expressed in its own promotional material and website,[4] is undermined by the fact that the network roll-out begins in large metropolitan areas. Rather than act as a tool of spatial equalisation, the most remote areas will be some of the last to receive access, even though assisting the education of some of the most disadvantaged students has been argued as an important benefit.

Finally, the considerations of new policy perspectives will only be effective in a stable environment in which they can be explored, trialled and implemented. A student is after all at school for at least 13 years, and over this time policy approaches to schooling can change dramatically. Such changes are often linked to broader political issues that are typical of centralised high-scale policy issues (Hogan *et al.*, this volume), such that political attention on education may not result in the best, and most consistent, policy outcomes. In the last few years alone we have seen the abolition of the main equity programme for rural schools, the Country Areas Programme, only to have it suggested by the same government that they will introduce new equity loadings for rural schools as part of their new funding reforms. Recently we have seen high profile debates about the quality of teaching and national target setting that have distorted the research base upon which the genuine focus is founded (Dinham 2012). To counter this constant shifting, a third party and independent body similar to the Schools Commission of the 1970s and 1980s would be an important addition. With arms-length political control, the Schools Commission was able to conduct thorough research, over appropriate timeframes to ensure quality work, and was therefore able to suggest and implement sensible research-informed policies – most notably, the Disadvantaged Schools Programme and the Country Areas Programme cited earlier in this chapter, and seminal reports such as 'Schooling in Rural Australia'. Therefore, an important step in exploring an enlarged, spatially aware, form of localism in education is the re-establishment of such a body to investigate issues pertinent to rural education from the perspectives of the communities it is designed to represent.

Notes

1 *Sydney Morning Herald* 16–17 April 2011, p. 7. Supporting data cited at: www.det.nsw.edu.au/detresources/min-mr106O2000_RcvvxtSuUW.pdf. Further details of Australia's performance are available at www.acer.edu.au/ozpisa/key-findings/.

2 It is scantly mentioned twice in list form within another concern, but not considered in its own right.

3 Mining is not considered as an issue of community economic sustainability as the vast majority of mining operations now employ more fly-in, fly-out workers and subsequently do not benefit the community in any sustainable way.

4 See: www.nbn.gov.au/nbn-benefits/digital-economy-goals/education/why-is-this-important/.

References

Brett, J 2011, 'Fair Share: Country and City in Australia', *Quarterly Essay*, no. 42, Black Inc, Collingwood, Victoria.

Campbell, C and Sherington, G 2006, *The comprehensive public high school: Historical perspectives*, Palgrave Macmillan, New York.

Cloke, P 2006, 'Conceptualizing Rurality' in Cloke, PJ, Marsden, T and Mooney, PH (eds), *Handbook of Rural Studies*, Sage, London.

Commonwealth of Australia 2010, *Regional Participation: The Role of Socioeconomic Status and Access*, Department of Education, Employment and Workplace Relations, Canberra.

Corbett, M 2007, *Learning to leave: The irony of schooling in a coastal community*, Fernwood, Black Point NS.

Country Areas Program 1997, *Issues facing students living in rural and geographically isolated areas*, Commonwealth of Australia, Canberra.

Craven, R 2011, *Teaching Aboriginal studies (2nd ed.)*, Allen & Unwin, Crows Nest, NSW.

Creswell, J and Underwood, C 2004, *Location, Location, Location: Implications of Geographic Situation on Australian Student Performance in PISA 2000*, Australian Council for Educational Research (ACER), Camberwell, Victoria.

Cuervo, H and Wyn, J 2012, *Young people making it work: continuity and change in rural places*, Melbourne University Publishing, Carlton, Victoria.

Dalley-Trim, L and Alloway, N 2010, 'Looking "outward and onward" in the outback: regional Australian students' aspirations and expectations for their future as framed by dominant discourses of further education and training', *Australian Educational Researcher*, vol. 37, no. 2, pp. 107–125.

Dinham, S 2012, 'The Hijacking of the Teacher Quality Movement', *Professional Educator*, vol. 11, no. 7, pp. 8–11.

Donehower, K, Hogg, C and Schell, EE 2007, *Rural literacies*, Southern Illinois University Press, Carbondale, IL.

Downes, N 2013, 'The Challenges and Opportunities Experienced by Parent Supervisors in Primary School Distance Education', *Australian and International Journal of Rural Education*, vol. 23, no. 2, pp. 31–41.

Green, B and Letts, W 2007, 'Space, equity, and rural education: A 'trialectical' account', in Gulson, KN and Symes C (eds), *Spatial Theories of Education: Policy and Geography Matters*, Routledge, New York.

Howley, CB, Theobald, P and Howley, AA 2005, 'What rural education research is of most worth? A reply to Arnold, Newman, Gaddy, and Dean', *Journal of Research in Rural Education*, vol. 20, no. 18, pp. 1–6.

HREOC 2000, *Emerging Themes: National Inquiry into Rural and Remote Education*, Commonwealth of Australia, Canberra.

Interim Committee for the Australian Schools Commission 1973, *Schools in Australia*, AGPS, Canberra.

MCEETYA 2008, *Melbourne Declaration on Educational Goals for Young Australians*, Commonwealth of Australia, Canberra.

Reid, J, Green, B, Cooper, M, Hasting, W, Lock, G and White, S 2010, 'Regenerating rural social space? Teacher education for rural-regional sustainability', *Australian Journal of Education*, vol. 54, no. 3, pp. 262–227.

Roberts, P 2005, *Staffing an Empty Schoolhouse: Attracting and retaining teachers in rural, remote and isolated communities*, New South Wales Teachers Federation, Sydney, NSW.

Roberts, P and Green, B 2013, 'Researching Rural Place: On Social Justice and Rural Education', *Qualitative Inquiry*, vol. 19, no. 10, pp. 765–774.

Skilbeck, M and Connell, H 2003, *Attracting, Developing and Retaining Effective Teachers: Australian Country Background Report*, Commonwealth Government Australia, Canberra.

Smith, S 2001, *Deregulation and National Competition Policy and its Effects on Rural and Regional Areas*, Briefing Paper No. 7/01, NSW Parliamentary Library Research Service.

Thomson, S 2011, *PISA in brief: highlights from the full Australian report Challenges for Australian education: results from PISA 2009: the PISA 2009 assessment of students' reading, mathematical and scientific literacy*, ACER, Camberwell, Victoria.

Vinson, T 2002, *Inquiry into the provision of Public Education in NSW*, NSW Teachers Federation, Pluto Press, Sydney.

Welch, A, Helme, S and Lamb, S 2007, 'Rurality and Inequality in Education: The Australian Experience', in Teese, R, Lamb, S and Duru-Bellat, M (eds), *International Studies in Educational Inequality, Theory and Policy, Volume 2: Inequality in Education Systems*, Springer, Dordrecht.

Wilkinson, I, Caldwell, B, Selleck, R, Harris, J and Dettman, P 2006, *A History of State Aid to Non-Government Schools in Australia*, Department of Education, Science and Training, Canberra.

9 Commonwealth employment and welfare policies in post-war regional Australia

Sharon Wheller

Australian Government welfare and employment policy initiatives have played a vital role in shaping rural and regional Australia in the period following World War II. Post-war reconstruction, economic management, full employment and national security were all key drivers in the formation of a Commonwealth social security system. National programmes replaced state-based pensions and charitable relief payments assisting those in need in both rural and urban communities alike. The welfare system that has evolved since 1945 is now a vast and convoluted mix of income support payments and allowances, supplementary benefits and tax rebates and concessions (Kewley 1980). Programmes have been universally applied or targeted to specific groups. Few, however, were designed solely with country Australia in mind.

This chapter provides an overview of the Commonwealth welfare and employment policies and programmes that have influenced rural and regional post-war Australia in the pursuit of full employment and social security. Changes in the economic, social, political and technological environment since the 1970s, in Australia and internationally, gave rise to growing poverty and inequality in some parts of rural and regional Australia. In both employment and welfare policies, a neoliberal shift occurred as welfare was replaced with workfare. To counter growing rural hardship a series of adjustment policies promoted a business model of self-reliance. More recent government policies have included several spatially based initiatives designed to support the rural sector. While a plethora of employment and welfare programmes have sought to assist those in need through times of major social, economic and environmental change, these have also had consequences for country communities and rural livelihoods that have not always been foreseen. A discussion of how future welfare and employment initiatives could be shaped to better meet the needs of modern country Australia concludes this chapter.

Building blocks of the Australian welfare state

Australian colonial pastoralism was extremely successful during the boom period of the Victorian industrial revolution from 1850 to 1890, resulting in the emergence of an elite group of large rural landowners (Wheelwright 1989,

p. 29). At the same time, trade union movements developed and workers commanded high wages due to labour shortages and a prosperous export sector. This prosperity was not to last and the depression of the 1890s had a catastrophic impact on the population, with very few institutional safety nets and no state welfare available to alleviate the poverty and desperation that ensued. Brian Dickey points out that social welfare in Australia developed in earnest following this significant economic depression. The appalling conditions people experienced at this time arose as a result of the volatility of the market system. In consequence, a key policy principle emerged in colonial parliaments at the time, which held that the state had a role in 'civilising capitalism, that is to moderate its worst effects upon the working classes by mobilising what they believed to be the neutral powers of the state' (Dickey 1987, p. 73). Dickey (1987) observes that social security, such as an aged pension, initially developed in a number of states, before being adopted as a national scheme in 1908 by the Commonwealth government – a scheme he notes rapidly became widely accepted. Such legislation introduced the notion of universal entitlement (however, only for white citizens) into policy and was accompanied by the rise of a large centralised state bureaucracy to facilitate the distribution of benefits. Universal entitlement was extended to the provision of a maternity benefit in 1912 and initial steps were also taken to introduce systems of child protection. However, Dickey (1987, p. 109) maintains the universality of social security was not without debate during the period before World War II. At the same time social security was being established, Justice Higgins' Harvester Judgement (1907) was brought down. It established a minimum living wage for a (male) worker and their family and became the guiding principle for industrial relations. Dickey (1987, p. 95) contends,

> No other single decision of the twentieth century in this field in Australia has done more ... to transform the lives of a whole sector of the community whose welfare in the nineteenth century had so often been a problem of selective charity.

Together social security and wage setting cemented the concepts of equity and fairness into the Australia psyche. It also set a precedent for centralised regulation and interventionism (Beilharz 1989, p. 139). However, during World War II the pressures on social security changed significantly as did the level of suffering, death and disability. State governments and charitable institutions were unable to finance the level of welfare payments required (Dickey 1987, pp. 131ff.). Many new federal structures were put in place including family support, widow's pensions, and a national welfare fund including unemployment, sickness and old age pensions, maternity and funeral benefits. Full employment emerged as a government objective as early as 1942 as a means to foster 'economic security and social justice' (Dickey 1987, p. 139). During the war years a Parliamentary Joint Committee on Social Security was set up to review the provision of social welfare in Australia. This would have a lasting impact.

Post-war reconstruction and the 'New Social Order'

Emerging from World War II with a vision for a 'new social order' premised on full employment, the Federal Government's policy for the Australian 'welfare state' would shape the social policy for decades to follow. Many of the major components of this policy had their origins in the imperatives of wartime, particularly the need to manage the war economy, fund the war effort and contain inflation (Watts 1987). Murphy (2011) contends that the social policy debate taking place during the war was not just a social necessity but a symbolically important and critical element of the war economy. The war had necessitated major economic and constitutional reforms that were unpopular to the states, including the introduction of Commonwealth income taxation. Social security measures helped make these federal measures more palatable. More importantly they provided a flexible mechanism by which Keynesian economic intervention could be undertaken to curb inflation and control wages (Murphy 2011).

The post-war reconstruction efforts further cemented social security and employment as federal government responsibilities and powerful aspects of rebuilding the nation. By 1946 when the Committee completed its final report the fundamental structure of the social security system that remains in place today was largely set out (Shaver 1987). The government's objectives for employment were defined in a White Paper *Full Employment in Australia* in 1945, and in 1946 the Commonwealth Employment Service was established. In the wake of the depression, Kewley (1980) contends that unemployment was envisaged as the leading economic issue for post-war Australia. New welfare measures shifted the emphasis from unemployment relief and an associated charity mentality to the idea of security through full employment as a Government objective and social right (Harris 2001). Full employment remained a guiding principle for government social and economic policy and from the end of the war to the early 1970s the unemployment rate seldom exceeded 2 per cent.

Many existing federal welfare measures were consolidated into a single piece of legislation, the *Social Services Consolidation Act 1947* (also known as the *Social Security Act 1947* and the *Social Services Act 1947*). The Act provided national programmes for payment of pensions, benefits and allowances for social purposes, including the aged pension, invalid's pension, widow's pension, supporting mother's benefit, funeral benefit, maternity allowance, child endowment, double orphan's pension, unemployment and sickness benefits, special benefits, sheltered employment allowances, and Commonwealth Rehabilitation Service. An Australia-wide system, in replacing previous state-based measures, ensured that risks were pooled and costs could be borne across all states (Shaver 1987). Shaver (1987) also notes a relationship of mutual obligation between the citizen and the state was apparent with the linkage between taxation and income security.

The social security system had at its foundations the principles of income security and national unity (Shaver 1987). Income security took the form of a secure and sufficient family wage. The concept of the nuclear family was central, with the notion of a male breadwinner, wife and children featuring prominently in policy documents. This, however, seems primarily modelled on the urban male wage labourer. The Commonwealth-wide social security system became the embodiment of national unity, building on the enormous nationalism engendered during World War II (Shaver 1987). With this came the idea of Australia as a single community. Country Australia was essentially subsumed into this concept of the nation as community, and a welfare system built around urban wage labour. The new scheme provided for more assistance to farmers and the self-employed who were out of work than the previous *National Insurance Act* of 1938. However, primary producers were not eligible for unemployment relief if they remained on their farms and worked the land (Kewley 1980).

From welfare to workfare and the great country adjustment

The Australia-wide social security system built on the notion of full employment remained largely unchanged until the 1970s. At this time unemployment had become increasingly widespread and poverty was growing more prevalent. There was growing recognition that Keynesian economic policy and the associated growth of the state had been ineffective and was unsustainable. A new approach was needed to address the scale of need generated by the downturn in the economy. The focus of the policy agenda at this time moved to economic liberalism and a belief in the powers of the free market intent on withering the state and thereby reducing the taxation burden. Saunders and Deeming (2011) maintain that the period prior to the first oil shock saw extensive changes to social policy, however the timing of the recession meant that much of the major reform was not enacted. For those gaining their livelihoods off the land, this period is contextualised with changes in Government agricultural policy including the removal of tariffs and market driven emphasis on efficiency and productivity (Lawrence 1987, see also Cockfield, this volume, and Smith and Pritchard, this volume). A major concern at the time was farm poverty and the unproductiveness and inefficiency of many of the 'traditional' small family farm businesses. The deterioration of farm income resulted in calls for farmers' eligibility for the unemployment benefit to be reviewed, and in 1976 provisions were introduced that enabled producers to be classified as unemployed if seeking full-time work off the farm (Watts 1987). From this period to the present the primary methods of Commonwealth government welfare assistance to those involved in agriculture, over and above the universal social security system, have been programmes designed to create economically viable individual rural enterprises. Throughout Australia neoliberal reforms led to an increase in social inequality through the introduction of a less progressive taxation system, reductions in social security, changes in industrial relations, increased wage inequality and job insecurity (Quiggin 1999).

Rural adjustment

The Rural Reconstruction Scheme was introduced in May 1971 to alleviate critical issues within rural industries resulting from economic distress, and to provide longer term structural adjustment for the sector (ABARE 1975). Other industry specific schemes included the Marginal Dairy Farm Reconstruction Scheme in July 1970 and the Fruit Growing Reconstruction Scheme (October 1972). Rehabilitation grants were introduced at the same time, providing incentives to farmers to leave economically unviable farms. This formed part of the structural realignment of the industry to remove uncompetitive players.

Reconstruction schemes were replaced by Rural Adjustment Schemes from 1977, providing Commonwealth funding for debt reconstruction, farm build-up and farm improvement. Funding was also made available to those experiencing financial hardship, particularly as they transitioned out of farming, under the *States Grants (Rural Adjustment) Agreement Ratification Act 1977*. This scheme was designed to hasten the process of industry adjustment and was applied to all primary industries. Policies changed only incrementally during the period from 1977 to 1992 with farm welfare and income support being provided as part of the 'adjustment' process. In 1992 the welfare component of the Rural Adjustment Scheme was shifted into the Farm Household Support Scheme, with the adjustment policy being used to address extreme events such as drought and 'exceptional circumstances' (Botterill 2000). The Household Support Scheme included re-establishment grants and farm help advice and training as well as exit allowances for dairy farmers and exceptional circumstances allowances.

In 1997, the Agriculture–Advancing Australia (AAA) package sought to provide an integrated policy approach to the rural sector with measures that included improved welfare support to the farming sector. The Farm Family Restart scheme replaced the welfare component of the Farm Housing Support Scheme. Provision for continuation of adjustment support remained a focus, with specific support for particular industries. An example of this was the Dairy Industry Adjustment Programme in 2000 which sought to ameliorate the effects of deregulation. This programme continued until the end of 2008. The Agriculture–Advancing Australia package included the Retirement Assistance for Farmers Scheme 1997–2001 which allowed retiring farmers to transfer the family farm to younger generation family members and be eligible for the aged pension. Prior to this asset testing had meant that farmers had been unable to access retirement assistance due to asset thresholds. This scheme aimed to encourage farmers experiencing financial hardship to retire and maintain an income (Department of Families 2007). Other welfare measures included the exceptional circumstances hardship assistance aspects of the Rural Adjustment Scheme (1992). These measures were repackaged several times (Drought Relief Payment (1994) and the 1997 Exceptional Circumstances Relief payments) as part of policy to address the effects of droughts on the rural community. These schemes provided assistance to farm businesses and farm households where extreme events had occurred and the region had been designated an Exceptional Circumstances declared area.

Growing unemployment

Growing long-term structural unemployment signalled the failure of the Keynesian notion of full employment. During the period from 1974–1975 to 1996–1997 unemployment averaged 7.6 per cent of the labour force, more than three times higher than during the preceding period from 1940–1941 (Borland and Kennedy 1998). The downturn in agricultural and manufacturing industries resulted in structural changes in the demand for rural and regional labour. Numerous programmes were introduced to address the growing phenomenon of rural and regional unemployment. In 1972 the Non-Metropolitan Unemployment Relief Scheme was established to create employment and in 1974 the Regional Employment Development Scheme (REDS) was introduced by the Whitlam Government. The REDS and a National Employment and Training Scheme (NEAT) aimed to specifically address rural unemployment as well as unemployment for other key groups such as women (Harris 2001). In 1976 several programmes were implemented to address growing youth unemployment. These included the Special Youth Employment Training Programme (SYETP) providing wage subsides for those employing youth, and the Community Youth Support Scheme (CYSS). Commonwealth Rebates for Employment of Apprentices on Full-time Training (CRAFT) were also offered from 1977 (Cook 2008). As the range of programmes offered expanded from the mid-1970s, work tests were tightened for eligibility to benefits (Harris 2001). Requirements to relocate to find work or accept work at lesser skill levels plus waiting times for benefit eligibility if 'voluntarily unemployed' were also introduced.

During the early 1980s the policy focus emphasised job creation with programmes such as the Community Employment Programme (CEP) in 1983. Programmes for disadvantaged indigenous job seekers included the National Employment Strategy for Aboriginals and the Community Employment Development Programme (CEDP). A New Enterprise Incentive Scheme (NEIS) 1985 encouraged unemployed workers into self-employment while receiving the unemployment benefit for one year. In the mid-1980s the policy emphasis had shifted from job creation to training after an inquiry by Kirby found there were too many programmes and they were far too complex (Cook 2008). Boreham (2004) contends there was growing lack of enthusiasm for political interference in the workings of the market to create full employment at this time. The reduction in tariffs at the same time meant major job losses over a range of industries including textiles and motor vehicles. This hit hard in communities with specialised labour markets servicing vulnerable industries.

In the late 1980s there was a further shift from welfare to workfare with 'active' labour market and social security policies emphasising active participation and a move away from the notion of dependency. A major overhaul of social security and unemployment resulted in the introduction in 1988 of the job search allowance, job search training and job clubs. Existing training programmes for adults and youth were reconfigured into Jobtrain. The Newstart programme commenced in 1989 aimed at alleviating long-term unemployment.

This programme introduced reciprocal obligations for those unemployed receiving benefits. These mutual obligations included an activity test, participation in training, and requirements for accepting part-time and casual work.

This emphasis on workfare programmes was taken further in the 1990s with an increased push to move other welfare recipients, including people with disabilities and single parents, into the workforce – a policy direction still pursued today. Programmes such as the Jobs, Education and Training Scheme (JET) for sole parents and the Disability Reform Package were put in place to this end. More generally, the Active Employment Strategy launched in July 1991 put in place a 'new' Newstart programme and a Jobsearch Allowance which replaced the unemployment benefit. Increasingly, the responsibility was placed on the beneficiary to seek and accept employment that was deemed reasonable.

The Keating Government introduced a raft of measures under the Working Nation banner in 1994. These policies sought to address the increasing number of long-term unemployed, who had been unemployed for 12 months or more. The Working Nation policies included a Job Compact which provided subsidised work, training wages and wage subsidies. Other policies fostered self-employment, work experience and training including Landcare and Environment Action Plan (LEAP), and the New Work Opportunities programme. Refusal of 'reasonable' job offers resulted in withdrawal of welfare benefits under the concept of reciprocal obligations.

The Howard Government introduced major labour market and welfare reform which, although applied universally throughout Australia, had significant effects on rural communities. The 1996 *Workplace Relations Act* brought the introduction of voluntary unionism, non-union contracts and individual contracts at the same time reform of welfare and unemployment administration was underway. The establishment of Centrelink as a 'one stop shop' for income support in 1997 was followed by the contracting out of employment service functions and the disbanding of the Commonwealth Employment Service. Employment services were delivered via the Job Network, a network of private, public, and not-for-profit sector providers (Junankar 2000). Employment assistance programmes included Job Matching, Job Search Training, and Intensive Assistance. Job seekers were required to keep a diary documenting their job search to maintain eligibility for financial assistance as part of the mutual obligations requirements, and failure to do so resulted in 'breaches' and subsequent loss of benefit. In 1997 a Work for the Dole programme (WFD) was put in place for 18 to 25 year olds who had been unemployed for six months or more.

Further labour market deregulation was underway with the increasing free market reforms and 'hard line' policies of the coalition government (Lansbury 2000). This reform culminated in the *Workplace Relations Amendment (Work Choices) Act 2005*. Amendments included removing the unfair dismissal laws for smaller companies, and extending individual workplace agreements. This was followed by a Welfare to Work policy in 2006 that introduced strict part-time work and mutual obligation requirements for single parents, limiting access to parenting payments.

Keeping the country working – spatial solutions to social problems

As with the Keynesian approach to welfare previously, the neoliberal policy rhetoric failed to provide a long-term sustainable solution to welfare provision. In the absence of any viable alternative, the neoliberal policy agenda continued while policymakers sought new directions or the third way. Dialogue shifted from social security to social inclusion, however for many welfare recipients this 'inclusion' equated to an obligation to participate in the labour market however precarious that involvement was. Policy solutions took on an additional spatial focus in the attempt to address growing inequalities often clustered in communities of multiple disadvantage.

Country Australia has not traditionally been a major focus for federal government policy in the areas of welfare and employment. However, the allocation of public funds on geographic terms is fundamental to the nature of federation and lies at the heart of the Australian political structure (Fincher 2005). More recently there has been a growing recognition in the policy discourse of regional disparities in social and economic disadvantage and the acknowledgement of social exclusion occurring in some country communities. With the balance of power being held by regional interests, policies have stressed the increasing diversity of the Australian social and economic landscape in an attempt to address the uneven impact experienced as a result of the global financial crisis and devastating climatic events. In particular, recent employment initiatives set out to tackle the growing inequality in unemployment rates between regions.

Government welfare policy was embodied in Centrelink's 'Supporting Rural Australia 2009–11' strategy which aimed to enhance services to rural Australia through better understanding the needs of rural people and communities and better coordination of services. The policy set up Rural Support Network Coordinators, bringing together various community and social welfare services for individuals, families and communities within a region (Centrelink 2009).

Drought assistance programmes were also administered through Centrelink including the Climate Change Adjustment Programme 2008 that provided advice and training grants as well as transitional income support for primary producers likely to be affected by climate change, including drought. The adjustment programmes and re-establishment grants required farmers to sell their farms. Other measures to address the difficulties faced as a result of the recent drought were piloted in Western Australia. Linked to the Climate Change Adjustment Programme, the Transitional Farm Family Payment programme provided payments to low income farm families facing hardship. Again the objective was to assist families as they financially adapted to changing conditions.

Employment policy was embodied in the *Fair Work Act 2009* which replaced the *Workplace Relations Act*. The Act brought together a set of National Employment Standards (NES) and modern awards to establish a set of minimum employment conditions and minimum wage orders, creating a 'safety net' for employees. In 2009 Job Services Australia (JSA) replaced Job Network and six other employment services as the Government's chief mechanism to provide services and support for job seekers, with objectives of establishing sustainable employment outcomes. Other mechanisms included Disability Employment Services and an Indigenous Employment Programme.

The Keep Australia Working initiative sought to maintain employment in the wake of the global financial crisis and ensure that the Government's economic stimulus packages generated employment related outcomes. The focus was on localities hardest hit by the downturn of 2008–2009, as the rise in unemployment had hit hard in some communities across Australia. A set of Priority Employment Areas were determined according to the likelihood of labour market disadvantage. Keep Australia Working forums were held with key local stakeholders 'to discuss and develop on-the-ground solutions to local employment issues' (Department of Education Employment and Workplace Relations 2009: 15). Local Employment Coordinators (LECs) were appointed in 20 priority employment areas to develop regional employment plans and generate local employment and training projects (Department of Education Employment and Workplace Relations 2011b). In addition to these programmes, the Jobs Fund created jobs for youth, retrenched workers and local communities. Programmes included Local Jobs, Get Communities Working, and Infrastructure Employment Projects.

Local Connections to Work (LCTW) was another place-based employment programme for disadvantaged locations. This programme aimed to remove barriers to social exclusion, assist in participation, reduce long-term unemployment particularly among youth in disadvantaged areas and improve local service delivery through community partners in these areas (Department of Education Employment and Workplace Relations 2011b). In order to provide sufficient workers for major projects within the resource sector a National Resource Sector Workforce Strategy and Taskforce was set up by the Government. A single project alone was expected to generate 10,000 jobs, and it was expected that up to 70,000 skilled resource related workers would be required nationally (Department of Education Employment and Workplace Relations 2011a).

National Green Jobs Corps, a 26-week environmental training programme for young people to work on projects within local communities, offered a combination of work experience and training. Another environmentally based scheme was the 2008 Working on Country programme, set up to address Indigenous unemployment. The programme provided wage subsidies for the employment of Indigenous rangers in environmental protection projects and built on traditional knowledge (Department of Sustainability 2008). Other more general programmes aimed at increasing participation among specific disadvantaged groups, such as older workers being targeted with an 'experience +' programme.

While some regional areas experienced high unemployment, others faced labour shortages. Several migrant schemes were put in place to address this. The Pacific Seasonal Worker Pilot Scheme enabled horticultural businesses to employ Pacific seasonal workers for up to six months to meet seasonal harvest needs in the absence of local workers. Participating countries included Kiribati, Papua New Guinea, Tonga and Vanuatu. Workers were employed under the same pay and conditions as local workers.

The Regional Education, Skills and Jobs programme funded 34 coordinators to work with Regional Development Australia committees and local stakeholders in 46 Regional Development Australia areas throughout non-metropolitan Australia (Department of Education Employment and Workplace Relations 2012c). This initiative sought to improve employment, education and training participation in regional localities. Four key areas of focus were largely education and training based and provided a framework for specific regional and community level strategies including early childhood education, school education, tertiary education and training and workforce development, jobs and skills (Department of Education Employment and Workplace Relations 2012c). These programmes demonstrated a further shift in policy emphasis to include workforce development in addition to unemployment, job creation and training. At the same time, large-scale resource sector construction projects demanded ongoing security of labour supply that was not readily available in areas that had experienced long-term declines in the population and skilled labour force.

More recently, Commonwealth policies addressing Indigenous rural and remote employment and training have replaced the Community Development Employment Projects Scheme (CDEP). These include the Remote Jobs and Communities Programme (RJCP) established to increase Indigenous and remote community job participation and skill development. This aimed to facilitate a variety of employment and training related activities in remote communities including employment participation and engagement, case management and job placement, training and mentoring (Department of Education Employment and Workplace Relations 2012a). Addressing issues and barriers relating specifically to young people's employment and training in remote communities, policies also targeted youth leadership and development (Department of Education Employment and Workplace Relations 2012b).

While the above policies sought to address some of the spatial disadvantages faced in regional communities, others did not and in effect may have further increased social inequality. Recent changes to parenting payment entitlements and the application of workfare concepts and obligations to single parents while cutting back financial assistance appear to pay no heed to differences in local and regional labour markets across Australia. Nor do they appear to take account of factors impacting on employment for women and in particular women with children in such communities. Although the overall Australian unemployment rate may be relatively low and women's employment participation historically high, women are more prone to precarious work and disrupted employment. Women are more likely to experience employment transitions that result in exclusion from the labour market. Issues of adequate childcare provision in rural areas are complex and have far reaching and potentially dangerous consequences (Kingwill and Dalton 2005).

Policy consequences for rural and regional communities

From their inception, it was apparent that Commonwealth employment and welfare policies were never developed with country matters in mind. However, even the most forward thinking politicians and policymakers of the time would have had difficulty imagining the magnitude of change that would take place within rural and regional communities and the impact that this would have on rural livelihoods. Since World War II, employment and welfare policies have had, and continue to have significant consequences for rural people and their communities. While the impetus for much of the change that has taken place may have resulted largely from external factors, Commonwealth policies have influenced the evolution of social and economic issues that now exist within this sphere.

Saunders (2004) asserts that although welfare policies can and do lead to actions which may undermine their success, little research has been undertaken on the effects of this in Australia. The impact of various welfare and employment policies can have very different consequences in different rural, regional and urban communities and families throughout Australia. However, it is difficult to isolate such changes from the many factors that have shaped social transformation including global political, economic and technological developments affecting agriculture and rural life. Structural changes within the agricultural industry since the 1970s have contributed to the long-term decline of farming as a way of life and an associated demise of the agricultural labour force in Australia. This in turn has resulted in significant population changes (see Gross, this volume). Between 1970 and 2008–2009 the number of agricultural establishments declined by 28 per cent while the number of people employed in agriculture dropped by almost 18 per cent (ABARES 2010). This decline is all the more significant when taken within the context of the Australian population as a whole, which increased by more than 67 per cent during this period. However, the failure to provide adequate policy measures for sustainable rural livelihoods from the inception of Australian federal welfare programmes has contributed to an industry that was highly vulnerable to competitive forces and external conditions.

Even in the early days of the restructuring schemes it was apparent that such measures were not successful in preventing farm poverty (ABARE 1975). However, these schemes were continued for more than 20 years after this. The heavy reliance on subsides in turn created an industry that was locked in to a cycle of dependency and therefore disempowered (Herbert-Cheshire 2000: 211). This cycle of welfare dependency is somewhat contradictory with the neoliberal rhetoric of the farm as a commercial entity and the farmer as business manager (Gray and Lawrence 2001). The rise in farm poverty has also meant an increasing requirement for off-farm labour to supplement the farm incomes. Gray and Lawrence (2001) maintain that in the 1990s 30 per cent of broadacre farm family incomes in Australia were derived from off-farm income sources, and a third of operators' spouses derived income from off the farm.

The significant decline in the farm labour force over the period from the 1970s has created an industry that is nearing crisis point, with an ageing workforce and very little if any succession planning taking place, and poor recruitment and retention of younger workers (Agrifood Skills Australia 2012). This brings into question not just the sustainability of the industry but also the future of the country's food security as well as export security. Anecdotal evidence is that many working in agriculture have moved to the mining industry due to the current boom. While this may be the case, evidence also suggests that large numbers have simply left the workforce while others moved to manufacturing and construction industries where jobs were available in local areas. These two industries are also characterised by instability, including the long-term decline of manufacturing and the fluctuations inherent in the construction industry with business cycles and changes in government infrastructure spending. Off-farm labour, where members of farming households are employed in enterprises other than the family farm, may also be highly susceptible to economic fluctuations with many regional towns now heavily reliant on retail and service industry employment.

Deregulation of the labour market and 'workfare' employment and welfare policies have vastly changed the workplace. While on one hand creating a so-called flexible labour market, deregulation has also resulted in a growing proportion of workers for whom work is precarious and fragmented (Watson *et al.* 2003). The growth in casual employment has been phenomenal and is often accompanied with cycling in and out of unemployment or in and out of the labour force. The mutual obligations and responsibility requirements embodied in workfare pave the way for other forms of employment disadvantage such as underemployment (both time related and skill related) as well as people who are marginally attached to the labour force or discouraged job seekers. Time related underemployment is where a person is working fewer hours than they would ideally like, whereas skill related underemployment is where people accept work at a skill level that is lower than preferable.

Since the 1970s changes in rural communities have been far reaching. The heavy reliance on the economy of the farming sector that has undergone extensive structural changes has meant that many rural communities are struggling to survive (Collits 2000). The withdrawal of many government services and agencies in an efficiency drive has coincided with the centralisation and withdrawal of many businesses such as banks, telecommunications and professional organisations. But the sustainability of regional towns is more than just an economic issue. Incentives for people to leave the farming industry have long-term effects on community capability. For many areas the experience of population decline and associated demographic change, with young people leaving for education and employment and not returning, has meant that the responsibility for community development has fallen on the few older people remaining (Herbert-Cheshire 2000). Rural and regional towns have also been disadvantaged through the provision of welfare services being contracted out during the 1990s as part of the efficiency measures and the separation of service provision and funding.

While metropolitan areas had larger and more diverse voluntary and service sectors this was not the case in many rural and regional areas, where changes have left small communities with inadequate infrastructure and the people both isolated and alienated (Alston 2010).

Shaping the future

Welfare and employment policies for working aged Australians were founded upon the urban male breadwinner model. The central notion of these policies was full employment where all, that is working aged men, were willing and able to engage in the labour force. The labour market was perceived to have equilibrium between the number of unemployed people and the number of job vacancies at a broad national level. Neoliberal discourse holds that unemployment results from a mismatch in location or a mismatch in skills between available workers and available jobs. This mismatch is believed to be remedied by labour mobility, capital mobility or improvements in human capital through education and training. However, in policy terms the labour market is commonly seen as a transaction between workers and employers taking place within a context that is devoid of the spatial and generally lacking in human dimensions. Individual responsibility is strongly emphasised with welfare provision also taking contractual forms with mutual obligations, rights and responsibilities. Taking this neoliberal shift even further has been the separation of policy development from implementation. Programme implementation is undertaken through the provision of services to clients with service provision often contracted out to a variety of service providers.

Questions have been raised regarding the overreliance on business models for the delivery of social services. The contracting out of services and the increased focus on the achievement of agreed performance measures do not necessarily provide the best outcome for the 'client' or job seeker. Payments per job seeker placement for example, provide a strong commercial focus on quick job placements to achieve business targets which may or may not be in the best interests of job seekers looking for adequate stable employment. Such placements may also not be in the best interest of the employer. Recent reviews have suggested that there is little collaboration between contracted job service providers regarding vacancies, to the detriment of both the job seeker and employers (Department of Education Employment and Workplace Relations 2011b). The focus on long-term unemployment means that those who may benefit from immediate assistance with job searching may not be eligible for many programmes until they have 'failed', the effects of which have long-term consequences and 'scarring' for the unemployed person.

For nationwide policies to be effective in a diverse range of communities it is important that local conditions are allowed for. Spatially there is enormous variation in the workings of local labour markets, the structures and operations of industries, and individual businesses at a local level, as well as in the human and social capital of workers and the community support structures. A clear understanding of the nature of the spatial division of labour in rural and regional Australia is imperative. The major changes that have shaped country Australia have resulted in a vastly different labour geography from the 1940s – one that is both multidimensional and multi-scalar, simultaneously encompassing the local, regional, national and international. Global corporations work alongside family based businesses, and agriculture, mining and non-metropolitan based industries utilise the latest technological advances. This is no longer the 'bush' glorified in our folklore and policies based on an urban/regional divide will necessarily fall short. Stimson (2001) argues that socio-economic differentiation has resulted in a far more complex and spatially divergent Australia, including those that have adapted to the changing structure of the economic and employment environment and those that have not.

Within recent policy discourse there has been growing recognition that special consideration is needed in disadvantaged localities to ensure positive outcomes. Keep Australia Working and Local Connections to Work policies both provided for collaborative place-based processes to address the variable regional impact of joblessness. It is uncertain, however, how these alone can address issues relating to the size of local labour markets in many areas without significant investment in regional development strategies which look at long-term sustainability and community capacity building. Such solutions are of much broader scope than the responsibilities of those agencies currently involved, and would also benefit from transcendence of the traditional sector based boundaries that have characterised the sphere to date. Community-based plans developed under the Regional Education, Skills and Jobs initiative provide scope for greater stakeholder engagement and locally driven strategies for employment and training to potentially cross these boundaries and provide for more integrated programmes. How these plans translate into better welfare and employment outcomes for these communities will be heavily dependent upon the detailed implementation across a broad range of agencies largely within existing budgets. The integration of local, regional, state and Commonwealth policies and programmes and a greater understanding of the regional development needs, both economic and social, may go some way to improving rural and regional futures.

Much policy discourse surrounding unemployment in regional areas has been based on the notion of spatial mismatch in which unemployed job seekers will move to areas with lower unemployment to gain work, thus balancing employment. Adjustment policies and relocation allowances are more overt illustrations of this, but many barriers to labour mobility remain in place including state-based occupational licensing, education systems and an array of taxes and duties. Not all personal and household decisions are made on purely economic terms. For many farmers stewardship of the family farm for future generations is as emotional as it is economic. Botterill (2000) contends many families would choose poverty over losing the farm for future generations. Family ties and community connections which contribute to social embeddedness are not accounted for in policy, but rather would be considered as barriers to obtaining employment elsewhere. Other questions arise around the singular focus on labour force participation for all welfare categories below the retirement age. Social inclusion does not simply equate with labour force participation for all vulnerable groups.

Employment and welfare policy innovation in a rural setting must look beyond the context of wage labour for those gaining their livelihoods from the land. For many, the adequacy and security of an income above the poverty level is far more complex than working or not working, being employed or unemployed. Future welfare and employment strategies for rural and regional areas would benefit from a policy approach that reinvents the model that has existed for almost 70 years. This model was never designed for country needs and has evolved in a haphazard and piecemeal fashion to address changing social, economic and political needs that have been primarily urban. The way forward may not be an adaptation of person-based or place-based policies that depend upon an ethos of neoliberal self-reliance. For country Australia, a whole of government solution needs to take into account the social reality of today's rural living and the business of farming with all the complex risks that this entails.

References

ABARE, Australian Bureau of Agricultural Economics 1975, *The Rural Reconstruction Scheme: A Review of Progress 3rd Report*, Canberra. Available at: www.abare.gov.au/publications_html/economy/archive/rural_scheme.pdf. Accessed: 26 July 2011.

ABARES, Australian Bureau of Agricultural and Resource Economics and Sciences 2010, *Australian commodity statistics 2010*, Australian Government, Canberra. Available at: http://adl.brs.gov.au/data/warehouse/pe_abares99001762/ACS_2010.pdf. Accessed: 7 February 2012.

Agrifood Skills Australia 2012, *2012 Environmental Scan of the Agrifood Industry*, Australian Government, Canberra. Available at: http://c.ymcdn.com/sites/www.agrifoodskills.net.au/resource/resmgr/publications/agrifood_2012_environmental_.pdf. Accessed: 20 July 2011.

Alston, M 2010, 'Australia's rural welfare policy: overlooked and demoralised', *Research in Rural Sociology and Development*, vol. 15, pp. 199–217.

Beilharz, P 1989, 'The Labourist Tradition and the Reforming Imagination', in Kennedy, R (ed.), *Australian Welfare, Historical Sociology*, Macmillan, South Melbourne, Australia.

Boreham, P 2004, 'The labour market and the future of employment', in Hall, R, Boreham, P and Stokes, G (eds), *The Politics of Australian Society: Political Issues for the New Century*, Pearson Education Limited, Frenchs Forest, NSW.

Borland, J and Kennedy, S 1998, *Dimensions, Structure and History of Australian Unemployment*, HC Coombs Centre for Financial Studies, Kirribilli: Economic Group, Reserve Bank of Australia, and Centre for Economic Policy Research, Australian National University, Canberra.

Botterill, L 2000, *Rural Adjustment and Drought Policy in Australia*, Australian National University, Canberra. Available at: http://apsa2000.anu.edu.au/confpapers/botterill.rtf. Accessed: 29 July 2011.

Centrelink 2009, *Supporting Rural Australia 2009–11*, Australian Government, Canberra. Available at: www.centrelink.gov.au/internet/internet.nsf/filestores/se124_0910/$file/se124_0910en.pdf. Accessed: 7 February 2012.

Collits, P 2000, *Small Town Decline and Survival: Trends, Success Factors and Policy Issues*, The Regional Institute Ltd, La Trobe University, Bendigo. Available at: www.regional.org.au/au/countrytowns/global/collits.htm. Accessed: 7 February 2012.

Cook, B 2008, *National, regional and local employment policies in Australia*, University of Newcastle. Available at: http://e1.newcastle.edu.au/coffee/pubs/wp/2008/08–06.pdf. Accessed: 22 July 2011.

Department of Education Employment and Workplace Relations 2009, *Keep Australia Working*, Australian Government, Canberra. Available at: www.keepaustraliaworking.gov.au/documents/PDFs_RTFs/KAW_report%20_29%20Oct__final.pdf. Accessed: 8 August 2011.

Department of Education Employment and Workplace Relations 2011a, *National Resources Sector Workforce Strategy*, Australian Government, Canberra. Available at: www.deewr.gov.au/Skills/Programs/National/ResourcesWorkforce/Documents/AGAnnouncement.pdf. Accessed: 7 February 2012.

Department of Education Employment and Workplace Relations 2011b, *Taskforce on Strengthening Government Service Delivery for Job Seekers*, Australian Government, Canberra. Available at: www.deewr.gov.au/Employment/Documents/TaskforceReport.pdf. Accessed: 8 August 2011.

Department of Education Employment and Workplace Relations 2012a, *Funding Agreement 2013–2018, Remote Jobs and Communities Program; Remote Activity Conditions 1 – Remote Employment and Participation Activities*, Australian Government, Canberra. Available: www.deewr.gov.au/Employment/EmploymentServicesProcurement/Documents/RJCPFundingAgreement_RemoteActivityConditions1.pdf. Accessed: 5 November 2012.

Department of Education Employment and Workplace Relations 2012b, *Funding Agreement 2013–2018, Remote Jobs and Communities Program; Remote Activity Conditions 2 – Remote Youth Leadership and Development Corps*, Australian Government, Canberra. Available at: www.deewr.gov.au/Employment/EmploymentServicesProcurement/Documents/RJCPFundingAgreement_RemoteActivityConditions2.pdf. Accessed: 5 November 2012.

Department of Education Employment and Workplace Relations 2012c, 'Regional Education, Skills and Jobs', Australian Government. Available at: www.deewr.gov.au/Employment/Programs/RESJ/Pages/default.aspx. Accessed: 5 November 2012.

Department of Families, Housing, Community Services and Indigenous Affairs 2007, '1.2.3.80 Retirement Assistance for Farmers Scheme (RAFS) – Description', Australian Government, Canberra. Available at: www.fahcsia.gov.au/guides_acts/ssg/ssguide-1/ssguide-1.2/ssguide-1.2.3/ssguide-1.2.3.80.html. Accessed: 26 July 2011.

Department of Sustainability, Environment, Water, Population and Communities 2008, *Working on Country, Fact Sheet 3*, Australian Government. Available at: www.environment.gov.au/indigenous/publications/pubs/workingoncountry.pdf. Accessed 7 February 2012.

Dickey, B 1987, *No Charity There, A Short History of Social Welfare in Australia*, Allen & Unwin, Sydney, Australia.

Fincher, R 2005, 'Spatial Difference and Public Policy', in Walter, J and Saunders, P (eds), *Ideas and Influence, Social Science and Public Policy in Australia*, University of New South Wales Press, Sydney.

Gray, I and Lawrence, G 2001, *A Future for Regional Australia, Escaping Global Misfortune*, Cambridge University Press, Cambridge.

Harris, P 2001, 'From relief to mutual obligation: welfare rationalities and unemployment in 20th-century Australia', *Journal of Sociology*, vol. 37, no. 1, pp. 5–26.

Herbert-Cheshire, L 2000, 'Contemporary strategies for rural community development in Australia: a governmentality perspective', *Journal of Rural Studies*, vol. 16, no. 2, pp. 203–215.

Junankar, PN (Raja) 2000, 'An Evaluation of the Howard-Reith Labour Market Reforms', *The Drawing Board: An Australian Review of Public Affairs*, vol. 1, no. 1, pp. 15–27.

Kewley, TH 1980, *Australian Social Security Today*, Sydney University Press, Sydney.

Kingwill, S and Dalton, H 2005, *Current State of Play in Child Care for Australian Farming Families*, Australian Centre for Agricultural Health and Safety, University of Sydney for Farmsafe Australia Inc., Moree, NSW.

Lansbury, R 2000, 'Workplace Change and Employment Relations Reform in Australia: Prospects for a New Social Partnership?', *The Drawing Board: An Australian Review of Public Affairs*, vol. 1, no. 1, pp. 29–45.

Lawrence, G 1987, *Capitalism and the Countryside*, Pluto Press, Leichhardt.

Murphy, J 2011, *A decent provision: Australian welfare policy, 1870–1949*, Ashgate Publishing Limited, Farnham, Surrey.

Quiggin, J 1999, 'Globalisation, Neoliberalism and Inequality in Australia', *Economic and Labour Relations Review*, vol. 10, no. 2, pp. 240–259.

Saunders, P 2004, 'The welfare reform agenda', in Hall, R, Boreham, P and Stokes, G (eds), *The Politics of Australian Society: Political Issues for the New Century*, Pearson Education Limited, Frenchs Forest, NSW.

Saunders, P and Deeming, C 2011, 'The Impact of the Crisis on Australian Social Security Policy in Historical Perspective', *Social Policy & Administration*, vol. 45, no. 4, pp. 371–388.

Shaver, S 1987, 'Design for a welfare state: The joint parliamentary committee on social security', *Historical Studies*, vol. 22, no. 88, pp. 411–431.

Stimson, R 2001, 'Dividing Societies: The Socio-Political Spatial Implications of Restructuring in Australia', *Australian Geographical Studies*, vol. 39, no. 2, pp. 198–216.

Watson, I, Buchanan, J, Campbell, I and Briggs, C 2003, *Fragmented Futures, New Challenges in Working Life*, The Federation Press, Sydney.

Watts, R 1987, *The Foundations of the National Welfare State*, Allen & Unwin, Sydney.

Wheelwright, T 1989, 'World Economic Crises and the Welfare State in Australia', in Kennedy, R (ed.), *Australian Welfare, Historical Sociology*, Macmillan, South Melbourne, Australia.

10 Youth policy in Australia since World War II

The more things change

Seán MacDermott and Susan Taylor

> What can we take on trust in this uncertain life? Happiness, greatness, pride – nothing is secure, nothing keeps.
>
> Euripides, *Hecuba*

Introduction

Youth as a demographic or market segment originated in Australia in the boom-times of the 1950s and 1960s. However it was not until the early 1980s that youth were identified as a group for whom formal government policy was to be developed. In an environment where youth unemployment was high and school retention and university attendance were low (Smart *et al.* 1986) the first Hawke ministry established a department to tackle youth affairs as well as education. In the 1960s, government investment in education – especially secondary and tertiary education – gathered momentum and successive governments since then have continued to view education as crucial to the nation's economic success and prosperity. The majority of Australia's higher education institutions have been established from the 1960s onwards and a university education has become commonplace.

In the 1970s and 1980s government economic policy turned away from the Keynesian principles of state intervention that had dominated Australian politics from World War II. During this period, in the 1980s, rural and regional Australia suffered possibly the most severe drought of the twentieth century (Australian Bureau of Meteorology 2004). Public services were withdrawn from country towns, 'country-mindedness' (Aitkin 1985, cited in Davison 2005) lost traction as a nationally-subscribed philosophy validating the special status of rural life (Brett 2011), and rural towns started to die.

As in every civilisation, every country, every life, time changes all things. This might seem like a platitude but nevertheless change is the underlying theme of this chapter, because a fundamental question facing rural and regional Australia is how to deal with the changes that have occurred in the last 30-odd years. Are they changes that can be reversed to restore the previous state of play or, as change involves a process of becoming something different, is it having the patience, fortitude and foresight to become 'the something different' that should be the present challenge for rural and regional Australia? Is it time for the culture of 'country' to be renegotiated?

Given that formal approaches to youth policy are relatively new, being a little over one generation old, identifying rural youth as a separate group from youth in general has not yet occurred in statements of government policy. To understand issues around rural youth and youth policy in regional Australia it is helpful to view them through the context of the history of rural and regional Australia and the times in which these issues have arisen. Such an approach involves consideration of events that have occurred and changes that have happened historically in the rural and regional environment in which young people live their lives. Since World War II many changes have occurred with regard to the experiences, expectations and opportunities available to youth, and during this time there have also been significant changes to the rural and regional experience and the 'country's' contribution to the nation. In fact it seems that the development of a youth culture has paralleled the demise of the 'country'. As well as change that occurs in communities and cultures due to political, social and other events, young people are by nature in a state of flux. Young people (15–24 year olds) are in various stages of development and are dealing with other personal and individual issues of change. This time presents a series of important crossroads for young people who have to make decisions about education options, choices for work and careers, navigating relationships and progressing through rites-of-passage, or, alternatively, not making active choices about any of these weighty issues.

For societies and governments there are some fundamental issues that never really go away. In Australia, as will be described, colonial administrations and governments after federation have sought to manage underprivileged, uncared-for and neglected youth. Whatever motivated these administrations and governments to intervene, and however well or poorly the interventions were executed, the fact remains that *problem youth* or *youth with problems* have been a constant element of the social fabric of Australia since white settlement. Furthermore, young people from the bush have always been confronted with opportunities and temptations offered by the cities and, like moths to flame, have been drawn to the apparent glow of city life.

Within the overarching theme of change and flux this paper considers five propositions. The first proposition is that youth policy to date has not differentiated between rural and regional and metropolitan and city-urban youth.[1] The second proposition is that, historically, education in one form or another has predominated policy affecting youth and continues to do so – the paradox for rural and regional areas at the moment is that these places need better educated young people, but better education often leads to the development of aspirations that rural and regional areas cannot satisfy. The third proposition is that although there is currently a concern amongst rural and regional communities about the exodus of their young people, this is not a new phenomenon. The fourth proposition is that concern for young people in regional and rural areas is maybe being confused with concern for preserving a way of life. The fifth proposition is that the current federal government youth strategy is consistent with a model of localism but that localism may require the existence of particular qualities of relationships that are no longer prevalent.

Government approaches to youth policy: youth is youth

It has been claimed that it was in the 1980s under the Hawke Labor government that youth were first explicitly identified as a client group, although policies affecting youth in Australia had been implemented from the early days of white settlement (Pyvis 2006). Pyvis (2006) contends that policies such as those introduced in Australia have been directed toward national interest (youth as a resource for the state) and addressed youth as a problem that had to be corrected (miscreants, delinquents, larrikins, bodgies and dole bludgers). Thus, throughout Australia's white settlement history government intervention has been directed towards turning troubled youth into *useful citizens*, with usefulness determined by the transition to either an economic contributor or a contributor to national security.

Although the policy area of youth has only recently been added to government's portfolio, the history of the education and training of young people to create useful citizens is a long one. Pyvis traces this history right back to the juvenile ships that were introduced in the 1830s to separately transport young convicts to Australia:

> On board their ships the 'juveniles' were taught moral and religious laws, and also received instruction in reading and writing. The teachings were fairly rudimentary but the schooling was purposeful.
>
> (Pyvis 2006, p. 36)

Prior to this, in the early 1800s, there was the 'policing' of the rising generation (also known as the Currency lads and lasses who were the white, native-born youth) whereby children were sometimes removed from their parents and placed in Orphan and Industrial schools (Burns and Goodnow 1979, cited in Pyvis 2006; King 1800, cited in Macnab and Ward 1962). Throughout the nineteenth century, successive administrations in Australia attempted to provide moral and practical skills education to children. Originating from the 1850s gold rushes when the numbers of destitute young people swelled, training ships, industrial schools and reformatories were established. The public school system of state schools was only fully developed in the 1870s, prior to which time state aid was given to religious schools (Horne and Sherington 2010). In response to concerns about 'juvenile depravity' and larrikinism, between 1870 and 1895 elementary schooling became compulsory (Pyvis 2006).

During the first half of the twentieth century, government intervention into the development of young people continued with the military training scheme enacted in 1909 and made operative in 1911 (Pyvis, 2006). There was also an attempt to connect technical education with apprenticeship training in order to produce skilled labour in the manufacturing industry (Irving, Maunders and Sherington 1995). It was in the 1930s that adolescence was first recognised as a particular phase of growing-up by psychologists and educators. This was considered to be a 'problematic stage in life' that primarily affected males (Irving, Maunders and Sherington 1995, p. 10). Delinquency was an issue again in the 1940s, being attributed to 'lack of parental control, uncontrolled association with members of the allied armies (both boys and girls), insufficient opportunities for profitable spare time training, truancy and ineffective vocational guidance' (First Constable Loftus, cited in Irving, Maunders and Sherington 1995, p. 53).

Since World War II major policies implemented by government that have directly affected youth (especially male youth) include: the National Fitness movement (which originated in 1938 as the National Fitness scheme, in preparation for the War); Child Endowment in the 1940s; the provision in the 1950s of Commonwealth scholarships for university; the National Service scheme of the 1950s, and; selective conscription in the 1960s (Irving, Maunders and Sherington 1995). At the height of the 1974–1975 stagflation the rate of unemployed youth (15–19 years) reached almost 14 per cent and it was at the same time that the term 'dole bludger' entered the Australian vernacular (Archer 2009). As stereotypes emerged and some groups of young people who lacked the skills for work were characterised as 'dole bludgers', government turned to education to supply the solution (Pyvis 2006). In the 1980s retaining young people in education was the primary goal of government in policy regarding young people (Smart *et al.* 1986). The retention rate of students to Year 12 was low at just 36 per cent in 1983, but it was increased to 65 per cent by 1992 (Pyvis 2006). Retention of young people in education has continued to be a primary aim of government's policies targeting youth.

A review of government interventions on behalf of youth as outlined above suggests that the issues faced by administrators and governments of Australia in relation to youth have been issues of behaviour and non-behaviour: getting young people to behave in a way that is beneficial to the state. Inasmuch as this has been the goal, the distinction between rural and regional and metropolitan and city-urban has not been relevant. Nevertheless, the policies affecting young people have perhaps tended to be more oriented toward youth living in the cities because the reformatories and industrial schools were more likely to have been populated by children from the cities, as it was a problem of places where there was a concentration of population. Larrikinism was mob-style behaviour which, by definition, was predicated on congregation in groups and was more likely to occur in centres of population. Apprenticeship and training was a response to industrialisation, which was centred in the cities and manufacturing industries. The youth culture that sprang up in the 1950s and created the bodgie and widgie was suburban (Macintyre 2009). In 1975 there were 19 universities in Australia, 15 of which were located in the major cities (Australian Education Network). Furthermore the aim to have young people complete Year 12 or an equivalent qualification, which has occupied governments since the 1980s (Smart *et al.* 1986), does not differentiate between rural and regional young people and their metropolitan and city-urban counterparts: youth is youth.

Education policy as youth policy

In 2012 Australia's Attorney General Nicola Roxon said about education, '[I]t is actually key to unlocking all of our productivity for the future and we need to get it right' (*Q&A* 2012). Identifying young people as a national resource seems still to be a driver of policy, since the education of Australia's young people will be of economic benefit to Australia. Utility of a citizenry seems in a common-sense fashion to be a reasonable expectation of a community or a nation because it serves to create a robust, prosperous and healthy society. Also, from the individual's perspective, having an occupation contributes to well-being through having a purpose, status within society and the freedom through self-determination that an income affords. Roxon's statement implies that it was considerations for the economy that shaped education policy in 2012. This is the same 'economic imperative' that affected education policy after World War II (Roberts, this volume).

Since World War II commitment to formal education has predominated policies affecting youth, and successive federal governments have become increasingly interested in education. National investment in higher education reached a peak of 1.5 per cent of GDP in 1974–1975 at a time when the Commonwealth assumed full funding responsibility, and until the late 1980s 90 per cent of the funding continued to be provided by the Commonwealth (Marginson, 2001). In 1951 32,000 students were being educated in tertiary institutions compared with 850,000 in 2001 (Aitkin, 2005). Proportionate to Australia's population, which was about 8.5 million in 1951 and 19 million in 2001, the number of students in tertiary education had swollen. It is bewildering to think that 'most of the careers they [the 2001 cohort] were preparing for had not existed in 1951' (Aitkin 2005, p. 78). While there has been entrepreneurship and development in rural areas, the majority of these new careers and industries are urban rather than rural. This highlights a problem faced by rural and regional Australia: how to accommodate the career aspirations of young people with such diverse specialisations.

The growth in secondary schools was also a phenomenon of the second half of the twentieth century due to governments having more money to spend and the education of children becoming more important to families (Aitkin 2005). As high schools sprang up across Australia (Aitkin 2005) five government reports into Australian education were published between 1975 and 1987 (Wyn *et al.* 2001). Wyn *et al.* (2001) list these as: *Schools Commission Report (1975)*, *Poverty and Education in Australia (1976)*, *Report on Poverty in Education (1976)*, *Quality of Education in Australia (1985)* and *Schooling in Rural Australia (1987)*. These reports identified factors of rural disadvantage in relation to education, such as,

> early school leaving; the need for qualifications; low aspirations and expectations; lack of access to post-compulsory education, except for wealthy families who sent their children to private boarding schools in cities; reluctance of teachers to teach in rural schools; and the lack of linkage of curriculum to local experience.
>
> (Wyn *et al.* 2001, p. 15)

Although the problems were acknowledged, opportunities to address the issues were limited as 'policies driven by concerns with efficiency and the need to reduce public spending result[ed] in the withdrawal of health, social welfare and educational services to rural communities across Australia' (Wyn *et al.* 2001, p. 21).

In 1983 the Hawke government had made improving school retention and completion rates, through the Participation and Equity Programme (PEP) 'the centrepiece of the overall framework of youth policies' (Ryan 1983, cited in Smart *et al.* 1986). Governments' enthusiasm for increasing the participation of young people in secondary education continues, such that the aim of the Council of Australian Governments is to lift the Year 12 or equivalent or Certificate III attainment rate for 20–24 year olds to 90 per cent by 2020 (Council of Australian Governments 2012).[2]

While the aspirations regarding school attainment apply nationally, there are differences in the proportions of young people in major cities and those in rural and regional areas attaining Year 12. The Australian Bureau of Statistics (2011) report into Year 12 attainment relates that in 2010 a greater percentage (81 per cent) of 20–24 year olds living in the major cities had attained a senior secondary certificate of education in comparison with those living in inner or outer regional areas (67 per cent) or remote and very remote areas (64 per cent). It is not made clear in the report whether 'living in the major cities' encompasses 20–24 year olds living in a major city at the time the data were collected but who did not grow up or did not complete their schooling there. Therefore the statistic might under-represent young people *from* rural and regional areas attaining Year 12 because those who do may afterwards move to the cities, especially if they are pursuing university education.

Rural and regional areas need intellectual capital but in order to build intellectual capital young people need to pursue further education, which for rural and regional youth probably necessitates leaving the place they call home. There are options for studying off-campus in many fields of study, but if presented with the opportunity most young people choose to relocate for tertiary education (McKenzie 2009). Having left home and having gained higher order skills and an expanded view of the world, young people have more choices for a life trajectory. Therefore there is a conflict of interest here: rural and regional areas have to let their young people go in order for them to gain the skills that rural and regional Australia need, but it is at the risk that they won't come back.

Youth exodus: not a new phenomenon

There is a paradox about Australian history. The national memory seems to remember its rural past in idyllic terms: the story of prosperity, the creation of a wealthy nation through wool, and the pioneer spirit. What we don't remember so readily is the sheer hardship of life on the land, the failed attempts at closer settlement because the land was not productive enough, of succeeding generations of women right up until the mid-twentieth century or even later who found themselves isolated and alone on the family farm. The general ongoing pattern of decline since the late nineteenth century has been largely neglected in the telling of Australia's rural and regional history (Davison and Brodie 2005). Nostalgia for country life and the bush means that we prefer to remember the wealth that was created from colonial sheep rather than that early pastoral life (experienced by both the squatters and the shepherds they employed) was rife with disease, pests, malnutrition, loneliness, filth and squalor, and little material comfort (Pickard 2008). So difficult was life in the bush that some squatters preferred to live a civilized 'town' life and spent more time in the city than on their stations (Dingle 1984). Children under ten tended sheep and 16-year-old girls were shepherding in Western Australia in the 1860s (Pickard 2008). Although fortunes were made, what also tends to be forgotten is that as well as the making of fortunes, there was the breaking of fortunes or the breaking of dreams as one 'crash' followed another and boom-times have really only been intermittent (Dingle 1984; De Garis 1974). In this context it is little wonder that the children of those who lived the hard life on the land were attracted to the prospect of city life. The young have always been leaving rural Australia – it is not a new phenomenon:

> But while experts thought that country life was superior to city life, a growing number of country boys and girls evidently disbelieved them, and were heading in their thousands down the railway to Sydney and Melbourne. In 1914 the Victorian parliament established an official inquiry into what it called, ominously, 'the drift of population to the city'.
>
> (Davison 2005, para. 9)

Nevertheless retention of young people is an important issue for rural and regional communities. In the years between 1996 and 2001, rural and regional areas within Australia lost 85,871 young people aged 15 to 24 years who moved to capital cities (ABS 2003, cited in Gibson and Argent 2008). Gibson and Argent (2008) urge:

> We can only assume that the movement of young people out of virtually all non-metropolitan settlement zones (whether coastal, dry, remote or inland) signifies a central, if not *the* central, issue of contemporary research concern regarding young people in rural areas.
>
> (Gibson and Argent 2008, p. 135)

Outmigration of young people is such a significant issue that in 2006 there was a Victorian State parliamentary inquiry into the retention of young people in rural and regional areas (Gibson and Argent 2008). Rural leaders believed that presenting media images of outmigration as a negative aspect of rural and regional life 'only hastened the impulse of young people to leave' (Gibson and Argent 2008, p. 136).

In the nineteenth century it was the locomotive that provided the impetus for life in rural and regional Australia to be potentially more agreeable – it offered fast and easy access to the cities – whilst simultaneously provoking some inhabitants of the country to become unsatisfied with such a life, for the railway brought with it travellers who spoke of 'city fashions in dress, food, health, art and public opinion, creating a taste for urban ways of life' (Davison 1987, cited in Davison 2005). Perhaps the 'locomotive' of the twenty-first century is new technology; broadband, the internet and social media, available constantly and instantly on phones, tablets and 'ultrabooks', have expanded the world in which we live without the need for travel. Such technology offers opportunities to study at a distance from the institution that will confer our qualification, to purchase goods from anywhere in the world, to start a global business in a garage, as well as experience a diversity of events that would otherwise be inaccessible. The potential is that living rurally and regionally will not seem so isolated and any sense of deficit will be mitigated by our ability to 'connect' to others, pursue special interests and participate in careers or businesses all online. However, just as with the arrival of the locomotive, the other aspect of this phenomenon may be that with a new awareness of all of the possibilities available elsewhere, combined with the effect of the negative media images of hardship in the country (Brown 2006, cited in Gibson and Argent 2006), there will be a greater dissatisfaction with a life lived remote from perceived opportunities and the nucleus of action in the cities.

Gabriel (2002), exploring the issue of the exodus of youth from regional areas (particularly from Tasmania), noted that the issue for communities was 'not just about how to keep youth at home but specifically how to keep the best and brightest at home' (Gabriel 2002, p. 211). In accordance with the later views of Pyvis (2006), Gabriel contends that the underlying motivator for youth policy is the betterment of the state – the state as client:

> Again, the 'best and brightest' narrative is articulated predominantly by politicians and technical experts who are interested foremost in the State, as opposed to the interests of a diverse youth population.
>
> (Gabriel 2002, p. 211)

Later Gabriel (2006) observed that young people were caught in a paradox whereby their home communities wished for them to stay and contribute whilst at the same time there was a push for them to become better educated, requiring them to move away. Furthermore, the current marketplace for jobs and careers requires that young people be mobile and improve their qualifications with the attendant risk that having had a taste of university life, lived in a city, or had the opportunity to travel their expectations and aspirations will change and they will be 'lost' to the country (Gabriel 2006). The conflict confronting rural and regional communities is that the health and viability of such communities is dependent on maintaining an adequate population of young people to sustain the community. Such a community-driven requirement may not be in the individual young people's best interests. Put another way, communities need young people who are educated to participate in the local workforce and young people need to have the opportunity to pursue their dreams.

In the Australia of today, the departure of young people from rural and regional areas is in part due to young people viewing leaving home or the hometown as a rite-of-passage (Drozdzewski 2008; McKenzie 2009). Drozdzewski's (2007) study of youth outmigration intentions in coastal New South Wales found that young people outmigrate to larger centres for a number of reasons. Higher education and employment opportunities featured as reasons why young people wanted to leave even though there was a university presence in the town. Furthermore, the prospect of additional educational facilities in the area did not affect their intentions to leave. It was also found that having a sibling who had left (had paved the way) increased the likelihood of a young person intending to leave. McKenzie (2009) found that the idea of city life was a factor that motivated young people to attend university in a city, and that decisions to stay were dependent on how established their lives became in the new place of residence. Nevertheless the thought of moving back to the country to raise a family was appealing – a potential 'pull' factor for return-migration in the future.

Traditionally the term 'push-pull' refers to factors that 'push' one in a certain direction (such as the need to pursue an education) and those that 'pull' one in the same direction (such as the 'rite-of-passage' and the lure of the city). Pretty *et al.* (2006) posit another interpretation of 'push-pull' wherein the 'push' and 'pull' factors act in conflict. For example an individual might experience 'push' reasons for outmigrating such as employment opportunities and access to services but also 'pull' factors for staying such as community relationships and kinships. Pretty *et al.* (2006) conducted a study of young people in the Darling Downs region of Australia, which discovered that 'the larger the community (less structural disadvantage), or the higher the sense of belonging, sense of community, community support, and subjective quality of life, the greater the intention to stay' (Pretty *et al.* 2006, p. 235).

In contrast to studies investigating young people leaving rural and regional areas, some studies have investigated migration patterns of young people moving *to* rural and regional areas. Corcoran, Faggian and McCann (2010) used data (65,661 individual records) from the 2006 Australian Graduate Survey (2005 cohort of graduates) and applied the Australian Standard Geographical Classification Remoteness Areas to investigate spatial employment patterns of university graduates in non-urban locations. Looking at the location of the universities, the results showed that major cities retained the greatest percentage of graduates (86 per cent) and that 62 per cent of people graduating from inner regional areas relocated to major cities. Outer regional areas lost 39 per cent of graduates to major cities and 20 per cent to inner regional areas. However, Corcoran *et al.*'s (2010) study also found that in 2006 just over 1,000 graduates relocated to remote or very remote areas.[3]

Since 2008–2009 a number of incentive schemes have been implemented by various governments to encourage professionals such as doctors and nurses, teachers and lawyers to migrate to rural areas (Corcoran *et al.* 2010). These schemes have included attracting graduates by offering above average salaries and it was found that the schemes had an effect (Corcoran *et al.* 2010).

Other findings were that Australian-born graduates were more likely than foreigners to be willing to live outside major cities; younger graduates preferred the major cities; graduates in creative sectors and post-graduates were more likely to prefer an urban location upon graduation; and there was some evidence that job experience in the first year of studies reduced the chances of leaving the city (Corcoran *et al.* 2010). Self-employment, including freelancing, was found to be more prevalent in urban adjacent or core rural areas. The study did not investigate return migration or whether graduates remained in the communities to which they relocated for any length of time.

As noted by Corcoran *et al.* (2010) various governments have recently instituted incentive schemes that have met with some success in attracting recent graduates to move to remote and very remote places. The professions that were targeted by the schemes were service professions (especially allied health and education), which do not contribute to expanding a town's 'economic foundations' (Keneley 2005). Writing about the urban development of the Western District in Victoria between 1890 and 1930, Keneley (2005) demonstrates that historically the types of functions that a 'settlement' performed determine the potential for the settlements to survive. The functions can be categorised into basic and non-basic functions (Alexander 1959, cited in Keneley 2005). According to Keneley:

> [T]he basic functions are those which form the town's economic foundations – those relationships and activities which generate income for the town and provide impetus for growth and economic development. Non-basic activities are those that support the town itself. They are the service industries which develop as the town grows and improve the quality of life of the urban population. They are non-basic because they are not the primary function of the town or the purpose for which it was initially established. Whilst they are important to the residents of the town they do not provide the rationale for its existence.
>
> (Keneley 2005, para. 12)

Keneley's classification of the non-basic activities of the time include: professional, government, clergy, teachers, hotels/accommodation, personal service, commerce, contractors, transport and clerical. Consideration of the mix of basic and non-basic activities is as pertinent today as it was over 100 years ago. If a town is to prosper and grow, be sustainable and attract young people, then it needs to be more than a service centre for the surrounding region or the single major industry that is present. Today as in the past, rural and regional towns need industries which 'service markets beyond the boundaries of the immediate region' (Keneley 2005, para. 12). Promoting creative industries may be one way to expand the economic foundations of rural and regional areas (Gibson 2008) and 'ameliorate youth unemployment problems' (Gibson 2008, p. 187).

The professions that have been targeted by the recent graduate incentive schemes fall into the category of non-basic activities and it can thus be supposed that they will not diversify the function of the communities and will not therefore generate new prosperity.

Concerns for youth: or preserving a way of life?

The previous section of this paper considered the issue of youth outmigration as well as schemes to attract new young people to rural and regional areas. These may be construed as 'state issues' whereby it is the sustainability and well-being of the region (population demographics, economic vitality, etc.) that is of concern rather than the well-being of the individual (employment prospects, mental health, etc.). Young people who choose to stay in rural and regional areas are disadvantaged in comparison to those who move to the city in the spheres of education, employment (Kilpatrick and Abbott-Chapman 2002) and well-being (Baume and Clinton 1997; Dudley *et al.* 1997), but may be advantaged in terms of retaining links to their families and communities (Kilpatrick and Abbot-Chapman 2002).

Life in regional communities and on the land has been tough in recent years and while Australia's urban economies continue to advance, 'the regional experience is increasingly equated with high unemployment rates, low school retention rates, extensive contraction of services and amenities, high levels of farm debt, and rising suicide rates' (Gabriel 2002, p. 209). The suicide rate of young males in rural and regional areas has been especially concerning. Between 1964 and 1993 the rate of suicides of young males aged between 15 and 24 years increased four-fold in towns with populations between 4,000 and 25,000 and 12-fold in towns with populations of less than 4,000 (Baume and Clinton 1997; Dixon and Welch 2000; Dudley *et al.* 1997). In the literature both psychiatric and social correlates are given in explanation of completed suicides (Dudley *et al.* 1997) and suicide rates have also been correlated with unemployment rates (Morrell *et al.* 1993). For example, in Victoria's Swan Hill teenage rates of self-harm have been reported to be seven times the state average (*7.30 Victoria* 2012). Well-being of young people in rural and regional areas is therefore deserving of attention by policymakers.

One indicator of well-being is position in society or social status (ACT Government 2007; OECD 2011). With the rapid changes in the status of the country in Australia's history, it is possible that status may be a factor impacting on young people's satisfaction with life in rural and regional areas. In a report investigating the differences in health status of rural people in comparison with their metropolitan counterparts, Dixon and Welch (2000) reported:

> Social status is another psychosocial factor that is receiving epidemiological attention. In cross-national comparative work Wilkinson (cited in Dixon and Welch 1999) concluded that over a certain threshold, income levels are not related to health status in OECD countries. Instead, income as a proxy for social status is the important factor.
>
> (Dixon and Welch 2000, p. 258)

Up until World War II and even for a short time afterwards with the soldier settlement schemes, encouraging people to inhabit rural Australia was part of a nation-building strategy. A big Australia – Australia Unlimited – meant that inland Australia would be closely populated. The vision of a 'society of self-sufficient producers that would channel the energies of the people into productive contentment' (Macintyre 2009, p. 98) had persisted since at least the 1850s. This vision prevailed well into the twentieth century. The enormous cost of populating country Australia was overlooked and governments were prepared to subsidise programmes (settlement schemes, postal services, railways, etc.) in order to attract people to the country (Brett 2011). Although there were many attempts, the vision never became a reality and it took until the mid-twentieth century to finally accept that this was not feasible due to Australia's climate and resources – even science and technology were not going to combat the bush. Nevertheless there was one-more great era for agriculture between then and now. The outbreak of war in Korea in 1950 brought such a high demand for wool that its price increased seven-fold during 1951 (Macintyre 2009), but by the end of the 1960s, returns had declined although production had increased. Wool had sustained Australian growth and prosperity for a century (Macintyre 2009) but government belief in the country and commitment to its progress waned and the status that the country had long held as being intrinsic to Australia's prosperity waned with it. By 1971 the rural population was just 14 per cent of the national total at less than two million (Macintyre 2009). Brett (2011) observes that in the 1980s '[t]he contributions of country people to the nation were dismissed by policy makers as so much special pleading' (Brett 2011, p. 14).

Nevertheless, as recently as 2000 at the opening ceremony of the Olympic Games in Sydney, when all of the world's eyes were on Australia, we presented ourselves first as bushmen. On that stage the Olympic Games were heralded in by 120 riders in Driza-Bones and Akubras careering across the arena on galloping stockhorses to the stirring musical score of *Man from Snowy River*. It seems that in the new millennium the bush was still part of the Australian psyche, and in 2006, Australian Prime Minister, John Howard, confirmed it when announcing drought assistance funding for family farmers:

> It is part of the psyche of this country, it is part of the essence of Australia to have a rural community.... Not only would we lose massively from an economic point of view [but] we would lose something of our character. We would lose something of our identification as Australians if we ever allowed the number of farms in our nation to fall below a critical mass.
>
> (Peatling 2006, cited in Merlan and Raftery 2009, p. 1)

The implication for rural and regional areas of Australia that are dealing with issues of economic stagnation, ageing local populations and the outmigration of young people is that understanding the difference between rurality as a geographic location and rurality as an ideal (or idyll) may be imperative in order for them to imagine and progress toward a new future:

> As locality, rurality is a specific type of space that has a concrete geographical location where its character is objectified in the physical and social attributes of that location.... In the mode of social representation, rurality is a de-spatialised cultural concept that has a 'disembodied and virtual character' because it is not linked to a concrete geographical location.... Instead, it is a discourse about a type of space that is usually morally charged and about the kind of social life that occurs in it.
>
> (Gray 2009, p. 16)

In Australia the concept of rurality has been summed up in Aitkin's term 'country-mindedness' (Botterill 2009). This is a form of agrarianism that 'rests on the belief that agricultural pursuits are inherently worthwhile and wholesome' (Botterill 2009, p. 61). As Prime Minister Howard's remarks indicate, there seems to be some residual empathy for, and continuing identification with, the rural way of life. From a 'pragmatic' economic perspective agriculture's contribution to Australia's GDP has dropped significantly between the first and second half of the twentieth century and further again from the 1980s to the 2000s. In the first half of the twentieth century the contribution hovered between 20 per cent and 30 per cent of GDP and, after the Korean War peak in 1950–1951, it steadily declined to between 4 per cent and 5 per cent of GDP from the 1980s onwards, reaching a low of 2.9 per cent in 2002–2003 (ABS 2005). As contribution to GDP has declined over recent decades, the average age of farmers has risen such that farming has increasingly become 'an occupation for older men in four-wheel drives and air-conditioned tractors' (Davison and Brodie 2005, p. xi). The median age of farmers in 2010–2011 was 53 years (ABS 2012). Victorian wool-growers are a sector of the Australian agricultural industry that are declining in numbers as well as ageing (Wilkinson, Barr and Karunaratne 2002). Wilkinson *et al.* (2002) noted that young people were not entering the industry (including not taking over the family farm) in part because of modest returns from wool but mainly because of cultural forces: 'career and lifestyle opportunities in the city are much greater than on the farm' (Wilkinson *et al.* 2002, para. 2). Wilkinson *et al.* (2002) anticipated that a return to higher prices would not be enough to reverse the trend because it was not the short-term market fluctuations that were causing young people to turn their backs on the industry.

With the average age of farmers being 53 years this would mean that most were probably born in the late 1950s. The 1950s and 1960s were an agricultural boom, and consequently '[f]or farmers who grew up in this period, it took on the image of a "golden age" that came to represent the full flowering of the closer settlement ideology and the pioneer legend' (McCann 2005, para. 9). The 1950s and 1960s were boom times for all of Australia, metropolitan as well as rural. It was in the 1950s that the experience of urban-metropolitan life shifted from austerity to prosperity: dreams rolled off production lines in the form of Holden cars, washing machines and refrigerators. These were the times of urban development: the growth of the suburb, the family car and the commuter lifestyle. It was also a time when industrialisation rather than agriculture became the focus of Australian nation-building (Brett 2011). Youth came into their own, developing their own identity through consumerism: fashion, rock 'n' roll, cinema and comics. Youth were a new market and the teenager was a new demographic. The bodgies and widgies who embodied this new consumerism presented a threat to the status quo and there was a fear that these were the new young deviants requiring 'management' by government (Irving, Maunders and Sherington 1995; Pyvis 2006). This was a time when the surfer, 'cool, modern, uncommitted' (McGregor 1966, cited in Jaggard 1997), evolved as an Australian icon (Jaggard 1997), superseding previous incarnations of Australian youthful masculinity that included the 'rugged bushman, gold digger, warrior at Gallipoli' (Saunders 1998, p. 96) and surf lifesaver. Also, sports men and women were successfully representing Australia at elite level, especially at the Melbourne Olympics and in the Davis Cup (Macintyre 2009). Such pursuits were the new domain of youth (young, virile, athletic and active) and could be integrated with an urban-metropolitan lifestyle.

Whilst youth was undergoing a transformation so were the cities. Many young people may have suffered in dead-end jobs (Irving, Maunders and Sherington 1995) but they were compensated for by new entertainments: cinema, radio and music. In Melbourne the architectural landscape of the Central Business District changed with the removal of the decorative aspects of Victorian buildings, including verandahs and even whole buildings, which were replaced with high-rises and modern structures with curtain-walls. The social and cultural landscape of Melbourne also changed with the clearance of slums (School of Historical Studies 2008) and the arrival of European immigrants. The country's zeitgeist was middle-class and urban: the great aspiration of the time was to own a brick-veneer in one of the new suburbs. By 1961 in the cities home ownership had reached 70 per cent (Berry 1999). Previous to this period, owning a farm probably provided the best opportunity for an individual or family to be landowners.

Although the trajectory of wealth creation that began in the 1950s has not continued unabated, since there have been intermittent periods of economic downturn and high unemployment, upon reflection what that period seemed to have done is create a conceptual and relational rift between the country and the city. The city became established as the place of opportunity, independence and expressions of individuality, and with the development of new city-based industries it also no longer depended on the productivity of the country to create its jobs.

The point of raising these issues of country as a geographical location versus a social representation, agrarianism, the current state of agriculture's contribution to Gross Domestic Product, and of 'painting a picture' of how Australian culture has changed since World War II, is to posit considerations of how to progress rural communities in the future, and how to nurture the well-being of the young people living in them, in a broader context.

Localism and youth policy

The prevailing style of government from World War II until the late 1970s was interventionist – Keynesian. It was the time of post-war reconstruction and planning and no unemployment. Rural and regional Australians experienced old-style regionalism incorporating state intervention, regulation and welfare/safety net provision and protection (Swan 2009). For the Australian Government in the 1960s the perspective was 'that all social problems were inherently soluble' (Aitkin 2005, p. 52), but in the 1980s 'it was now asserted that governments could not solve some problems which were best left for the citizens themselves to grapple with' (Aitkin 2005, p. 52) and '[n]ation-building, once the almost explicit first priority of the national government, was now sidelined' (Aitkin 2005, p. 52).

According to Davison (2005) the Country Life ideal has disintegrated:

> [O]ver the last twenty-five years its slow decline has accelerated. Drought, declining export prices, and environmental degradation have compounded the historical difficulties of the inland towns, especially those in the old sheep-wheat belt. For more than a century, politicians believed that country life was a national good that should be supported by the taxpayer. Later they had believed that the state could promote and strengthen it. Since the 1970s, however, as the country's reliance on rural exports has lessened, and both the major parties have embraced neo-liberal doctrines of smaller government, the subsidies for rural communities have been quietly withdrawn.
>
> (Davison 2005, para. 32)

Since the 1980s rural Australia has also experienced the collapse of the Australian wool reserve price scheme (Bardsley 1994), the deregulation of the dairy industry (Edwards 2003) and changes in the financial facilities available to farmers (small businesses) as a result of the deregulation of the financial sector (Jones 2002), as well as several periods of severe drought. In this context governments place the onus of community development on the local community. Tonts and Haslam-MacKenzie (2005 p. 185) observed that 'new forms of intervention are emerging' that 'involve new forms of governance, centred around partnerships with communities, business groups and local government' and that this type of intervention transfers responsibility 'downwards and sideways' but without financial resources or political power.

Localism is the catchword of the day, although the idea that local communities should take responsibility for themselves has been popular since the late 1970s (Swan 2009). As the Minister for Regional Australia from 2010 to 2013, Simon Crean advocated for regional communities to take responsibility for developing their sustainability, through diversifying their economies and using the structure of the Regional Development Australia committees to support this (Hogan *et al.*, this publication). Localism as an advocated approach is in accord with expectations of how government strategies, such as the National Strategy for Young Australians, would be implemented. The National Strategy for Young Australians launched in 2010 identifies eight priorities for 'supporting young people to succeed and build lives of their own choosing' (Australian Government 2010, p. 3). The priorities comprise health and well-being, education, support within families, participation in communities, skills for employment, safe online participation, early intervention and establishing legal consequences for behaviours that endanger others (Australian Goverment 2010, p. 3). Realisation of the aims of the youth strategy is dependent on partnerships between organisations and the community as well as other levels of government and non-government agencies working together. The strategy is a set of statements about 'what' the government seeks to achieve but not 'how' the outcomes will be delivered. The strategy seems to present a broad, overarching theme, but does not articulate specific problems confronting particular sectors of Australia, which implies that identifying those problems and solutions is a local responsibility. In contrast, in the area of education policy, the Federal Government is currently working toward a national curriculum thereby effectively standardising education across Australia. A criticism of uniformity of education provision was made over 20 years ago in relation to the structures then present in the education system (D'Cruz 1990, cited in Wyn *et al.* 2001). D'Cruz (1990 cited in Wyn *et al.* 2001) indicated that such uniformity was not appropriate to tackle the issues experienced by schools in rural (and perhaps regional) areas. This concern may be just as relevant today because although there may be a reason for communities to consider how they might manage education at the local level, it is conceivable that with the implementation of a national curriculum local communities will have less ability to respond to their unique circumstances than is currently the case.

Gibson and Argent (2008), citing Stockdale (2006), observe that 'the fashionable call for endogenous development or "locally-led" economic development as the panacea for rural demographic and economic decline is simply incompatible with overall population decline and youth net migration loss.' (p. 136). As the population in rural and regional areas ages and decreases in number, the result is often that there is no appropriate core community in place to instigate community initiated strategies. Furthermore the irony is that for localism to work even at the basic level of developing meaningful relationships, communities would need to draw on aspects of 'country' culture such as generosity, kindliness and community effort: aspects which have been devalued over the last 30 years. If localism is about individuals being active in their communities then a relevant question to ask is 'To what community do I belong?' Aitkin (2005) points out that in the 1950s Australian communities had a strong spatial definition but that by the end of the twentieth century that sense of the local had been changed by wealth and communications. Localism as envisaged by the then Minister for Regional Australia, Simon Crean (Crean 2011, cited in Hogan *et al.*, this publication) focuses on regional economic development. While a goal of economic progress is important, this in and of itself will not bind a community together even when such economic development is shared. Margaret Alston

(2004) considers the limitations of economic capital development in isolation of other investments in rural communities:

> If rural communities are to thrive economic capital development is but one ingredient. Equally important are human, institutional and social capital. Key stakeholders should abandon their reliance on a market led recovery and communities helping themselves and address the strategies needed for rural revitalisation. A message that community self-help is the key to a community's future is particularly simplistic as it cannot be effective without government and non-government support for rural community development. It ignores the real need for government and non-government investment in human, institutional and social capital in rural areas.
>
> (Alston 2004, p. 311)

Conclusion

This chapter began by asserting that an overarching theme for the chapter was one of change and flux as it related to young people and country Australia. Each section of the chapter has addressed a different proposition regarding government approaches to youth issues, rural youth issues and the rural context. Each time, the social and cultural changes that have occurred in rural and regional Australia and the broader Australian society have been referred to in an attempt to provide a richer context for considering those propositions.

The first proposition was that youth policy to date has not differentiated between rural and regional and metropolitan and city-urban youth. The section provided an overview of schemes and programmes affecting youth that administrations and governments of Australia have introduced since white-settlement and it was argued that these schemes originated to deal with problem youth and youth problems, and as such did not define youth by geographical location. It just happened that most schemes probably impacted on city rather than country youth because it was in the social and cultural sphere of the cities that the problems were concentrated.

The second proposition was that historically education in one form or another has predominated policies affecting youth and continues to do so. There is a common thread of education, whether moral, technical, school or university, as the means to change the lives of young people running throughout the history of government policies affecting the young. Education has been consistently seen as a means to apprehend delinquent behaviour and to make young people into *useful* citizens who contribute to the economic prosperity of Australia. Education is currently at the centre of youth policy, with governments aiming to continue to increase the Year 12 or equivalent attainment rates and to encourage young people to pursue post-compulsory education. This situation creates a paradox for rural and regional Australia because on the one hand rural and regional communities need and want their young people to be better educated, but on the other hand when young people move away after schooling, they usually don't return.

The third proposition was that although there is a concern amongst rural and regional communities about the exodus of their young people, this is not a new phenomenon. For as long as there has been a country Australia, young people have been leaving it, but that doesn't make the current exodus of young people from rural and regional Australia any easier to bear. Young people leave rural and regional Australia for a variety of reasons, including as a rite-of-passage and because of push-pull factors like seeking further education, employment and access to the social and cultural amenities of the city. In contrast, some young people, recent graduates, can be lured to rural and regional areas through government schemes, but in order to sustainably increase the population of young people in rural and regional areas these areas may need to diversify the industries present.

The fourth proposition was that concern for young people in regional and rural areas may be confused with concern for preserving a way of life. This section opened with a consideration of young people's mental health and well-being in rural and regional areas, noting that rates of suicide among young males are greater than in metropolitan areas. The notion of country as a geographical place or a social representation was discussed and the idea of agrarianism was examined. It was noted that these *ideas* about country need to be understood and debated if the future of rural and regional Australia is to be successfully cultivated.

The fifth proposition was that the current federal government youth strategy is consistent with a model of localism, but that localism may require the existence of particular qualities of relationships that are no longer prevalent. With the dwindling of country communities the community relationships that once existed have been whittled away, but localism seems to require that form of unity in order to function appropriately. Currently the National Strategy for Youth does not differentiate between spatial locations. This is where localism could have a role, whereby particular issues experienced in communities together with any unique opportunities that may exist, could lead to tailor-made solutions. Furthermore the sphere of education policy, which has underpinned almost all of Australia's policies regarding youth, is becoming possibly less open to adaptation, and therefore responsive to local situations, as the Federal Government moves toward a national curriculum.

Rural and regional Australia is faced with a conundrum: there is an expectation that young people growing up in these areas will have access to the same levels of education, services and employment opportunities as their metropolitan city-urban counterparts – which will probably change expectations of life after home – and there is also a desire that young people will continue living in the places where they were raised. As much as communities desire to retain their young people for the benefit of their communities, this should not be the motivation for educating them. Young people need to be equipped to make decisions about their life-trajectory and have the resources (especially resources such as fortitude and confidence) to act on those decisions. In this respect, young people in rural and regional areas may be treated no differently to young people from other parts of Australia.

This chapter opened with a quotation from Euripides noting the uncertainty of life and the constancy of change. Every account of the history of regional Australia focuses on adaptability and change – entire settlements have come and gone – some to reappear again in a different guise. Modes of transport and communication have changed dramatically and with that has come many attendant changes in the way we do business. Such changes in transport and communication with the rest of Australia (indeed the entire planet) have contributed to changes in aspirations. Young people growing up in rural and regional Australia are entitled to equity in terms of access to education, training, health services and employment opportunities. The difficulty for any administration is how to achieve this.

A 'one size fits' all approach does not equate to equity of service or opportunity and that is one of the conundrums facing any administration. While, on the face of it, such an approach might appear fair it does not recognise underlying differences. For example, setting national targets with respect to Year 12 attainment or university entry rates on the basis that further education is associated with increased well-being or prosperity will not, in itself, be beneficial to all communities or individuals. As this chapter has shown, one of the difficulties facing small communities is that the well-educated often leave not to return. At the same time, those who remain may benefit from increased access to training and development but their needs are often tightly tied to their immediate environment in terms of industry, values, family and community.

So the challenge for any administration is to strike a balance between supporting the aspirations of young people in regional Australia while, at the same time, allowing latitude in terms of the pathways that individuals and communities follow in pursuit of their goals. This is very much in accordance with the localism approach underlying the National Strategy for Young Australians described earlier. We recommend that the focus be on providing young people with the basic tools such as public transport and broadband to allow access to education and mental health services, while at the same time allowing communities more discretion in how services and programmes are tailored and deployed. The success or failure of such a localism model is dependent on partnerships between organisations and the community as well as other levels of government and non-government agencies. Such partnerships do not simply materialise – like young people they need to be conceived, developed, nurtured, allowed to make mistakes, and given the freedom to choose their own destiny.

Notes

1 There are six categories of remoteness defined by the ABS Remoteness Structure under the Australian Geography Standard (Australian Institute of Health and Welfare 2004). These are: Major Cities of Australia; Inner Regional Australia; Outer Regional Australia; Remote Australia; Very Remote Australia, and; Migratory. The existence of four regional and remote classifications amongst the six categories is indicative of the problems of discussing rural and regional issues as though rural and regional Australia was a homogenous entity, everywhere experiencing the same problems. For instance, in

NSW, Outer Regional Statistical Local Areas (SLAs) include (but are not limited to) places such as Coffs Harbour, Dubbo, Forbes and Glen Innes. Also in Victoria, Outer Regional SLAs include areas such as Ararat, Baw Baw and East Gippsland whilst Inner Regional SLAs include Ballarat, Bendigo, Warrnambool and Southern Grampians Shire – Hamilton. Southern Grampians Shire – Wannon, on the other hand, is classified as Outer Regional. Furthermore, areas within an SLA may be defined as being of mixed classification. For instance Moyne SLA in Victoria is divided into three areas and each area is partially Inner Regional and partially Outer Regional. In this respect the classification does not provide elucidation but becomes somewhat cumbersome. Therefore, for the purposes of this paper the Australian Statistical Geography Standard (ASGS) classification serves to provide a conceptual framework of rural and regional difference but, in discussing regional and rural issues, this paper does not rely solely on these categories. It is acknowledged that different places and communities will be experiencing unique issues, but in much of this paper 'country' is contrasted with 'city', construed variously as attitude, perspective, experience and geographical location. Where a specific definition of rural and regional is required it is provided.

2 The recognised international standard of equivalence of upper secondary education is Certificate III (ABS 2011).

3 The definition of rural and remote is based on the five Australian Standard Geographical Classification Remoteness Areas developed by the Australian Bureau of Statistics and is dependent on 'proximity to public services' (Pretty *et al.* 2006, p. 231).

References

7.30 Victoria 2012, television broadcast, Australian Broadcasting Corporation, 10 August.

ACT Government 2007, *Community well-being indicators. A discussion paper prepared for the ACT Community Indicators Board*, Social Policy and Implementation Branch, Policy Division, Chief Minister's Department. Available at: www.cmd.act.gov.au. Accessed: 2 September 2012.

Aitkin, D 2005, *What was it all for?: the reshaping of Australia*, Allen & Unwin, NSW.

Alston, M 2004, '"You don't want to be a check-out chick all your life": The outmigration of young people from Australia's small rural towns', *Australian Journal of Social Issues*, vol. 39, no. 3, pp. 299–313.

Archer, V 2009, 'Dole bludgers, tax payers and the New Right: Constructing discourses of welfare in 1970s Australia', *Labour History*, pp. 177–190.

Australian Bureau of Meteorology 2004, *Drought, dust and deluge: a century of climate extremes in Australia*, Commonwealth of Australia.

Australian Bureau of Statistics 2005, *Year Book Australia 2005*, Australian Bureau of Statistics. Available at: www.abs.gov.au/AUSSTATS/abs@.nsf/lookup/1301.0feature+article212005. Accessed: 2 September 2012.

Australian Bureau of Statistics 2011, *Australian Social Trends: Year 12 Attainment*, Australian Bureau of Statistics. Available at: www.abs.gov.au/AUSSTATS/abs@.nsf/DetailsPage/4102.0Mar%202011?OpenDocument. Accessed: 10 August 2012.

Australian Bureau of Statistics 2012, *Labour force and other characteristics of farmers*, Australian Bureau of Statistics. Available at: www.abs.gov.au/ausstats/abs@.nsf/Lookup/1301.0Main+Features3032012. Accessed: 22 July 2012.

Australian Education Network. Available at: www.australianuniversities.com.au/history-of-australian-universities.php. Accessed: 2 September 2012.

Australian Government 2010, *National strategy for young Australians*, Australian Government. Available at: www.youth.gov.au/ayf/media/Pages/NationalStrategyforYoung-Australians.aspx. Accessed: 9 August 2012.

Australian Institute of Health and Welfare 2004, Rural, regional and remote health: a guide to remoteness classifications, AIHW Cat. No. PHE, 53, Australian Institute of Health and Welfare, Canberra.

Bardsley, P 1994, 'The collapse of the Australian wool reserve price scheme', *The Economic Journal*, pp. 1087–1105.

Baume, P and Clinton, M 1997, 'Social and cultural patterns of suicide in young people in rural Australia', *Australian Journal of Rural Health*, vol. 5, no. 3, pp. 115–120.

Berry, M 1999, 'Unravelling the "Australian Housing Solution": The post-war years', *Housing, Theory and Society*, vol. 16, no. 3, pp. 106–123.

Bessant, J 2002, 'Risk and Nostalgia: The problem of education and youth unemployment in Australia – a case study', *Journal of Education and Work*, vol. 15, no. 1, pp. 31–51.

Bolton, G 1996, *The Oxford history of Australia. Vol. 5, 1942–1995*, 2nd edn, Oxford University Press Australia, Melbourne.

Botterill, L 2009. 'The role of agrarian sentiment in Australian rural policy', in Merlan, F and Raftery, D (eds), *Tracking Rural Change: Community, Policy and Technology in Australia, New Zealand and Europe*, ANU E Press, Canberra, pp. 59–78.

Brett, J 2011, 'Fair Share: Country and City in Australia', *Quarterly Essay*, no. 42, pp. 1–67.

Cheshire, L and Lawrence, G 2005, 'Neoliberalism, individualisation and community: Regional restructuring in Australia', *Social Identities*, vol. 11, no. 5, pp. 435–445.

Corcoran, J, Faggian, A and McCann, P 2010, 'Human capital in remote and rural Australia: the role of graduate migration', *Growth and Change*, vol. 41, no. 2, pp. 192–220.

Council of Australian Governments 2012, *Review of the National Education Agreement Performance Framework*. Available at: www.coag.gov.au/node/440. Accessed: 1 September 2012.

Day, D 1996, *Claiming a continent: a new history of Australia*, HarperCollins Publishers, Sydney.

Davison, G 2005, 'Country life: the rise and decline of an Australian ideal', in Davison, G and Brodie, M (eds), *Struggle Country: The Rural Ideal in Twentieth Century Australia*, Monash University ePress, Melbourne, pp. 01.1–01.15.

Davison, G and Brodie, M 2005, 'Introduction', in Davison, G and Brodie, M (eds), *Struggle Country: The Rural Ideal in Twentieth Century Australia*, Monash University ePress, Melbourne, pp. ix–xvi.

De Garis, B 1974, '1890–1900', in Crowley, F (ed.), *A New History of Australia*, Heinemann Educational Australia, Port Melbourne.

Dingle, T 1984, *Settling*, Fairfax, Syme & Weldon Associates, Melbourne.

Dixon, J and Welch, N 2000, 'Researching the rural-metropolitan health differential using the "social determinants of health" ', *Australian Journal of Rural Health*, vol. 8, no. 5, pp. 254–260.

Drozdzewski, D 2008, 'We're moving out: youth out-migration intentions in coastal nonmetropolitan New South Wales', *Geographical Research*, vol. 46, no. 2, pp. 153–161.

Dudley, M, Kelk, N, Florio, T, Howard, J, Waters, B, Haski, C and Alcock, M 1997, 'Suicide among young rural Australians 1964–1993: a comparison with metropolitan trends', *Social psychiatry and psychiatric epidemiology*, vol. 32, no. 5, pp. 251–260.

Edwards, G 2003, 'The story of deregulation in the dairy industry', *Australian Journal of Agricultural and Resource Economics*, vol. 47, no. 1, pp. 75–98.

Everingham, JA, Cheshire, L and Lawrence, G 2006, 'Regional renaissance? New forms of governance in nonmetropolitan Australia', *Environment and Planning C: Government & Policy*, vol. 24, no. 1, pp. 139–155.

Gabriel, M 2002, 'Australia's regional youth exodus', *Journal of Rural Studies*, vol. 18, no. 2, pp. 209–212.

Gabriel, M 2006, 'Youth migration and social advancement: How young people manage emerging differences between themselves and their hometown', *Journal of Youth Studies*, vol. 9, no. 1, pp. 33–46.

Gibson, C 2008, 'Youthful Creativity in Regional Australia: Panacea for Unemployment and Out-Migration?', *Geographical research*, vol. 46, no. 2, pp. 183–195.

Gibson, C and Argent, N 2008, 'Getting on, getting up and getting out? Broadening perspectives on rural youth migration', *Geographical Research*, vol. 46, no. 2, pp. 135–138.

Gray, J 2009, 'Rurality and rural space: the "policy effect" of the Common Agricultural Policy in the Borders of Scotland', in Merlan, F and Raftery, D (eds), *Tracking Rural Change: Community, Policy and Technology in Australia, New Zealand and Europe*, ANU E Press, pp. 15–40.

Herbert-Cheshire, L 2000, 'Contemporary strategies for rural community development in Australia: a governmentality perspective', *Journal of Rural Studies*, vol. 16, no. 2, pp. 203–215.

Hogan A, Cleary J, Lockie S, Young M, and Daniell K 2015, 'Localism and the policy goal of securing the socio-economic viability of rural and regional Australia', this volume.

Horne, J and Sherington, G 2010, 'Extending the educational franchise: the social contract of Australia's public universities, 1850–1890', *Paedagogica Historica*, vol. 46, no. 1–2, pp. 207–227.

Irving, T, Maunders, D and Sherington, G 1995, *Youth in Australia: policy, administration and politics*, Macmillan Education Australia Pty Ltd, South Melbourne.

Jaggard, E 1997, 'Chameleons in the surf', *Journal of Australian Studies*, vol. 21, no. 53, pp. 183–191.

Jones, E 2002, 'Rural Finance in Australia: A troubled history', *Rural Society*, vol. 12, no. 2, pp. 160–180.

Keneley, M 2005, 'The dying town syndrome: A survey of urban development in the Western District of Victoria, 1890–1930', in Davison, G and Brodie, M (eds), *Struggle Country: The Rural Ideal in Twentieth Century Australia*, Monash University ePress, Melbourne, pp. 10.1–10.16.

Kilpatrick, S and Abbott-Chapman, J 2002, 'Rural young people's work/study priorities and aspirations: The influence of family social capital', *The Australian Educational Researcher*, vol. 29, no. 1, pp. 43–67.

Lingard, B 1991, 'Policy-making for Australian schooling: the new corporate federalism', *Journal of Education Policy*, vol. 6, no. 1, pp. 85–90.

Macintyre, S 2009, *A concise history of Australia*, 3rd edn, Cambridge University Press, Melbourne.

Macnab, K and Ward, R 1962, 'The nature and nurture of the first generation of native-born Australians', *Australian Historical Studies*, vol. 10, no. 39, pp. 289–308.

Maude, A 2004, 'Regional development processes and policies in Australia: a review of research 1990–2002', *European Planning Studies*, vol. 12, no. 1, pp. 3–26.

Marginson, S 2001, 'Trends in the funding of Australian higher education', *Australian Economic Review*, vol. 34, no. 2, pp. 205–215.

McCann, J 2005, 'History and memory in Australia's wheatlands', in Davison, G and Brodie, M (eds), *Struggle Country: The Rural Ideal in Twentieth Century Australia*, Monash University ePress, Melbourne, pp. 03.1–03.17.

McKenzie, F 2009, *Regional youth migration and the influence of tertiary institutions*,

Department of Planning and Community Development. Available at: www.dpcd.vic.gov.au/home/publications-and-research/urban-and-regional-research/Regional-Victoria. Accessed: 2 September 2012.

McQueen, H 2004, *Social sketches of Australia 1888–2001*, 3rd edn, University of Queensland Press, St Lucia.

Merlan, F and Raftery, D 2009, 'The rural future in Australia and New Zealand: mapping the terrain of cultural change', in Merlan, F and Raftery, D (eds), *Tracking Rural Change: Community, Policy and Technology in Australia, New Zealand and Europe*, ANU E Press, pp. 1–14.

Morrell, S, Taylor, R, Quine, S and Kerr, C 1993, 'Suicide and unemployment in Australia 1907–1990', *Social science & medicine*, vol. 36, no. 6, pp. 749–756.

OECD 2011, *Compendium of OECD well-being indicators*. Available at: www.oecd.org/std/. Accessed: 2 September 2012.

Pickard J, 2008, 'Shepherding in colonial Australia', *Rural History*, vol. 19, no. 1, p. 55.

Pretty, G, Bramston, P, Patrick, J and Pannach, W 2006, 'The relevance of community sentiments to Australian rural youths' intention to stay in their home communities', *American Behavioral Scientist*, vol. 50, no. 2, pp. 226–240.

Pyvis, D 2006, *Government youth policy in Australia, 1788–2000: the control of military training, employment and socialization*, The Edwin Mellen Press Ltd, Wales.

Q&A 2012, television broadcast, Australian Broadcasting Corporation, 23 July.

Saunders, K 1998, '"Specimens of superb manhood": The lifesaver as national icon', *Journal of Australian studies*, vol. 22, no. 56, pp. 96–105.

School of Historical Studies 2008, *eMelbourne*, The University of Melbourne. Available at: www.emelbourne.net.au/home.html. Accessed: 31 May 2012.

Smart, D 1991, 'Higher education policy in Australia: corporate or coercive federalism?', *Journal of Education Policy*, vol. 6, no. 1, pp. 97–100.

Smart, D, Scott, R, Murphy, K and Dudley, J 1986, 'The Hawke government and education 1983–1985', *Politics*, vol. 21, no. 1, pp. 63–81.

Smith, R and Wearing, M 1987, 'Do Australians want the welfare state?', *Politics*, vol. 22, no. 2, pp. 55–65.

Swan, H 2009, The search for policy coherence: Australian regional governance in a Federal framework, 1996–2007. Unpublished doctoral thesis, University of Canberra, submitted to the Australian Government in response to the discussion paper *Our cities: building a productive, sustainable and liveable future.*

Tonts, M and Haslam-McKenzie, F 2005, 'Neoliberalism and changing regional policy in Australia', *International Planning Studies*, vol. 10, no. 3–4, pp. 183–200.

Waterhouse, R 2000, 'Australian Legends: Representations of the Bush, 1813–1913', *Australian Historical Studies*, vol. 31, no. 115, pp. 201–221.

Wilkinson, RL, Barr, N and Karunaratne, K 2002, '"The Kids Don't Want to Take Over the Farm": What's happening to the Demographics of Victoria's Wool Industry?', *Wool Technology and Sheep Breeding*, vol. 50, no. 3, pp. 295–301.

Williams, C 1983, 'The "Work Ethic", Non-Work and Leisure in an Age of Automation', *Journal of Sociology*, vol. 19, no. 2, p. 216.

Wyn, J, Semmens, B, Falk, I and Guenther, J 2001, 'Education for rural development in Australia 1945–2001', *Working Paper 22*, Youth Research Centre, University of Melbourne.

Wyn, PJ and Woodman, D 2006, 'Generation, youth and social change in Australia', *Journal of Youth Studies*, vol. 9, no. 5, pp. 495–514.

11 Rural policy

Shaping women's lives

Margaret Alston

Introduction

Since European settlement the lives of Australia's rural women and men have been shaped by a prevailing *gender order* (Connell 1987, 1997, 2009) that prescribes and defines socially desirable gender expectations. These gender relations are reinforced by policies that emerge from institutions that are themselves highly gendered, and supported by media. This process has resulted not only in the virtual absence of women from bush folklore and perceptions of national identity, but also in their tenuous access to power, ownership of land and resources, rural and agribusiness leadership positions and political influence. In this chapter I argue that rural women's invisibility and a dominant masculine hegemony is supported and enhanced by agricultural and rural policy. Policy is never innocent, and in Australia, through language, assumptions and traditions, rural and agricultural policies have fostered and supported a male normative position. Further I will argue that a lack of gender mainstreaming as a fundamental principle of policy formulation has not only facilitated and prioritised masculine power and control of resources – thereby shaping the ways women and men live their lives – it has also ignored and trivialised the contributions women make to their families, industries and communities. Indicating the level of their invisibility, as late as 1994 Australia's farm women were officially recorded as 'sleeping partner, non-productive' (ABS 2002). In more recent times, this has led rural women to adopt resistant actions to highlight their individual and collective positions.

Family farming is officially recognised as the dominant mode of agricultural production and in 2011 there were 93,300 Australian farm families (ABS 2012). Not surprisingly given recent climatic conditions and a harsh economic environment, there has been a significant decline in the number of families engaged in farming, with a drop of over 106,000 in the 30 years to 2011, equating to a loss of 294 every month for that period. While officially 72 per cent of Australia's farmers are male, this is an occupational, self-defined category in an industry that often requires family effort. It ignores farm partnership arrangements and women's various economic contributions. Nonetheless women reportedly make up 28 per cent of the farm workforce and over 35,000 women are known to work off the farm supporting the farm income – 57 per cent of these working 15 hours or more. This equates to at least one-third of family farms being dependent on women's income.

In this chapter I particularly discuss rural policy and the lack of gender mainstreaming, noting the ways policies have historically shaped and constrained rural women's lives and their relationship to land, industry and resource control. Further, I discuss how a primary focus on agricultural productivity and agricultural or *sectoral* issues overshadows a regional development or *territorial* approach (Shucksmith 2008) to rural policy. This reduces attention to education, health and service infrastructure, factors that would improve the lives and working opportunities of rural women and their children. Taking a historical perspective enables us to learn from the past, allowing an understanding of the way future rural policies might more effectively enhance and support gender equality. I argue that a radical change in policy assumptions, the introduction of gender mainstreaming and a territorial rather than sectoral approach is necessary if rural communities, and the women and men who live in them, are to survive and thrive.

Gender mainstreaming

Many countries, including Australia, endorse gender mainstreaming as a principle of policy development. The United Nations defines gender mainstreaming as:

> The process of assessing the implications for women and men of any planned action, including legislation, policies or programmes, in all areas and at all levels. It is a strategy for making women's as well as men's concerns and experiences an integral dimension of the design, implementation, monitoring and evaluation of policies and programmes in all political, economic and societal spheres so that women and men benefit equally and inequality is not perpetuated. The ultimate goal is to achieve gender equality.
>
> (ECOSOC 1997)

Essentially gender mainstreaming is designed to bring about gender equality, by exposing gender as a socially constructed phenomenon and making transparent new possibilities for reshaped, and more equitable gender arrangements. Successful gender mainstreaming requires gender-sensitive policies to emerge from all government departments, and not just from women's policy units. A global shift to gender mainstreaming principles in the late 1990s had one unfortunate result. This was that many national governments adopted gender mainstreaming rhetoric, subsequently cutting resources to women's policy units and downgrading women-focused infrastructure without creating compensatory gender mainstreaming processes and operations (Prugl 2009; Alston 2006). This is evident in Australia where the Office of the Status of Women, previously located in the Department of Prime Minister and Cabinet, experienced budget and staffing cuts under the Howard government in 1996, was renamed the Office for Women and moved to the Department of Family, Community Services, Housing and

Indigenous Affairs. In this department it was removed from central government and, by implication, assigned to address family and community matters rather than whole of government policy. No gender mainstreaming instrumentalities were established to compensate for its downsizing and removal from its central role in whole-of-government policy assessments. While the Abbott government has shifted the Office back to the Department of Prime Minister and Cabinet, it remains sidelined from mainstream policy deliberations.

In the 1990s Rural Women's Policy units were also established in the Federal Department of Agriculture, Forests and Fisheries and in the then Department of Regional Affairs, following years of activism and representations by committed rural women tired of being written out of history and their economic contributions being ignored. These policy units have since been gradually eroded, renamed and/or disbanded. State-based women's rural policy units and networks followed a similar path with the Victorian Rural Women's Network being the latest to 'restructure' in 2013.

Studies of these women's policy units in national and state government departments indicate that their work had become marginalised and co-opted to support the goals and power relations of organisations and dominant industry bodies. Evidence for this is found in my own research with heads of national and state rural women's units in Australia undertaken in the early 2000s before many were disbanded (Alston 2006). Women in these organisations noted that their work was trivialised, ignored, ghettoised and largely left outside core departmental business. Yet many bureaucrats in these departments argue that gender goals have been achieved, or that gender equality is no longer a 'problem'. Another Australian researcher Connell (2006, p. 444) reinforces this view noting that, 'across much of the public sector, gender is regarded as a non-problem'.

Thus while the women's units have been eroded or removed, gender mainstreaming has not been facilitated by alternative resourcing. Gender mainstreaming requires dedicated institutional infrastructure, a budget, support from Ministerial and Head of Department levels and staff appropriately educated about gender equality (Alston 2013). In the case of rural women, once their dedicated policy units were disbanded, downgraded, reshaped or renamed, very little policy attention or resource allocation has focused on gender equality measures. Largely this is because of a long-standing and misguided perception that rural women are located outside mainstream power and industry hierarchies and are not engaged in agriculture. Thus very limited attention has been paid to rural women's empowerment through rural/agricultural institutional structures, policy processes, government appointments or agenda setting items.

Another factor of significance to rural women's intersection with policy processes is the way departmental budgets are allocated. To ensure this is transparent, gender budgeting has become one mainstreaming process being employed in other parts of the world to assess how public funding is distributed through departments and organisations for the benefit of women and men. Anne Summers developed this process in Australia in the 1980s when Head of the Office of the Status of Women, a process since adopted in many other countries, but now dismantled in Australia. Yet when introduced in the 1980s it immediately met with great support from women's groups and significant resistance from other quarters. At the time all Federal departments were required to assess the distribution of public wealth to determine if women or men were unfairly benefiting. This process was also adopted in some Labor states, and when introduced to Victoria by then Premier John Cain, the Department of Agriculture and Rural Affairs was forced to admit that from a budget of $50 million, just $100.00 had been targeted to women (Eisenstein 1996). This embarrassing assessment led to the immediate appointment of women's policy officers and widespread consultation with rural women. This example indicates how gender budgeting allows an assessment of who is benefiting from public funds, and presumably being prioritised in the policy processes, consultations and appointments to decision-making bodies. Agricultural and rurally based departments and organisations rarely see women as clients, despite their active engagement and contribution to rural industries and communities. It is therefore easy to see why gender mainstreaming and gender budgeting are essential to exposing the way policies and public resources reinforce gender inequalities.

Another widely used indicator of gender mainstreaming is the assessment of leadership positions by gender, and the way these reflect the composition of the society/sector, the way this composition shapes the agenda of an organisation and the processes used to fill these positions. In research funded by the Australian Research Council in the late 1990s it became clear that leadership positions in agriculture are filled largely by older white males and that they are rarely representative of the sector as a whole (Alston 2000). These government-sponsored and agricultural organisations advise governments on policy and make representations on issues of concern to all rural people. Thus the lack of female representation is a cause for significant concern raised by women in a number of forums undertaken as part of the research. Women argued that this failure of representation impedes gender equality, promotes a neoliberal, economic approach to policy and reduces attention to social, community and health issues (Alston 2000). Importantly, what was happening here is also well articulated by Ferree (2012, p. 14). Women's claim for rights was not about adding to an existing rights framework but about 'changing the meaning of "rights" and extending the sense in which women's experiences were validated as human.' Women's actions during this period were about transforming 'the language of politics' (Ferrer 2012, p. 14) and challenging the existing institutional structures and agendas of agricultural politics.

The arrival of a conservative period of government from the mid 1990s brought a neoliberal philosophy that championed individualism, responsibility and mutual obligation. It also signalled an end to gender budgeting, a steady erosion of women-focused policy, a reduced focus on equity, leadership positions, and minimal attempts to incorporate gender mainstreaming. Australia's rural and agricultural policy has rarely adopted a mainstreaming lens and this failure not only reduces gender equality in budget allocation, leadership and support structures, it also places additional burdens on women. To understand how this failure to incorporate fair and equitable processes in policy infrastructure and processes disadvantages women, I turn now to an example of gender-blind policy relating to women's off-farm income generation.

Drought policy – a failure of gender mainstreaming

Australian rural women are more highly educated than their male counterparts, and are more likely to be in paid work and thus supporting their enterprise and family through income generation than at any time in previous history (Alston and Whittenbury 2012; Alston 2000; ABS 2004). It is arguable that this transformation in women's economic contribution to the historically dominant family farming mode of production comes as a result of long years of drought and economic hardship caused by deteriorating terms of trade, low production and a cost-price squeeze.

Farm families have adopted various strategies to remain in agriculture, including increasing production, reducing costs, reducing the standard of living enjoyed by family members and replacing hired labour with family labour. Additionally, one of the most important strategies adopted by families in recent times has been to access off-farm income generation activity to assist family viability, most often done by women but also increasingly by men working as fly-in, fly-out workers in the mining industry. This creates significant issues in relation to farm, household and care work. The increasing economic significance of off-farm income generation is of particular note for a number of reasons, not least being that women's paid work which previously added to family income to pay for children's education and items such as family holidays, is now more likely to be covering living and farm costs (Alston and Whittenbury 2012). Further, rather than a career or personal development opportunity, women's off-farm work is now more likely to be viewed as a *farm survival strategy* (Alston and Whittenbury 2012), and their labour commodified for the good of the *farm*.

This is a point worth stressing because it indicates the divide between the broader institutional level structures, where rural leaders and policymakers are predominantly focused, and the individual farm level. While agribusiness and rural leaders endorse a commitment to neoliberal economic policies, free trade and deregulated markets at national levels, at individual farm level this has had major repercussions for farm income by exposing individual farm family units to a volatile global marketplace. This exposure has had a significant impact on the social relations of production on-farm, changing the way women and men work. At the farm level, or what Connell (1987, 1997, 2009) calls the *gender regime* level, women and men are negotiating new working arrangements, reshaping the way they work on and off the farm and in the household. Because women often have reduced power in farm family business arrangements and intergenerational negotiations, and are open to community censure should they protest, their labour has been co-opted for the good of the farm and family, often at the expense of their health and well-being (Alston and Whittenbury 2012).

This was demonstrated during the drought years when off-farm income generation was vital for family survival in agriculture. The impact of the drought of the late 1990s and early 2000s on-farm incomes was dramatic (ABARE 2007) and many families slipped into poverty (Alston and Kent 2004). Drought policy focused initially on the productive side of agriculture with the government adopting the attitude that drought was a risk to be managed rather than a natural disaster (Botterill and Fisher 2003). Because farm families are largely excluded from traditional poverty alleviation payments the main measure designed to give farm household support was Exceptional Circumstances Relief Payments. The Drought Review Panel (2004) and families themselves (Alston and Kent 2004) criticised not only the lengthy and complex process that families were forced to go through to secure income, but also the uncertain outcome. One result was that many women went off-farm to work or increased their paid work hours.

The generation of off-farm income often involves driving long distances or living away from home during the week (involuntary separation) (Alston and Kent 2004, 2006). What was not clear to families early in the drought, and representing a failure of gender mainstreaming of drought policy, was that off-farm income rendered them ineligible for income support payments. Consequently the efforts of women to cover basic necessities often resulted in their families being penalised. Following widespread community concern the government introduced a provision in 2005 that families could earn up to $10,000 before they were classified as ineligible. Nonetheless the lack of a gender assessment of this policy caused widespread hardship and despair for many women. Further, it was often the most vulnerable families – those with young children and a high debt burden – that were assessed as ineligible by this process. Many women in these families who took off-farm work for the good of the farm, often had no ownership or partnership involvement, but were working to ensure their families could buy groceries.

While the drought has now officially ended, women continue to work off the farm in significant numbers to provide much needed income. Yet because the state and farm organisations are themselves so highly gendered, there remains little industry or policy acknowledgement that the off-farm work done by women is ensuring the continuance of the farm family mode of production. There is also no recognition that this work often places significant burdens on women relating to travel, moving away from home, childcare, traditional household expectations and a lack of workplace flexibility. In the mid-twentieth century a popular concept was that agriculture *rode on the sheep's back*, a reference to the high price Australian producers were receiving for their wool. Because agricultural leaders and commentators fail to see that agriculture is now dependent on women, there is inadequate industry or policy attention to facilitating women's various work, care and community roles. This represents both a failure to gender mainstream policy and a flawed focus on neoliberal economic policy at the expense of health, well-being and quality of life. To understand how an economic focus, and a lack of attention to social issues, shapes and constrains agriculture, gender relations and women, it is useful to take a historical perspective on the development of agricultural production in Australia.

Rural Australia – a changing policy landscape

Rural Australia has changed remarkably during the time of European settlement. From the opening of the inland and the establishment of rural settlements fostered by growth, development and agricultural expansion policies, rural Australia reached something of a peak in the 1950s, before falling into a steady decline through the remainder of the twentieth century. A number of issues discussed in other chapters in this volume are significant to the declining fortunes of rural people and places.

For the purposes of this chapter it is useful to briefly acknowledge the way each stage of this growth and decline was shaped by policies with implicit gendered overtones, either through unstated expectations of a traditional farm family or overt policies that restricted women's lives. These have further been fostered and developed by media creating a dominant discursive construction of women as helpmates and partners, but rarely as owners and farmers.

Arguably Australian agriculture has always been highly dependent on women's labour. The opening up of the inland regions for farming in the nineteenth century was largely done through Settlement Acts that drew on the European 'yeoman' style of farming. This was very much based on a model that included a family where the male partner was awarded ownership, with an unspoken assumption that women and children would provide the workforce. The work of women was rarely acknowledged in the nineteenth century and in fact in 1893 an Act of the Victorian Parliament determined that women's labour on farms would no longer be recorded in the census to remove any perception that Australia was a developing rather than a developed nation. The idea that Australian women might work in the fields was a view that parliamentarians did not want held up to scrutiny (Lake 1987). This decision ensured that women's farm work would be invisible in censuses or be defined as 'sleeping partners, non-productive' (ABS 2002). Because this continued throughout the twentieth century it ensured that policy developed on the basis of statistical information which favoured men and framed farming as a male occupation.

The establishment of family farming as the dominant mode of production and of men as the farmer was further reinforced through additional policies such as the Soldier Settlement Schemes instituted following World Wars I and II. Under these schemes large squatter runs were broken up into smaller farms to reward returning soldiers. Following World War I, 23,000 farms were created, a policy as much about establishing law and order amongst returning soldiers as a reward for effort (ABC 2010). Three aspects of these schemes are worth noting – the first is that the soldiers were men and therefore the reassignment of farm land precluded women; the second was that these schemes ignored the women who had been drafted into the Womens' Land Army during World War II, excluding them from any ballots for land; and the third is that many of these farms were marginal, unable to support a family. By 1939, 60 per cent of the World War I soldier settlers had left the land (ABC 2010) and Marilyn Lake's (1987) study of World War I Soldier Settlements provides heartbreaking accounts of women and men struggling to survive. These accounts give insights into women's historical contribution to agriculture. For example, farmer Norris applied to the Soldier Settlers' Commission to sell his land because 'the doctor had "ordered" him to "keep his wife away from the farm work" '. Norris explained to the Commission that it was impossible to run the farm without her (Lake 1987). Lake also quotes from a letter written by 'Una' to the *Countryman* newspaper, published on 10 September 1926. Una stated,

> The men's hours on the machine may be long and laborious, but not so long as those of the woman who has to tend them. After the men's last meal for the day is over they can lie down and rest, or have a smoke, but not the women.... If a farm won't pay without women having to make slaves of themselves in this fashion, well the quicker we give them up the better.
>
> (Lake 1987, pp. 177–178)

Despite the failure of the World War I scheme, the Soldier Settler Scheme was repeated following World War II and many small, 20-acre, irrigation farms were established along the rivers and larger farms in dry country. However, often the size of farms was less than could generate an income that could support a family and again many families were left to flounder. Nonetheless many did survive, and instant communities sprang up patterned on implicit but highly structured gender role expectations. These gendered policies on land redistribution did much to ensure male predominance in agriculture and fostered patrilineal inheritance practices.

Despite this, it is significant to note how these highly gendered arrangements can be changed when necessary. The entry of Japan into World War II in 1941 signalled the need for a rapid build up of the armed forces. Farm labourers were no longer exempt and a serious farm labour shortage loomed. From 1942 until the end of World War II, the Australian Women's Land Army (AWLA) was formed under the Director-General of Manpower. By 1943, nearly 2,500 permanent, and just over 1,000 auxiliary members, formed the AWLA and provided the farm labour workforce (Australian War Memorial 2013). This scheme was so successful that draft legislation was developed to name it a fourth national service. Unfortunately the end of the war prevented this from being formally enacted and it was not until 1997 that the women of the Land Army were officially recognised for their national service. The Land Army demonstrates that policy can be developed that can radically change gender roles in farming, that a national emergency overthrew established norms and values if only for a time, and that these were very quickly reinstated when the war ended.

Not only can government policy change gender roles, it can also reinforce them. Nowhere has this been more radically introduced than with the Australia-wide ban on married women working in public service positions following World War II. Designed to ensure that returning soldiers were given priority in the labour force, it was also a heavy-handed way of ensuring that women were encouraged back into the home. Until 1966, women were forced to resign their paid positions in the Commonwealth Public Service on marriage. In rural areas many gifted teachers, nurses and other professionals were lost from the paid workforce and this policy as much as any other ensured that women's contribution remained very much in the realm of the family and that gender roles were reinforced. Women clearly did not support this workforce ban, and this is most tellingly indicated by the rise in workforce participation of married women from 29 per cent to 53 per cent in the 25 years following the lifting of the ban (ABS 1995). Yet while the bar was withdrawn from 1966, women have still not achieved equal pay, and those who entered the rural workforce from the 1960s and beyond have done so on lower pay with less secure conditions, limited workforce flexibility, without the benefits of maternity leave and ultimately without similar superannuation benefits.

Despite their rapid entry into the workforce, rural women still carry the major burden of care work for children, aged relatives and disabled family members, and are more likely to be undertaking volunteer community work as they paper over the cracks of declining infrastructure. Further, until very recently legislation such as the *Family Law Act* restricted rural women's access to farm resources should their marriages break down. Daughters rarely figure in inheritance of farmland with best estimates being that 5 per cent of inheritors are women (Dempsey 1992; Alston 2000). The most likely entry point is through marriage and there remains an attitude of fear and suspicion surrounding daughters-in-law who enter family farm partnerships through marriage (Pini 2007).

Women's resistance

There have been various resistance movements among Australia's rural women for much of our European history. Women took part in suffrage movements, property, marital and child custody rights campaigns, right to work rallies and fought for child endowment payments to go to women (see for example Lake 1999). Rural women were and are part of these ongoing movements. In this section I will focus on rural women's activism in more recent times as their movement into the paid workforce accelerated their call for visibility and rights. In the 1990s several elements came together to enable rural women to have, if only briefly, a strong and united voice. Australian Women in Agriculture under Mary Salce organised the first rural women's international conference in Melbourne in 1994. This conference brought together over 800 women from 34 countries and was deemed by the then Governor-General, Bill Hayden in his opening address as the largest agricultural conference ever held in this country. At this conference the then Minister for Agriculture, Bob Collins, agreed that 50 per cent of all agricultural and rural board positions would be held by women by 2000, a promise that never came near to being realised. In their evaluation of the conference, delegates noted the chief barriers to their involvement were the commodity groups and farmer organisations, gender stereotyping and lack of time because of their work obligations (Dietrich 1995). Nonetheless the conference gave the impetus to rural women to continue their activism and to argue for greater visibility, representation and rights.

The establishment of Rural Women's units in several national and state departments following this conference was a critical factor in the progress of women gaining access to policy channels and for a time these were not only highly successful in raising women's profile, but also in facilitating women's access to ministers and department heads. These units emerged at a time when women were uniting and building their own representative organisations and were staffed by strong, capable women who took senior, highly influential roles in the bureaucracy. Critically the grassroots Australian Women in Agriculture movement was building strength at the same time and gave women a representative vehicle to the policy units and to ministers. The third element that made this a highly successful period for women was academic research that exposed the multiplicity of roles being undertaken by women, and more importantly gave it a monetary value (Alston 1995; RIRDC and DPIE 1998). The appraisal that rural women contributed 48 per cent of real farm income through their off-farm and community work was a spark for more intense activism and lobbying.

In 1995 the Federal Labor government responded by funding a National Rural Women's Forum in Parliament House, Canberra which drew together 80 delegates of these emerging and established organisations to plan a national blueprint for rural women. The writer organised and ran the Forum and developed the report that emerged from the negotiations (Alston 1995). Reading the report to government that emerged from the Forum some 18 years later, it is significant to see the very different focus of rural women from the prevailing neoliberal economic policies that dominate agriculture. The vision that emerged from the Forum called for:

- Recognition of the contribution of rural women to all spheres and across all socio-economic groups.
- The formation of a national rural women's network.
- Access to and participation in all areas of the decision-making process for rural women.
- Sustainability of rural and farming communities (including social sustainability).
- Access to and equity in service delivery to rural areas including government, private and community services; and
- Recognition of the citizenship rights of all Australians (Alston 1995, p. 3).

Women were calling for communities that were sustainable and provided them and their families with services, jobs and an adequate quality of life. They also wanted their rights as Australian citizens recognised through more encompassing social policies. The full document calls for education, training, workforce development, sustainability, visibility and recognition of voluntary community work.

What happened following this forum was a mushrooming of rural women's policy units, and a growth of Australian Women in Agriculture and more rigorous research outputs. One of the several significant documents to emerge during this period was the *Vision for Change: National Plan for Women in Agriculture and Resource Management* (Standing Committee on Agriculture and Resource Management (SCARM) 1998). This document detailed a comprehensive plan to improve women's visibility based on principles of equity, sustainability, participation, diversity and research. The document is a world-leading example of good policy action for gender equality.

Women were enthusiastic for a time as they felt they were being heard and included, and that their energy for the task would change policy directions. What happened instead was a change of government, a reduction and erosion of women's policy units, a loss of gifted senior bureaucrats (their positions taken by more junior staff, and eventually even those were lost), and funding for women's organisations such as Australian Women in Agriculture withdrawn.

These actions emerged from a very conservative government whose leader, Howard, famously argued that it was his intention to do away with special interest groups and to govern for mainstream Australia (Johnson 2000). According to Howard, special interest groups included women! His government's actions coincided with the terrible drought years, and both the climate and a changed policy environment eroded the spirit of many activists and reduced attention to women's disadvantage.

One initiative of the Howard years was the establishment of the National Rural Women's Coalition (NRWC) in 2002. This body brought together the heads of the five most prominent rural women's organisations at the time. While President of the Foundation for Australian Agricultural Women (FAAW), the writer was a member of the NRWC. The NRWC's intentions were good in that it was expected to provide coordinated policy advice on a range of nationally relevant issues. However, it was grossly under-funded and placed significant expectations on already busy women. The leaders of these national organisations were not paid for their time on the NRWC and this expectation was placed on top of the unpaid role of leading a national organisation, other work and family commitments. The writer recalls having to pay for her hotel room because members were only covered if they shared rooms. The writer's experience was that this model drew on society's unstated expectations of rural women – that they would work for no pay, providing unique and nationally based advice to policymakers at no cost. A further extension of the NRWC occurred in 2010 when the National Rural Women's Network (NRWN) was established giving rural women access through the NRWC to a newsletter and other information-sharing forums.

Meanwhile the failure to realise ambitious leadership and Board targets for rural women in decision-making and the tireless work of liberal women such as Senator Judith Troeth, led to a further evaluation of agricultural and rural leadership in 2005. The Department of Transport and Regional Affairs undertook an analysis of the composition of decision-making bodies and published *A Snapshot of Women's Representation on Regional Bodies* (DOTARS 2005). This indicated that women held 9 per cent of positions on agricultural commodity councils, 16 per cent of Rural Industry Research and Development Corporation positions, 13 per cent of rural representative positions, and 7 per cenr of positions in publicly listed agricultural bodies – nowhere near the 50 per cenr target promised by 2000. In 2006 Senator Troeth led a Senate Inquiry into the poor representation of rural women, producing a report, *At the Table, Getting the best people and making the right decisions for regional and rural Australia* (DOTARS 2006). The report notes the need for change, but sometimes veers dangerously close to blaming women, rather than the gendered structures, for their absence because they lack 'confidence' or 'time'. In 2013 Australian Women in Agriculture remains a small disciplined group of women, there are few if any rural women's policy units and women's representation on decision-making bodies remains non-existent or marginal.

The 1990s golden age of Australian rural women's activism represents the most highly visible public resistance by women, and their profile was raised for a time. This created the possibility that policy would finally address the issues of concern to women – strong, active, well-serviced communities where they and their children might find education and satisfying work and where agriculture developed in vibrant family-friendly communities. What we have instead is a draining of the inland, many small and remote communities with few services, a continued loss of young people, and work options being so sparse that many women must leave to find the income necessary for their partners to remain in farming. The contrast between the vision of women in the 1990s and the resolution forged by neoliberal conservative policy is stark.

What then of rural women's resistances? Arguably these have become individualised and less public, but are evident in trends across rural regions. These include the higher numbers of young women outmigrating from rural areas and leaving a growing number of young men without marriage partners; the higher numbers of marriage breakdowns, divorces and separated couples; the growing incidence of gender-based violence in rural areas (Whittenbury 2011); the lower numbers of women able to commit to voluntary work; the growing numbers of women working and studying off-farm; and the growing disenchantment with supporting the *farm* as opposed to improving lifestyle choices (Alston and Whittenbury 2012). Meanwhile there are escalating tensions between women and men, with many men yearning for a traditional family farming lifestyle (unrealisable in current financial circumstances) and many women who are working long hours, often away from home becoming increasingly disenchanted with their lifestyle (Alston and Whittenbury 2012). What we see now is the result of the lost opportunity of the 1990s and a growing resistance by women of all ages to committing to a farm family system that so obviously ignores their efforts, reduces attention to sustainable communities and fails to capture their views in decision-making bodies. Without gender mainstreaming policy family farming and small rural community life is unsustainable.

Rural policy shaping gender and rural spaces

There is no doubt that the state is critical to gender politics in rural areas. Rural policies, emerging as they do from a gendered state apparatus that fails to recognise or validate women's experiences, ensures and encourages significant gender inequalities. Through policies, programmes and underpinning principles the state is the 'most important institutional player in gender politics' (Connell 2009, p. 145). It is a place and site of gender formation, imposing and reinforcing processes and practices that shape and distort the way women and men are viewed within, and hence respond to, prevailing customs and sanctions. There is no doubt that Australian governments through the creation of rural policies collude, accept and sanction patriarchy, patrilineal inheritance, globalising forces, destabilised communities and centralised power.

The state also sanctions a sectoral rather than a territorial approach. Thus a regime that supports neoliberal economic policy has led to a downturn in rural place-based fortunes; resulted in growing wealth inequalities between rural and urban areas; led to a loss of services and infrastructure and a very evident differentiation between rural and urban quality of life indicators; and failed to support socially sustainable communities and therefore a healthy farm sector. Further the focus on sectoral policy, in this case equating agricultural with rural policy, masks the significant interaction between the agricultural sector and sustainable communities. A globally competitive agricultural sector is largely dependent on the health of its people and communities. The agricultural industry takes place across the inland. Therefore it would seem wise to support the people who live in these areas and provide the country with $43 billion in gross income per year (Australian Government 2011).

What is required into the future is gender mainstreamed rural policy that is territorially focused. This policy must address regional development, acknowledge and encourage women, build skills, better utilise the existing skills base, adopt flexible work plans, build retirement plans and create a future that satisfies and develops all who choose to live in rural places. Neoliberal policies have not worked for rural places because the target of smaller government and the focus on globalised agriculture has crippled rural communities, destabilised families and fractured once vibrant areas.

Further, rural policies relating to service infrastructure have increasingly been shaped around a notion of service delivery costs to rural areas being prohibitive and therefore unacceptable. As a result, rural people have been progressively denied equitable access to health, welfare, education and employment opportunities. This notion ignores the citizenship rights of rural people and the obligations of governments. It also leads to a lazy notion of service development that is based on currently understood urbo-centric models. With the roll out of the National Broadband Network (NBN) new services are possible and new ways of delivering and administering these services are achievable. With a critical investment in rural human capital, ideas will emerge for place-based, locally relevant services. The alternative is a decline in the resilience of rural people, further reductions in rural infrastructure and services and a rapidly escalating divide between urban and rural areas. The notion of Australia divided, with rural areas typified by poverty and lack of opportunity, is unsupportable.

New policy frameworks underpinning rural areas are necessary. These should attend not only to the new realities of globalisation and changing societal structures, but also to the type of society we want in our rural areas. Rural communities require the National Broadband Network (NBN), place-based development, investment in local young people as future leaders, the development of human capital through education and training, the development of services around locally identified needs, at the same time as building local jobs and skills. To cover shortfalls in volunteers so necessary to rural community revitalisation, Australian Governments could introduce innovative policies such as the allocation of 20 per cent of rural paid work to be directed to community work – training a sports team, running a volunteer centre, providing meals on wheels, etc. – thereby building the networks of support so necessary to rural life which have been eroded over the last two decades.

Above all, gender mainstreaming is essential to achieving gender equality, increasing the numbers of women in decision-making bodies, and incorporating the ideas and values of rural women to create sustainable place-based development. Rural policies should therefore mandate that no rural bodies or organisations receive government funds unless they practice gender mainstreaming and achieve regularly monitored gender targets. Rural policy shapes a certain type of society and can therefore be manipulated to produce equality of opportunity and outcome for all.

Conclusion

A socially sustainable rural Australia is threatened not only by globalisation, new market forces and climate-based challenges, but also by policies that fail to support and sustain individuals and communities. Arguably the historical equation of rural policy with all things agricultural – the sectoral rather than territorial approach – has created a destabilised rural Australia. While this has affected all who live in rural areas, it has been particularly challenging for rural women. Policy is never innocent. It has shaped and changed gender roles depending on circumstances, and at the expense of women's advancement throughout our European history. The example given in this paper of the Women's Land Army indicates the way policy can adjust gender relations to provide greater equality, while the example of the restriction on married women working indicates how it can also retract equality.

The activism of women in the 1990s indicates the types of development women desire – recognition, representation and rights. The growth of the Women in Agriculture movement during this period, and the successful intersection of funded women's organisations, vibrant women's policy units and academics, indicates how this rich combination can provide gender sensitive policy. The failure to build on this during the Conservative years, the erosion of the women's units, the loss of funding for women's organisations, the failure to provide equity in leadership and decision-making positions and the failure to develop gender mainstreaming institutional structures has returned women to a secondary position in rural decision-making and place shaping.

For agriculture and rural areas to survive and thrive we must draw on all our knowledge and skills, incorporate the skills and talents of everyone and shape an enhanced quality of life for rural people. This demands gender equality and territorial policies; enhanced infrastructure, particularly including the National Broadband Network (NBN); and secure, senior positions in health, welfare, education and service delivery that are located in rural communities. Most tellingly what is required is a change in rural policy to ensure that future generations of rural women, having committed to agriculture and/or rural positions, can stay and thrive in their local areas.

References

Alston, M 1995, *Women on the Land: the hidden heart of rural Australia*, UNSW Press, Kensington.

Alston, M 1995b, *Report from the National Rural Women's forum*, Wagga Wagga, Charles Sturt University.

Alston, M 2000, *Breaking through the Grass Ceiling: Women, Power and Leadership in Rural Organisations*, Harwood Publishers, Amsterdam.

Alston, M 2006, 'Gender Mainstreaming in Practice: a view from rural Australia', *National Womens' Studies Association Journal*, vol. 18, no. 2. pp. 123–138.

Alston, M 2013, 'Gender Mainstreaming and Climate Change', *Women's Studies International Forum*, Special Edition.

Alston, M and Kent, J 2006, *Impact of Drought on Rural and Remote Education Access: a Report to DEST and Rural Education Fund of FRRR*, Centre for Rural Social Research, Charles Sturt University, Wagga Wagga.

Alston, M and Whittenbury, K 2010, *Impacts of Declining Water Availability in the Murray–Darling Basin: Short report*, Gender, Leadership and Social Sustainability (GLASS) research unit, Monash University, Melbourne.

Alston, M and Whittenbury, K 2012, 'Does climatic crisis in Australia's food bowl create a basis for change in agricultural gender relations?', *Agriculture and Human Values*, vol. 30, no. 1, pp. 115–128.

Alston, M, Kent, J and Kent, A 2004, *Social Impacts of Drought: Report to NSW Agriculture*, Centre for Rural Social Research, Charles Sturt University, Wagga Wagga.

Australian Broadcasting Commission (ABC) 2010, *Landline: From Battlefields to Bush Blocks*, broadcast 27 April 2010. Available at: www.abc.net.au/landline/content/2010/s2882249.htm. Accessed: 7 March 2013.

Australian Bureau of Research Economics (ABARE) 2007, *Farm Financial Performance: Australian Farm Income, Debt and Investment 2004–5 to 2006–7*. Available at: www.abareconomics.com/interactive/ac_mar07/htm/a3.htm. Accessed: 21 May 2007.

Australian Bureau of Statistics (ABS) 1995, *Australian Social Trends 1995. Employment Arrangements – the Working Week*. Available at: www.abs.gov.au/ausstats/abs@.nsf/2f762f95845417aeca25706c00834efa/5d57bee8f25280f0ca2570ec0075276a!OpenDocument. Accessed: 16 March 2013.

Australian Bureau of Statistics (ABS) 2002, *The invisible farmers – women in agriculture*, cat. no. 1384.6. Available at: www.abs.gov.au/ausstats/abs@.nsf/7d12b0f6763c78caca257061001cc588/dd316da6a444df9eca256c320024784b!OpenDocument. Accessed: 19 March 2013.

Australian Bureau of Statistics (ABS) 2004, 'Perspectives on Regional Australia: Women's Employment in Urban, Rural and Regional Australia', *2001 Census*, cat. no. 1380.0.55.001. Available at: www.abs.gov.au/AUSSTATS/abs@.nsf/Lookup/1380.0.55.001Main+Features12001. Accessed: 7 March 2013.

Australian Bureau of Statistics (ABS) 2012, *Australian Social Trends – Australian Farmers and Farming*, cat. no. 4102.0. Available at: www.abs.gov.au/AUSSTATS/abs@.nsf/Lookup/4102.0Main+Features10Dec+2012#MEN. Accessed: 16 March 2013.

Australian Government 2011, *Australian Farms and Farming Communities*. Available at: http://australia.gov.au/about-australia/australian-story/austn-farms-and-farming-communities. Accessed: 19 March 2013.

Australian War Memorial 2013, *History of Australian Women's Land Army, 27 July 1942–31 December 1945*, cat. no. AWM54 1025/4/1 [Original record available only at the Australian War Memorial]. Available at: www.awm.gov.au/encyclopedia/home-front/land_army/. Accessed: 7 March 2013.

Botterill, L and Fisher M 2003, 'Introduction', in Botterill, L and Fisher, M (eds), *Beyond Drought, People, Policy and Persepctives*, CSIRO Publishing, Collingwood, Victoria, pp. 1–8.

Connell, RW 1987, *Gender and Power*, Allen & Unwin, Sydney.

Connell, RW 1997, 'Masculinities and Globalisation', *Men and Masculinities*, vol. 1, no. 1, pp. 3–23.

Connell, RW 2006, 'The Experience of Gender Change in Public Sector Organizations', *Gender, Work and Organisations*, vol. 13, pp. 433–452.

Connell, R 2009, *Gender: In World Perspective* (2nd ed.), Polity, Cambridge, UK.

Dempsey, K 1992, *A Man's Town: Inequality Between Women and Men in Rural Australia*, Oxford University Press, Melbourne.

Department of Transport and Regional Services (DoTARS) 2006, *At the Table: Getting the best people and making the right decisions for Regional and Rural Australia: Report of the Inquiry into Women's Representation on Regional and Rural Bodies of Influence*, Commonwealth of Australia, Canberra.

Department of Transport and Regional Services 2005, *A snapshot of women's representation on selected regional bodies*, Department of Transport and Regional Services, Canberra.

Dietrich, L 1995, *Agents for Change: Farming for our Future. Evaluation of the First International Women in Agriculture Conference, Melbourne 1994: Agents for Change: Farming for our Future*, Women in Agriculture 1994 International Conference Committee Inc.

Drought Review Panel 2004, *Consultations on National Drought Policy: Preparing for the Future*, Commonwealth of Australia, Canberra.

Economic and Social Council (ECOSOC) 1997, *Gender Mainstreaming Extract from REPORT OF THE ECONOMIC AND SOCIAL COUNCIL FOR 1997 (A/52/3, 18 September 1997)*. Available at: www.un.org/womenwatch/daw/csw/GMS.PDF. Accessed: 18 June 2012.

Eisenstein, H 1996, *Inside Agitators*, Allen & Unwin, Sydney.

Ferree, Myra Marx 2012, *Varieties of Feminism German Gender Politics in Global Perspective*, Stanford University Press, Stanford California.

Johnson, Carol 2000, *Governing Change*, University of Queensland Press, St Lucia.

Lake, Marilyn 1987, *The Limits of Hope: Soldier Settlement in Victoria 1915–1938*, Oxford University Press, Oxford.

Lake, Marilyn 1999, *Getting Equal: The History of Australian Feminism*, Allen & Unwin, Crows Nest.

Pini, B 2007, 'Always an outlaw: Daughters-in-law and Australian family farming', *Women's Studies International Forum*, vol. 30, no. 1, pp. 40–47.

Prugl, Elisabeth 2010, 'Feminism and the Postmodern State: Gender mainstreaming in European Rural Development', *Signs*, vol. 35, no. 2, pp. 447–475.

Rural Industries Research and Development Corporation (RIRDC) and Department of Primary Industries and Energy (DPIE) 1998, *Missed Opportunities: Harnessing the Potential of Women in Australian Agriculture*, Commonwealth of Australia, Canberra.

Shucksmith M 2008, 'New Labour's Countryside in International Perspective' in Woods, M (ed.), *New Labour's Countryside: Rural Policy in Britain since 1997*, The Policy Press, Bristol, pp. 57–76.

Standing Committee on Agriculture and Resource Management (SCARM) 1998, *Vision for Change: National Plan for Women in Agriculture and Resource Management*, Commonwealth of Australia, Canberra.

Whittenbury, K 2011, *Paper presented to the Gender and Climate Change conference*, Prato, Italy, September.

12 Three decades of rural health[1]

Gordon Gregory, Rebecca Phillips and Susan Brumby

Introduction

On average, Australians have a life expectancy that is very high by international standards and that continues to improve. Although Australians living in rural areas (including all rural, regional and remote areas) have shared in absolute improvements in morbidity and mortality, in relative terms they remain disadvantaged compared with their metropolitan cousins.

The Australian Institute of Health and Welfare (2012) reports that people living in rural areas

> tend to have shorter lives and higher levels of illness and disease risk factors than those in major cities … (and that) people living in rural Australia do not always have the same opportunities for good health as those living in major cities. For example, residents of more inaccessible areas of Australia are generally disadvantaged in their access to goods and services, educational and employment opportunities, and income.[2]

There is also a substantial body of evidence which identifies the critical contributions made by the social and economic determinants of health (Marmot and Wilkinson 2005; Dixon 2000). Distance itself is a substantial barrier to the effective prevention of disease and the management of health. There is a significant and unacceptable gradient in the status of health and well-being for individuals as one moves from major cities to rural and then to remote areas. Health outcomes generally worsen with distance from the major cities. This gradient is caused by a combination of the health risk factors experienced by people in different areas, by their differential access to health services, social factors and cultural attitudes such as a commitment to stoicism. As a consequence of metropolitan-rural differences in these factors, people living in rural and remote communities have quite distinct needs not readily met by models of care and intervention designed for metropolitan application.

This is the essence of the perception of people in the rural and remote health sector: that they stand within but separate from the mainstream of the Australian health system. The development of that separateness – the main narrative of this chapter – has been an essential underpinning of activity to remove the rural health inequity.

Chapter overview

Health is a major policy issue to be considered in a book such as this. However within the space available it is only possible to provide a brief overview of the trials, tribulations and successes of the rural and remote health sector in Australia over the past three decades.[3] This chapter is broad in scope, its concern being to assess the extent to which national health programmes implemented in the last 20 years, as well as those specifically targeted to rural and remote areas, have succeeded in reducing the gap between metropolitan and rural health and well-being.

Health status is determined by many factors and a comprehensive analysis of the health gap would therefore require considerations well beyond the health system. Programmes affecting rural health span local, state and federal governments; health and health-related portfolios; and whole-jurisdiction programmes as well as those specifically targeting, and only available in rural areas.

The chapter will:

- Provide an overview of the health status of rural Australians.
- Discuss the factors influencing health status.
- Describe and comment on the emergence of 'rural and remote health' as a separate and distinct part of Australia's health system.
- Comment on the impact of some of the major *national* health developments on the health status of the residents of rural and remote areas; and
- Discuss some of the outstanding barriers to resolving rural health challenges.

Rural health outcomes

People in rural areas are persistently documented to have poorer health outcomes and higher mortality rates than those in metropolitan areas. When compared with metropolitan areas, mortality rates in rural areas are 1.05–1.7 times higher, with mortality rates for Indigenous Australians over three times higher than the general population in rural areas (Phillips 2009). The higher mortality rates have been shown to be due to coronary heart disease (CHD), diabetes, chronic obstructive pulmonary disease and cancers (particularly lung and prostate cancers) (Phillips 2009). When specifically looking at the farming community there is a higher prevalence of cardiovascular disease (CVD) risk factors and psychological distress than national averages suggest (Brumby *et al.* 2012).

The prevalence of disability across rural and metropolitan areas is similar for women but is 20 per cent higher for men in rural areas, with higher incidences of psychiatric disability, sensory/speech disability, acquired brain injury and physical disability (Phillips 2009). Coupled with the high rate of psychiatric disability is the increase in male suicides over the past 20 years (Alston 2012; Phillips 2009). Suicides are continuing to increase as climatic conditions force farmers to make major decisions about whether to leave agriculture (Alston 2012).

The health of Aboriginal and Torres Strait Islander people is also a separate and significant national issue. The Australian Institute of Health and Welfare reports that,

> Indigenous Australians experience lower levels of access to health services than the general population, are more likely than non-Indigenous people to be hospitalised for most diseases and conditions, to experience disability and reduced quality of life due to ill health, and to die at younger ages, than other Australians. Indigenous Australians also suffer a higher burden of emotional distress and possible mental illness than that experienced by the wider community.[4]

Factors influencing the health outcomes of people living in rural areas are discussed in the following sections. These factors include access to services, social determinants and rural culture.

Access to services

The documented poorer health outcomes are in part the result of limited access to services. Living in a rural area impacts on the ability to access health services, with fewer services available per capita and greater distance to travel, potentially on poor quality roads, to reach the available services (Alston *et al.* 2006; Dixon and Welch 2000; Smith, Humphreys and Wilson 2008). Australian Bureau of Statistics figures reveal that the number of doctors per head of population varies from 308 per 100,000 in major cities to 77 per 100,000 in very remote areas. A survey of rural women has identified that as well as a lack of medical services, there is a paucity of general health and well-being support such as maternity services, mental health services, care and respite services and domestic violence services (Alston *et al.* 2006).

Attracting and retaining health professionals is a key issue in the delivery of rural health services (Alston 2007; Moore, Sutton and Maybery 2010). Although there are positives of working in a rural area such as feelings of personal and professional belonging, the rural lifestyle, supportive networks and ease of childcare, there are also barriers to attracting staff (Fisher and Fraser 2010). These include: professional isolation, limited access to educational opportunities and supervision, shortage of employment opportunities for spouses, lack of career structure, lack of anonymity, large caseloads and excessive travel (Fisher and Fraser 2010; Struber 2004). There is also a lack of recognition of the skill base required for effective rural practice.

In an attempt to address health professional shortages the Federal Government has introduced a scheme to encourage overseas-trained doctors to work in rural areas. However, there are limitations associated with this initiative such as language and cultural differences as well as ensuring standards of care are met (Alston 2007). There is also a large body of literature investigating rural intention (what it is that drives health professionals to work in rural areas). Those who have spent time living or studying in rural areas, have a partner who has lived in a rural area, intended to work in generalist rather than specialist practice and who held a scholarship during university are more likely to work in rural areas (Laven *et al.* 2003; Jones, Humphreys and Prideaux 2009).

Social determinants

Poorer health outcomes are not solely the result of limited access to services; social determinants, including economic, social and cultural factors, are also influential (Marmot and Wilkinson 2005; Smith, Humphreys and Wilson 2008). These include a higher prevalence of short-term high-risk alcohol consumption, psychological distress and obesity (Brumby, Kennedy and Chandrasekara 2013). The nature of a farmer's work (long working hours, limited social interaction, increasing automation of tasks and increased sedentary activities) may make it difficult for farmers to participate in physical activity for the associated physical and psychological benefits (Brumby *et al.* 2012).

Rural culture

Men in rural areas have shown a commitment to stoicism in which they will keep going through hardship or illness, not acknowledge difficulties and blame themselves for failures (Alston 2012; Hogan *et al.* 2012). This attitude can be linked to reluctance to access health services and to increasing psychological distress and suicide rates during the ongoing drought (Alston and Kent 2004; Alston 2012; Brumby *et al.* 2011; Brumby *et al.* 2012). While both men and women in rural areas may theoretically understand when they should seek medical assistance (e.g. for chest pain), the greater the distance they live from a health service, the longer they will wait to seek assistance, not wanting to travel the distance unnecessarily (Baker *et al.* 2011).

A brief history of rural health

In Australia, governments were slow in starting to acknowledge and respond to the distinctive health needs of rural and remote communities. Once started, progress was relatively rapid on some fronts, such as support for general practice, and relatively slow on others, such as in recognising the importance of allied health. However, given the economic, social and cultural importance of Australia's rural areas to the nation, the particular circumstances relating to health in rural areas were always given at least a nod. For instance, in a 1976 report the Hospitals and Health Services Commission (p. 2) stated that:

> Many country people find it difficult to obtain adequate health care. There is a shortage of doctors, dentists and other health personnel, and difficulties in maintaining health facilities in many districts … even where an adequate range of services is available, access may be impeded by lack of public transport or poor roads…

Since the focus of a good deal of rural health policy today is still on these same issues, it might be argued that not much has changed in the intervening 35 years and more. In what follows, however, it will be shown that there have in fact been notable advances and achievements in rural health policies and in health outcomes. The precise relationship between better health policies and better health is uncertain because of the critical impact of the social determinants of health such as income, education, housing and food.

The 1976 report by the Hospitals and Health Services Commission was followed in 1978 by a seminal event: the *Country Towns-Country Doctors Conference*. Organised by the Royal Australian College of General Practitioners (RACGP), this conference highlighted many of the issues confronting rural health, albeit through a largely medical lens. Its key concern was the shortage of doctors in rural areas, an issue that was to become overtly political a decade later. Despite this focus on GPs, and with the benefit of hindsight, that conference certainly played an important early part in claiming the distinctiveness and significance of rural health issues. However, over 30 years later, following the implementation of the strategies and programmes below, the shortage of health professionals in rural areas is still of utmost concern.

Institutional and political developments continued. In 1982 the Council of Remote Area Nurses of Australia (CRANA) was established. It was, at least in part, a response to the recognition of the benefit of collective action in getting governments to respond to the health care issues experienced by the residents of remote (as distinct from rural) communities. The uniqueness of remote issues remains an important principle for many in the 'rural health' sector.

In 1990 a report from the Australian Health Ministers' Advisory Council (AHMAC) Rural Health Care Task Force identified the following priority rural health issues (AHMAC 1990):

- The health needs of rural and remote communities, and specifically those of particular population groups.
- Improving education, training and career structures in rural practice.
- Overcoming disincentives for rural practice.
- Improving resource allocation mechanisms and rural infrastructure.

The New South Wales (NSW) doctors' dispute of 1988 led directly to the establishment of the Rural Doctors' Association of NSW and then, in turn, to the Rural Doctors' Association of Australia (RDAA). It was RDAA that took the lead in running the *1st National Rural Health Conference* in Toowoomba in 1991, which was a watershed moment in rural health (a chronology of major rural health policies in the decade that followed is listed in Table 12.1). It was joined in this venture by CRANA, some much older bodies like the Country Women's Association and the Australian Nursing Federation (ANF), and a number of passionate and resilient individual rural nurses, allied health professionals, consumers and public servants engaged in health. Because of that 1991 Conference, Toowoomba is widely regarded as the birthplace of Australia's rural health movement. And thanks to the Cunningham Centre and the Toowoomba Hospital Foundation, the city retains a special place in the sector through its continued support for some awards at the Conference, which has been held biennially since 1991.

The report from the Toowoomba Conference was entitled *A Fair Go for All*. Its recommendations resulted in the first significant national programmes for rural health. They included the Rural Health Support Education and Training (RHSET) grants programme, commitment to the development of a National Rural Health Strategy, and a range of special programmes for rural general practice.

The *Australian Journal of Rural Health* was launched in 1992, while the 1990s also saw three national rural health policy documents endorsed by the Australian Health Ministers' Conference. They were the 1994 *National Rural Health Strategy*, the 1996 *National Rural Health Strategy Update* and, in 1999, the first iteration of *Healthy Horizons*. These were instrumental in guiding early changes and initiatives designed to address rural health issues and problems.

Such developments would not have occurred without the consistent support of a small number of public servants and ministers of the day who became committed – in various measures and for various reasons – to rural and remote health. From the beginning the Federal Government had an unequivocal and widely accepted responsibility for the general practice workforce, but not for nurses and allied health professionals. One of the main reasons was of course the existence of Medicare, with the Commonwealth responsible for open-ended, demand-driven payments under the Medical Benefits Schedule (MBS). This clear responsibility is what underpinned the development of a plethora of programmes relating to general practice – and rural and remote general practice in particular.

Like the Commonwealth, the state and territory Health Departments grew their specific capacity to deal with policy issues relating to rural and remote areas, including through the establishment of Rural Health Policy Units. However, this was always an uneven and vacillating process, with the wheel turning from time to time on what was deemed necessary and desirable, just as it did on the 'best structure' for a jurisdiction's administration of health services (small Areas; large Regions).

In 1996 the first University Departments of Rural Health were established. This was a major initiative for the support of health workforce programmes in selected regional areas, and the importance of these entities has grown steadily over time. That year also saw the publication of *Healthy Horizons*, a joint development of the National Rural Health Policy Forum and the National Rural

Table 12.1 A chronology of major rural health policies during the decade 1992–2002

Year	*Policy/event*	*Policy impact and programme activity*
1991	National Rural Health Conference in Toowoomba – *A Fair Go for Rural Health.*	Landmark document setting the agenda for many of the Commonwealth initiatives of the 1990s.
	• Rural Health Support Education and Training programme.	Funded specifically rural health initiatives across Australia.
	• Beginnings of the National Rural Health Alliance.	Australia's peak NGO for rural health, providing significant impetus for profiling rural health and associated policy development.
1992	• Australian Association for Rural Nurses established.	Organisation to provide leadership and focus for rural nursing issues.
	• Australian Journal of Rural Health established.	National and international focus for disseminating rural health research.
1993	• 2nd National Rural Health Conference, Armidale, NSW.	Minister proposes national Office of Rural Health and funding for National Rural Health Unit.
	• General Practice Rural Incentives Programme.	Funding to encourage doctors to practise in rural and remote areas, and measures to provide professional support in the form of appropriate education, training and locum relief for practising rural and remote area GPs.
	• Review of nursing workforce issues.	Broadening the national rural health agenda to include nursing.
1994	• Divisions of General Practice established.	Regional support for GPs who opt in to membership.
	• National Rural Health Strategy endorsed by Australian Health Ministers' conference.	National framework to guide Commonwealth, State and Territory rural health funding and programmes.
	• Establishment of Rural Health Policy Units within some State Health Departments.	Became the focus for National Forum of Commonwealth-State representatives on rural health matters.
	• Establishment of Rural Health Training Units in all States.	
1995	• 3rd National Rural Health Conference, Mt Beauty, Victoria.	The first to be managed by NRHA; the last small community-based one.
1996	• National Rural Health Strategy Update endorsed by Australian Health Ministers' conference.	Progress in achieving rural health proposals set in the National Rural Health Strategy reviewed and new strategic directions outlined.
	• Announcement of University Departments of Rural Health to be established.	Significant ongoing funding initiative in establishing major rural health nodes in seven regional centres.
	• Formation of SARRAH.	The first peak organisation for individual rural and remote allied health practitioners.

1997	• 4th National Rural Health Conference, Perth.	Numbers rise to *c.* 700.
	• Australian College of Rural and Remote Medicine	Peak professional association for rural medical education and training in Australia.
	• John Flynn Scholarships.	To provide on the ground rural experience to medical students.
1998	• National Review of General Practice Training and General Practice Strategy Review.	Significant leap forward in setting the parameters of ongoing General Practice activities.
	• 1st National Rural Public Health Conference, Adelaide 1998.	Major initiative focusing attention on public and population health and towards a primary health care approach.
1999	• 5th National Rural Health Conference, Adelaide.	Management of AJRH passes from AARN to NRHA.
	• Healthy Horizons endorsed by the Australian Health Ministers' Conference.	National framework for improving the health of rural, regional and remote Australians.
	• Budget provides funding for GP retention grants, James Cook University medical school, Wagga Wagga clinical school and new Regional Health Service Centres.	Largest yet integrated package of new measures for rural and remote health.
	• Regional Australia Summit convened by Deputy Prime Minister in Canberra.	National gathering provides major impetus for 2000–2001 Budget initiatives.
2000	• *More Doctors, Better Services* Regional Health Strategy.	$562 million Budget to fund more rural health professionals, regional clinical schools and regional health services programme.
	• Rural Health Stocktake and NHMRC Rural Health review.	Independent reviews of investments to date.
2001	• 6th National Rural Health Conference, Canberra.	
	• Minister Wooldridge announces new University Departments of Rural Health (UDRH) and Regional Clinical Schools (RCSs).	Settles significance and role of UDRHs and, for rural medical education, of RCSs.
	• General Practice Education and Training Limited established.	Political decision to locate GP training money with a new, independent body.

Health Alliance (NRHA) for the Australian Health Ministers' Conference. For the first time Commonwealth, state and territory governments recognised the wisdom of involving and locking in national associations and interest groups with the capacity to deliver on some of the content of the statement. Having awakened the sleeping giant, the interest groups were invited by it to commit themselves to the agreed action. For this reason the National Rural Health Alliance was a co-signatory to *Healthy Horizons*. No longer a strategy, this national policy document was endorsed as a 'framework for improving the health of rural, regional and remote Australians'. It gave highest priority to addressing 'the worst first', including the poor health of Aboriginal and Torres Strait Islander people.

The Federal Budget of 1999 saw the largest package yet of new measures specifically for rural and remote health. They included funding for GP retention grants, the establishment of the James Cook University Medical School and the Rural Clinical School in Wagga Wagga. The 1999 Regional Australia Summit[5] convened by Deputy Prime Minister John Anderson had a rural and remote health stream. Most of the health issues highlighted in it were by then familiar.

This was followed in Budget 2000 by *More Doctors, Better Services*, regarded by many people as Minister Michael Wooldridge's greatest success and gift for rural and remote areas. In 2001–2002 health was not much on the front pages, except for the challenges of medical indemnity. The sector saw few significant structural alterations but continued to be characterised by ongoing tensions and generally uncooperative relationships between the Commonwealth and the states. These were typified by the acrimonious 'negotiations' over new Australian Health Care Agreements (AHCA) in 2003. A chronology of major rural health policy initiatives and events between 2002 and 2011 has been outlined in Table 12.2. As far as the rural health sector was concerned, 2003 saw Michael Wooldridge's 2000 *Regional Health Strategy* rebadged as the *Rural Health Strategy* under Health Minister Kay Patterson. That year also saw the release of a little-noticed report from the Australian Institute of Family Studies (AIFS) on child abuse in the Northern Territory (Stanley 2003). Four years later that report was to be detonated with considerable collateral damage – and ongoing ramifications.

In the meantime there was fallout from the Australian Health Care Agreements (known as the 'AHCAs'). A number of specialised working groups had been established to provide input to the negotiations for the AHCAs. When nothing came of this work and governments retreated once more to bickering and point scoring, many of the experts who had gathered for another purpose threw their support behind a new health reform body: the Australian Health Care Reform Alliance (AHCRA).[6] Led initially by John Dwyer, AHCRA provided a new voice for many in the health sector who believed that major reform of the sector was essential and long overdue.

In the next few years this push for reform by 'health experts' was joined by a far more powerful force: the weight of public opinion. It was highlighted – perhaps led – by the situation facing Australia's mental health system. Much public attention was given in 2004–2005 to the unlawful detention for ten months of Cornelia Rau, whose unstable behaviours were caused by schizophrenia and other disorders. Then there was considerable publicity in 2005 given to the unlawful removal to the Philippines of Vivian Solon, whose mental and physical health problems were not given due attention. These and other cases provided the background for consideration of two publications skilfully prepared and promoted by the Mental Health Council of Australia (MHCA): *Out of Hospital, Out of Mind* (published in 2003) and *Not For Service: Experiences of Injustice and Despair in Mental Health Care in Australia* (2005).

Importantly, on 2 April 2007 the Close the Gap campaign was launched in Sydney. There was then an unexpected explosion relating to child abuse in the Northern Territory. The *Little Children Are Sacred* report was handed down in June 2007. This led swiftly to the Northern Territory National Emergency Response, also known as 'the Intervention'. With widespread awareness of such tragic situations as these in Indigenous health and mental health, the reformist views of health experts gained greater traction. It became impossible for politicians and the public to remain complacent about the health system. Very fertile ground was created for a Prime Minister with aspirations for extensive health reform which broadened the focus from predominantly medical care to include broader health and well-being.

The Rudd Government was elected in November 2007. This ushered in an ambitious agenda of health reform relating to the structure and funding of the health system as a whole, a national approach to primary care, and greater emphasis on preventive health. The stronger focus on prevention gave brief hope that the planned health reform might result in some increased appetite within both the government and the sector for a true primary health care approach – one part of which is primary care. This would involve greater attention to the social determinants (education, housing, employment) and to holistic, interdisciplinary action on health. However, despite more widespread and undisciplined use of the term 'primary health care', it was a false dawn.

Five different models have been identified for providing primary care in rural areas and have been shown to be successful in meeting their stated goals (Wakerman *et al.* 2008). These models are 'discrete services' where GP services are delivered from an identifiable site in the community, 'integrated services' emerging from a community health service approach in which multiple services work in a team, 'comprehensive primary health care services' of which primary care is a part, such as the Aboriginal Community Controlled Health Services, 'outreach models' and 'telehealth' (Wakerman *et al.* 2008).

Medicare Locals have been introduced to improve the coordination of primary care service delivery and ensure the needs of each local community are met (Russell *et al.* 2013). It is hoped and expected that, like Aboriginal Health or Medical Services, they will also have some capacity to provide broad primary health care, through such things as special services for the unemployed, those with a disability, the homeless and the incarcerated. First and foremost, however, Medicare Locals will better link local GPs, nursing and other health

Table 12.2 A chronology of major rural health policy initiatives and events in Australia, 2002–2011

Year	*Initiative/event*
2002	• $740 million in drought relief for financial assistance, counselling and employment services; tax relief. • Funding for *HealthConnect*, a proposed electronic health records information network.
2003	• *Healthy Horizons: Outlook 2003–2007* released. • *MedicarePlus:* $2.4 billion to increase bulk billing and convenience for patients to claim rebate. • $47.3 million for rural and remote GP retention payments. • New Australian Health Care Agreements: Federal funding for public hospitals. • 7th National Rural Health Conference, Hobart, Tasmania.
2004	• The Rural Health Strategy: $830 million over four years, mainly to improve distribution of GPs. • Rural Procedural Grants to help procedural GPs maintain skills. • Bonded Medical Places Scheme introduced. • *MedicarePlus* extends MBS to selected dental and allied health procedures.
2005	• Rural Nursing Scholarships: $20.6 million to help remove barriers to recruitment and retention. • *Australia's Health Workforce*: Productivity Commission Report on health workforce issues. • Rural undergraduate scholarships for allied health. • 8th National Rural Health Conference, Alice Springs, Northern Territory.
2006	• MBS Better Access Programme: $507 million for Psychiatrists, Psychologists, GPs and Allied Health Professionals. • E-health: $70.2 million to establish a national electronic health records system. • Public disclosure of sexual abuse and violence in Central Australia.
2007	• Close the Gap Campaign launched. • *Highway to health:* Senate Report on Patient Assisted Travel Schemes. • Public release of the *Little Children Are Sacred Report.* • NT National Emergency Response (*the Intervention*). • New $223.4 million Royal Flying Doctor Service Funding Agreement 2011–2015. • National Health and Hospitals Reform Commission (NHHRC) established. • 9th National Rural Health Conference, Albury, NSW.

2008	• *Audit of Health Workforce in Rural and Regional Australia.* • Office of Rural Health established in response to Audit of Rural Health Workforce. • *Beyond the blame game:* NHHRC's proposals on the next Australian Health Care Agreements. • Evaluation of University Departments of Rural Health Programme and Rural Clinical Schools Programme. • COAG establishes Australian Health Practitioner Registration Agency for ten health professions. • GP Super Clinics: $275.2 million for 31 GP Super Clinics. • Rural Health Workforce Strategy: $134.4 million to encourage doctors to rural areas. • Royalties for Regions – political principle features in WA State Election. • Apology to the Stolen Generations. • Review of *Healthy Horizons.*
2009	• NHHRC's Interim and Final Reports: *A Healthier Future for all Australians.* • ASGC-RA classification system to rep*lace RRMA* as basis for funding rural health programmes. • *Primary health care reform in Australia*: Strategy to guide future policy and practice in Australia. • *Australia: the healthiest country by 2020*: National Preventive Health Strategy providing roadmap for tackling obesity, tobacco and alcohol. • Rural and Remote Health Workforce capacity: Australian National Audit Office report on programmes administered by the Department of Health and Ageing. • National Rural and Remote Health Infrastructure Programme: Health and Hospitals Funding for rural and remote communities. • Health Workforce Australia established: Responsible for implementing COAG $1.6 billion health workforce package. • First Minister for Indigenous, Rural and Regional Health (Warren Snowdon). • 10th National Rural Health Conference, Cairns, Queensland.
2010	• *National Health and Hospitals Network*: foreshadows Medicare Locals and Local Hospital Networks. • $1.8 million Health and Hospital Funding – Regional Priority Round for health infrastructure. • $632 million to increase GP training places from 700 to 1,200 a year; specialists from 360 to 900. • MBS and PBS benefits for specific services of nurse practitioners.
2011	• New expenditures for mental health. • Medicare rebates payable for specialist video consultations with patients in rural areas and eligible aged care facilities and Aboriginal Medical Services. • Rural and Regional Health Australia established in Department of Health and Ageing. • House of Representative Inquiry into Registration Processes and Support for Overseas Trained Doctors. • National Advisory Council on Dental Health established. • 11th National Rural Health Conference, Perth, Western Australia.

professionals, hospitals and aged care, identify where local communities are missing out on services they might need and coordinate services to address those gaps (Department of Health and Ageing 2011).

Much of the impact of the 2007 reform agenda on health outcomes and the distribution of health services for rural and remote people remains to be seen, including the extent to which the expectations of Medicare Locals can be met. Already, however, several mooted reforms (such as having a single funder for health, or making the Commonwealth responsible for policy and funding in primary care) have been significantly compromised 'until the next time'.

In 2008 there was an *Audit of Health Workforce in Rural and Regional Australia* – a modest piece of work compared with the three national health reviews then in train. It resulted in the establishment of an Office of Rural Health in the Department of Health and Ageing. The wheel was still a-turning. Kevin Rudd's health reform aspirations led to three particular pieces of work and resulted in three reports, all published in 2009 – each of which was and remains highly regarded. They are *A Healthier Future for all Australians* from the National Health and Hospitals Reform Commission; *Primary Health Care Reform in Australia* from the Department of Health and Ageing and its External Reference Group; and *Australia: the healthiest country by 2020* from the National Preventative Health Taskforce.

These were all valuable pieces of work, conscientiously undertaken and with a raft of potentially valuable recommendations. Unfortunately, however, the health sector poses more challenges to fundamental structural reform than almost any other, and the people of rural and remote areas remain among those most seriously disadvantaged by what remains undone.

Australia's first *National Primary Health Care Strategy* (Department of Health and Ageing 2010) and the *National Preventative Health Strategy* (National Preventative Health Taskforce 2009) both highlighted the critical part played in determining health status by taxation, employment, education, housing, transport, regional development, reconciliation, the arts and social security. Unfortunately, it remains very difficult to implement a whole-of-government approach to health, with the competition for resources between portfolios and the very purpose of the central agencies (Treasury and Finance) both acting against such a thing.

There was optimism about the establishment in 2011 of Rural and Regional Health Australia, an agency mandated to take on a strong advocacy role within government to promote a joined-up government approach to rural health, and to provide high-level input to budget and policy development on key rural, regional and remote health and ageing issues. The promise of that organisation is yet to be seen.

The dependence of the Gillard Government on the support of two independent rural MPs has been instrumental in the recent orientation of national policies and programmes to deliver more focus on and resources to non-metropolitan regions. The importance of a rural voice holding the balance of power in the parliamentary arena is also illustrated in Western Australia, where the National Party negotiated a 'royalties for regions' agreement, such that 25 per cent of the state's mining and onshore petroleum royalties are returned to regional areas each year as an additional investment in projects, infrastructure and community services. Despite its critics, the hung Parliament has been beneficial for rural regions. It has provided an opportunity for some much-needed 'catch-up' for infrastructure, workforces and services associated with rural health and well-being.

Barriers to improvements

Throughout the period since 1991, in its health activity the Commonwealth government remained overwhelmingly involved with general practice and Medicare. Despite some initiatives designed to support nurses and allied health professionals, there is still a very long way to go to achieve any sort of equivalence between medicine and the other health professions, especially in rural areas. The major education, training, service provision and population health initiatives set in place in the 1990s are now beginning to improve the lives of rural and remote Australians. University Departments of Rural Health (UDRHs) and Regional Clinical Schools (RCSs) have become established as vital infrastructure supporting the devolved education and training of Australia's future rural and remote health workforce.

Substantial funding made available through the Health and Hospitals Fund, the National Rural and Remote Health Infrastructure Programme and others boosted health-related infrastructure in rural areas. Other initiatives, such as the Medical Specialist Outreach Assistance Programme (MSOAP) and Medicare rebates for video consultations to link specialists and consultant physicians with patients are also helping to improve the access of rural and remote patients to health care.

Despite such progress, the persistence of poorer health in rural Australia suggests that much more is required. A focus on medical solutions, whilst positive, has missed other opportunities to reduce the divide. In rural communities there are so many occasions to contribute to health, well-being and safety and these occasions exist not just in the health and medical domain.

Crossover and interaction occurs routinely and commonly in the lives of rural people between health, education, agriculture, welfare, transport and communication and in all tiers of government. Whilst this interaction should in theory provide an opportunity to address poor rural health from numerous angles through cross-sector collaboration it has mostly remained a siloed approach across departments, and sadly within them (Brumby 2013). Collaboration is required to grow within the health department and its numerous health disciplines and between the common departments that service rural areas. Delineation and shifting the buck ('it's not a health problem, it's an industry problem', 'it's not industries, it's education and training') must cease, and instead the focus should be on a population that is missing out. For a country that prides itself on innovation and 'can do' there is still much to do.

A fundamental reason why rural health status is not being improved as quickly as it should is the nation's and the health sector's failure to address the barriers in the system in which decisions are made, resources allocated and programmes implemented.

Resource availability

There is a consistent health underspend in rural areas compared with what is both fair and needed (AIHW 2011; NRHA 2011). Lack of funding for rural health is further complicated by Australia's complex health financing arrangements, and a failure to resolve Commonwealth-state relationships (especially 'cost shifting').

Problems associated with programme duplication, lack of coordination and integration of programmes, cost-shifting, cross-border issues, and lack of mutual professional recognition continue to inhibit the quest to overcome workforce problems and to deliver efficient and appropriate health services effectively. These problems were highlighted in the National Hospitals and Health Reform Commission's report (2008), but the opportunity for change under that reform agenda appears to have passed.

Much more remains to be done on the resourcing front. Allocation of health dollars according to health need would see people in rural and remote areas among the main beneficiaries. But such a system would require substantial revision of the architecture of the nation's health system, including two of its best features: Medicare and fee-for-service medicine.

Workforce shortages

Rural health workforce shortages remain a critical first-order problem, often being the main reason why an effective health service cannot be provided in a rural area. Even large regional centres suffer significant health workforce shortages, requiring residents to seek health care from capital cities.

The difficulties of workforce recruitment and retention are exacerbated by the persistence of some negative images of rural communities, including among some of those who are teaching and mentoring the health professionals of the future. The 'good news' rural health stories seldom warrant a priority, despite ample evidence that rural Australia has long been the incubator of successful innovation. One promising development is the increasing capacity of social media and internet sources like *Croakey* and *Crikey* to provide more broadly based views on health than are found in 'mainstream' media.[7]

Contextual considerations

Rural context and the portrayal of regional and rural communities are important in shaping the health behaviours and health actions of its communities. Messages that reinforce rural stoicism and a 'she'll-be-right' attitude are unhelpful in addressing rural health inequity. Rural populations are often shocked to learn they experience higher rates of morbidity and premature death through accident and preventable diseases. To be knowingly stoic one must be informed and aware of the consequences of choosing not to act, rather than not knowing how or where to act (Brumby 2014). Much remains to be done to communicate health messages that recognise and address rural context rather than using a backwash of metropolitan campaigns or reinforcing stoic behaviours that promote inequity.

Cross-sector collaboration

The opportunity for improved health, well-being and safety outcomes through cross-sector collaboration is promising for rural populations. However, it is easy to talk about but difficult to do beyond physically or virtually meeting about it. Whole of government approaches that address critical social and economic determinants of health will provide more collateral strength in resourcing to address rural equity. This multi-pronged collaboration should be on every local, state and federal government departmental strategy.

Commonwealth-state relations

Despite the existence of a range of National Healthcare Agreements and many jointly funded health programmes, the rural health scene is littered with problems associated with poor delineation of responsibilities, lack of coordination and integration of programmes, cost-shifting, cross-border issues, and lack of mutual recognition.

One thing that would help greatly is a better data set for 'current effort'. It is not surprising that the Commonwealth has found it challenging to be involved again in the funding of oral health programmes. Its fear is that for every extra dollar it puts into child oral health, for example, the states could divert an existing child oral health dollar to some other use.

Conclusion

In the last three decades considerable progress has been made in addressing the barriers to improved rural health outcomes. However the deficits and the gradient from major cities to very remote areas remain. There are still urgent challenges in a number of areas, including in Indigenous health as a whole, oral health and mental health. Some health risk factors are still much worse in rural areas than the major cities, including rates of smoking, dangerous levels of alcohol consumption and obesity.

Rates of smoking have been coming down in the cities at much faster rates than in rural and remote areas, which suggests the need for a fresh look at how health promotion is undertaken in rural areas. Without greater success on smoking rates in rural areas, Australia is very unlikely to meet its target of 10 per cent nationally by 2018.

A key question is the extent to which major improvements in rural health can be achieved without extra resources: how much more and better can be done with existing allocations. The prospect of increases in real expenditure on rural health is limited by fiscal fears and realities. Australians are now familiar with the scenario in which China sneezes and Australia catches a cold, and Europe and the US have not been in the best of economic health for some time. A strong aspiration to balance the national budget or achieve a surplus will increase the drive for a financially sustainable national health system and, as this chapter has clearly demonstrated, the rural health sector is a part of that. This provides an opportunity for seeing health promotion and illness prevention as good investments for the economy as well as for the people.

If this argument is not won, however, there will need to be zero-net-cost changes, including in relation to the health workforce. Most of the desirable changes of this kind have been canvassed in the 'health reform' processes of the last five years. For example the National Health and Hospitals Reform Commission's (NHHRC) *Final Report* (2009) included specific recommendations about the redistribution of resources to rural areas, but redistribution means that some will get less. This perhaps explains why those ideas fell on barren ground. The fact that there has been no national rural health strategy since the expiry of *Healthy Horizons* in 2007, and no rural health plan either, does not help the rural case.

The Council of Australian Governments (COAG) Reform Council is reporting annually on targets set in National Healthcare Agreements and its special rural supplement is a bright spot in terms of the use of evidence and public accountability. AHMAC's current work on progress with key performance indicators in the National Strategic Framework for Rural and Remote Health may also deliver some much-needed means by which governments and other stakeholders can be held more publicly accountable.

People matter. Maximising their health status and life chances can only be assured through the provision of appropriate health care services – preventive, acute and rehabilitative. In the interests of people and national and state budgets, but particularly for residents of rural and remote communities, greater attention must be paid to a primary health care approach. This will see greater focus on the determinants of health, upstream of the health sector itself. True primary health care includes relevant activity in preschools and schools, health promotion initiatives such as fluoridation of water or quit smoking campaigns, workplace initiatives, targeted work relating to food, exercise and parenting and cross-sector collaboration. A good primary health care system includes access to good primary care: from a doctor, a community nurse, an allied health professional or dentist. In the health sector per se, there needs to be more emphasis on health promotion and illness prevention, the implementation of cross-sector collaborations and not so much on acute care and hospitals.

Such shifts in Australia's health system will require changed attitudes and behaviours, and this will take time and patience. However, once achieved it will put the health system on a financially sustainable basis and the people of rural areas will be among the main beneficiaries. For, despite the improvements of the last three decades, there is still a significant metropolitan-rural health inequity. And it is large enough for us to be sure that, given any erosion in the general capacity of the national health system, it will be felt worst by the people of rural areas.

Notes

1 This chapter began life loosely based on two review articles published in the *Australian Journal of Rural Health* (AJRH): Humphreys *et al.* 2002; and Humphreys and Gregory 2012.
2 See www.aihw.gov.au/rural-health.
3 More reports on various aspects of rural and remote health can be found at www.ruralhealth.org.au.
4 See www.aihw.gov.au/indigenous-health/.
5 See www.infrastructure.gov.au/department/annual_report/1999_2000/RegionalAustraliaSummit.aspx.
6 Some of the history of AHCRA can be found at www.healthreform.org.au/history-of-ahcra/.
7 See http://blogs.crikey.com.au/croakey/ and www.crikey.com.au/.

References

Alston, M 2007, 'Globalisation, rural restructuring and health service delivery in Australia: Policy failure and the role of social work?', *Health and Social Care in the Community*, vol. 15, no. 3, pp. 195–202.

Alston, M 2012, 'Rural male suicide in Australia', *Social Science and Medicine*, vol. 74, no. 4, pp. 515–522.

Alston, M, Allan, J, Dietsch, E, Wilkinson, J, Shankar, J, Osburn, L, Bell, K, Muenstermann, I, Giorgas, D, Moore, E, Jennett, C, Ritter, L, Gibson, R, Wallace, J, Harris, J and Grantley, J 2006, 'Brutal neglect: Australian rural women's access to health services', *Rural and Remote Health*, vol. 6, no. 475.

Alston, M and Kent, J 2004, *Social impacts of drought: Report to NSW agriculture*, Centre for Rural Social Research, Charles Sturt University, Wagga Wagga.

Australian Health Ministers' Advisory Council Rural Health Care Task Force 1990, *Preliminary report to the Australian Health Ministers' Advisory Council*, Australian Health Ministers' Advisory Council, Canberra.

Australian Institute of Health and Welfare (AIHW) 2011, *Australian health expenditure by remoteness: a comparison of remote, regional and city health expenditure*, Health and welfare expenditure series No. 41, Cat. No. HWE 50, AIHW, Canberra.

Australian Institute of Health and Welfare (AIHW) 2012, *Australia's Health 2012*, AIHW, Canberra.

Baker, T, McCoombe, S, Mercer-Grant, C and Brumby, S 2011, 'Chest pain in rural communities; balancing decisions and distance', *Emergency Medicine Australia*, vol. 23, no. 3, pp. 337–345.

Brumby, S 2013, Farm work and family health: A study on farming health across selected agricultural industries in Australia (Doctoral dissertation), La Trobe University, Bendigo. Available at: http://library.latrobe.edu.au/record=b3415647~. Accessed: 10 July 2014.

Brumby, S, Chandrasekara, A, McCoombe, S, Kremer, P and Lewandowski, P 2012, 'Cardiovascular risk factors and psychological distress in Australian farming communities', *Australian Journal of Rural Health*, vol. 20, no. 3, pp. 131–137.

Brumby, S, Chandrasekara, A, McCoombe, S, Kremer, P and Lewandowski, P 2011, 'Farming fit? Dispelling the Australian agrarian myth', *BMC Research Notes*, vol. 4, no. 89.

Brumby, S, Kennedy, A and Chandrasekara, A 2013, 'Alcohol consumption, obesity and psychological distress in farming communities: An Australian study', *The Journal of Rural Health*, vol. 29, no. 3, pp. 311–319.

Department of Health and Ageing 2010, *Building a 21st Century Primary Health Care System: Australia's First National Primary Health Care Strategy*, Commonwealth of Australia, Canberra.

Department of Health and Ageing 2011, *Improving primary health care for all Australians*, Commonwealth of Australia, Canberra.

Dixon, J 2000, 'Social determinants of health', *Health Promotion International*, vol. 15, no. 1, pp. 87–89.

Dixon, J and Welch, N 2000, 'Researching the rural-metropolitan health differential using the 'social determinants of health', *Australian Journal of Rural Health*, vol. 8, no. 5, pp. 254–260.

Fisher, KA and Fraser, JD 2010, 'Rural health career pathways: Research themes in recruitment and retention', *Australian Health Review*, vol. 34, no. 3, pp. 292–296.

Hogan, A, Scarr, E, Lockie, S, Chant, B and Alston, S 2012, 'Ruptured identity of male farmers: Subjective crisis and the risk of suicide', *Journal of Rural Social Sciences*, vol. 27, no. 3, pp. 1–17.

Hospitals and Health Services Commission 1976, Rural health in Australia, Australian Government Publishing Service, Canberra, p. 2.

Humphreys, JS and Gregory, G 2012, 'Celebrating another decade of progress in rural health: what is the current state of play?', *Australian Journal of Rural Health*, vol. 20, no. 3, pp. 156–163.

Humphreys, J, Hegney, D, Lipscombe, J, Gregory, G and Chater, B 2002, 'Whither rural health? Reviewing a decade of progress in rural health', *Australian Journal of Rural Health*, vol. 10, pp. 2–14.

Humphreys, JS, Wakerman, J, Wells, R, Kuipers, P, Jones, JA and Entwistle, P 2008, '"Beyond workforce": A systemic solution for health service provision in small rural and remote communities', *Medical Journal of Australia*, vol. 188, no. 8 (suppl.), pp. S77–80.

Jones, M, Humphreys, J and Prideaux, D 2009, 'Predicting medical students' intentions to take up rural practice after graduation', *Medical Education*, vol. 43, no. 10, pp. 1001–1009.

Laven, GA, Beilby, JJ, Wilkinson, D and McElroy, HJ 2003, 'Factors associated with rural practice among Australian-trained general practitioners', *Medical Journal of Australia*, vol. 179, no. 2, pp. 75–79.

Marmot, M and Wilkinson, R (eds) 2005, *Social determinants of health*, 2nd edition, OUP, Oxford.

Moore, T, Sutton, K and Maybery, D 2010, 'Rural mental health workforce difficulties: A management perspective', *Rural and Remote Health*, vol. 10, no. 1519.

National Health and Hospitals Reform Commission 2008, *Beyond the blame game: Accountability and performance benchmarks for the next Australian Health Care Agreements*, National Health and Hospitals Reform Commission.

National Health and Hospitals Reform Commission 2009, *A healthier future for all Australians: Final Report*, National Health and Hospitals Reform Commission, Canberra.

National Preventative Health Taskforce 2009, *Australia: the healthiest country by 2020. National Preventative Health Strategy – the roadmap for action*, National Preventative Health Taskforce, Canberra.

National Rural Health Alliance (NRHA) 2011, *Australia's health system needs re-balancing: a report on the shortage of primary care services in rural and remote areas*, National Rural Health Alliance.

National Rural Health Policy Forum and the National Rural Health Alliance 1999, *Healthy Horizons 1999–2003: a framework for improving the health of rural, regional and remote Australians*, report to the Australian Health Ministers' Conference, Canberra.

Phillips, A 2009, 'Health status differentials across rural and remote Australia', *Australian Journal of Rural Health*, vol. 17, no. 1, pp. 2–9.

Ranmuthugala, G, Humphreys, J, Solarsh, B, Walters, L, Worley, P, Wakerman, J, Dunbar, JA and Solarsh, G 2007, 'Where is the evidence that rural exposure increases uptake of rural medical practice?', *Australian Journal of Rural Health*, vol. 15, no. 5, pp. 285–288.

Russell, DJ, Humphreys, JS, Ward, B, Chisholm, M, Buykx, P, McGrail, M and Wakerman, J 2013, 'Helping policy-makers address rural health access problems', *Australian Journal of Rural Health*, vol. 21, no. 2, pp. 61–71.

Smith, KB, Humphreys, JS and Wilson, MGA 2008, 'Addressing the health disadvantage of rural populations: How does epidemiological evidence inform rural health policies and research?', *Australian Journal of Rural Health*, vol. 16, no. 2, pp. 56–66.

Stanley, J 2003, *Child abuse and neglect in the Northern Territory*, Australian Institute of Family Studies (AIFS).

Struber, JC 2004, 'Recruiting and retaining allied health professionals in rural Australia: Why is it so difficult?', *The Internet Journal of Allied Health Sciences and Practice*, vol. 2, no. 2.

Wakerman, J, Humphreys, JS, Wells, R, Kuipers, P, Entwistle, P and Jones, J 2008, 'Primary health care delivery models in rural and remote Australia – A systematic review', *BMC Health Services Research*, vol. 8, no. 276.

13 Rural research and regional innovation

Are past and present research funding policies building future resilience in the bush?

Richard Price

Introduction

Over millennia, Australia's traditional owners found ways to adapt to the harsh and diverse environments of the Australian continent. This adaptation process no doubt involved trial and error, the use of human imagination and creativity to go beyond the bounds of the known, the collaboration of expertise and the sharing of knowledge through stories. If you could fold time, compress this experience, encrypt the process, codify the learning practice, box it up and label it, then the label might read 'Rural Research: Institutionalised for the Modern World.' The author would add, 'Handle with Care. Not Guaranteed Against Defect.'

Over the past 200 years, Australian farmers and the communities dependent upon them have relied upon institutionalised research in order to adapt to harsh Australian landscapes. The term *institutionalised* here is used in two senses: first, the codification of research practice through formal methods of experimentation; and second, the creation of organisations, laws, policies and funding mechanisms to support, undertake and communicate research and its findings. The subject of this chapter is the latter, now valued to be at least $2.9 billion per annum (RRDC 2011, p. 3) and considered relatively novel and worthy of emulation elsewhere around the globe (Price 1994; Lovett 1997).

In visioning the future of rural and regional Australia, particularly within the context of the role of government and analysis of key policy developments since World War II, Australian rural research can proudly hold its place. Just as this research effort has sought to make Australian agriculture and rural communities resilient to the exigencies of highly variable terrain, climate and markets, the evolution of rural research policy too can be seen in the light of formulating support mechanisms resilient to farmers' capacity to pay for innovation and inter-sectoral competition for public research funds.

There are many forms of knowledge and many means of generating it. Visioning the future does not require institutionalised research (see Gross, this volume, for example), but creating the means of attaining a preferred future will certainly rely on forms of creativity, collaboration and knowledge-generation that policies and institutions can potentially facilitate. Whether or not this potential can be realised in terms of achieving resilience in rural and regional Australia will depend on how the research agenda is set and who is involved.

A historical perspective of rural research

Pre-WWII

Understanding the post-World War II rural research policy regime requires at the very least a brief consideration of what preceded it. Starting with Elizabeth Macarthur's experiments with sheep breeding from 1806, for a significant part of the nineteenth century farmers undertook much of their own research and technology development (Price 1994). Technologies such as Smith's stump-jump plough (1876), Walker's wire strainer (1884) and Wolseley's shearing machine (1887) are examples of farmers having to construct, trial and refine their own technologies in order to overcome the harsh reality of taming Australian landscapes, or to gear-up to levels of production achievable over the enormous areas of land available to them. The results of homespun research and technology development were shared through many avenues; occasionally through formal commercial arrangements that followed patenting, but more commonly through generous community co-dependence that supported free exchange. Naturally for the time, some forms of sharing took the form of theft or illegal copying. By the late nineteenth century, however, farmers were beginning to realise that formalising and implementing sharing arrangements prior to the research process taking place made better sense in terms of having the right people with the right expertise work on the right innovations. Indeed, injecting some competition into this process also made sense as a means of improving the chances of solutions to problems being reached. Some farmers started to pool funds for innovation prizes at agricultural fairs, and while the source of funding may have changed over time, we can still see the legacy of this today in the livestock and produce competitions of agricultural shows across Australia.

Of course, the farmers were not alone in their efforts for too long. From the late 1800s, the colonial ministries of agriculture and the emerging institutions of education and research (such as the Roseworthy Agricultural College (1883) and the agriculture schools established in the Universities of Sydney (1910) and Melbourne (c. 1910)) began to institutionalise and dominate rural research activity, providing both the infrastructure and experimental stations necessary to support it (Jarrett and Lindner 1982). The Commonwealth government also became directly involved in undertaking rural research following the establishment of the Institute of Science and Industry (now CSIRO) in 1920.

The concept of farmers pooling their funds for research paralleled the concept of pooling their produce for marketing, first through voluntary cooperatives and then through statutory marketing organisations. And just as they had experienced in their cooperative marketing arrangements, farmers found that the voluntary nature of pooling – such as in the wool-growers' Pastoral Research Trust or the wheat-growers' Soil Fertility Research Fund – presented problems of fairness and equity sometimes described as free-rider or spillover effects (Productivity Commission 2010), with those not participating benefiting from those that did. As a consequence, farmers sought for voluntary funding to be made compulsory, through politically influential industry bodies and their relationships with political representatives (there was a greater percentage of rural representation in governments at the time). At the state-level, a statutory-based levy imposed on sugar growers in 1900 to support the Bureau of Sugar Experimental Stations set a precedent for compulsory farmer contributions to rural research. Nationally, the Commonwealth government marked its intervention through the establishment of a compulsory wool levy in 1936 and subsequent creation of the Australian Wool Board (AWB). In 1945 the Commonwealth introduced matching government contributions for wool research on a one-for-one basis. This coincided with the transfer of control of the research account from the Australian Wool Board to a committee of four government departments. In 1953, control of the funds was transferred back to the Board, but with input on funding decisions from a mandatory government board member. In 1957, a statutory advisory committee, comprising representatives from the Department of Primary Industries, the CSIRO and producer groups, was given the power to administer the funds. Funding decisions were made by the Minister on the basis of the committee's recommendations. This scheme remained in place for the next 28 years.

Post-World War II

The AWB arrangement opened the doors for other industries to follow, particularly where these industries had a presence in more than one state. Over the decades following World War II several Rural Industry Research Funds (RIRFs) were established, each involving compulsory producer levies matched by government appropriation. The administration of the funds was largely performed within the Commonwealth ministry of the day responsible for agriculture. Commodity-specific producer-dominated Rural Industry Research Committees (RIRCs) were established to determine rural research priorities and guide the allocation of funds to research activities. The main beneficiaries of the funds were the State agricultural agencies, CSIRO and those universities with agricultural science faculties.

The growth of these bodies reflects the productivist hegemony that has dominated Australian rural policy (Lockie, Lawrence and Cheshire 2006). The focus of nearly all rural research funded under these arrangements was on increasing agricultural production and productivity. Where investments were made in areas dealing with natural resources, these were largely about overcoming constraints to production, such as constraints in soil fertility. Of course, conservation research was undertaken, but largely through government bodies such as CSIRO and soil and water conservation authorities, and the results were rarely incorporated into the mainstream industry extension mechanisms that were more closely aligned with the agricultural ministries (Dunn, Gray and Phillips 2000, p. 17).

By the 1980s, problems with the RIRF arrangements begin to emerge. The RIRFS had become a significant part of the total rural research funding pool, particularly as a result of the matching Commonwealth contribution. Researchers argued that producers should not have such high sway over both industry and government funds, and pointed to the narrow focus of issues being addressed as a result of limited producer appreciation of both technical and commercial issues. At the same time, the Joint Review of Research Administration by the Department of Primary Industries and the Public Service Board in 1983 criticised the RIRCs for being too passive in the selection of proposals and not considering the rates of return from projects (PSB 1983).

In response to the review, Commonwealth rural research legislation was overhauled, essentially in two steps. The first step, commencing in 1985, was an interim arrangement establishing Research Councils with improved governance arrangements taking into account wider representation of expertise. Like the RIRCs, their administration remained largely housed within government – the then Bureau of Rural Research. The second step entailed the corporatisation of these Councils into Research and Development Corporations (RDCs) in 1989. Each of these corporations was intended to be more strategic and flexible in making rural research investments directed towards making their industries more competitive and sustainable. They were to be directed and managed under skills-based boards and non-government professional staff, commercially focused and unchained from bureaucracy and inflexible financial management (Kerin and Cook 1989).

In all, 15 RDCs were established under different Commonwealth legislation, including 12 RDCs under the *Primary Industries and Energy Research and Development (PIERD) Act* (Commonwealth 1989). Five Research Councils were retained under this Act, with their administration transferred from the Bureau of Rural Research to the newly created Rural Industries Research and Development Corporation. It should be noted that the RDCs established under the PIERD Act were not the first RDCs, with the Australian Meat & Livestock Corporation and Horticulture Research Corporation having been established in 1985 and 1987 respectively. As with the RIRCs before them, the RDCs were funded by statutory-based levies, matched dollar-for-dollar up to 0.5 per cent of each industry's gross value of production, and were accountable to the Commonwealth Minister for Primary Industries and Energy and to each RDC's relevant peak industry body.

During the formative years of the RDCs, another significant Commonwealth research initiative was introduced by way of the Cooperative Research Centre (CRC) programme, which sought to increase the level of applied research collaboration between research funders, providers and users, as well as across disciplines. In 2012 there were 11 agricultural-specific CRCs and a further seven CRCs with strong rural and regional interests. Many of these CRCs, including the agricultural-specific ones, reflect a weakening of the productivist hegemonic stranglehold on rural research, with most having significant mandates to undertake environmental or natural resource management research and development

(R&D). It is no coincidence that the publicly-funded CSIRO should be a partner in nearly all of these centres, for together with the university research sector it has dominated Australian environmental research activity (McFarlane 1999). It is also no coincidence that much of the recent public investment in rural research is directed towards farmers and rural communities becoming self-sufficient, at one time in the face of drought and climate variability but more recently in the face of climate change. The drive for self-sufficiency has been closely tied to a neoliberalist perspective seeking to increase efficiency through reducing unnecessary government intervention (Cockfield; Smith and Pritchard, both this volume). Some go further, and see it as a cynical approach to justify withdrawal of government support from areas of traditional rural investment, such as in regional development (Sher and Sher 1994) and research and extension where the lines between public and private benefits are not black and white (Marsh and Pannell 2000).

Rural research funding and its contribution to the triple bottom line

Table 13.1, prepared by the Rural R&D Council as part of the *National Strategic Rural Research and Development Investment Plan* (RRDC 2011) estimates the total current rural research investment to be around $2.9 billion, based on 2008–2009 budgets. Of this, the Productivity Commission (Table 13.2) estimates that around $1.5 billion is specifically related to agricultural production. The $490 million RDC investment in 2008–2009 outlined in Figure 13.1 therefore suggests that the funding from the RDC model amounts to around one-third of all production research and around 16 per cent of all forms of rural research undertaken in Australia.

The recent Productivity Commission review of rural research provides examples of the contributions this research has made to economic, environmental and social outcomes for rural and regional Australia (Productivity Commission 2011). To detail that work here is not justified, however, in brief, these benefits include:

Economic

- lower costs of production;
- improved productivity, yields and quality, including through increased; genetic potential and agronomic performance;
- improved supply chain logistics;
- reduced impact from pests and disease.

Environmental

- reduced externalities, including through reduced pesticide use and reduced runoff and associated sedimentation;
- sequestering of carbon;

Table 13.1 Rural R&D expenditure in Australia (total), 2008–2009

R&D focus	*Government $m*	*Higher education $m*	*Business $m*	*Total $m*
Agriculture, Fisheries and Forestry	479.7	301.8	294.9	1,076.4
Expanded along the value chain	180.8	110.2	688.9	979.9
Related to rural	457.6	237.1	130.0	824.8
Total expenditure	1,118.1	649.2	1,113.8	2,881.1

Source: RRDC 2011, based on ABS Rural expenditure on research and experimental development – government, higher education and business sectors, by socio-economic objective, 2008–2009 (special extraction from cat. nos 8109.0, 8111.0 and 8104.0).

- improved natural resource monitoring and risk management;
- improved environmental amenity.

Social

- reduced food-borne illness through improved product quality and handling;
- support for indigenous employment through growth of new industries;
- improved animal welfare to address societal concerns;
- improved standard of living through the provision of cheaper and better quality food;
- improved capacity of individuals and communities to adjust to changing circumstances (such as in markets or in climate).

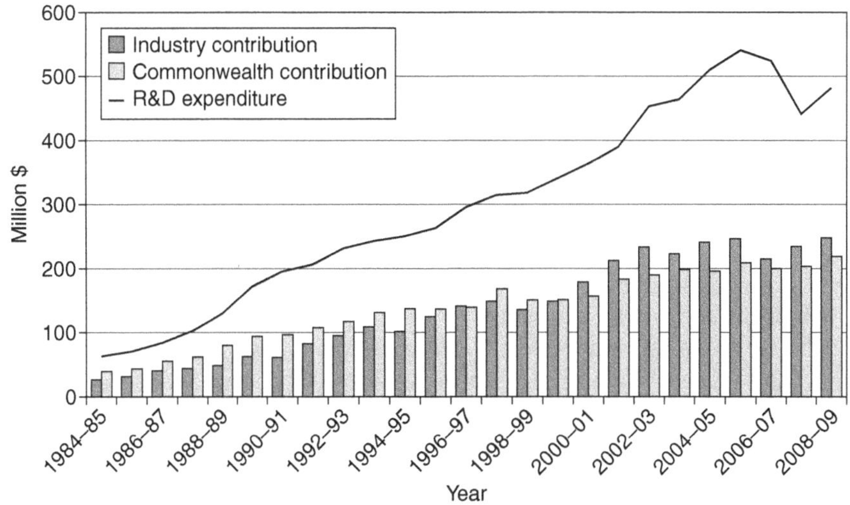

Figure 13.1 RDC contributions and estimated R&D expenditure[a] (source: Productivity Commission 2011, based on RDC annual reports and information from DAFF).

Note

a Includes expenditure on associated extension activities.

Table 13.2 Rural R&D funding (production), 2008–2009[a]

Organisation type	*Funding $million*	*Share %*
Australian Government[b]		
Cooperative Research Centres	63	
Core funding for the CSIRO	193	
Core funding for the universities[c]	118	
Research and Development Corporations (RDCs)	218	
Other departmental programmes[d]	114	
Foregone tax receipts arising from R&D tax concessions	9	
Total Australian Government	*715*	*48*
State and Territory Governments		
Project-related budget allocations[e]	348	
Capital investment in R&D facilities	47	
Payments to other funders and suppliers	21	
Total State and Territory Governments	*416*	*28*
Private/Industry		
Levy payments provided to RDCs	248	
Other (for which a tax concession is claimed)[f]	116	
Total Private/Industry	*364*	*24*
Total	**1495**	**100**

Source: Productivity Commission 2011. (a) These data do not include funding from royalties and other intellectual property income (on the basis that these have been generated by past funding from governments and private parties). Also, the data do not include in-kind contributions from the private sector, such as through the provision of land and facilities for experiments. (b) Only the portion of the budget assigned to rural R&D is included. (c) Estimated by applying the rural share of total university funding received from contestable sources and the portion of university students studying in agriculture-related areas to the three largest university block grants. (d) Includes programmes aimed at wider issues (such as climate change), programmes with no sector-specific focus and any one-off payments. (e) Includes rural R&D and associated extension funding for programmes facilitated within the primary industries department (or its equivalent). Any funding for rural R&D from State and Territory Government Environment Departments and the like is not included. (f) Calculated using tax concession data (including an estimate for concessions claimed for R&D on agricultural chemicals). Also includes payments made to the Australian Animal Health Laboratory.

In acknowledging these and other benefits of rural research, the Productivity Commission questions the accuracy of some of the quantitative estimates made of the returns from rural research. These estimates have varied significantly, although some of the more reliable analyses suggest the benefits are in the order of between 14–40 per cent (Mullen 2007) and 50 per cent (CRRDC 2010), rates which the Commission agrees deliver *significant benefits for both primary producers and the broader community* (Productivity Commission 2011, p. 46). Where the Commission has particular concern is that the return on investment estimates are used indiscriminately in justifying arguments for public investment. In many cases, the distribution of benefits between different beneficiaries is not so clear. Moreover, the Commission argues that correlations between levies paid and rates of return achieved are problematic given that R&D is not the only influence on productivity growth; that in the absence of R&D it is unlikely levy payers could have maintained productivity; that there can be long adoption lags for some technologies; that the benefits are not always provided to the individual levy payer in terms of productivity gain; and that the benefits may be more distributed in terms of environmental and social gain (Productivity Commission 2011).

Decentralist-centralist tides in rural research policy and the loci of power

If this chapter is to discuss the capacity for rural research policy to build future resilience in the bush, it needs to explore who exactly will be setting the agenda in which the meaning of resilience is framed. Sociologically speaking, this is a question of power. For this reason, it is worthwhile revisiting rural research policy since World War II in terms of the loci of power and where it is heading.

The evolution of progressing through voluntary research funds, research committees, research councils and finally RDCs should not be seen as a smooth, clearly planned, ordered or plotted path (Lovett 1997). Historically, rural research funding policy has mostly followed global shifts in the dominant institutional, economic and political hegemony of the time. On occasion, however, it has stood at the forefront of emerging shifts. Yet it also appears that Australia's rural research reforms have resisted shifts from time to time. Cockfield (2011) notes in a cognate area of rural reform, namely regionalisation, that government support for self-sufficiency has been in contrast to a policy history of intervention.

In recent years the re-centering and centralisation of the state as the dominant political force across the western world has seen a number of statutory organisations disappear in many countries, including in Australia, with their roles supposedly absorbed into central agencies (Halligan 2006). From this perspective, the 2009 demise of Land and Water Australia (LWA) as one of the rural RDCs can be seen merely as an inevitable outcome of a dominant administrative reform blueprint. To a centralist mindset it makes no sense for one government agency (Department of Finance) to be providing funds to another government agency (Department of Agriculture) to devolve to another government agency (LWA) to then distribute, no matter how strategically, to research organisations that are more often than not closely tied to government if not totally government-owned themselves. Yet at the same time, we have seen some of the RDCs being further decentralised, becoming industry owned corporations (IOCs) still in receipt of matching Commonwealth funding.

For much of the period following World War II, there have been two interrelated principles in rural research policy that have remained relatively stable. First has been the principle of co-investment between industry and government. Second, and as a consequence of the first, has been the principle of mutual accountability to both industry and government for the expenditure of research funds (Price 1992). Despite the relative stability in these principles, the power relations between these two actors has been in a constant state of flux. The shifts in power and influence might be seen to be aligned to the cycles of centralisation and decentralisation that have taken place more broadly in the global policy environment (Halligan 2006; De Vries 2000). In this light, we ought to view policies as snapshots that are floated across a sea of time in which the tides are constantly either moving in or moving out.

The privilege of mutual accountability, in which statutory authorities are in theory equally accountable to government and a sub-set of non-governmental society (Rhodes 1975), was not simply handed to rural industries on a platter. It had to be negotiated, and this negotiation process is one perspective through which we might understand how rural and regional communities have interacted with government in the policy development process. In this respect, the evolving nature of rural research arrangements following the establishment of the AWB holds considerable historic interest in public administration theory.

Since World War II, statutory arrangements for primary industry functions have been at the forefront of developments in wider statutory organisation design, funding, management and control. Implicit in their evolution has been an accountability framework which transcends the traditional Westminster model. Over time this transcendence has become more explicit, to the stage that acknowledgement of the fundamental right of rural stakeholders to be directly accounted to is enshrined in rural research legislation. In essence, government has formalised the processes of mutual accountability, the more significant aspects of which are those that go beyond open administration to embrace participatory administration (Mackenzie and Hood 1975; Rhodes 1975; Barker 1982). Such forms of accountability focus on aspects of horizontal as well as vertical accountability (Guillermo O'Donnell in Schedler 1999).

When the cyclonic rural research reforms of the 1980s were taking place, the predominant tide was a decentralist one. These reforms were formulated following a formidable period of review, of which the Royal Commission on Australian Government Administration, also known as the Coombs Commission, was the most significant (RCAGA 1976). The review laid the foundation for the disentanglement of semi-government operations being performed as core functions and institutions within central government. Essentially what we are talking about here are applications of the concepts of *devolution*, *corporatism* and *managerialism*. At the time, a major challenge for public administration was the difficulty in balancing the pursuit of managerialism within a broader push for pluralism and public choice (Campbell and Halligan 1992). This dilemma had arisen most notably in debate on the appropriate balance between the delegation of authority to institutions outside the traditional framework of government, and the desire for popular control and accountability.

While these reforms are described here as occurring during a decentralist tide, some observers at the time, the neo-pluralists, believed that the influence of public participation in the policy sphere was elsewhere dwindling (Dunleavy 1982). This tends to suggest that the demarcation of tides is not always clear, and that the key message for policymakers is that policy development should always be seen as occurring in an environment of permanent transition. That said, many of the neo-pluralists recognised that the segregation and decentralisation of statutory enterprise authority functions from the policy arena taking place provided enormous opportunity for participation in government decision-making by relevant interest groups and the general public (Dunleavy 1982; Barker 1982).

Gerritsen (1987) has argued that the only area of public administration where corporatism has worked is in the policy realm of primary industries, largely because participation has been formal and compulsory, and that the vertical linkages have existed through producer interest groups. Mauldon and Schapper (1974) observe that Australia has a history of negotiation between government and farmers in rural policy matters, and that it was partly to break the nexus of such negotiations that the Australian Labor Government in 1973 created the Industries Assistance Commission. This arrangement, however, continued through and beyond the 1980s. As Martin (1990, p. 155) observes:

> The first six years of the Hawke government saw significant reform in Australian rural policies. Many of the major policy changes were brought about by consensus rather than confrontation, although the pursuit of consensus was not an end in itself. Rather, the broad direction of policy was influenced by the economically rationalist goals of efficiency, restructuring and equity set by the Minister and the government.... The reforms were largely negotiated with, rather than being imposed upon, the agricultural sector.

What we can take from the preceding discussion is the notion that rural communities, at least through the representative interest-groups that helped direct the operations of the RDCs, have played a role in setting the agenda for rural research. Indeed, Figure 13.1 suggests that this influence extends to at least one-third of all production research. That said, the nature of participation, representation, power and influence is not clear cut. What we can observe from the RDC process has been the reinforcement of productivism through a focus, by and large, on commodity-specific goals. This is a historic artefact arising from the product specialisation of large numbers of farmers across the Australian continent and the influence this had on the development of local commodity associations prior to their amalgamation into powerful producer organisations (Mauldon and Schapper 1974). Traditionally, farmers and governments have tended to see farmer prosperity and specific commodity sales as being inextricably linked, and hence government agricultural bureaucracy has also been organised along commodity lines. This model has favoured rural research serving the interest of farmers as producers of commodities rather than as citizens of rural communities. The question arises as to how well rural communities, including research levy paying farmers, are served when their interests are assumed to be taken into account in representational arrangements that are in fact more narrowly framed.

Such questions no doubt were being asked within government during the 1990s. By this time, many governments around the world, including in Australia, saw the limits of a decentralist approach to governance as having been reached (Halligan 2006). In particular, politicians were concerned about public perceptions of the performance of delivery agencies. They were also concerned about the dangers imposed by bureaucratic proliferation (DoFA 2004) and the negative perception engendered by knowing that only 22 per cent of public sector employees were employed in mainstream departments, while the remainder were engaged in around 180 agencies, of which many had statutory independence (Shergold 2004). The solution was seen as extending central control to remove implementation blockages and delays. In seeking advice on how to rationalise statutory authorities, or at least to improve their corporate governance, the Government established the Uhrig Review of the Corporate Governance of Statutory Authorities and Office Holders in 2002 (Uhrig 2003).

Even before the Uhrig review, the RDCs were beginning to feel their sense of independence being whittled away. From the late 1990s they were required to formally demonstrate how their priorities aligned to the Australian Government's objectives for rural research. Later, on advice arising from the Uhrig review, the Government ceased to appoint specific Government representatives to RDC Boards in a move to remove any conflict of interest arising whereby Commonwealth public servants would be seen to be accounting to themselves. On the surface this gave the appearance that the Boards were gaining greater independence, but in reality it ensured that the Government provided a greater level of scrutiny to the activities of the RDCs, through its bureaucrats in the Department of Agriculture, Fisheries and Forestry. Many of the RDCs objected to losing their Government Director, arguing it had led to a deterioration in the quality of communication with Government, such as in jointly setting directions for future rural research (Productivity Commission 2011, p. 234). This desire for a close relationship between industry and government is in contrast to a certain level of disdain some rural communities have shown for government interference in, or monopoly over, agenda setting in rural Australia (Sher and Sher 1994).

The growing environmental awareness and concern among regional communities has been reflected in the rural research agenda, not simply in response to the edicts of government priorities. Indeed, where industry groups have recognised that environmental issues might severely threaten the livelihoods of their members, either by reducing their incomes as a result of consumer backlash to practices perceived to be polluting or by reducing social cohesion as a result of community ostracisation, the rural research agenda has been significantly broadened beyond investments in production R&D. Cotton research into reducing pesticide spray-drift is a prominent of example of this and is often cited as representative of the investments made across all RDCs in natural resource management research.

While Table 13.1, Table 13.2 and Figure 13.1 suggest that the majority of rural research, and in particular research outside the productivist domain, is supported largely through the activities of government, in truth industries have steadily increased their contribution towards research that may be considered environmentally and socially responsible (Day 2005). The thrust of the recent review of rural research by the Productivity Commission is therefore somewhat at odds with the directions the RDCs have taken in recent years. In contrast to RDCs increasing their contributions to natural resource management, and in response to declining rates in productivity improvements evident across agriculture, the Commission's review seeks to refocus RDC expenditure on production priorities. To more clearly delineate the various responsibilities for different outcomes from rural research the Commission argues that – as the primary beneficiaries of production research – industry should carry the greater burden of funding. Commensurately, it recommends reducing the matching government contribution that has been in place for over half a century, and further recommends the establishment of a separate body (nominally called Rural Research Australia) to deal with the many cross-sectoral issues once handled by Land and Water Australia or through multi-RDC collaboration. In essence, the Commission is advocating specialisation in the rural research funding system that will reinforce compartmentalisation of the voice of rural Australians to negotiate their shared future. While levy payers will have a say over production research through the accountabilities of RDCs to powerful industry organisations, the broader rural research agenda will be determined through less tangible, transparent and certain means.

Competing tensions that need to be addressed in future

Rural research policy since World War II has attempted to engage rural Australians in fostering a more resilient future through co-investment in rural research via the RDC model. However, this engagement has been dominated by well-organised industry bodies that largely support the productivist elements of the wider rural and regional research agenda. This model has served rural communities well, no doubt by enhancing the economic viability of farming in Australia. But by the same token, the model may inadvertently act to reduce rather than enhance resilience in the bush in future, particularly as the social, economic and environmental dynamics in rural Australia have changed. From the author's perspective, these changing dynamics create tensions in terms of what has gone on before in rural research and what might be needed in future to underpin resilient industries and communities. These tensions, framed as questions, include: (i) Who should be responsible for natural resource management research and how should it be conducted? (ii) How do we break the mindset of focusing on single issues to live up to the rhetoric of integration? (iii) How can we reconcile evidence-based policy with adaptive management? (iv) What place is there for social science in a future rural research agenda?

i Who should be responsible for natural resource management research?

The institutional history of rural research in the twentieth century has been less kind to natural resource management research than it has been to agricultural research. This has not only been in terms of funding, but more importantly in terms of institutional placement. By separating the funding mechanisms as well as the research organisations responsible for this research, we have also separated the results of this research from the context in which potential adopters make their adoption decisions. The evolution of extension theory and practice in the context of sustainable agriculture supports the need for integration of production and natural resource management research at the planning, conduct, adoption and monitoring/reflection stages of research activity (Vanclay 2004; Nicholson *et al.* 2003; Vanclay and Lawrence 1994).

As state agencies continue to withdraw their support of agricultural and natural resource management extension, the opportunity to align sustainable agriculture messages within the context of farmers' decision-making frameworks may in fact be enhanced in favour of extension models that work (Marsh and Pannell 2000). This will only happen, however, if there are community, private sector or industry forces at work to facilitate the alignment. Any model that reinforces a notion that industry is responsible for production research while government is responsible for other research immediately compromises the capacity to exercise best practice extension by achieving alignment up-front, during the planning stages. From the author's first-hand experience as a manager within Land and Water Australia (LWA), the sustainable agriculture collaborations of LWA proved to be more successful where it invested in industry-managed RDC initiatives than where it sought industry contributions to the initiatives it managed itself. The most likely reason for this is that it required the industry partners, which had greater credibility among the farming community, to plan, integrate, facilitate and engage in ways that enhanced their commitment to a natural resource management agenda. It saw an overall increase in funding committed to natural resource management research, engendering a sense of ownership in the prospective research results (Day 2005). Perhaps most importantly, it acted to remind industry groups that their constituents have interests beyond agricultural production that need to be taken into account in order for them to attain or maintain a level of resilience conducive for their agricultural practices to improve.

The argument for specialisation as a means of improving productivity can be compelling, but in the context of rural research it can also be limiting. Here is the tension: have productivity levels in agriculture declined in recent years because the resources of industry have been diverted away from production to take into account other issues facing farmers? Or have they declined due to the inherent difficulties in undertaking integrative research, particularly where it involves many institutions? Integration of research already has a high transaction cost (Dovers and Price 2007), and further moves towards specialisation may only serve to increase the cost beyond the point where integration will occur. The future of rural research ought to lie in building the resilience of individual farmers and communities in ways that support their capacity to achieve a range of aspirations, including productivity increases. This will require integration of the research effort, best achieved through mechanisms of integration that start with priority setting and funding.

ii How do we break the mindset of focusing on single issues?

The challenges confronting rural and regional research are no longer simply about resolving diametrically opposed stresses represented through conflicts such as production wealth versus environment health, community expectations versus farmers' rights, urban growth versus rural values, and regionalisation versus centralised governance. Although these tensions remain, they now embed an even more complex entanglement of discords: environment versus environment (e.g. trade-offs between plantation forestry benefits and potentially reduced environmental flows); one form of production versus another (e.g. conflicts between farming and mining); rural versus rural (e.g. trade-offs between water allocation for growing rural towns and water to maintain large irrigation industries); and empowerment versus subsidiarity in managing environments locally (i.e. balancing the incentives and uncertainties of trust and the transaction costs and certainties of accountability). Dealing with these tensions is all grist for the rural research mill; however, each tension carries with it ethical dimensions as well as economic, biophysical and other social research ones. By describing this as a *complex entanglement*, the intention is to convey the enormity of the challenges to rural and regional research that the interrelationships between these problem domains present.

This does not bode well for research funding mechanisms which have tended to deal with more narrowly defined issues. The competitive nature of research funding often acts to reinforce this constricted focus so that projects can be neatly categorised and include feasible methods and achievable outputs that are easily peer-reviewed by disciplinary-based panels (Gannon 2005). Moreover, in a tide of centralism the range of research priorities tends to get contracted into narrow themes, while the demand for research agencies to lever complementary research funding sources helps ensure these narrow themes pervade the wider research funding infrastructure. This phenomenon has been observed in Europe, where each change in European Union Framework Programme research priorities is followed by a corresponding shift in the wider research activities of research institutions, both public and private (Breschi and Cusmano 2004).

While this may be appropriate for addressing some short-term research problems, the phenomenon is highly problematic where issues are complex, long-term and deeply interconnected (Sprinz 2009), such as those associated with climate change (Hovi *et al.* 2009). Under these circumstances, Sprinz (2009) argues that although governments should be best placed to deal with the multidimensional complexities of problems, they are hampered by the fact that 'long-term policy problems pose a rather difficult class of challenges that are beyond the scope of single parliaments and political or bureaucratic tenures in office' (Sprinz 2009, p. 2). This would seem like a good argument for models of research priority setting and funding that are tied to the long-term interests of society through its communities, and that are resistant to the ebbs and flows of centralist agendas.

Bello poses three questions about a post-neoliberal world that, although placed in the context of dealing with the global financial crisis, could just as well be placed in the context of establishing research agendas:

> Will government ownership, intervention, and control be exercised simply to stabilize capitalism, after which control will be given back to the corporate elites? Are we going to see a second round of Keynesian capitalism, where the state and corporate elites along with labour work out a partnership based on industrial policy, growth and high wages – only with a green dimension this time around? Or will we witness the beginnings of fundamental shifts in the ownership and control of the economy in a more popular direction? There are limits to reform in the system of global capitalism, but at no other time in the last half century have those limits seemed more fluid.
>
> (Bello 2008, p. 1)

Here, one could easily substitute the terms *capitalism* and *economy* for *research agenda* and consider a future rural research funding model that, working alongside the RDCs, might take into account a wider and truer representation of the rural community. The establishment of catchment management boards across the country gave some promise to this; however these have largely become on-ground implementation organisations constricted by the priorities of the government of the day. Generally, they have little responsibility for setting and funding research agendas, and in any case typically have no rural mandate beyond natural resource management.

iii How do we reconcile evidence-based policy with adaptive management?

Research, including rural research, is supported on many grounds, one of which is the need to underpin sound policy. The pursuit of evidence-based policy seems universal across western democracies at present, perhaps because of its universal appeal:

> It is difficult to imagine anyone arguing that policy should be based on anything but the best available evidence. The concept of evidence based policy has an intuitive, common sense logic, which partly explains how it has become naturalised in a diverse range of policy settings.
>
> (Marston and Watts 2003, p. 144)

In reality, evidence-based policy is contested because the very nature of evidence is contested. This is not simply because different forms of evidence are derived from different philosophical approaches, but also because, as British studies certainly suggest, there appears to be a hierarchy of evidence in terms of perceived credibility, with lay forms of evidence coming down in the hierarchy (Nutley *et al.* 2002). This hierarchy tends to favour policy elites such as

Ministerial advisers and senior public servants who have greater access to those forms of evidence seen to be more credible, such as research and statistics, policy evaluation, economic modelling and expert advice (Marston and Watts 2003). In the context of many regional issues, this hierarchy also gets messy because of interest group activism and political reactivism, and because of inherent uncertainties in the science due to the complexity of the issues faced.

In the context of building future resilience in the bush, the role of rural research needs to take into account the nature of resilience. Important elements of resilience are the capacity to self organise, learn, adapt and cope with nonlinearities and uncertainties (Lebel *et al.* 2006). These are also important elements in dealing with multiple problem domains (Reynolds 2001). Most critically, these aspects of resilience support an adaptive management approach to dealing with the growing complexity of rural issues. Unfortunately, the fluid nature of these concepts can be at odds with what constitutes good evidence from a policy perspective. Here, the notions that support evidence-based policy and adaptive management come into conflict. Although advocates of adaptive management argue that adaptation must be based on good science (Lindenmayer 2009; Holling 1978), in reality the availability of good science and the need to adapt do not always coincide (McDonald 2007). Moreover, the investment level required to support good science tied to adaptive management processes can be prohibitive (Walters 1997). If other forms of knowledge are taken into account in the process of developing adaptive management strategies, then a similar problem of hierarchical evidence arises, particularly where groups such as Aboriginal people, women or the elderly are marginalised in communities (Tompkins and Adger 2004; Hunt, this volume). These groups may be cut out of the decision-making process altogether, or their evidence may be given less weighting. Without an adaptive management framework for dealing with rural research in the future, issues of community resilience are likely to be subjugated in favour of traditional forms of single-domain production research with narrow, incremental benefits.

iv What place is there for social science?

In the 1970s many of the social science disciplines started to shift their focus from more academic pursuits of rural research to the applied challenges that were emerging in rural communities, particularly where these included natural resource management. This focus began with studies on property rights and co-management (Hanna and Munasinghe 1995). The transition arose partly from the perceived inability of the biophysical sciences alone to resolve the full range of issues facing communities, and partly because of an increasing interest among decision-makers in emerging forms of governance (Gibbons *et al.* 1994).

The limited success of the biophysical sciences to resolve the broad range of rural issues should not be seen as a failure of the disciplines themselves or the quality of the research, but rather a breakdown in the interpretation of science into policy (Luks and Siebenhuner 2007). There also was, and still is, a strong tendency to assume that most problems can be solved by identifying the optimal solution and developing a method to apply that solution. Such an approach to framing problems lends itself to the development of 'scientific tool kits', the forte of the biophysical sciences. In the 1990s the idea of 'post-normal science' emerged (Funtowicz and Ravetz 1992), which proposed that problems are perceived differently by different people and that addressing such problems requires understanding different perceptions (or 'truths') before proposing solutions. Indeed, there is rarely one solution that will suit everyone when dealing with these so-called 'wicked problems', and managing the process of consultation with stakeholders becomes the key to finding a solution that most will accept (Kane and Bishop 2002).

Social science comes into its own in identifying and dealing with multiple perceptions of problems, understanding their basis, and finding ways to bring people to the point of acceptance of imperfect solutions. It is therefore an essential element of adaptive management as well as a means of addressing the conflict raised previously, between evidence-based policy and adaptive management.

Conclusion

The history of rural research and its institutionalisation in Australia has been about the search for resilience in two ways. First, it has been directed towards taming a harsh country and then aligning agriculture to fit, so that farmers and communities dependent upon them can thrive in the bush. Second, the policies underpinning rural research funding have been directed towards supporting models of investment that in themselves are resilient. The evolution of the RDC system, for example, has seen a relatively stable model of funding in place for the greater part of history since World War II. Even the Productivity Commission's recent recommendations to change this model have been rejected by the current government (Ludwig 2011).

Past rural research has largely followed a productivist pathway, shaped by a coalition between government and industry bodies that voices the concerns of Australia's farmers. However, resilience of rural communities, and even of individual farmers, will in future require a rural research map and supporting mechanisms that are better suited to addressing multiple problem domains. This will require greater levels of inspirational, intellectual, financial and physical collaboration at every level, both horizontally and vertically, in future. An important feature will be the capacity of institutions involved in rural research to take an adaptive management approach to knowledge generation, sharing and implementation as a means of both identifying problems as well as addressing them. It will require rural research institutions to listen to the voice of a greater range of stakeholders in the bush, including those who do not have formal bodies of representation.

References

Barker, A 1982, *Quangos in Britain*, Macmillan, London.

Bello, W 2008, 'The Coming Capitalist Consensus', *Foreign Policy in Focus*, 24 December.

Breschi, S and Cusmano, L 2004, 'Unveiling the structure of an European research area: Emergence of oligarchic networks under E.U. Framework Programmes', *International Journal of Technology Management*, vol. 27, pp. 747–782.

Campbell, C and Halligan, J 1992, *Political Leadership in an Age of Constraint*, Allen & Unwin, Sydney.

Cockfield, G 2015, 'From state direction to community self-efficacy: The devolution of responsibility for regional development in Australia', this volume.

CRRDC (Council of Rural Research and Development Corporations Chairs) 2010, *Impact of Investment in Research and Development by the Rural Research and Development Corporations: Year 2 Results*, CRRDC, Canberra.

Day, PR 2005, *RDC Profiles 2004–05: A Summary of Rural Research & Development Corporations and Companies*, Land and Water Australia, Canberra.

De Vries, MS 2000, 'The Rise and Fall of Decentralization: A Comparative Analysis of Arguments and Practices in European Countries', *European Journal of Political Research*, vol. 38, pp. 193–224.

Dunleavy, P 1982, 'Quasi-Governmental Sector: Some Implications for Public Policy-Making in Britain', in Barker, A (ed.), *Quangos in Britain*, Macmillan, London.

DoFA (Department of Finance and Administration) 2004, *List of Australian Government Bodies 2002–2003, Financial Management Reference Material No. 1*, Commonwealth of Australia, Canberra.

Dovers, S and Price, RJ 2007, 'Research and the Integration Imperative' in Hanna, K and Slocombe, D (eds), *Integrated Resource and Environmental Management*, Oxford University Press, Toronto.

Dunn, T, Gray, I and Phillips, E 2000, 'From Personal Barriers to Community Plans: a Farm and Community Planning Approach to the Extension of Sustainable Agriculture', in Schulman, AD and Price, RJ (eds), *Case Studies in Increasing the Adoption of Sustainable Resource Management Practices*, Land and Water Resources Research and Development Corporation, Canberra, pp. 17–33.

Funtowicz, SO and Ravetz, JR 1992, 'Three Types of Risk Assessment and the Emergence of Post-Normal Science' in Krimsky, S and Golding, D (eds), *Social Theories of Risk*, Prager, Westport.

Gannon, F 2005, 'Is the system dumbing down research?', *EMBO Reports*, vol. 6, p. 387.

Gerritsen, R 1987, 'Collective action problems in the regulation of Australia's common property rebewable resources', *Australian Journal of Public Administration*, vol. 46, no. 4, pp. 390–401.

Gibbons, M, Limoges, C, Nowotny, S, Schwartzma, P, Scotland, P and Trow, M 1994, *The New Production of Knowledge: The Dynamics of Science and Research in Contemporary Societies*, Sage, London.

Gross, C 2015, 'Understanding the aspirations of people living in rural and regional Australia', this volume.

Halligan, J 2006, 'The Reassertion of the Centre in a First Generation NPM System', in Christensen, T and Lægreid, P (eds), *Autonomy and Regulation. Coping with agencies in the modern state*, Edward Elgar, Cheltenham.

Hanna, S and Munasinghe, M (eds) 1995, *Property rights and the environment: social and ecological issues*. Beijer International Institute of ecological economics and the World Bank, Washington DC.

Holling, CS (ed.) 1978, *Adaptive environmental assessment and management. International series on applied systems analysis 3*, International Institute for Applied Systems Analysis and John Wiley and Sons, Toronto.

Hovi, J, Sprinz, D and Underdal, A 2009, 'Implementing long-term climate policy: Time inconsistency, domestic politics, international anarchy', *Global Environmental Politics*, vol. 9, no. 3, pp. 20–39.

Hunt, J 2015, 'The Commonwealth's policies and Aboriginal people in regional Australia', this volume.

Jarrett, FG and Lindner, RK 1982, 'Rural Research in Australia' in Williams, DB (ed.), *Agriculture in the Australian Economy*, Sydney University Press, Sydney.

Kane, J and Bishop, P 2002, 'Consultation and Contest: the danger of mixing modes' *Australian journal of public administration*, vol. 61, no. 1, pp. 87–94.

Kerin, J and Cook, P 1989, *Research Innovation and Competitiveness: Policies For Reshaping Australia's Primary Industries and Energy Portfolio Research and Development*, Commonwealth of Australia, Canberra.

Lebel, L, Anderies, JM, Campbell, B, Folke, C, Hatfield-Dodds, S, Hughes, TP and Wilson, J 2006, Governance and the capacity to manage resilience in regional social-ecological systems, *Ecology and Society*, vol. 11, no. 1, p. 19. Available at: www.ecologyandsociety.org/vol. 11/iss1/art19/. Accessed: 3 October 2011.

Lindenmayer, DB 2009, 'Forestwildlife management and conservation', *New York Academy of Sciences*, vol. 1162, pp. 284–310.

Lockie, S, Lawrence, G and Cheshire, L 2006, 'Reconfiguring rural resource governance: the legacy of neo-liberalism in Australia', in Cloke, PJ, Marsden, T and Mooney, PH (eds), *Handbook of rural studies*, Sage, London.

Lovett, S 1997, 'Reforms to rural research and development viewed in a new light: the importance of the individual', *Australian Journal of Public Administration*, vol. 56, no. 2, pp. 81–94.

Ludwig, J 2011, *Rural research and development: Statement by the Minister for Agriculture, Fisheries and Forestry*, 15 June 2011, Commonwealth of Australia, Canberra.

Luks, F and Siebenhuner, B 2007, 'Transdisciplinarity for social learning? The contribution of the German socioecological research initiative to sustainability governance', *Ecological Economics*, vol. 63, nos 2–3, pp. 418–426.

Mackenzie, JM and Hood, CC 1975, 'Administrative Control, Collusive Conflict and Uncoupled Hierarchies' in Hague, DC, Mackenzie, WJM and Barker, A (eds), *Public Policy and Private Interests: The Institutions of Compromise*, Macmillan Press, London.

Marsh, SP and Pannell, DJ 2000, 'Agricultural extension policy in Australia: The good, the bad and the misguided', *Australian Journal of Agricultural and Resource Economics*, vol. 44, no. 4, pp. 605–627.

Marston, G and Watts, T 2003, 'Tampering with the evidence: A critical appraisal of evidence-based policy-making', *An Australian Review of Public Affairs*, vol. 3, no. 3, pp. 143–163.

Martin, W 1990, 'Rural Policy', in Jennett, C and Stewart, RG (eds), *Hawke and Australian Public Policy*, Macmillan, Melbourne.

Mauldon, RG and Schapper, HP 1974, *Australian Farmers Under Stress in Prosperity and Recession*, University of WA Press, Perth.

McDonald, J 2007, 'Is new policy evidence based – and is it working?', in Wilson, AL, Dehaan, RL, Watts, RJ, Page, KJ, Bowmer, KH and Curtis, A (eds), *Proceedings of the 5th Australian Stream Management Conference. Australian rivers: making a difference*, Charles Sturt University, Thurgoona.

McFarlane, J 1999, 'Collaborative Research: The Australian Experience', *International Journal of Technology Management*, vol. 17, no. 4, p. 387.

Mullen, JD 2007, 'Productivity growth and the returns from public investment in R&D in Australian broadacre agriculture', *Australian Journal of Agricultural Economics*, vol. 51, pp. 359–384.

Nicholson, C, Barr, N, Kentish, A, Dowling, PM, McCormick, LH, Palmer, M, Simpson, I, Simpson, K and Walsh J 2003, 'A research-extension model for encouraging the adoption of productive and sustainable practice in high rainfall grazing areas', *Australian Journal of Experimental Agriculture*, vol. 43, pp. 685–694.

Nutley, S, Davies, H and Walter I 2002, '*Evidence-Based Policy and Practice: Cross Sector Lessons from the UK*', Working Paper 9, Research Unit for Research Utilisation, University of St Andrews, St Andrews Scotland.

Price, RJ 1992, 'Dual Accountability in Primary Industries Statutory Enterprises', Masters Thesis, University of Canberra, Canberra.

Price, RJ 1994, 'From Governor Phillip to Captain Collins – The evolution of rural research funding in Australia', *Agricultural Science*, vol. 7, no. 3, pp. 26–30.

Productivity Commission 2011, *Rural Research and Development Corporations, Report No. 52, Final Inquiry Report*, Commonwealth of Australia, Canberra.

PSB (Public Service Board) 1983, *A Joint Management Review of the Administration of Research Schemes in the Primary Industry Portfolio*, Urwick International, Melbourne.

RCAGA (Royal Commission on Australian Government Administration) 1976, *Appendix to Report: Volumes 1 and 2*, Commonwealth of Australia, Canberra.

Reynolds, KM 2001, 'Fuzzy logic knowledge bases in integrated landscape assessment: Examples and possibilities', *General Technical Report PNW-GTR-521*, USDA Forest Service Pacific Northwest Research Station, Portland.

Rhodes, G 1975, 'Accountability and Social Innovation: Some British Experience', in Hague, DC, Mackenzie, WJM and Barker, A (eds), *Public Policy and Private Interests: The Institutions of Compromise*, Macmillan Press, London.

RRDC (Rural Research and Development Council) 2011, *Draft National Strategic Rural Research and Development Investment Plan*, RRDC, Canberra.

Schedler, A 1999, 'Conceptualizing Accountability' in Schedler, A, Diamond, L and Plattner, M (eds), *The Self-Restraining State: Power and Accountability in New Democracies*, Lynne Rienner, Boulder, pp. 12–28.

Sher, J and Sher, K 1994, 'Beyond conventional wisdom: Rural development as if Australia's rural people really mattered', in McSwan, D and McShane, D (eds), *Issues Affecting Rural Communities*, Townsville Rural Education Research and Development Centre, James Cook University, pp. 9–32.

Shergold, P 2004, 'Plan and Deliver: Avoiding Bureaucratic Hold-up', paper presented to Australian Graduate School of Management/Harvard Club of Australia, 17 November, Canberra.

Smith, E and Pritchard, B 2015, 'Australian agricultural policy: the pursuit of agricultural efficiency', this volume.

Sprinz, DF 2009, 'Long-term environmental policy: definition, knowledge, future research', *Global Environmental Politics* vol. 9, no. 3, pp. 1–8.

Tompkins, EL and Adger, WN 2004, 'Does adaptive management of natural resources enhance resilience to climate change?', *Ecology and Society*, vol. 9, no. 2, p. 10.

Uhrig, J 2003, *Review of the Corporate Governance of Statutory Authorities and Office Holders Report*, Commonwealth of Australia, Canberra.

Vanclay, F 2004, 'Social principles for agricultural extension to assist in the promotion of natural resource management', *Australian Journal of Experimental Agriculture*, vol. 44, pp. 213–222.

Vanclay, F and Lawrence, G 1994, 'Farmer rationality and the adoption of environmentally sound practices: a critique of the assumptions of traditional agricultural extension', *European Journal of Agricultural Education and Extension*, vol. 1, pp. 50–90.

Walters, C 1997, 'Challenges in adaptive management of riparian and coastal ecosystems', *Conservation Ecology*, vol. 1, no. 1. Available at: www.consecol.org/vol. 1/iss2/art1. Accessed: 3 October 2011.

Part III

Emerging issues in rural and regional policy

14 Assessing adaptability in regional economies

Kim Houghton and Thomas Fell

Introduction: irrigation and the economics of drought in rural and regional communities

Water availability has long been thought to be the key driver of agricultural economies, and many economic tools have been used to assess the quantitative links between water availability, water use, production and regional economic activity. Preparation of the Murray–Darling Basin Plan has seen several studies done that model the economic impacts of various levels of water availability. These models take high-level data on the structure of agricultural economies and use it to model the effect on smaller regions, typically postulating a linear relationship between availability of irrigation water and economic activity. As the Murray–Darling Basin Authority states, 'The relationship between water availability and economic activity is more or less a straight line' (2010, p. 776).

Is this statement accurate? Through the early 2000s, and in particular through the drought years, while water availability and production were highly variable, the flow-on effects through regional economies appeared very mixed. Despite the concerns raised at the height of the drought, and despite the genuine economic hardship clearly experienced by businesses in regional communities, no towns appear to have 'died' as a result of reduced water availability. Better understanding of the links between these economic relationships will help communities identify their economic 'tipping points' and adaptive capacity.

It is crucial for the future of the Murray–Darling Basin that policymakers, researchers and community members have a good understanding of how the many different parts of the Basin have reacted to variations in water availability, and how they will react to future variations. But the research findings on these relationships are often in conflict, and there also seems to be a disconnect between the results of the modelling and the observed experience through the drought in many Basin communities. This chapter sets out an alternative approach to modelling the relationship between water availability in agricultural communities and economic activity, an approach which is grounded from the outset in the local, lived experience of the study sites.

This chapter is a summary of the report *Securing Wealth and Wellbeing of Regional Communities*, prepared by Strategic Economic Solutions for Cotton

Catchment Communities CRC. By investigating the socio-economic histories of three case study regions (St George, Gunnedah and Waikerie), and then collecting first-hand information along local agricultural supply chains, the project sought to better understand the linear and non-linear relationships between agricultural production and local economies. The project wanted to map local examples of economic adaptability in small communities to assess the scale of adaptation over the decade of the drought, and beyond.

Economic adaptation

A 2011 study into regional economic sustainability for the National Institute for Rural and Regional Australia (NIRRA) explores the characteristics of long-term sustainability in regional Australia, focusing on the impact of population movements, economic growth and investment cycles, and adaptation to external drivers like commodity/resource prices and consumer/resident preferences (Houghton and Fell 2012).

Population has long been thought to be the driver of economic development in regional Australia. But in the study mentioned previously, economic sustainability in regional Australia appears to be more dependent on adaptation and the capacity for transitions than on population growth per se, which is better seen as a means to an end, rather than an end in itself. As discussed in other chapters in this book, the nineteenth and twentieth century notions of 'populate or perish' have no real basis in Australia's current economy, with investment and jobs being drivers in the twenty-first century.

Economic diversification is also seen as another component of the path to economic sustainability. The importance of diversification reflects the changes seen in most regional economies as economic structural adjustments have seen whole industry sectors become uncompetitive and disappear. Industry sectors such as Tasmanian apples in the 1960s or Victorian textiles and clothing in the 1990s lost competitiveness, with the policy response being to diversify the economies to reduce dependence on individual sectors, thereby improving prospects

Table 14.1 Typology of population and diversification dynamics

Working population	**Increasing**	Growing around dominant industries, exposure to external shocks *muscle town*	Growing and diversifying *thriving/reviving town*
	Decreasing	Consolidating around dominant industries – no structural adjustment *dying town*	Effective 'structural adjustment' *turnaround town*
		Decreasing	**Increasing**
		Employment diversity	

Source: Houghton and Fell 2012.

for long-term sustainability. But even in regards to employment, diversification of employment in a local economy – typically thought to be a prerequisite for economic sustainability – is in fact not always necessary. Over-emphasis on diversification would see potential windfall gains be foregone if a region failed to capitalise on an opportunity in a particular sector in which it had some competitive advantage. Even if this competitive advantage was short lived, economic gains could be wrung from it, and the real issue is managing the adaptation once the opportunity has passed (Houghton and Fell 2012).

A four-quadrant approach depicts the pressures on regional communities in terms of working population (growth or decline) and employment mix (diversity increasing or decreasing).

This typology shows that population growth can co-exist with decreasing economic diversity, if a regional economy grows around one of its existing strengths – such as a mining related 'muscle town'. It also shows there is place for a regional economy which is diversifying without population growth, as structural adjustment occurs and new employers take the place of those displaced, with no net growth.

This depiction is useful in thinking about enhancing economic adaptation in the three study sites, as it highlights the importance of changes in both the axis variables: size of the working population and employment mix. Long-term structural challenges tend to reduce employment diversity in the short term, with a positive adjustment bringing subsequent increases in employment diversity as the economy reconfigures itself. These changes either increase the working population if the town is in a 'boom' area, or decrease it if not.

The three study sites can be situated in this typology to give a snapshot of their current economic environment. The Queensland town of St George has been through its 'cotton boom' and is now consolidating, whereas Gunnedah in New South Wales is restructuring, creating (slowly) a broader economic and population base. In the other study site, the South Australian town of Waikerie, more than one in three employed people work directly in the agricultural sector (*Waikerie Economic Profile* 2007, p. 5), with the main enterprise being grapes and citrus fruit. Based on the typology above, if the working population is not increasing, it is crucial that employment diversity does. In fact, Waikerie is in the midst of structural change to the citrus industry, and is taking active steps (through the Riverland Sustainable Futures process) to build industry diversity. An exacerbating factor is that in Waikerie there is less scope for changing crops to suit different environmental conditions, because of the significant investment required in infrastructure for orchards and vineyards.

Understanding adaptation and water

Regional economic modelling is commonly done using either computable general equilibrium (CGE) models or Input-Output models. Both these approaches start with national level data on sectoral activity and the linkages between sectors using national ABS data on economic activity. Derived ratios such as employment per dollar of output or employment per dollar of value added are then used to approximate the mix of economic activity in a regional study area. These approximations are central to the modelling processes, as accurate and detailed regional data on economic activity are not available in Australia. The most common proxy measure is the regularly-measured number of people employed in an industry sector in a specified region. This measure for each sector is then multiplied by one of these derived ratios to estimate the total value of output or value added from the sector.

Enhanced computing power has given these models much greater ability to produce more sophisticated and sensitive results, but the underlying weakness is that the economic performance measures (like productivity per worker, or value-added) come from national averages. This means that regional specialisations which generate region-specific productivity rates or value-adding rates are effectively washed out of the modelling, and national averages are imposed instead. This is one of the reasons why there is often some criticism of 'top-down' economic modelling on regional economies by stakeholders in those regional communities, and is one reason why modelled projections are often seen as unrealistic.

Because of this inherent washing away of local specialisations, these 'top-down' modelling approaches are not very useful in understanding local and regional economic adaptation, for example predicting the local or regional economic impacts of reduced water availability.

In work undertaken for the MDBA (Marsden Jacobs and Associates 2010), people in 12 irrigation areas in the Basin were asked how they would respond to water availability reductions of 20 per cent, 40 per cent and 60 per cent. The interviews and surveys showed that businesses (including farm businesses) in each sub-region expected little change to operations if water reductions were up to 20 per cent. On the other hand,

> ...removing 20% or more water from the consumptive pool without compensation would trigger widespread and large scale change within all irrigation regions in the Murray–Darling Basin.
>
> (Ibid., p. xiii)

Furthermore, reductions of 40 per cent or more would see reduced production and processing of cotton, rice, dairy and horticulture (ibid., p. xiv).

These findings suggest some elasticity in the ability of growers and others in these sub-regional economies to adapt to changes in water availability, and some important tipping points as water availability reduces. The presence of both elasticity and tipping points suggests that responses to water availability will not be linear – i.e. it would not be prudent to align economic activity with water use by imputing a certain level of activity (e.g. output or employment) per gigalitre consumed.

Nevertheless, the quote at the beginning of this chapter shows that this assumption was in fact central to the 2010 study. It was also made in another study done at the same time where employment predictions were made for the Balonne Shire in relation to 10 per cent, 25 per cent and 50 per cent reductions in water availability (Judith Stubbs and Associates 2010). The 25 per cent water allocation scenario job loss prediction was 2.5 times the 10 per cent scenario, and the 50 per cent water allocation scenario job loss prediction was five times the 10 per cent scenario. These predictions were made despite the evidence that small reductions would have little effect on economic activity and that much bigger impacts were expected once the 40 per cent reduction threshold had been crossed.

The assumption of linear relationships between water availability and economic activity does not fit well with the observed changes through the drought, nor with adaptability expectations of people interviewed in Basin sub-regions. These adaptability expectations reflect characteristics of elasticity and tipping points rather than linearity. Another approach is needed if predictions and modelling are to be closer to the reality of economic life in basin communities, and if the predictions are to pass the 'town meeting reality-check test'.

A more 'bottom-up' approach was taken by the Centre for Agricultural and Regional Economics (CARE) in another study analysing the impact of water availability (2003). The study gathered farm performance data over several years and over several farms to determine farm production functions – with the production functions relating farm level economic activity to a range of inputs, including water.

This approach provides a much more locally-responsive modelling framework, as adaptive behaviours are based on the observed experiences of farmers in the study region. The outcomes of each farmer's adaptive strategies were then aggregated and fed in as inputs into a regional Input-Output model to estimate the overall impact of reduced water availability. This approach is able to better capture local specialisations, but is very labour-intensive and expensive as considerable local data needs to be gathered before modelling can be undertaken.

The local supply chain approach undertaken here seeks a more efficient and cost-effective way of incorporating local economic specialisations into adaptability and impact analysis.

Managing change: supply chain interviews

Brief economic histories of St George, Gunnedah and Waikerie investigated social change associated with primary industries in these three rural towns. In a general sense the pattern in each community has been similar, in that each has gone through major structural changes in the last 100 years or so. Each local economy and each community has demonstrated its capacity for adaptation: changes in crop varieties, changed practices and scales of production, and changes in the people involved and the economic infrastructure around them. For example, St George was founded as the district centre of what was then a wheat-sheep area. Now, St George and its surrounding region are highly dependent on irrigated agriculture both directly and indirectly as a major source of economic activity and employment; in 2005–2006 crops accounted for approximately 60 per cent of the total value of agricultural production (Murray–Darling Basin Authority 2010, p. 890).

While seasonal water availability, irrigation infrastructure and climate variability clearly take their places in the influences on the agricultural enterprises in the study areas, longer-term sustainability is also about retaining people and business in the community, as well as seeing the business mix adapt to and change with external drivers. An example is the way in which the town of Gunnedah has had to adapt over time to the decline of its mining industry and the more recent closure of a local abattoir.

The complexity of economic and social change in the three case study sites means that community adaptation is best understood at the local level. Local level information and data reflect the realities of local agricultural and downstream business activity in a way that the top-down economic performance ratios do not. In the approach followed here, interviews with farmers and farm-servicing businesses in the three case study areas provided detailed information about the practicalities of supply chain economics in each area. In St George and Gunnedah the research was focused on the cotton supply chain, and in Waikerie it was focused on citrus and grapes. The following is a summary of the results from St George.

The cotton supply chain

Figure 14.1 shows a simple representation of the cotton supply chain in St George. Cotton moves along the middle line from growers to gins (where fibre is separated from the seed) and then to buyers. The major buyers of Australian cotton are currently China, Indonesia, Thailand, South Korea and Japan, and there is no government intervention in the growing or marketing of the crop

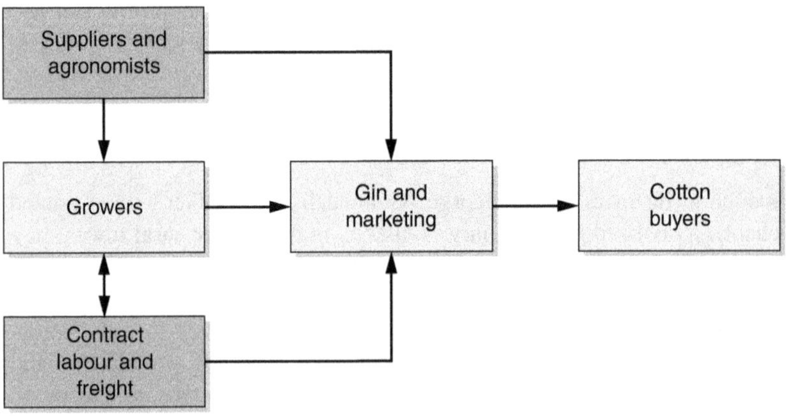

Figure 14.1 The cotton supply chain (source: Houghton and Fell 2012).

(Roth 2010, p. 23). The cotton supply chain in St George is quite tightly controlled, with one major company operating the three gins in the area, and also providing marketing services to many growers. Most of the other services required by the growers in both areas, such as machinery, agronomy and chemical supplies, are provided by local businesses. Growers use freight and contract labour from outside sources but in many cases may also provide these services for other growers. The whole supply chain in the area is therefore quite contained and interdependent.

Interview findings

Three cotton growers and seven businesses (including gins, suppliers and contractors) were interviewed in St George. The interviews revealed that it there is no simple way to quantify the changes to local economy for small communities that rely on agricultural industries. For example, if water availability is reduced in St George, how will this affect employment in the town or through the supply chain? Each grower or business interviewed set out their own approach to this familiar challenge and most of the farmers and non-farm businesses interviewed had strategies aimed at retaining staff through difficult periods. For example, one grower commented:

> I didn't lay off staff [during the drought] because I knew that they were going to be hard to replace, and I had one fella coming up for retirement anyway, and it's very hard to pelt [*sic*] someone for two years and then say can you come back now ... everyone knew that we should be decreasing staff but I actually decreased hours and I worked around it that way...

The reluctance to lose staff (except when absolutely necessary) suggests that the relationship between employment loss and reduced water availability is non-linear. In other words, there appeared to be no simple, consistent ratio linking declining production, subsequent loss of business and declining employment. The reasons for this include difficulty in attracting new staff when times get better, and the fact that employers know the impact that job loss will have on individuals and the community, and therefore try to avoid it. The one exception to this was the cotton gins, which reduced the hours of casual staff in direct relationship to the amount of cotton available for processing – though they minimised the impacts on their full-time staff. Most businesses also mentioned issues of labour availability, including competition with mining and lack of skilled candidates.

The 'tipping points' for adaptation were also an important subject of the interviews. Farmers and businesses were asked to predict their actions if water availability (and its impact on cotton related businesses) was decreased or increased by 10 per cent, 25 per cent or 50 per cent, respectively. Business owners (non-farm businesses) reported that they take some action if activity levels drop by over 25 per cent, but at that level the main actions involve monitoring and reducing costs. For growers, a reduction of water availability of 10 per cent or even 25 per cent is within normal business parameters and growers will use immediately available tools, such as varying the mix of farm operations, to minimise any negative impacts on their farm businesses. If activity levels drop by 50 per cent then more drastic action follows. For businesses this could include active diversification into other business income, overall reductions in staff and contractors, and reduced spending on other operating costs. A 50 per cent reduction in water availability means that growers will review the viability of the farm in that season and will consider selling assets, finding other income or employment, leaving farming and perhaps even leaving the community.

The case studies of farm businesses in this study confirmed that the relationship between production, profitability and water availability is highly complex and non-linear. It depends on many factors including the timing of the water and the ability of the farmer to employ opportunistic cropping, severity of pests, localised climatic conditions, management decisions and the ongoing financial position of the grower. This means that the flow-on effects to on-farm employment and economic activity in the surrounding economy are difficult to predict. However, in the case of the cotton gins there is a clear impact on casual employment, which is directly related to the amount of cotton available in any one season. Other businesses are more adaptable and can find other income sources. The effects are thus varied across the supply chain and elasticity is a key feature of the interactions within it.

Modelling local economic adaptation

Based on the economic information collected by the interviews, including employment and production data, a simple model of local production was devised. This approach was selected to try and create an accurate picture of the scale of activities along the local agricultural supply chain, as well as business responses to increased or decreased activity. The inability to properly account for these localised effects is a key weakness on the more common 'top-down' input-output or general equilibrium modelling approaches.

The approach used here is based on a pragmatic approach to gathering local information (which can be an expensive process) alongside making appropriate use of higher level (national) data and economic relationships. In this way, this approach seeks to draw out the best aspects of both the top-down and bottom-up approaches into a methodologically sound and cost-effective tool for communities to predict the impact on their specific local economy.

Three scenarios were modelled:

- High level of planting and water availability.
- Medium level of planting and water availability.
- Low level of planting and water availability.

The modelling showed the extent to which the localised impacts are predicted to vary across each site, and vary widely across each scenario – confirming the inappropriateness of imposing linear relationships between water and economic activity in these supply chains. For the two cotton communities, on-farm employment is likely to vary by a factor of four between the low planting and high planting scenarios. Flow-on employment would vary in the range of two-fold to five-fold.

For St George, it is likely that the total on-farm and immediate flow-on employment would vary by a very significant 307 employees between the best scenario (445 people) and the worst (138 people). These projections take into account the changed employment response for the high/medium and worst scenarios, and amount to some 14 per cent of the Balonne Shire workforce in 2006. For Gunnedah, the variance would be 390, between the best scenario (633 people) and the worst scenario (243 people). This is a smaller proportion (8 per cent) of the larger Gunnedah workforce. The higher water and labour costs anticipated from the worst case have also been factored in, leading to ten-to-twelve-fold differences in the amount of discretionary spend from growers into the community.

The modelling for Waikerie shows that the direct and flow-on levels of employment vary from 440 in the best scenario, to 210 for the worst scenario. This is a change of 230 people, some 32 per cent of the jobs in Waikerie. The Waikerie modelling shows nearly three-fold variances in grower discretionary spend between the best and worst scenarios, indicating significant flow-on impacts across the local economy.

It is clear that in modelling local economic activity in these rural study areas, the main players in the supply chains are experienced in handling variability in agricultural activity levels, and that there is not a simple, linear relationship between planting, harvest and local flow-on spending. In particular, it is not accurate to predict flow-on spending by growers, or employment levels on farms or in processing businesses, as a fixed proportion of the area that is under crop in any given region. There is a tipping point for grower and business adaptation of between 25 per cent and 50 per cent reductions in water availability, with practices for both groups changing significantly beyond 50 per cent reduction.

It is important to understand the nature of these tipping points and improve understanding of the impacts of changes on agricultural production, so that communities have access to more robust and more intuitively believable modelling. Earlier simplifications which base modelling on fixed relationships like employment per gigalitre of water used have had little traction in communities. The interviews, local histories and modelling done for this project have shown that these relationships are not linear, and that to base further research on such an erroneous assertion is to invite community criticism.

While some level of variation is expected as ‘the norm’, the scale of the downstream consequences is significant. The best/worst scenarios showed an 8 per cent impact on total employment in Gunnedah, 14 per cent in St George and 32 per cent in Waikerie. The modelling also showed that a five-fold increase in area planted (or of water available) could lead to a ten-to-12-fold increase in discretionary spending in these regional economies – a very significant ‘topping up of the economic tank’.

Conclusion

This project has been about testing proof of concepts in an alternative approach to understanding the linkages in small agricultural economies. It has tested a 'bottom-up' approach built around local intelligence about the flows within supply chains important to three local economies, and how these have adapted to external changes over the last decade or so. This approach seems useful in being able to generate believable scenarios for local futures, but will require more breadth (analysis of other supply chains) and depth (closer analysis of firm-level responses to changing circumstances) before it can be used as an holistic approach.

The credibility of predictive modelling in farming communities is much enhanced when it is obvious that key local supply chains, and even key local businesses, have been included. This requires a measure of local information gathering to understand the nature of changes experienced to date, how much 'petrol is still in the tank' to contribute to further adaptations, and therefore how the local economy will respond to the next challenge. Some local economies will be highly dependent on particular crops, and even on the performance of particular businesses tied to those crops, while others will be responding to a more diversified agricultural base.

Incorporating local information is crucial in generating more realistic predictions of adaptations, and in passing the 'town hall test' in that the predictions are broadly accepted by the community. This process empowers communities to be more active in planning their responses to different scenarios, and understanding the strengths and weaknesses of their capacity to adapt in future.

Based on the case study areas, adaptation is 'the norm' for rural communities; they clearly have elastic businesses and 'spongy' labour markets that adapt well within quite wide ranges. Businesses are generally reluctant to let staff go, especially full-time staff, and workers are generally reluctant to move.

For governments, the implication of this and of the companion work by NIRRA (see Houghton and Fell 2012) is that assistance with adaptation or transition, based on an understanding of the local flows in employment growth and diversity, is much better than 'knee-jerk' assistance to declining businesses or industries. However, it is also important to acknowledge that there is clearly a breaking point if the lean times continue. As one farmer said in the *Beyond the Farm Gate* study (Department of Transport and Regional Services 2005): 'There's nothing worse than drought following a couple of dry years'. Elastic businesses clearly have a limit to the amount of stretch they can manage, and it is vital that policymakers considering intervention in markets or specific support measures are well informed about just how much flexibility is left in a small local economy.

References

Centre for Agricultural and Regional Economics 2003, *A socio-economic analysis of the impact of the reduction in groundwater allocations in the Namoi Valley*, Department of Transport and Regional Services, Canberra.

Department of Transport and Regional Services 2005, *Drought Impacts Beyond the Farm Gate: Two Regional Case Studies*, Department of Transport and Regional Services, Canberra, pp. 1–46.

Houghton, K and Fell, T 2012, 'Characteristics of economic sustainability in regional Australia', in *Scoping a Vision for the Future of Rural and Regional Australia: Collection of Papers*, unpublished proceedings from the Sustaining Rural Communities Conference 2012, National Institute for Rural and Regional Australia, Australian National University, Canberra.

Marsden Jacobs and Associates 2010, *Synthesis Report of the Economic Profiles and Impact Assessments for the Murray–Darling Basin Plan*, unpublished report.

Murray–Darling Basin Authority 2010, 'Lower Balonne Community Profile', in *Appendix C of The Guide to the Proposed Basin Plan*, Murray–Darling Basin Authority, Canberra.

Roth, G 2010, *Economic, Environmental and Social Sustainability Indicators of the Australian Cotton Industry*, Cotton Catchment Communities CRC, Australia.

Stubbs, Judith and Associates 2010, *Report 4: Exploring the relationship between community resilience & irrigated agriculture in the Murray Darling Basin. Social and economic impacts of reduced irrigation water, Balonne Case Study*, Cotton Catchment Communities CRC, Australia.

Murray–Darling Basin Authority 2010, *The Guide to the Proposed Basin Plan*, Murray–Darling Basin Authority, Canberra.

Waikerie Economic Profile 2007, District Council of Loxton-Waikerie, Australia.

15 Localism and the policy goal of securing the socio-economic viability of rural and regional Australia

Anthony Hogan, Jen Cleary, Stewart Lockie, Michelle Young and Katherine Daniell[1]

Introduction: setting the context for the emergence of localism

As the Organisation for Economic Co-operation and Development (OECD) (2006) has made apparent, rural decline is a common feature across all OECD countries. Within the Australian context, not only is such decline common, it is also not a new phenomenon. As Gutman (2007, p. 384) points out, in the past 100 years agriculture has declined from generating 80 per cent of Gross Domestic Product to less than 5 per cent. Lockie (2000) observes that international economic pressures on Australian agriculture have been cyclically impacting on the industry since late in the nineteenth century. Alston and Kent (2004, p. xiii) observe that 'small town rural decline and depopulation have been a common factor of rural life at least since the 1970s'. Rural decline has been particularly evidenced in a reduction in the number of people living in rural Australia, an ageing of the residual rural population, and a sustained decline in the number of jobs in agriculture, averaging 2.3 per cent per annum (Bureau of Rural Sciences 2008).

However, industries such as agriculture and mining have not been the only drivers of either non-Indigenous settlement or population decline in rural and regional Australia. Initially people also settled in rural and remote locations to provide services not only to agriculture and mining but also as a result of the need for labour to build and maintain critical forms of infrastructure. With regard to services, the town of Dubbo (for example), situated in the north-west of New South Wales, was first established as a settlement serving an emergent pastoral industry. Similarly settlements were established in regard to the development of the overland telegraph, servicing horse driven coaches, railway towns, dams, irrigation systems and the hydroelectricity scheme to name a few. These populations of course in turn needed access to goods and services. And so a positive cycle of development ensued. In support of the role played by people living in these settlements, there was acceptance that urban and country Australians played a significant, interdependent, yet distinctive role in contributing to the viability of the nation state. Central to this value position was the view that all Australians were equally 'deserving' of access to services and other social entitlements. This was reflected in policy aims and ideals that strove for a state of national ‘equality’ that was concomitant with ‘being Australian’. This policy manifested itself in ‘country’ Australia through the provision of compensations for the costs and impost of living outside the metropolitan areas (Brett 2007, p. 4).

As a result of economic and technological development (such as satellites, broadband communication, helicopters used to inspect telephone and power lines, improved transport systems) the need for local people to be locally based to fulfil many roles has also declined over time. The development of the motor car alone has changed what it means to live in a given place vis-à-vis the accessibility of goods and services available in other settlements. In the 1930s, it was a common event for example, for children to ride a horse (30 minute ride) or walk distances of five miles to the local school. Churches and settlements were also situated within riding distance of rural properties.[2] As a result of the motor car, larger distances could be travelled in relatively short periods of time, making schools, services and shops in other localities more accessible. The multiplicative effect of many small changes over a long period of time (80 years) has resulted in subsequent changes in the placement of, and support for, services and shopping. And while many people have moved away from these smaller towns and villages, others have chosen to stay. Such a decision may have been informed by economic necessity or social and cultural factors such as attachment to people and place. Similarly, the push for agricultural efficiency (see Smith and Pritchard, this volume) realised in the increased mechanisation of farm processes meant the need for fewer waged labourers and fewer labourers meant fewer country residents over time.

From 1997, and particularly between 2002 and 2008, these problems of decline were exacerbated when large parts of Australian agriculture were subjected to a significant drought (BRS 2008; Kenny 2008) with negative economic impacts on agricultural production and the subsequent social and economic flow on effects on the viability of rural towns. Over time, the cumulative impacts on rural towns of globalising economic forces, informed as they were by neoliberal policies and drought, has meant not just socio-economic decline (Alston and Kent 2004, p. xiii) but the increasing risk that ‘regional towns and cities are sliding towards welfare-dependency’ (Marsden Jacobs *et al.* 2010, p. xii). With many jobs and businesses at risk, concern about the viability of rural towns is once again uppermost in the minds of the community.

It was within this context that localism re-emerged as a policy strategy designed to enable local communities to address the socio-economic challenges which beset them. As a policy strategy localism is neither new nor uniquely Australian. Indeed, as our analysis shows, in developing its policy approach to localism, Australian policymakers drew heavily on policy work undertaken in Europe. However, Australia is geographically distinct from Europe and policies that relate to either space or place need to take spatial, demographic and cultural differences into account. Spatially, Australia differs enormously from Europe. Switzerland, for example, occupies 41,290 square kilometres and is smaller than

Australia's smallest state of Tasmania, which occupies more than 60,000 square kilometres. Some of Australia's national parks are physically larger than some European countries (such as Belgium). In addition, Australia is far less densely populated than Europe (OECD 2006). In remote Australia, approximately 3 per cent of the population lives on 70 per cent of the landmass.

Earlier chapters drew attention to the way policy processes have constructed regions as productive spaces. Population approaches to settlements also construct a certain image as to what constitutes a region. In a report from the Bureau of Rural Sciences (BRS 2008) the 'rural' was constructed as being those spaces not occupied by small towns or larger settlements. A working definition of regional could also be derived from these analyses. By default, regional did not encompass major urban centres but was also likely to encompass settlements which were greater than 250,000 people which were not also one of the centres of state governance. Regional was also likely to encompass settlements of up to 100,000 people, and of 100,000 to 250,000 people. Notably, while smaller towns and villages may be in decline, so-called regional centres are growing in population. The Bureau of Rural Sciences (BRS 2008) reports that regionally Australia has seen growth in centres such as the Gold Coast (Queensland), Geelong and Bendigo (Victoria), Mandurah (Western Australia), the Tweed, Newcastle and Maitland (New South Wales), and Alexandrina, Victor Harbour and Mount Barker (South Australia). Interestingly, only 9 per cent of Australians now live in rural Australia (BRS 2008, p. 3).

There are of course a variety of other ways to think about the notion of what constitutes a region, particularly when considered from a community perspective. For Goffman (1969, p. 107) regions 'may be defined as any place that is bounded to some degree by barriers to perception … they are bounded according to the media of communication in which the barriers to perception occur'. For Kinnear *et al.* (2013, p. 6) 'a definition of regional Australia requires a subjective and fluid interpretation: a collection of areas surrounding non-capital settlements; with common features, cohesive functions and/or shared purpose and variable boundaries according to context'. Note that in these definitions of space, the words place and purpose arise. Creswell (2004) makes a specific distinction between space and place, with the idea of space being more readily associated with the idea of a region. For Creswell (2004, p. 39), a place is 'constituted through reiterative social practice – place is made and remade on a daily basis. Place provides a template for practice – an unstable stage for performance'. Contrasting Kinnear *et al.* with Creswell, regions might be thought of in terms of physical spaces which are purposeful, perhaps, as an example, with regard to industrial or productive activity, whereas place is 'a way of being' (Cresswell 2004, p. 16). Notably, the everyday use of the word place is often associated with the possessive, such as 'my place' as well as 'your place' and 'our place'. Place is also associated with identity and culture, taking in such phrases as *my place in the world*, or *my connection to country*. Notions of place have as much to do with feelings and relationships to space as they do with lines on a map. We return to these issues of place as distinct from space below as we develop our discussion on the issue of localism.

Competing constructions then exist around the idea of regions which can be understood as an exploitable economic resource, as a means for local livelihoods and as a place which has differing social and cultural meanings and attachments. Each understanding of region is also underpinned by a history of policy approaches and such approaches, like the assumptions which underpin them, are not always consistent with each other. It is against this background that we consider localism as a policy strategy which attempts to address these issues. The chapter in turn provides an overview of localism before providing a critique of its application within the Australian context. As with earlier chapters within this book, the apparent links in policy between constructions of regional and economic policy are drawn out and contrasted with a social approach to space, centred on the notion of place. At its heart, localism raises questions of how best to structure governmental processes in order to facilitate the socio-economic and environmental sustainability of communities. To this end the chapter concludes with a consideration of alternate ways of governing rural and regional Australia into the future.

Localism

Gray (2010) points out that the recent developments of localism policy originated in Europe. The policy, developed by the European Commission, was concerned with diversifying the economic base which underpinned its regions, seeking in particular to move on from a specialist focus on agriculture (European Commission 2011a) to an integrated territorial development which supported not just agriculture, but also the development of infrastructure and education as well as addressing social and economic issues at a local level (Gray 2010, p. 31). The European Union's (EU) localist strategy included 'economic diversification, infrastructural improvement, rural heritage, protection of the environment, maintenance of the countryside, restoration of landscapes, extensification and set aside' (Gray 2010, p. 32). The European Commission's overall strategy for economic development was designed to enable Europe 'to become a smart, sustainable and inclusive economy' where smart is understood with regards to the development of the digital economy, innovation and youth employment (European Commission 2011b). As Hogan and Lockie (2013) observe, the EU strategies also had regard to sustainable (e.g. creating a low carbon economy and green technologies) (European Commission 2011c) and inclusive communities (e.g. addressing poverty, employment and social cohesion) (see also European Commission 2011d and 2011e).

The OECD (2009, p. 3) argues that in addressing change and stimulating growth, public policy needs to 'unlock the potential of regions and support long-term economic, social and environmental objectives'. The OECD points out that such a strategy 'is all the more crucial given the very limited resources that are available to national, regional and local governments and the tight fiscal constraints likely over the coming years' (2009, p. 3), noting that a mix of market, environmental and social strategies are required to achieve a sustainable outcome. The OECD (2006) proposed that policy coherence could be achieved by situating place, rather than sector, at the heart of the rural and regional question.

Consistent with policy developments in Europe, the Australian Government has developed a place-centred localism policy, which is focused on rural and regional Australia. Australian localism also seeks to diversify rural and regional economies away from agriculture in order to drive 'growth, liveability and sustainability' (Crean 2011, p. 1). The Australian Government proposed that:

> ...if communities are stronger and more connected at the local level, overall productivity rises at the national level (...). We want to enable regions to broaden their traditional economic base – through new partnerships, new skills and new technologies. In this way, communities will become more resilient, more viable and more sustainable in the longer term. A one size fits all approach will not achieve these goals. Empowering regional communities to take ownership of their future (...). We need to look at individual regions through their eyes – through the local lens. The people who live and work in regional Australia know their patch best (...). They are best placed to identify the drivers for change and the potential for partnerships and new markets.
>
> (Ibid.)

Localism is concerned to promote self-sufficient, socio-economically viable regional communities. Localism proposes that regions can and should invest in their own growth through the mobilisation of local assets and resources, so as to capitalise on their specific competitive advantages. Within localism, sustainably developing regional Australia requires an effective multi-sector partnership. Such a partnership is created and sustained within a developmental framework which catalyses the process. To achieve this outcome, communities are required to establish a unique collaboration with key industry groups and (following Europe again) create *smart* local strategies that can lead to economic development for their region. The Australian Government (2011) takes the position that in order to realise sustainability, regional development has to pivot on the ability of communities to enact a place-based vision of effective partnerships with industry centred on technological innovation. For the Australian Government then, technological innovation is central to national productivity. Echoing the strategy of the European Union (Europe Commission 2010), the Australian Government (2011) also takes the view that the development of broadband internet services and the digital economy are central to this change strategy. Australian localism, consistent as it is with broader OECD policy, is seen as the mechanism that can take the regions to a new level by *unleashing their economic potential*, by addressing four key policy objectives:

- Delivery of concrete economic and social benefits.
- Commitment to innovation and building capacity in local communities.

- Linking regional communities across traditional boundaries; and
- Creating the ability to leverage additional funding across government and the private sector (Crean 2011).

Within this vision, regional industries are seen as having the capacity to generate the economic foundation upon which communities can prosper. In addition to their own local spending and the multiplicative effect this has on the local economy, spending resulting from state government and industry initiatives provides people with incomes to live on, income which in turn is spent on goods and services in the local community, creating a virtuous cycle of socio-economic well-being.

The Australian Government (2011) created the Regional Development Australia (RDAs)[3] initiative as the mechanism through which this change process would be driven and managed. Not dissimilar in design to the regionalised strategy Hunt (this volume) noted was used in Indigenous policy, the Australian Government created 55 regional development committees across Australia to manage the localism process. In the Australian Government's view, the RDAs were the key mechanism through which it planned to progress localism and regional decision making:

> So I want the RDAs to join the dots. Your work has to go beyond thinking about a single Government portfolio, it needs to be cross portfolio, cross governments but also through engaging with the private sector and NGOs. The role of RDAs should be seen as one that complements the work of Local Government. RDAs are there to perform a strategic role – one that is rooted in strong engagement with Local Government, Regional Organisations of Councils and other stakeholders. RDAs are there as facilitators, mentors and brokers on regional development. As such, I see RDAs and Local Government playing a collaborative role. A relationship that should be embraced for the opportunities it presents, because if we are to deliver effective regional development in Australia we need strong, creative partnerships.
>
> (Crean 2011)

Notably, innovation, development of human capital, networks and social interaction were seen as being critical to the success of regional development (McCall 2013). Local governance, McCall noted (2013, p. 79), was therefore a 'key strategy' moving forward. Kinnear *et al.* (2013, citing Cooke 2006) note policymaker interest in designating regional sites as places of innovation and that innovation is central to long-term regional, and in turn (as policy suggests) national development and well-being. This kind of discourse draws on iconic themes of the historic place which rural and regional Australia has held within the nation's identity and seeks to reframe it within a new policy context, which moves beyond the confines of agriculture.

Strengths of localism

As detailed in Table 15.1, localism seeks to engage local communities in progressing decision-making processes that will shape critical strategic decisions concerned to secure their social and economic futures. A funding base, that has been provided by the Australian Government to enable local visions to be realised, supports the policy. As was observed in the British House of Commons, localism is based on a level of self-evident common sense that is difficult to argue with (House of Commons 2011). Localism seeks to provide a vision for rural and regional areas, a vision that is based on the idea of a future centred on socio-economic self-sufficiency. Central to this vision is the notion of sustainability, which is inherently linked with economic development. This policy has been operationalised with local communities developing strategies which seek to diversify their economic base, enhance their access to markets, and to enhance the accessibility of the community through improvement in transport and broadband infrastructure.

The design of Australian localism is highly consistent with other Australian Government policy strategy, which is concerned with the long-term sustainability of the economic base and productive systems. In the case of agriculture for example, the government has promoted market liberalisation and facilitated structural adjustment (Botterill 2003) such that 'less efficient' operators could leave the industry, resulting in a more highly competitive primary industry. In drought policy the Australian Government has made it explicit that it is the responsibility of farmers to manage their own risks in the face of climate change, and in water policy it is the responsibility of farmers to manage their own water needs. Central to this policy strategy is the principle that individual producers are responsible for themselves, their financial viability and their place within the industry. Localism, as it is being developed in Australia, extends this principle to a community level with resources put in place to facilitate change at a community level where communities also take responsibility for their

Table 15.1 Benefits of localism

Localism strategy	*Requirement for local implementation*	*Accountability*
Bottom-up decision-making.	A highly participative, community-based decision-making process.	Government partners with local areas.
Power to make local decisions.	Local legislative power.	Specific government agencies address their financial responsibilities in rural Australia.
Resources to implement decisions.	Access to and control of sufficient resources across government. Capacity to raise revenue.	Specific government agencies provide appropriate resources.

viability and their futures. In the face of forces demanding adaptation at a societal level, localism seeks to put in place a mechanism whereby local people can have control over decision-making processes, which will impact on their livelihoods and well-being. In keeping with earlier policies under localism, the decision about the viability of a specific settlement rests with local people. In the Australian context, resources are made available to support 'drivers for change and the potential for partnerships and new markets' (Crean 2011). The OECD (2009) particularly notes that regional development occurs not simply as a result of access to economic resources, but through a systems-based approach, which takes into account a community's capacity for innovation, adaptation, education and skills development combined with the potential to realise investment in infrastructure. Localism seeks to avoid a centralist approach to local decision-making by enabling communities to identify how best they can move forward. Inherent within such a process is the possibility that a community may conclude that there is no enduring socio-economic basis to sustain their community.

The opportunity to progress Australia's localism policy was to have been provided through the potentially large resource base created from proceeds of a mineral resources rent tax (MRRT). However, in its early years, the tax only raised about half of the expected $5–7 billion (Alan Kohler 2013), which the Australian Government could have made available for infrastructure development in regional and rural Australia. Access to funds was also subject to local areas securing collaborative funding from state and local governments or industry partners. In one region alone, this has resulted in the investment of over $45 million in the area over a three-year period. Extrapolated nationally, such a level of total spend in the regions would equate to a not insubstantial $2.5 billion over three years. However, we return to the question of the extent to which this kind of expenditure, at a national level, is an effective and efficient use of public funds.

Limits to localism

Significantly, localism differs from other forms of policy rationalisation in that government policy does not provide for structural adjustment at a community level. Unlike initiatives where it provided financial incentives for producers to leave an industry (e.g. agriculture), the Australian Government has not provided community residents with financial incentives to leave an area, which might be considered either economically unviable or practically unserviceable. Similarly, the Australian Government has avoided taking on the role of Solomon; it does not explicitly decide which communities will survive and which ones will not, save that specific funding decisions will have the same, but less apparent effect.

As noted previously, localism, as it is being developed within Australia, potentially creates democratic pathways through which adaptive challenges to the socio-economic viability of given settlements can be considered by those most likely to be impacted by change. Localism, however, is not without its limitations and it is to these concerns which attention is now given.

In a review of literature on localism, Hogan and Lockie (2013) identified a number of limitations with localism as a social policy strategy. This literature (which is summarised in Table 15.2) highlights the fact that localism can be a strategy which:

- Forces communities to address local economic pressures in isolation from global economic forces.
- Results in government retreat from their commitment to local communities.
- Shifts responsibility for social policy outcomes to local communities which presently lack the constitutional right to raise their own revenues.
- Can lead to regulatory dumping.
- Further centralises decision making, keeping actual decision-making power out of the hands of local people (Bland 1944; Collits 2008).
- Disempowers local communities when control over decision making remains centralised (Bland 1944).
- Fails if critical investments are poorly resourced (Collits 2008).

This use of the word localism is problematic in that localism inherently refers to a bottom-up community-based approach to decision-making, whereas in the Australian context it inherently refers to the community having inputs into regional consultation processes with decisions made at a central level – what McCall (2013) refers to as a confusion between regionalisation (the latter) and regionalism (the former). Challenges arise between such competing approaches and include the inevitable tensions between centralised or higher-scale policy goals and processes and the aspirations of given communities. Additional challenges include the pace of regional development compared with national growth, balancing issues of equity and efficiency, and ensuring that social and environmental policy initiatives keep pace with economic initiatives (OECD 2009).

Infrastructure spending priorities were funnelled through the RDAs. The RDAs were required to identify local needs and priorities and provide a regional review process for any proposed infrastructure developments. Funds in the order of $25,000 were initially provided to RDAs to conduct research and help them write their development plans which documented identified local needs. In

Table 15.2 Limits to localism

Localist strategy	*Requirement for local implementation*	*Critique*
Bottom-up decision-making.	A highly participative, community-based decision-making process.	A retreat from government.
Power to make local decisions.	Local legislative power.	Shifting responsibility.
Resources to implement decisions.	Access to and control of sufficient resources across government. Capacity to raise revenue.	Power without resources.

addition, RDAs received, on average, $272,000 per annum to do their work. Notably a desk review of these regional plans, conducted by this team, found a huge disparity in the depth and breadth of research which went into regional plans. The extent of the work which went into regional plans in more highly urbanised regions suggests that these areas had access to far more resources than others.

Applications for infrastructure funding had to be applied for through a national process, with applications being vetted through the RDAs and a bureaucratic process prior to being subject to ministerial approval. Only local councils and incorporated non-governmental organisations (NGOs) could apply for these funds. In addition to the RDAs, an independent review committee was also convened to advise the minister on the advice of the RDAs in determining which of the proposed projects put forward by elected local governments and NGOs could be funded. RDA funding decisions also took into account the respective state infrastructure plans. However, as these plans were developed without priority consideration being given to non-metropolitan settlements, the capacity of such decision-making processes to address issues for people living outside the cities were limited. In South Australia, for example, only 15 per cent of the population lives outside the major metropolitan centre.

Assuming that in time the proposed $5–7 billion of federal funds for infrastructure development did become available, it is important to consider this budget in the light of the needs which the localism policy has to address. Having consulted with a number of RDAs, several factors quickly became apparent: that many of the plans were largely aspirational, and their collective total budgets greatly exceeded the total pool of available funds by an order of magnitude. As an example, in 2011, the Northern Inlands RDA (NIRDA) based in Armidale, New South Wales, had identified a wide range of infrastructure development needs necessary to secure its socio-economic viability. A significant agricultural area, this RDA required $225 million simply to bring its roads up to a reasonable standard in order to get its products more easily to port (NIRDA 2011, p. 16). Notably almost half (24/55) of the RDAs identified the development of some form of transport infrastructure as a priority area for securing their economic sustainability. Assuming that infrastructure funding is equitably allocated across all regions, the Northern Inlands RDA would receive just $20 million over five years. As Hunt (this volume) notes, criticism readily arises when policy strategies are seen to be more aspirational than functional, very thinly spreading a small amount of resource across a wide area, with resources in any given area being inadequate to genuinely meet the policy target set by an administration.

A focus on regions is not new. Like Bland (1944), Brown (2007) reported that regional approaches have been popular since the post-war period, noting that there are at least five forms of structured regionalism in Australia presently. The way localism is operationalised is very consistent with what Brown (2007, p. 16) referred to as a 'bastardisation' of regionalism. Brown (2007, p. 16) continues

> ...this particular reinvention of the term does demonstrate that 'regionalism' is not just a top-down administrative convenience, but also a live

> phenomenon in electoral politics. We know this because the renewed political interest in 'regional Australia' has arisen in response to a particular phase of political restiveness, or electoral instability, in rural regions – and indeed outer-metropolitan ones. Accordingly this bastardised definition reflects something of a hybrid between top-down and bottom-up concepts of regionalism. The response has also extended to a new suite of administrative initiatives in community engagement and place management, often targeted to less advantaged urban and peri-urban communities in addition to rural community renewal.

Brown (2007) argues that the problem with tendencies to centralise and localise decision-making processes, is that the two processes become like ships passing each other in the night; in other words that there is a discourse of localism, but it is centrally administered. Within the current Australian model, the government promotes the ideals of localism but in practice it maintains close control over the budget and the investment programme. Collits (2008, p. 305) argues that such 'national plans favour (central) intervention' and, as such, conflict with localist ideals. By contrast, localism as promoted in other countries proposes the devolution of power from central governments to local communities; yet the OECD observes that, 'unless issues of central control and local autonomy are addressed, the objectives and benefits of decentralisation will not be realized in practice' (OECD 2006, p. 128). While the challenges in getting the balance of power right are noted in the literature, localism cannot really function as localism if local communities cannot control both the resources and the decision-making process. Rather it becomes another form of governmental consultation. Notably however, taking into account Arnstein's (1969) classical framework on participative decision-making, consultative processes which provide participants with few assurances, if any, that their concerns would be taken on board or actioned, are generally considered to be tokenistic.

Localism policy assumes that the local economic base can be used to provide the necessary capacity for supporting the livelihoods of a specific rural economy (Malthus 1992), if only local initiatives can be applied, which unleash the potential in a given area. To be successful, localism assumes that key existing or new local industries will create and sustain the generative base for demand and opportunity for all other work and enterprises in a region, from hairdressers to dentists to music teachers (Parsons and Smelser 1956). Hogan and Lockie (2013) point out that the assumptions that underpin localism strongly echo functionalist social theory, which was rejected by mainstream sociological theorists many decades ago. Localism centres on Parsons' (Parsons and Smelser 1956) idea that the regional economy provides the adaptive base from which communities can secure their livelihoods, managing and integrating as they do differing internal interests towards the greater sustainability of the community. This style of functionalist social theory has been widely critiqued in the literature for its inability to recognise and deal with inequality within communities as well as its inability to provide for social change.

But what if it is the case that both theories have something important to say? What if it is true that when a society draws its livelihood from an advanced economy, the economic base has to be constantly monitored and changed, and that communities who draw their livelihoods from this base must constantly work together to adapt to such change in order to survive? And, if the elements which contributed to the operation of the economic base (which originally underpinned the vitality of that local economy) no longer exist (e.g. building/maintaining the overland telegraph), then such a community is faced with the need to find a new way to support their livelihoods or the community has to close. What we think Parsons and Smelser were saying, was that in such circumstances community, government and industry would work together to find a way through such a challenge. However, if the philosophy underpinning the operation of a society's economy has shifted from a market economy to a market society, then there is an increased readiness in the wider population to allow the costs of change to lie where they fall (Titmuss 2006). So in fact stakeholders do not necessarily pull together to resolve the socio-economic impacts of change. Industries and services can seemingly be pulled from communities without the decision-makers having to take responsibility for addressing the socio-economic dependencies which exist. Rather, under localism, communities are challenged to become economically self-sufficient. So while localist policy strongly resonates with Parsonian functionalist notions of systems theory, the application of a systems discourse potentially masks the real nature of the governmental process which is occuring; a process which is designed to secure the wider consent of the population to supporting a market society, without regard to the impact it has for individuals or their community (Foucault 1991; Burchell 1991).

Central to the success of localism is the capacity of rural economies to economically develop and innovate. Localist policy assumes that such communities have access to, and the capacity to utilise, exploitable assets (OECD 2006, p. 115), which exist and which are distinct to their particular locality, including natural and cultural amenities. Localism assumes that rural and regional communities have the resources and capacity to assess their natural, community and industry assets, with a view to optimising the benefits of these resources to provide livelihoods for current and future community members. It also assumes that local communities can utilise the proceeds of the sale of these assets to efficiently and equitably deliver public goods, an ability that will itself depend on the interplay between entrepreneurial capacities and the critical mass of resources which these capacities seek to mobilise (that is, 'the minimal combination of human capital, social capital, infrastructure and natural or human created amenities to trigger a developmental process' (OECD 2006, p. 115)). It is far from evident the extent to which communities in rural and regional Australia have either a diverse economic or natural resource base to draw upon or develop, and where such resources exist (e.g. yellowcake), whether it is ethical to do so. Certain crops, livestock or horticultural products are better suited to be produced in some environs rather than others, depending on their soil, climate and water needs. Moreover, given climate change, the scope of such productive capacities is changing (e.g. the wheatbelt in Western Australia). Minerals and ore deposits exist in specific geographic locations and not others. Notably though, even if the resources exist, it is quite feasible that small communities have no capacity to exploit such resources to their own ends, but rely on external parties to do so. In such cases the wealth generated in the regions typically does not stay in the region. A competitive advantage may be realised by regional communities who can develop an effective strategic working relationship with their local industry base (e.g. cotton or mining) or who have a unique environmental asset to draw on (e.g. a specific environmental amenity as a tourist attraction). Evidently there will be communities that do not have an environmental amenity to draw on, or whose industrial base may readily decline or change, leaving them with no economic base to draw upon. In a democratic society, which relies on a market economy to address its demands for goods and services, and in which communities have been established as a result of earlier national policy initiatives, is it not implicit within the kinds of processes proposed by Parsons and Smelser, that a transitional process would be deployed to assist not just industry, but also communities to undergo change? And where such change to the local economic base is not feasible, that a just process ensued to facilitate an equitable outcome for all?

Development and innovation evidently sit at the heart of localist notions of regional sustainability. In addition, localist policy echoes remarks made by other contributors to this text (e.g. Collits; Cockfield; Alston; and Phillips, this volume) that yet again policymakers essentially understand rural policy in the construct of economic or industry policy. But how can this be so, particularly when analysts have consistently observed (e.g. Lawrence 1987; and Smith and Pritchard, this volume) that the enhancement of the productive capacity of industry does not necessarily equate with the notion of vibrant rural communities? Industry intensification can inherently result in a reduced demand for labour and the reduced demand for labour has a cascading, downward impact on the local community. A variety of examples can be cited here. First, this kind of change was evident in the development of GM cotton, which significantly reduced the need for labour to manage weeds in the cotton industry. Second, enhanced transport infrastructure, such as better regional airports, facilitated the development of fly-in, fly-out (FIFO) workforces with a subsequent decline in people moving to live in specific rural localities. Third, the rapidly growing impact of the digital economy is being felt right across the retail, as well as service sectors. Australians can now readily buy their products online and they can also access transactional (accounting and law) and health services remotely. These kinds of services are set to develop further over the coming decade. As a case in point, some forms of ear, nose and throat services have already been provided to remote Aboriginal communities for many years in this way, reducing the need for specialist medical services to be remotely located. Various other forms of health and hospital care in the home are already in place or under further development (e.g. capacity for online hearing tests, remote heart monitoring, prosthetic programming and so on). After agriculture, health and retail are some of the biggest employers in country towns and the rise of the digital economy may further signal a decline in rural and regional employment opportunities. As Edwards (2013) points out, one should not confuse increasing gross domestic product with the sustainability of rural settlements; they are not necessarily connected. Carson and Cleary (2010) also found that improved technology serves to further isolate rural and remote places, because their capacity to adapt to the new technologies (particularly the regulatory factors) is limited.

Naively approached, localism can ignore the historical circumstances under which specific settlements were founded. Differing histories of settlement and settlement patterns, local resource stocks, service provision capacity, economic shocks and their impact, changing environments as well as changing policy environments and subsequent differences in both the pace and nature of development (and its associated economic activities) are all factors which differentially shape the viability of specific settlements. Some Australian regions (those most similar to 'normal' EU-like regions) have highly diverse local economies. They have larger, more demographically diverse economies and populations concentrated in relatively small areas (e.g. regional Victoria), while other regions are dominated by single, or a few industries that are agglomerative in nature (e.g. South Australia and the Northern Territory), containing smaller and less demographically diverse populations spread over vastly greater areas. Long lead times are also associated with the development of a productive capacity in a given place and such developments require the presence of specific local assets, including the capacity among local people to engage in entrepreneurial activities. Moreover, diversification requires a readiness within country communities to accept people from outside their localities, who may be different to people already living there. As Houghton and Fell (this volume) point out, growing the population or diversifying the local skills set are central to the sustainability of settlements. However there are documented barriers to such diversification when local people are resistant towards welcoming new people to town who are *not like them* (Carson and Carson 2011).

In countries like Australia and Canada, the competitive economic advantage of specific rural communities has more recently been promoted through the development of extractive (e.g. mining) industries. However, while such industries may once again contribute to national GDP, their local economic benefits, as Carson (2012) notes, may in fact bypass the local area, particularly once the construction phase has passed. Where economic bypass occurs, efforts to benchmark the productivity of local areas (from a centralist perspective) become misleading, if the benefits of that productivity are not actually accruing locally – which is of course the case in extractive industries and increasingly with regards to agribusiness. A seemingly unproductive localised economy may in fact be contributing more to securing local livelihoods than the presence of some large multinational enterprise. Undertaking research which enables a community to understand its local economic stocks and flows is far more useful as an indicator of the potential of a local economy, than just trying to compare regions using abstracted indicators (see Chapter 14).

The socio-economic viability of a regional economy then emerges in conjunction with place-based diversity in resources and the capacity for their utilisation. In a highly competitive global commodity market, economies of scale must also be achieved in order to be competitive. Small economies cannot generate the economies of scale required to become competitive (niche markets excepted), because their domestic markets are not large enough. Saupin (1997) points out that competitive advantage in the resources sector (citing the mining boom in Western Australia) centred on companies being able to develop specialised high technology industries servicing local resource producers. Such industries could then develop a competitive advantage, which could lead them to supply international markets. Saupin demonstrated that a growing demand for products and services from the resources sector in Western Australia generated research and development and the formation of a high technology 'cluster' of firms. However, the important point here is that such clusters feature interdependencies (Thompson 1967) between firms, and so geographic proximity becomes an advantage (O'Connor *et al.* 1998). O'Connor and colleagues point to the competitive advantages, for example, of firms based in Sydney and Melbourne. More recently we have seen the development of city-based service centres which support regionally based industries; mining being a case in point. Once again then the point emerges that infrastructure and industry development in rural and regional areas does not immediately mean that the socio-economic sustainability of the area is assured. Rather, resources need to be invested in economic development projects which are both labour intensive and which bring people to live in the specific areas (Gutman 2007); otherwise the economic benefits of given initiatives can bypass local people.

Finally, logical to the philosophy of localism is the potential question of place-based, and in time, per capita based, funding (Commons 2011, pp. 48–58). As the idea suggests, per capita based funding would be a model of funding where resources were allocated to an area on the basis of the percentage of people living as a share of the total resource pie. Such an approach would have grave equity consequences for people living in more sparsely populated parts of rural and regional Australia. An approach to per capita based funding, while superficially appealing, would in fact represent a significant shift in Australia's system of fiscal equalisation where revenue raised by the national government is redistributed to the states and territories on a per capita basis, but which in turn is modified by a formula which takes into account the cost to provide services in each location (Maude 2004). Similarly, systems of centralised government are underpinned by principles of market liberalisation, which focus on efficiency as a priority (McArdle 1999) and foster economies of scale that support benefits to the majority for the least cost. However, such principles are not readily extended to smaller rural communities in an effective manner. Within such communities, resources are often shared across different 'sectors', e.g. public libraries might exist in schools; various service providers might share vehicles and office space; and jobs might be shared, i.e. one person might work part-time for two different organisations where there is not enough work to justify two full positions, or one person might hold parts of different jobs in the one organisation. Such economies of scope (as distinct from scale) occur frequently in rural and regional Australia, and especially in more remote regions. Given the differences between 'normal' and 'different' regions in Australia, the application of policy and service delivery which supports *only* economies of scale may have detrimental effects on rural communities, and their capacity to mobilise local assets productively.

Implementing localism

Central to the effective implementation of localism, and as demonstrated across this text, is the need for the nation to reconcile the past and present with deliberate policies for the kind of future it wants for rural and regional Australia. With 20–20 hindsight, initiatives such as irrigated agriculture may not have been progressed in certain parts of Australia. However, such initiatives occurred and communities are in place. Progress in the life cycle of resource industries, climate change, global economic change and improved road transport are but a few of the factors (see for example Productivity Commission 1999) which may have undermined the socio-economic viability of specific settlements. Localism provides a framework for the nation to begin the difficult decision-making process of adapting to an ever-changing future. However, as a policy strategy it does come with its limitations, some of which have been noted previously. However, these limitations are not insurmountable. Communities and government can constructively move through the limits of localism to secure outcomes, which may be of greater mutual benefit. Neither farming groups nor members of rural or regional communities are inactive entities simply waiting to have their lives shaped by external forces. On the contrary, and as evidenced in 2010 by the significant and widespread public display of dissatisfaction with the Australian Government's Murray–Darling Basin Plan, Australian people are actively involved in the shaping of their socio-political futures. Central to their concerns is the maintenance of their livelihoods and well-being, including national concerns which address issues of equity as much as opportunities of economic development (OECD 2006).

But neither is there a magic bullet (Collits 2008), no one simple solution which will address the socio-economic viability needs of all rural or regional communities, save for the fact that durability seems to occur once communities achieve a certain size (see Houghton, this volume). Collits' work highlights in particular the fact that the rural space is truly heterogenic and that problems need to be worked in partnerships within local contexts. However, given the systemic nature of many of the problems facing the viability of rural and regional communities across the OECD, just as a purely centralist strategy has been unsuccessful, it is similarly unlikely that a purely localist strategy will be effective either.

In the Australian context, there has been much discussion about the problems of multi-level governance, and the need for constitutional reform to remove state and local government and replace them with a regional governance structure. Similarly, recognition of local government within the Australian constitution has also been suggested. Some form of national partnership is certainly required; one underpinned by a legislative framework which provides protection against the excesses of responsibility-shifting between jurisdictions, electoral demands for knee-jerk responses from policymakers in the face of crisis and the potential for local communities to be isolated and unsupported by this policy process. Without doubt, some difficult decisions will need to be made.

Intensified place-based policies will result in the further decline of some communities. To manage these challenges in an open and transparent fashion, Collits (2008) proposed a rural commission. But how would such a commission function to ensure that the process of rural governance is sufficiently depoliticised so as to be workable, taking into account the fact that differing levels of government have differing constitutional responsibilities? Approaches to multi-level governance (MLG) have great potential to resolve these issues. In a review of this literature Daniell *et al.* (2010) note that effective MLG systems can:

- Stabilise authority and provide for clear lines of accountability.
- Allow for participation in decision making.
- Be accountable, transparent and responsive.
- Provide opportunity to negotiate place-based and need-specific policies.
- Support flexibility in policy, accommodating strategy to local needs; and
- Increase efficiency in governmental processes.

Precedents for a multi-level approach to governance already exist both internationally and within Australia. Canada, for example, previously ran a Rural Secretariat, which was made up of representatives of nine regional councils, with participants appointed from an open process.[4] A key role of the Secretariat was to vet policy for rural user-friendliness before it was implemented. The Secretariat's work was supported by the Canadian Rural Partnership programme, which provided resources 'to overcome challenges and make the most of their opportunities created by the land'.[5] The Secretariat's work was also supported by Canada's Rural Development Network which brought

> federal departments, agencies and selected others together to achieve greater information sharing, collaboration and coordination on rural issues, with a view of developing better integrated federal policies and programmes that meet the diverse needs of Canadians living in rural, remote and northern communities.[6]

A key part of the network's role was to encourage collaboration by working across existing departmental boundaries to enable a readier transfer of knowledge and to facilitate information sharing.

Within Australia's governmental processes, partnered approaches to governance already exist and have successfully operated for over 30 years. Safework

Australia, for example was established to develop a national approach to workplace health and safety in Australia. It is governed by a tripartite board made up of governments, employers and employees. Safework Australia is an independent statutory body, which is responsible to drive 'national policy development on work health and safety and workers' compensation matters' with a view to protecting the well-being of people at work, to secure a nationally consistent approach to occupational health and safety and to improve approaches to managing workers' compensation. The statutory body is made up of an independent chairperson, a representative from each of the jurisdictions, industry (two positions), and union bodies (two positions). Safework Australia is supported by a substantively funded secretariat. Funds are also provided to the industry and union peak bodies so that they are able to properly participate in the process.

A Commission for Rural and Regional Australia could readily be established on a similar basis to Safework Australia. As a statutory body its responsibility would be to ensure that the socio-economic well-being of rural Australia is progressed by ensuring that governments adequately partner with, rather than abrogate, responsibility to local areas or leave them without adequate resources to progress their needs. As with existing bodies, the Commission could be made up of an independent chairperson, a representative from each of the jurisdictions, local government, and regional organisations; however resources would be required to support each of these functionalities. Botterill (2009) has previously proposed the establishment of an Office for Rural Australia, situated within the Department of Prime Minister and Cabinet. The role of the Office was to coordinate rural and regional policy across all Australian Government departments, providing input into all policy submissions impacting on rural and regional Australia. Under the Gillard government officers within the Department of Regional Australia undertook this role. However, this functionality did not provide the participative, stakeholder-based, decision-making process required to progress the interests of this sector in a strategic fashion. A more transparent and accountable decision-making structure, devolved from the current centralist model, could more adequately support such a mission.

The commission could be responsible for developing a national strategy for rural and regional Australia, including the identification of priority areas, outcome targets, minimum level of service delivery requirements and service delivery mechanisms. It would need to address challenges between spreading resources too thinly to be effective, or whether specific areas need to be progressed ahead of others. It would particularly need to clearly define the responsibilities of specific jurisdictions, therein reducing duplication of processes, as well as developing a whole of government approach to rural and regional Australia including addressing challenges to funding policy initiatives by addressing challenges such as 'single financial pots' (OECD 2006, p. 147) and per capita versus equity based funding models. It could identify the need for specific partnerships, and the mix of partners needed to achieve policy goals. It could oversee data collection concerned with benchmarking place-based outcomes. It could also oversee stock-takes of place-based governmental and private sector expenditure on infrastructure and services. Overall, such a commission would provide a mechanism to translate research and knowledge into policy action in a systemic way, with a focus on outcomes (Collits 2008). Its establishment could be achieved without constitutional change.

Concluding remarks

From the evidence provided within earlier chapters, it is quite evident that the philosophy of neoliberalism has been at the heart of national policy in Australia, at least since the 1970s. As a policy strategy, localism both extends and contradicts market-centred policy. Localism certainly extends neoliberalist policy by placing the self-sufficiency of rural and regional communities at the heart of policy strategy. In a country as vast as Australia, one might well argue that policymakers have few alternatives; that in the face of the consequences of historical outcomes, communities must now carve out a viable future for themselves through economic development and innovation. Localism seeks to place the opportunity for such future development in the entrepreneurial hands of local actors. Central to neoliberalist philosophy is Adam Smith's notion of the invisible hand of the market, working as it does, to generate economic futures for society through unregulated market activities. And yet by contrast, localism requires local communities to develop visions for their future, to identify infrastructure development projects that will be at least partly funded by the state, which are central to securing the socio-economic viability of the communities concerned. Similarly, localism requires the explicit collaboration of communities with all tiers of government and with industry, in order to secure the necessary mechanisms, developments and inputs required to bring about economic growth and the security of livelihoods. That is, the capacity for a society to satisfy the needs and wants of its citizens is not simply met by unconnected individuals pursuing their own interests without regard to others, but that social processes are required to be in place, which facilitate, if not mediate, the means through which people can secure their livelihoods. Well developed and participative governance processes are central to the success of such processes. Moreover markets, left to their own devices, are not sufficient to ensure the welfare of communities whose livelihoods depend on the economic flows which result from them. Where markets exist to provide for the meeting of a community's needs and wants, it remains evident that the design and functioning of such markets has to remain 'embedded' within and directed by a broader form of social relations, which has as its primary goal the maintenance of the well-being of community members (Holton 1992).

Approached from the perspective of a collaborative rather than a centralised process, localism offers the potential to enable a new form of regional governance to emerge. Within the nexus of environment, culture, community and industry, a shared policy space can open up. Here the needs and aspirations of people living in a given rural district can be tabled and addressed through a planning and development process which is collaborative and the outcome is seen by stakeholders to be just, irrespective of the outcome (Gross, this volume).

Notes

1 We gratefully acknowledge the input of Mark Hickman and Melanie Glavimans, whose discussions assisted us with the development of this paper.
2 These examples are based on the life experience of Anthony Hogan's father Max, who grew up on a property called Burkedale, outside the hamlet of Cumnock (district population of 613), in the central west of New South Wales.
3 We note that previous administrations have developed similar regional management structures over previous decades.
4 See www.exec.gov.nl.ca/rural/.
5 See www.rural.gc.ca/RURAL/display-afficher.do?id=1243600900010&lang=eng.
6 See www.rural.gc.ca/RURAL/display-afficher.do?id=1230073730882&lang=eng.

References

Arnstein, SR 1969, 'The ladder of participation', *Journal of American Institute of Public Planners*, vol. 215.

Australian Broadcasting Commission 2010. Available at: www.abc.net.au/news/2010–12–23/release-mining-tax-calculations-cormann/1884382. Accessed: 22 November 2011.

Australian Bureau of Statistics 2010a, *Year Book Australia 2009–2010*, Australian Bureau of Statistics, Canberra. Available at: www.abs.gov.au/AUSSTATS/abs@.nsf/Lookup/047D4BA4016F7A0BCA25773700169C25?opendocument. Accessed: 21 November 2011.

Australian Bureau of Statistics 2010b, *Year Book Australia 2009–2010*, Australian Bureau of Statistics, Canberra. Available at: www.abs.gov.au/AUSSTATS/abs@.nsf/Lookup/CEBE696C34C36C6ECA25773700169C5E?opendocument. Accessed: 21 November 2011.

Australian Bureau of Statistics 2010, *Household Income and Income Distribution, Australia, 2009–10*, Catalogue 6523.0, Australian Bureau of Stastics, Canberra.

Alston, M and Kent, J 2004, *Social impacts of drought: Report to NSW agriculture*, Centre for Rural Social Research, Charles Sturt University, Wagga Wagga.

Bland, FA 1944, *A note on regionalism*, The Institute of Public Administration, Australia, pp. 176–182.

Botterill, LC 2003, 'Beyond Drought in Australia: The Way Forward', in Botterill, LC and Fisher, M (eds), *Beyond Drought*, CSIRO Publishing, Collingwood, pp. 197–209.

Brett, J 2007, 'The country, the city and the state in the Australian settlement', *Australian Journal of Political Science*, vol. 42, pp. 1–17.

Burchell, G 1991, 'Governmental rationality', in Burchell, G, Gordon, C and Miller, P (eds), *The Foucault effect – Studies in Governmentality*, Harvester Wheatsheaf, London, pp. 1–53.

Carson, D 2011, *Mapping the "patchwork economy" in Australia – how employment in industry sectors plays out across regions*, National Institute for Rural and Regional Australia, The Australian National University, Canberra.

Carson, D and Carson, D 2012, 'Why Tourism May Not Be Everybody's Business: The Challenge to Overcome Tradition in Diversifying Peripheral Staples Economies', *Rangeland Journal*.

Carson, D and Cleary, J 2010, 'Virtual Realities: How remote dwelling populations become more remote over time despite technological improvements', *Sustainability*, vol. 2, pp. 1282–1296.

Collits, P 2008, 'The Howard Government and regional development', *Australasian Journal of Regional Studies*, vol. 14, no. 3, pp. 287–312.

Crean, S 2011, *Budget 2011–2012 – Investing in Regional Australia*. Available at: www.regional.gov.au/budget. Accessed: 15 September 2011.

Daniell, KA, Hogan, A and Cleary, J 2010, 'Breaking down the "one size fits all" approach to rural and regional policy in the face of climate change: enhancing policy initiatives through multi-level governance,' paper presented to the *Climate change, Adaptation and Governance, NCCARF Network for Social, Economic and Institutional Dimensions+ Workshop*, University of New South Wales, 16–18 November.

European Commission 2010, *Flagship Initiatives*. Available at: http://ec.europa.eu/europe2020/tools/flagship-initiatives/index_en.htm. Accessed: 17 November 2011.

European Commission 2011a, *Agricultural Policy Perspectives Brief No. 4: The future of rural development policy*. Available at: http://ec.europa.eu/agriculture/publi/app-briefs/04_en.pdf. Accessed: 27 July 2011.

European Commission 2011b, *Europe 2020: Smart Growth*. Available at: http://ec.europa.eu/europe2020/priorities/smart-growth/index_en.htm. Accessed: 27 July 2011.

European Commission 2011c, *Europe 2020: Sustainable growth for a resource efficient, greener and more competitive economy*. Available at: http://ec.europa.eu/europe2020/priorities/sustainable-growth/index_en.htm. Accessed: 15 September 2011.

European Commission 2011d, *Europe 2020: Inclusive growth – a high employment economy delivering economic, social and territorial cohesion*. Available at: http://ec.europa.eu/europe2020/priorities/inclusive-growth/index_en.htm. Accessed: 15 September 2011.

European Commission 2011e, *Europe 2020*. Available at: http://ec.europa.eu/europe2020/index_en.htm. Accessed: 15 September 2011.

DERREG 2011, *Developing Europe's rural regions in the era of globalization*. Available at: www.derreg.eu/content/about-derreg-project. Accessed: 15 September 2011.

Foucault, M 1991, 'Questions of method', in Burchell, G, Gordon, C and Miller, P (eds), *The Foucault effect – Studies in Governmentality*, Harvester Wheatsheaf, London, pp. 73–86.

Gray, J 2010, 'Rurality and rural space: the "policy effect" of the Common Agricultural Policy in the Borders of Scotland', in Merlan, F and Raftery, D (eds), *Tracking rural change: Community, policy and technology in Australia, New Zealand and Europe*, ANU E Press, Canberra, pp. 15–40.

Gross, C 2015, 'Understanding the aspirations of people living in rural and regional Australia', this volume.

Gutman, P 2007, 'Ecosystems services: Foundations for a new rural-urban compact', *Ecological Economics*, vol. 62, pp. 383–387.

Holton, RJ 1992, *Economy and Society*, Routledge, London and New York.

House of Commons (Communities and Local Government Committee) 2011, *Localism – Third Report of Session 2012–12. Volume 1: Report, together with formal evidence, oral and written evidence*. Available at: www.parliament.uk/clgcom. Accessed: 15 September 2011.

Kohler, A 2013, 'Those income tax cuts aren't looking so good now'. Available at: www.abc.net.au/news/2013-12-18/kohler-those-income-tax-cuts-arent-looking-so-good-now/5163338. Accessed: 18 December 2013.

Lawrence, G 1987, *Capitalism and the countryside: The rural crisis in Australia*, Pluto Press, Sydney.

Lockie, S 2000, 'Crisis and conflict: shifting discourses of rural and regional Australia', in Pritchard, B and McManus, P (eds), *Land of discontent*, University of NSW Press, Sydney, pp. 14–32.

Malthus, TR 1992, *An essay on the principle of population: A view of its past and present effects on human happiness*, edited by Winch, D, Cambridge University Press, Cambridge, UK.

Marsden Jacobs and Associates, RMCG, EBC Consultants, DBM Consultants, The Australian National University, McLeod, G and Cummins, T 2010, 'Synthesis report. Economic and social profiles and impact assessments in the Murray–Darling Basin. A report to the Murray–Darling Basin Authority', Canberra. Available at: www.mdba.gov.au/what-we-do/basin-plan/development/socio-economic-reports. Accessed: 29 April 2013.

Maude, A 2004, 'Regional development processes and policies in Australia: a review of research 1990–2002', *European Planning Studies*, vol. 12, no. 1, pp. 3–26.

McCall, T 2013, 'Transitions in regional development policy: comparative to competitive advantage', in Kinnera, S, Charters and K, Vitaetas (eds), *Regional Advantage and Innovation – achieving Australia's national outcomes*. Physica-Verlag, Springer, London. pp. 73–98.

Northern Inland Regional Development Association 2011, *Regional Plan 2011–2015*. Available at: www.rdani.org.au/our-region/regional-plan.php. Accessed: 22 November 2011.

Organisation for Economic Co-operation and Development (OECD) 2006, 'The new rural paradigm: policies and governance', *OECD Rural Policy Reviews*, Paris, France.

Organisation for Economic Co-operation and Development (OECD) 2009, *Regions Matter: Economic recovery, innovation and sustainable growth*, Paris, France.

Parsons, T and Smelser, NJ 1956, *Economy and Society*, Routledge and Kegan Paul, London.

Productivity Commission 1999, *Impact of Competition Policy Reforms on Rural and Regional Australia*, Report Number 8, Productivity Commission, Canberra.

Productivity Commission 2005, *Trends in Australian Agriculture*, Research Paper, Productivity Commission, Canberra.

Productivity Commission 2009, *Government Drought Support*, Report Number 46, Final Inquiry Report, Productivity Commission, Melbourne.

Pritchard, B and McManus, P (eds) 2000, *Land of discontent: The dynamics of change in rural and regional Australia*, University of New South Wales Press Ltd, Sydney, Australia.

Safework Australia 2011, available at: http://safeworkaustralia.gov.au/Pages/default.aspx. Accessed: 17 November 2011.

Saupin, MG 1997, 'Regional Competitive Advantage and Commonwealth Government Funding for Science and Technology: The Case of Western Australia', *Australian Journal of Regional Studies*, vol. 3, no. 2, pp. 121–134.

Stubbs, J and Associates 2010, *Exploring the Relationship Between Community Resilience & Irrigated Agriculture in the MDB: Social and Economic Impacts of Reduced Irrigation Water*, Cotton Communities CRC, Narrabri. Available at: www.cottoncrc.org.au/general/Research/Projects/3_03_05. Accessed: 17 November 2011.

Titmuss, R 2006, 'Universalism versus selection' in Pierson, C and Castle, FG (eds), *The Welfare State Reader*, Polity Press, Manchester, Great Britain, pp. 40–48.

16 Development of mining-affected regions

The influence of the Commonwealth in a state dominated sphere

Jo-Anne Everingham and Daniel M. Franks

Introduction

Since the nineteenth century gold rushes, mining has been significant in the development of population centres in regional Australia. Given this pre-Federation prominence and the extensive powers and responsibilities that lie with the states in Australia's federal system, it is not surprising that most policies directly related to the extraction of minerals and on-shore oil and gas sit with state governments that have sovereignty over these resources. Nevertheless, the Federal Government can intervene in situations involving foreign affairs and trade; international agreements and conventions; Federal Government territory, properties and activities; taxation, financial management and redistribution; as well as cooperation between states and territories (Bührs and Aplin 1999).

Some Federal Government policies and legislation directly influence the resources industry which, in turn, impacts on regional areas. Such legislation includes the *Environment Protection and Biodiversity Conservation Act 1999* (EPBC), *Native Title Act 1993*, and recently the *Mineral Resource Rent Tax Act 2012* (MRRT). In addition, the Federal Government's economic imperatives and responsibilities for national prosperity and development mean that general regional policy and socio-economic development programmes are relevant to mining-affected regions. Given these potential contradictions about responsibilities, there has been flux and at times confusion over the roles of various levels of government – and, indeed, other sectors – and the policy context for mining involves a complex interplay of factors at multiple levels.

This chapter provides a background to the scale and significance of extractive industries in Australia's regions and details some direct mining-related initiatives of the Federal Government. Primarily it profiles recent policy innovations that illustrate the indirect ways the Federal Government has influenced development in on-shore mining regions within the legal and administrative framework of a federation. Federal involvement is important to ensure that Australia's mineral and energy resources are utilised to maximum advantage in the national interest and that possible negative ramifications for regional communities associated with resource developments are addressed. The chapter finishes by suggesting some priority policy areas in this respect.

Background

Australia is well endowed with mineral resources and has a number of major mining regions in every state, with many important regional centres – including Mt Isa, Kalgoorlie, Broken Hill and Bendigo – being mining towns.

Ranking third in the world as a prominent target country for global mining investment, Australia received over 12 per cent of all investment for the decade to 2001 (Bridge 2004). In the subsequent mining boom that started around 2003–2004 investment levels increased, albeit with a temporary easing during the 2008 Global Financial Crisis. Other capital-intensive industries are rare in rural Australia.

Consequently, the resources industry is a significant contributor to the Australian economy – in terms of value of production, company taxes, payroll taxes and royalties and also, to a lesser extent, employment (and hence wage and salary incomes – see Table 16.1). The mining industry accounts for over 10 per cent of the national economy and is unevenly distributed over much of regional and remote Australia. It involves a range of commodities, processes and environmental and social contexts.

There are many claims, especially from industry bodies, about the national economic benefits from mining, for example:

> Since 2004–05 the resources boom has added about $250 billion to federal government coffers and over the same period, state governments have earned more than $30 billion from royalties … the Minerals Resource Rent Tax … will add another $6 billion to the industry's tax bill.
>
> (MCA 2012, p. 10)

In addition to royalties and taxes, one estimate (Lawrence 2011) is that in 2010–2011 the development of energy resources alone (coal and coal seam gas) in Queensland contributed direct spending to the state economy of $25.2 billion, including $4.7 million as wages and salaries associated with approximately 40,631 fulltime jobs, and $20.5 billion in purchases of goods and services from local businesses and contractors. In addition companies make voluntary community contributions and there are indirect, multiplier effects.

While many of these measures stand up, the claims are increasingly scrutinised amid counter-claims about the associated economic, environmental and social costs (Rolfe *et al.* 2011; Connolly and Orsmond 2011; Goodman and Worth 2008). A particular concern is that the positive impacts are unevenly distributed – differentially flowing to various localities, sectors, industries, workers and environments. For instance, economic benefits flow primarily to capital cities and major centres rather than the regional areas where the resources are extracted and which bear many of the associated costs. As well, within regional communities, divisions between 'haves' and 'have-nots' are exacerbated. Sixty per cent of Australia's mining operates in remote Australia (Walker *et al.* 2012). Consequently, the revenue derived from mining is

Table 16.1 Royalties, employment and production value of the resources industry for major mining states (and key regions)

State and year of data	*Region*		*Royalties ($M)*	*Employment Direct and Indirect (FTE)*	*Production Value ($M)*
QUEENSLAND 2010[1]	Darling Downs	Surat Basin	147	3,077	1,604
	South West		195	0	1,062
	Fitzroy SD	Bowen Basin	208	4,009	3,064
	Mackay SD		1,083	19,444	15,484
	North West		212	13,119	7,885
	Queensland Total		1,966	44,944	>29,099
WESTERN AUSTRALIA 2010–2011[2]	Pilbara				48,858
	Kimberley				998
	Perth Metropolitan				33
	Wheatbelt				1,946
	Goldfields – Esperance				8,451
	South West				533
	Gascoyne				141
	Peel				5,046
	Mid-West				2,592
	Great Southern Region				4
	Western Australia Total		3,867	85,163	~91,600
NEW SOUTH WALES 2010–2011[3]	Sydney			5,801	
	Hunter			17,232	
	Illawara and South East			5,638	
	Northern, Far West, North West and Central West			9,225	
	Richmond, Tweed and Mid North Coast			532	
	Murray-Murrumbidgee			576	
	New South Wales Total		1,240	~39,004	20,024

Sources: (1) http://lgaq.asn.au/c/document_library/get_file?p_l_id=189033&folderId=98699&name=DLFE-9119.pdf; (2) www.dmp.wa.gov.au/documents/StatsDigest2010a.pdf; (3) www.nswmin.com.au/Mining-in-NSW/Facts-and-Figures/default.aspx

largely the result of the efforts of the more than 200,000 people who are employed in the minerals sector of regional Australia, though increasingly metropolitan centres are contributing a greater share of the workforce (as a result of long-distance commuting) and in turn accrue a larger share of the economic multipliers. Rolfe *et al.* (2011) found the level of expenditure-capture by regional Queensland was in decline with an increasing share of economic benefits going instead to major centres and coastal zones. Indirect employee multipliers in mining ranged between 1.22 in Mt Isa, 2.08 in the Central Highlands and 4.53 in the Western Downs, rising to 4.72 in Gladstone, 6.74 in Mackay and 22.49 in Brisbane. This pattern is likely to be more pronounced in other, more centralised, states. There is the potential that mine-site automation may further contribute to relative declines in the regionally based mining workforce (McNab and Garcia-Vasquez 2011) and hence decrease flow-on benefits as well.

Nevertheless, the proportion of Australia's merchandise exports represented by mineral and energy exports makes Australia one of the most resource-dependent industrialised countries in the world and resource developments significantly influence the prosperity and well-being of many regional areas and of other rural industries (Goodman and Worth 2008; Stevens and Dietsche 2008). This means that policy settings affecting mining development have repercussions for regional development and there is value in exploring the evolution in Federal policy and in Federal-state relations with respect to the industry.

Mining-related Federal initiatives influencing rural and regional Australia since World War II

From the mid-twentieth century the Commonwealth Government has used instruments – including trade policy, obligations under international agreements, and tax policies – to advance its mining policy agenda within the context of prevailing Federal-state relations (Bührs and Aplin 1999).

Exploitation of newly-discovered minerals, oil and gas was a crucial part of the primary production that bolstered Australia's post-war economy. The Federal and state governments supported exploration and development with their own policy measures in line with what Cockfield dubs elsewhere in this volume a 'producer settlement and retention' approach. The Federal Government provided incentives and tax concessions, subsidised loans for infrastructure such as ports and railways, and established a Bureau of Mineral Resources. The protectionist trade policies of post-war decades included an embargo on iron ore exports (Stevenson 1976).[1] The state governments meanwhile entered into State Agreements with mining companies. These Agreements were highly favourable to the companies and encouraged them to open up often sparsely settled areas by building mining towns near their tenements. However, shifting policy priorities have removed many incentives and no purpose-built mining town has been constructed since Roxby Downs in the 1980s.

From the 1970s, international affairs provided an impetus for increased Federal Government intervention in resources policy. Factors behind this included the oil crisis and the reliance of the industry on foreign capital and foreign markets. However, there were also some contentious domestic considerations that the Commonwealth Government intervened to resolve. For instance, in 1976 they halted sand-mining on Fraser Island in Queensland. Such direct action was linked to rising environmental concerns and also manifested in national commitments to ecologically sustainable development that was subsequently formalised in the Rio Declaration on Environment and Development in 1992. The resultant Federal legislation gave impetus to a spate of new state regulations as well and to initiatives to achieve Federal-state cooperation through an evolving system of catchment and regional natural resource management (NRM) institutions (see the discussion by Tennent and Lockie, this volume). Although many of the government provisions had direct bearing on the extractive industries and have arguably modified outcomes of mining development, the coordination through regional NRM bodies had surprisingly little engagement with the industry until recently. However in 2009, one of these regional NRM institutions, the Fitzroy Basin Association in Central Queensland, commenced discussions with a range of stakeholders from government, agriculture and the coal mining industry about a waterway monitoring partnership to oversee a catchment severely affected by both agricultural activities and releases of saline mine-water (Eberhard *et al.* in press). This has progressed to formalisation of the Fitzroy Partnership for River Health, a promising example of adapting existing frameworks (in this case for NRM) to manage exploitation of energy resources as well.

Equally important was increased national recognition of Indigenous rights. This, in turn, was also reflected in legislation with the Commonwealth Government's *Land Rights Act (Northern Territory) 1976* and subsequent Federal legislation on Native Title, Cultural Heritage and Indigenous Heritage.[2] Like the environmental legislation, these laws proved to be a catalyst for both state legislation and for voluntary initiatives on the part of the private sector. Sometimes these Federal policy agendas with respect to environmental protection and Indigenous rights converged, as in the Hawke Labor Government's decision in 1991 to prevent mining at Coronation Hill in Kakadu National Park.

The major changes with respect to mining on Aboriginal land in Australia and Indigenous people's influence over resource development (O'Faircheallaigh 2006) are particularly notable, given that over 60 per cent of the Australian mining operations adjoin Indigenous communities (Australian Human Rights Commission 2006). As mentioned, the Federal enactment of the *Native Title Act 1993* stimulated subsequent state legislation over the ensuing decade that has, in turn, established new requirements and processes to support agreement making and Native Title holders' or claimants' direct negotiation of agreements (Harvey and Nish 2005). This provides a model of negotiation of reciprocal benefits with minimal government involvement. While Agreements, especially Indigenous Land Use Agreements (ILUAs), have become the prevalent means of documenting the mutual undertakings between mining companies and Indigenous communities, some resource companies operating in Australia, including BHP Billiton, QGC, Woodside, Wesfarmers and Transfield have adopted the Reconciliation Action Plan (RAP) approach espoused by Reconciliation Australia as their policy framework for Indigenous affairs. Such developments have facilitated progress, however limited, on national policy objectives such as Closing the Gap.

The Federal Government has also introduced a number of initiatives intended to support and encourage greater Indigenous involvement in the private sector and especially the mining industry. For example, the Department of Resources, Energy and Tourism's Working in Partnership programme fosters long-term relationships between Indigenous communities and the mining industry, to expand both employment and the business development opportunities for Aboriginal people in remote communities. Earned income from these two mining-related sources has been recognised as a key way Indigenous people directly benefit from the resources industry in the short to medium-term (Levitus 2008). One element of the Working in Partnership programme is the web-based Indigenous business directory, *Digedi*, intended to facilitate the participation of Indigenous businesses in the mining supply chain and assist major companies to buy from Indigenous businesses in the local communities where they operate. Some initiatives are aimed at coordinating measures introduced by various government departments, both national and state, with the undertakings and programmes of individual companies. One such whole of industry, whole of government response was a Memorandum of Understanding (MoU) between the Commonwealth Government and Minerals Council of Australia in 2005 to adopt a cooperative and coordinated approach to ensuring Indigenous people benefit from mining and building 'sustainable prosperous communities in which individuals can create and take up social, employment and business opportunities' (Australian Human Rights Commission 2006, p. 100). The MoU and subsequent Regional Partnership Agreements like the North West Queensland Indigenous Resource Industry Initiative (NWQIRII), involve the private sector and state industry peak bodies (in this case the Queensland Resources Council) and both state and Federal Governments.

Equitable and sustainable regional development with fair distribution of benefits has emerged as a dominant issue in mining regions in recent decades, reviving a recurring theme of services equity noted in the chapter by Cockfield (this volume). One concern is that regional infrastructure is inferior to that in metropolitan areas. The resources industry places additional pressures on transport, health and other infrastructure and services which are not the sole province of one level of government. It is notable that the rationale for introducing royalties was that they provided state governments with the means to respond to resources development and take over public responsibilities in mining towns from the private sector (encouraging the demise of the 'company town'). More recently, the popular pressure for distribution of benefits to the regions has prompted Western Australia and later Queensland to introduce a form of 'royalties for regions' funding, with similar ideas widely embraced in New South Wales as well.

Despite these state government resources and responsibilities, the Federal Government has assumed some responsibilities too, establishing the Regional Infrastructure Fund to invest part of the proceeds of resources development. Infrastructure Australia, an agency that reports to the Council of Australian Governments (COAG), administers the Regional Infrastructure Fund and implements programmes to deliver the priority infrastructure as determined by COAG. In Queensland, for example, Federal-state cooperation resulted in the development of a 50-year freight infrastructure plan for the Mt Isa-Townsville economic 'zone' which encompasses one of the state's major mining regions (Juturna and MITEZ 2012). This involved a study that examined the infrastructure supply chain and had the close participation of organisations including Regional Development Australia, Queensland Treasury, Queensland Geological Survey, the then Queensland Department of Employment, Economic Development and Innovation and the Queensland Resources Council.

The Commonwealth has also exercised the key redistributive mechanism at its disposal, taxation, primarily in the form of the hotly contested Mineral Resource Rent Tax (MRRT), to direct a greater share of profits from mining to public purposes including regional infrastructure and development. There has long been a concern about repatriation of profits to foreign owners, but the resources industry also demonstrates the priority that successive governments have placed on national equity and redistribution. This is evident in recent concern about a form of 'Dutch Disease' with inadequate returns to the public and weakened non-resource sectors (e.g. agriculture, manufacturing and tourism) and claims about a two-speed economy and regions missing out on the benefits of mining (Rolfe *et al.* 2006; Goodman and Worth 2008; Cleary 2012). Certainly research shows that current trends are for some rural communities experiencing resource extraction to have less equitable distribution of incomes than others (Reeson *et al.* 2012). The Federal Government's recent attempts to play a greater role in managing resource revenues by introducing a Mining Super-Profits Tax were stymied by political opposition which led to the much more circumscribed MRRT. Moreover, in practice, state governments' adjustments to their various royalty schemes, volatile market prices for the relevant commodities, and the impact of associated concessions meant the MRRT yielded only a fraction of the forecast revenue in its first year. In the absence of other budget provisions or alternative means of retaining windfall gains from mining to underpin regional infrastructure development, there are limited opportunities to harness resource industry revenues to fund the proposed development of regional Australia.

As a major producer and exporter of minerals and energy, Australia is cited as an exemplar in managing non-renewable resources by some (Wright and Czelusta 2007) and aspires to demonstrate leadership. To this end, AusAID's Mining for Development programme aims to support resource-rich developing countries to maximise sustainable benefits from mining while helping them overcome the associated challenges. In addition the Federal Department of Resources, Energy and Tourism administers a number of programmes aimed at building the capacity of Australian mining companies as internationally competitive and sustainable operators. One specific programme that illustrates this policy priority is the Leading Practice Sustainable Development Programme for the Mining Industry. This supports enhanced risk management, environmental performance and social performance of the Australian resources industry as a whole.

Though the outcomes for mining-affected regions of this initiative have yet to be assessed, its emphasis on environmental and social performance indirectly serves to advance the Federal Government's objectives of ecologically sustainable development in regional Australia. This agenda, though more central to NRM policies and exploitation of renewable resources, has ramifications for Australia's minerals, oil and gas industries and mining regions. This was illustrated in the debates accompanying the introduction of a national carbon pricing system. Australia's coal exports alone emit more carbon into the atmosphere than other industrial sources in this nation, so the coal mining industry has been integral to this mechanism for market-based emissions-reduction (Siriwardana *et al.* 2011).

Despite action on carbon pollution, there is evident concern that the lessons of proposed uranium mining at Jabiluka and sand mining on Fraser Island have not been learned. For example, there are fears that the ecological (and indeed world heritage) values of the Great Barrier Reef are under threat from state government-sanctioned port developments on the Queensland coastline to service the resources industry, and doubts about the Commonwealth's will or power to intervene.

Some other themes in recent policy developments and government programmes indicate contemporary policy challenges. With respect to the resources industry, one such challenge relates to expectations about community engagement and community development (Kemp 2005; Rolfe *et al.* 2006). This is in line with a general desire for greater community participation and increased recognition of industry's need for a social licence to operate. As a result, some state governments are adopting measures such as social impact assessment (Joyce and Macfarlane 2002; Franks 2011) for all major developments including mining and on-shore oil and gas projects. However, Federal initiatives also respond to these directions, as is evident in the national networks of regional bodies established as part of the NRM regime or the RDA committees – though the extent to which they constitute local, bottom-up participation has been questioned (see Tennent and Lockie, this volume).

Labour supply, labour relations and management issues are another policy preoccupation associated with this industry. In this respect the Commonwealth has responded with initiatives like the National Resources Sector Workforce Strategy to address the increasing demand for skilled labour for the mining, oil and gas industries. The National Resources Sector Employment Taskforce's 31 recommendations to the Federal Government are being progressively implemented. For example a fly-in, fly-out (FIFO) coordinator project, trialled in Cairns, has been extended to a further four locations around the country. The influence of the Federal Government on the mining workforce is also exerted through its authority over migration employment visas that allow importation of foreign temporary workers. As well, the Commonwealth has placed a particular emphasis on employment and training of Indigenous people for the mining industry (Trigger 2003; Tiplady and Barclay 2007).

Recent concerns about workforce conditions in the industry – including the impacts of long working hours, shifts and rosters (McCann 2005) – have focused on the increased use of fly-in, fly-out practices (Beach *et al.* 2003; State of Queensland 2011). Since it became increasingly prevalent from the 1990s, FIFO, or long-distance commuting, has been the focus of attention for reasons beyond workforce considerations and related to regional development as well (Houghton 1993; Storey 2001). To build understanding of the complex impacts of FIFO in the regions, a parliamentary committee conducted an inquiry into long-distance commuting workforce practices during 2012 (House of Representatives Standing Committee on Regional Australia 2013). The Committee's report bemoaned that, 'Corporate employment choices have become the regional Australia policy of many governments' (House of Representatives Standing Committee on Regional Australia 2013, p. viii). The committee expressed considerable ambivalence about growth based on resource extraction. It called for considerably more research and its findings highlighted problems with 'Dutch Disease', funding arrangements for local government, long-term quality of life in resource communities and the impacts of long-distance commuting on the health and well-being of workers and their families. One recommendation it made was for the Commonwealth Government to establish a dedicated secretariat within an existing government department with responsibility for consulting with state governments and the resources industry about matters including regional social and infrastructure impact assessments, development of regional plans and of community benefits agreements. In advocating this sort of coordination, the committee has endorsed the indirect role the Federal Government has played in many fields outside their direct authority.

Indirect Federal role – coordination

In their attempts to intervene in issues associated with mining, the Federal Government has adopted multiple governance strategies and used a range of policy levers including exercising their authority in terms of international trade and exports. For example, there have been tight controls on export of uranium since the Federal Labor Government introduced a 'three mines' policy in 1984 limiting uranium production to Ranger, Narbarlek and Olympic Dam. Export controls continued after the Howard Government overturned that policy in 1996. As well, Commonwealth powers with respect to foreign investment have been invoked to mandate Australian equity thresholds in the past; as mentioned Federal Indigenous Affairs initiatives such as the *Native Title Act* had far-reaching significance for the minerals industry; and taxation powers have allowed the MRRT and, less conspicuously, fringe benefits and other taxes that sometimes have unforeseen consequences for mining communities.

In some cases the Federal Government has assumed direct responsibility, as with regard to off-shore exploration and mining. In other cases, when the objective has been to achieve national standardisation, they have coordinated development of nationally consistent legislation under an inter-governmental agreement. Such legislation is proposed, for example, under the National Mine Safety Framework in order to achieve a standard occupational health and safety regime in the Australian mining industry, although reaching consensus is proving a challenge.

Other initiatives have involved encouraging new forms of regulation, including voluntary initiatives and certification schemes (Schiavi and Solomon 2007) and expanding the range of stakeholders influencing the regulatory environment (Brereton 2003). The Commonwealth Department of Resources, Energy and Tourism is, for example, convening a trial of the Extractive Industries Transparency Initiative (EITI) in Australia. The EITI is a globally developed standard that promotes revenue transparency at the local and national level to enhance resource governance and the benefits that flow to citizens from extraction of their natural resources. There are also many circumstances where Federal influence has encouraged involvement of a broader range of domestic stakeholders, particularly at local and regional levels, for example. These include the NWQIRII mentioned earlier as involving multiple departments of both the Queensland and the Commonwealth Governments, as well as resource companies through their state umbrella body the Queensland Resources Council.

Judiciously used, with alignment of the private sector and other interests involved, these diverse strategies can progress a national agenda for regional Australia, though at arm's length from the Federal Government. By adopting 'enabling' and 'influencing' interventions as identified by Schmidt (2009) the Federal Government can limit its direct involvement in mining matters over which states have legislative responsibility while still advancing its priorities for rural areas. As an 'enabling state', the Federal Government works in collaboration with market actors and/or with regional bodies, local governments, and other local organisations to plan and implement priorities. We see this role adopted for example in the model of the Regional Development Australia (RDA) committees and, in the Pilbara, the RDA, state government departments, mining companies, property developers and local councils are partnering over a number of major infrastructure projects worth around $4 billion. In 'influencing state' mode, market actors perform functions that might otherwise come under the purview of government, but with the state providing clear rules as to the responsibilities and accountabilities of the market actors. This approach, familiar in 'contract state' situations for example, has been evidenced in the Federal Environment Minister's conditions attached to approvals of resource extraction projects, though the grounds on which these can be imposed are quite constrained. Another example is the introduction of market mechanisms like the emissions trading scheme that involve the private sector engaging in market interactions, but at a carbon price set by government. Such modes of working are consonant with current emphases on localism and regional governance bodies, identified elsewhere in this volume (see for example chapters by Collits; Cockfield; and Hogan and Young).

The Commonwealth's quest for more cooperative inter-governmental relations has gained momentum in recent decades and led them to adopt a facilitative role and favour indirect intervention, consistent with Australia's federal system and also with trends to localism and regional self-sufficiency based on partnerships with industry, as detailed in other chapters. For mining, as for other policy domains, this is particularly evident in the COAG and the RDA Committees, both of which provide avenues for coordination and joint action though operating at different levels. It also manifests in the negotiation of formal agreements between the two levels of government whereby the Commonwealth delegates supervision of relevant processes to the states. This strategy has been used, for example, to streamline environmental assessments of mining projects under the *Environment Protection and Biodiversity Conservation Act*.

As well as general Federal-state agreements, negotiated through forums such as COAG, there have been bilateral inter-governmental agreements to cooperate on specific initiatives. For example, the Commonwealth and Western Australian Governments agreed in 2008 to conduct a joint strategic assessment of a proposed on-shore liquefied natural gas precinct for the Browse Basin under relevant environmental legislation. The exercise promised a better resourced and more robust assessment for key stakeholders, but in practice, the Western Australia Government's assertion of its interests and lack of patience undermined the process.

This has been the pattern overall, with none of these demonstrations of increasing rhetoric about collaboration and support between state and Federal Governments being wholly successful and a lack of integration and policy coordination as well as disputes between the two levels of government persisting. Examples of the Federal-state tensions include the Federal Environment Minister's condemnation of the Queensland Government's 2012 approval of the Alpha coal project and the Queensland Governments' reaction to proposals in 2012 to extend the Federal Environment Minister's powers to stop resources development on consideration of impacts on national water resources.

Despite the constraints of 'coordinate federalism' (see Cockfield, this volume), the range of policies, programmes and strategies relevant to the resources industry that have been employed by successive Federal Governments since the 1970s has enabled them to achieve various national policy objectives – economic, social and environmental. The fact that many of these achievements as well as some of the anomalous outcomes for mining-affected regions have flowed from general policy directions rather than mining-specific initiatives points to likely avenues for future action.

Indisputably, extraction of minerals, oil and gas has played, and will continue to play a significant role in the trajectory of rural and regional development in Australia. Hence, regional development policy is among the many federal policy areas that must engage with issues related to the extractive industries just as these are important considerations in macroeconomic policy, foreign policy and environmental policy. This is an iterative process and the direction all such policy areas take, in turn, influences regional development in mining-intensive states. Despite the changes outlined above, the legal, policy and institutional environment has been consistently favourable to expansion of Australia's resources industry. This environment contains significant current and emerging issues that are inadequately addressed, partly because they are not the exclusive domain of one level of government.

These issues relate to both policy focus and strategies. In terms of policy focus, the immediate challenge is enshrining holistic consideration of triple-bottom line sustainability as well as recognising the cumulative impacts (both positive and negative) that can arise through the interaction and aggregation of mining and other rural activities (Franks *et al.* 2010). In process terms the challenge for government is to collaborate effectively, operate at various scales as appropriate – especially regional and local – and perform a coordinating role. The Federal Government will need to address these challenges to move beyond reliance on boom and bust cycles associated with commodities production and achieve socio-economic sustainability of the rural and regional areas which remain the sites of production of diverse basic necessities: food, fibre, minerals and energy. This is especially the case in the face of rising concern about national and international food security, energy security and water security. It is not possible to advocate a definitive national mineral resources policy. Nevertheless a number of general principles mentioned throughout this book are highly pertinent. While many of these can be considered as governance issues they also relate in broad terms to sustainable development.

First, mining, oil and gas developments must be managed so as to bring broad economic benefits at both local and national scales. Resource operations are often situated in regional areas that have a declining population and workforce, relatively high levels of social disadvantage, and a limited economic base. Incomes and expenditure from resource companies currently provide an important stimulus to a number of such local and regional economies (Rolfe *et al.* 2011). Future resource developments can potentially generate economic benefits, such as employment and business expenditure, in areas that to date have had limited involvement with mining. This will especially be the case if a significant proportion of the workforce can be retained in the regional communities. The problem with this strategy for regional renewal is that it is beyond the power of any government to influence the location of the resource deposits! The Federal Government can, however, influence economic flows within and from well-endowed regions since it holds maximum taxing powers in the Australian system. Therefore, they can undertake reforms including of current taxation arrangements, for example in the fringe benefits tax, that limit the incentives of resource companies to provide local housing and services. They could also tackle changes to MRRT if they had the appetite for another political battle – and potentially shape the 'Future Fund' into a well-designed stabilisation fund or sovereign wealth fund to provide a buffer against the cyclical economic fortunes of the industry. Additional economic benefits could result from addressing elements of Federal funding of local government, and directing suitable resources to bodies to which responsibilities are devolved.

Second the identification, mitigation and management of the social disruption associated with mineral resource development should be explicitly addressed. The 'FIFO Enquiry' was a valuable initiative in that respect. However, mining will not be the panacea for all unwelcome social trends or persistent problems in rural areas. For instance, as a capital-intensive rather than labour-intensive industry there seems little prospect of a return to the situation of using mining for producer-settlement and retention to any significant extent, though the ambitious Pilbara Cities vision in Western Australia will be worth watching in this regard. Still, mining in general is unlikely to counter urban-drift even if governments, both Federal and state, introduce measures to influence the proportions of residential to FIFO workers for example. All governments have a responsibility to ensure that mining contributes to overall well-being and diversification rather than wholesale disruption of populations or livelihoods. There is an opportunity to explore options, in collaboration with state and local governments, for well-designed community agreements that could build on international examples, Australian experience with Indigenous Agreements, and also with recent experiments such as Social Impact Management Plans in Queensland.

Third, the environmental side-effects of the resources industry cannot be considered in isolation from overall management of natural resources. Pertinent lessons about coordination, appropriate scale, and adaptive and integrated management can all be drawn from regional NRM initiatives. The engagement of relevant institutions and programmes with the resources industry in cases like the Fitzroy Partnership for River Health or the Upper Hunter Air Quality Monitoring Network provides a foundation. Action on key national priorities like the Murray–Darling Basin Plan, and anti-salinity and stewardship of the Great Artesian Basin requires understanding of the cumulative impacts of all rural industries – especially mining and agriculture – on our soil, water and vegetation assets.

Resources booms, drought, deregulation of agricultural trade, and extensive NRM reforms have precipitated sometimes painful structural adjustments for rural Australians. History and our federal system show that there is some opportunity for direct legislative intervention by the Federal Government, but considerably more opportunity to contain the most negative consequences of such occurrences and minimise the ill-effects through working in collaboration with the private sector, other levels of government and local and regional stakeholders. In both direct and indirect ways, there is an opportunity to provide coordination and leadership and set a course that will deliver a legacy of sustainable regional development from extraction of the nation's endowment of mineral and energy resources. Improving flawed processes like joint strategic regional assessments, coordination through COAG, and currently fragmented approaches to regional planning and development that neglect cumulative impacts will be fundamental. So will coordinating, resourcing, empowering and building the capacity of existing institutions with the potential to plan, monitor and manage balanced development in regions seeking to leverage benefits from extraction of minerals, oil and gas.

Conclusion

Many of the controversies that have surrounded mining development involve important policy issues in Australia: Indigenous rights and Native Title, environmental protection, Federal-state relations, and even international relations. These cases illustrate that pursuing the sometimes conflicting objectives of the Commonwealth Government, state governments and corporations with regard to mineral resources within a federal context presents governance challenges.

In the decades following World War II, the consensus was that the Australian Government's aspirations with respect to mineral resources policy were a victim of the federal system. As Stevenson (1976, p. 82) expressed it:

> [T]he states have been able to frustrate the federal government's policy-making efforts to a considerable degree by virtue of their ownership of resources and the administrative powers which they derive from this fact. This has been counterbalanced to some extent by the distribution of legislative powers under the Australian Constitution, and particularly by the fact that the federal government has the power to control overseas trade. But the combination of fiscal dominance and the spending power given to it by Section 96, which enables the federal government to exercise great influence in other areas of policy, has not proved very significant in regard to mineral resource policy, an area in which spending power is no substitute for regulatory power.

Recent decades have seen some changes, with international commitments in areas such as environmental protection becoming more stringent, and considerable efforts directed to greater collaboration between state and Federal spheres with a coordinating role for the Federal Government. By working through and with other levels of government, the Commonwealth has indirectly advanced parts of its policy agenda. However, there is considerable popular concern that 'mining dominates our society, our economy and even our political system' (Cleary 2012, p. xi). Managing both the positive and negative impacts of this volatile industry sector remains a national policy goal in the interests of ensuring a positive, equitable and sustainable legacy for regional Australia from this inherently time-bound industry.

Notes

1 Notwithstanding Prime Minister Menzies' pre-war confrontation with waterside workers who refused to load scrap-iron for export to Japan, which earned him the nickname 'pig-iron Bob'.

2 Examples of relevant Commonwealth legislation include: *Aboriginal and Torres Strait Islander Heritage Protection Act 1984*; *Native Title Act 1993* (amended in 1998); *Environment Protection and Biodiversity Conservation Act 1999* (EPBC Act); *Environment and Heritage Legislation Amendment Act 2003*.

References

Aboriginal and Torres Strait Islander Social Justice Commissioner 2006, 'Chapter 3: The Memorandum of Understanding between the Australian Government and the Minerals Council of Australia and the East Kimberley Regional Partnership Agreement', in Aboriginal and Torres Strait Islander Social Justice Commission (ed.), *Native Title Report 2006*, Australian Human Rights and Equal Opportunity Commission, Sydney, pp. 99–111.

Beach, R, Brereton, D and Cliff, D 2003, *Workforce Turnover in FIFO Mining Operations in Australia: An Exploratory Study*, Centre for Social Responsibility in Mining (CSRM), University of Queensland, Brisbane.

Brereton, D 2003, 'Self-regulation of environmental and social performance in the Australian minerals industry', *Environmental Plannning and Law Journal*, vol. 20, no. 1, pp. 1–14.

Bridge, G 2004, 'Mapping the Bonanza: Geographies of Mining Investment in an Era of Neoliberal Reform', *The Professional Geographer*, vol. 56, no. 3, pp. 406–421.

Bührs, T and Aplin, G 1999, 'Pathways towards sustainability: The Australian approach', *Journal of Environmental Planning and Management*, vol. 42, no. 3, pp. 315–340.

Centre for Social Responsibility in Mining (CSRM) and Banarra Sustainability and Social Assurance 2006, *Voluntary Reporting and Accounting of Social Performance in the Mining Sector: State of Practice Voluntary Report Findings*, CSRM, University of Queensland, Brisbane.

Cleary, P 2012, *Mine-Field. The Dark Side of Australia's Resources Rush*, Black Inc, Collingwood, VICTORIA

Connolly, E and Orsmond, D 2011, 'The Mining Industry: From Bust to Boom', *Research Discussion Paper 2011–08*, Reserve Bank of Australia.

Davis, L 2001, 'The social responsibility of corporations', *Journal of Corporate Citizenship*, vol. 23, no. 8, pp. 2–8.

Eberhard, R, Johnston, N and Everingham, J in press, 'A collaborative approach to address the cumulative impacts of mine-water discharge: Negotiating a cross-sectoral waterway partnership in the Bowen Basin, Australia', *Resources Policy*.

Franks, D 2011, 'Management of the Social Impacts of Mining', in Darling, P (ed.), *SME Mining Engineering Handbook*, Society for Mining, Metallurgy, and Exploration, Colorado, pp. 1817–1825.

Franks, DM, Brereton, D, Moran, CJ, Sarker, T and Cohen, T 2010, *Cumulative Impacts – A Good Practice Guide for the Australian Coal Mining Industry*, Centre for Social Responsibility in Mining, Centre for Water in the Minerals Industry, and Sustainable Minerals Institute, The University of Queensland, and Australian Coal Association Research Program, Brisbane.

Goodman, J and Worth, D 2008, 'The Minerals Boom and Australia's "Resource Curse" ', *Journal of Australian Political Economy*, vol. 61, pp. 201–219.

Harvey, B and Nish, S 2005, 'Rio Tinto and Indigenous community agreement making in Australia', *Journal of Energy and Natural Resource Law*, vol. 23, no. 4, pp. 490–510.

Houghton, DS 1993, 'Long-Distance Commuting: A New Approach to Mining in Australia', *The Geographical Journal*, vol. 159, no. 3, pp. 281–290.

House of Representatives Standing Committee on Regional Australia 2013, *Cancer of the bush or salvation for our cities? Fly-in, fly-out and drive-in, drive-out workforce practices in Regional Australia*, Commonwealth of Australia, Canberra.

Joyce, S and Macfarlane, M 2002, 'Social impact assessment in the mining industry: current situation and future directions', *MMSD Report No. 46*, International Institute for Environment and Development and World Business Council for Sustainable Development, London.

Juturna and Mt Isa – Townsville Economic Zone (MITEZ) 2012, *50-year Freight Infrastructure Plan. Final report*, Juturna and Mt Isa – Townsville Economic Zone (MITEZ), May.

Kemp, D 2005, 'Between a Rock and a Hard Place: Community Relations Work in the Minerals Industry', PhD Thesis, University of Queensland, Brisbane.

Lawrence, R 2011, 'Economic impacts of the Resources Sector on the Queensland Economy 2010/11', prepared for the Queensland Resources Council. Available at: http://queenslandeconomy.com.au/images/stories/Economic-Impact-of-Resources-Sector-on-Qld-Economy-2010–11-Final-Report.pdf. Accessed 22 September 2012.

Levitus, R 2008, 'Aboriginal Organisations and Development', in Altman, J and Martin, D (eds), *Power, Culture, Economy. Indigenous Australians and Mining*, ANU E Press, Acton, ACT, pp. 73–97.

MCA 2012, *2011 Annual Report*. Available at: www.minerals.org.au/file_upload/files/annual_reports/AR_2011_Final.pdf. Accessed 28 September 2012.

McCann, D 2005, *Working Time Laws: a Global Perspective: Findings from the ILO's Conditions of Work and Employment Database*, International Labour Organisation, Geneva.

McNab, KL and Garcia-Vasquez, M 2011, 'Autonomous and remote operation technologies in Australian mining', *CSIRO Cluster Research Report No. 2.5*, prepared for CSIRO Minerals Down Under Flagship, Minerals Futures Cluster Collaboration, by the Centre for Social Responsibility in Mining, Sustainable Minerals Institute, The University of Queensland, Brisbane.

O'Faircheallaigh, C 2006, 'Aborigines, mining companies and the state in contemporary Australia: A new political economy or "business as usual"?', *Australian Journal of Political Science*, vol. 41, no. 1, pp. 1–22.

Reeson, AF, Measham TG and Hosking K 2012, 'Mining Activity, Income Inequality and Gender in Australia', *Australian Journal of Agricultural and Resource Economics*, vol. 56, no. 2, pp. 302–313.

Rolfe, J, Ivanova, G and Lockie, S 2006, 'Assessing the social and economic impacts of coal mining on communities in the Bowen Basin: summary and recommendations', *Research Report No. 11*, ACARP and Central Queensland University, Rockhampton.

Rolfe, J, Gregg, D, Ivanova, G, Lawrence, R and Rynne, D 2011, 'The Economic Contribution of the Resources Sector by Regional Areas in Queensland', *Economic Analysis and Policy*, vol. 41, no. 1, pp. 15–36.

Schiavi, P and Solomon, FL 2007, 'Voluntary initiatives in the mining industry: do they work?', *Greener Management International*, vol. 53 (special issue, Fall), pp. 27–41.

Schmidt, VA 2009, 'Putting the political back into political economy by bringing the state back in yet again', *World Politics*, vol. 61, no. 3, pp. 516–546.

Siriwardana, M, Meng, S and McNeill, J 2011, 'The Impact of a Carbon Tax on the Australian Economy: Results from a CGE Model', *Business, Economics and Public Policy Working Papers No. 2011–2*, University of New England, Armidale.

Solomon, F, Katz, E and Lovel, R 2008, 'Social dimensions of mining: Research, policy and practice challenges for the minerals industry in Australia', *Resources Policy*, vol. 33, no. 3, pp. 142–149.

State of Queensland (Queensland Treasury) 2011, *Surat Basin Population Report, 2010*, OESR, Brisbane, Queensland.

Stevens, P and Dietsche, E 2008, 'Resource Curse: an analysis of causes, experiences and possible ways forward', *Energy Policy*, vol. 36, no. 1, pp. 56–65.

Stevenson, G 1976, 'Mineral Resources and Australian Federalism', *Research Monograph No. 17*, Centre for Research on Federal Financial Relations, The Australian National University, Canberra.

Storey, K 2001, 'Fly-in/Fly-out and Fly-over: mining and regional development in Western Australia', *Australian Geographer*, vol. 32, no. 2, pp. 133–148.

Tiplady, T and Barclay, MA 2007, *Indigenous Employment in the Australian Minerals Industry*, CSRM, University of Queensland, Brisbane.

Trigger, D 2003, 'Mining Projects in Remote Aboriginal Australia: Sites for the Articulation and Contesting of Economic and Cultural Futures', *Proceedings of Mining Frontiers: Social Conflict, Property Relations and Cultural Change in Emerging Boom Regions*, Max Planck Institute of Social Anthropology, University of Leipzig, Germany, 16–18 June.

Walker, BW, Porter, DJ and Marsh, I 2012, *Fixing the Hole in Australia's Heartland: How Government needs to work in remote Australia*, Desert Knowledge Australia, Alice Springs.

Wright, G and Czelusta, J 2007, 'Resource-based growth, past and present', in Lederman, D and Maloney, W (eds), *Natural Resources: Neither Curse Nor Destiny*, The World Bank and Stanford University Press, Palo Alto, CA.

17 Understanding the aspirations of people living in rural and regional Australia

Catherine Gross

People living in rural and regional areas frequently feel that their perspectives and interests are neither understood nor valued by central policymakers or decision-makers. Protests are manifestations of the dissatisfaction with policies or decisions, such as those that occurred in 2010 with the release of the Murray–Darling Basin Authority's *Guide to the proposed Basin Plan* and in 2008 against the construction of the Victorian North-South pipeline. In an era of constant change, whether due to climate variability, government-initiated policy reform or changing market conditions, communities in many rural areas are facing an uncertain future. With food security an additional major global concern there are many reasons why agriculture and the future of rural and regional Australia should be high on the list of 'big issues' for the future of the country. A major challenge for decision-makers is in gaining acceptance for their decisions by those directly affected by policy reforms, particularly where people feel that they are disadvantaged and that their issues and concerns have not been understood.

This chapter explores the aspirations of people living in rural communities. It provides insights into the way people living in rural communities envisage their future and their perceptions of decision-making processes on issues that concern their livelihoods and future security. It does this by drawing directly from interview narratives in which people voice their stories, experiences, perspectives and thoughts about rural Australia. These interviews focused on people's aspirations for rural Australia and what they would like to see in a vision. Topics included government–community relationships, values and aspirations, water reform, consultation processes and decision-making processes.

The chapter is organised in three sections. The first section provides a background context for rural and regional Australia. It describes the complexity and change inherent in rural Australia and how differing perspectives have formed in response to government programmes and changing conditions. The second section presents the narratives and perspectives of people living in rural communities. The final section presents a summary of themes and highlights from these narratives and outlines a holistic vision for rural Australia.

Divided lines of rural, regional and urban Australia

Resources: wealth, conflict, fear and tension

The natural resources of the Australian continent are not only the foundation of its past and current wealth; they are also a source of anxiety and conflict in long-standing debates about how they should be used and shared. For example, disputes over the waters of the Murray–Darling river system have gone on for well over 100 years. It is commonplace for state governments and upstream and downstream communities to argue about water policies and who makes best or most efficient use of the water. As Boully and Maywald (2011, p. 103) describe it: 'No matter where you stand in the Basin, communities look upstream with envy and downstream with disdain'. This reflects a viewpoint that institutions and communities in one area often have little understanding of environmental conditions and institutional arrangements in other areas, in addition to seeing 'the problem through the lens of their own circumstances' (Boully and Maywald 2011, p. 103). People in irrigation communities frequently comment on what they perceive as the profligate use of water in other areas of the Murray–Darling Basin. For example, some irrigation farmers in NSW hold the view that maintaining constant water levels in the Lower Lakes of South Australia is wasteful due to the high evaporation losses. Unease and apprehension about the use of agricultural land for mining is another cause of conflict (Thompson 2012). Communities are concerned about land and aquifer pollution. This results in anxious communities, disputes about information and potential impacts, and a lack of confidence in institutional arrangements and decision-making processes. People fear for the future viability of their livelihoods, farms and communities.

There are a variety of underlying cultural dynamics and tensions between sections of Australian society that require understanding by policymakers and governments. Many tensions could be attributed to the rural-urban or country-city divide, a perception that there is a gap between people living in cities and those living in rural areas. This rural-urban divide and how it is manifested has been discussed in academia, community associations and the media (Rural Women's Network 2007; Adams 2011; Brett 2011a; Salt 2011). It can be attributed to a range of tangible and intangible factors, such as declining populations in some rural areas (Rural Women's Network 2007); differing levels of access to health and transport services (Adams 2011); and to a perceived lack of knowledge and understanding of rural and regional Australia by people who live in cities (Wahlquist 2003).

Change, uncertainty and 'crisis' in rural Australia

Recurring drought, unpredictable weather systems, environmental problems such as salinity and soil erosion, capricious markets, product trends and a variety of social factors contribute to a lack of constancy in Australian agriculture. Titles of books, book chapters and papers reflect the unpredictability inherent in

Australian agriculture with phrases such as 'Rural crisis' (Lawrence 1987), 'Crisis and conflict' (Lockie 2000) and 'Land of Discontent' (Pritchard and McManus 2000). The terms 'Structural adjustment' (Lawrence 1992) and 'restructuring' (Tonts 2000) reflect the dynamic and changing agricultural, social, institutional and economic landscape (Pritchard and McManus 2000).

Judith Brett in her 'Fair Share: Country and City in Australia' *Quarterly Essay* (Brett 2011a) has written about the past and current relationship between rural and urban Australia. Brett describes what she calls the 'country-city compact' in which country Australia has claimed special treatment (Brett 2011a, p. 26). There are three main reasons underlying the claim: the importance of the rural economy in the development of the nation; the need to live in and occupy the land as part of nation-building and defence of the nation; and the perceived larger contribution made by the country and its people to the nation's character (the notion of agrarianism). Brett describes aspects of the development of rural and regional Australia in which people settled as part of the government's nation-building imperative and in which large infrastructure schemes were part of the deal. These included dams and canals for irrigation, roads, railways, schools and hospitals. Some of these closer settlement schemes were more successful than others. The notion of decentralisation to rural areas was widely supported in the 1950s (Brett 2011a, p. 31). However, this changed as the neoliberalist economic worldview cut its swathe in the 1980s and 1990s. Markets and competition became the route to prosperity. Agriculture was no exception to this mandate. Farmers had to adapt to this new economic landscape in which the mantras were viability, efficiency, competition, and reduction of subsidies, tariffs and quotas. At the same time country areas saw a decline in the provision of services from both the public and private sector. People in government and agricultural offices were re-centralised to regional or city centres (Gerritsen 2000) and rural bank branches and post offices were closed across the country. The social fabric of rural communities was undermined by this 'restructuring' and the impact on employment, education, health services and the general well-being of communities was not only keenly felt but was also visible in the rapidly changing main street (Tonts 2000; Brett 2011a).

This history of the settlement and changing character of rural Australia is important in understanding the context in which rural people have come to feel forgotten (Lockie 2000) and 'abandoned and betrayed' (Brett 2011a, p. 51) by urban governments and city people. This context is important in understanding the idea of country-mindedness and agrarianism (Lockie 2000) and disagreements about water reform and resource use. The way in which people understand rural and regional Australia is dynamic and can shift in relation to changes in power and knowledge (Lockie 2000). One perspective is an agrarian or 'bush' outlook in which farmers and agriculture should be supported through subsidisation of infrastructure and other support initiatives. Others advocate free markets and reform to facilitate continual industry adjustment and the free-flow of resources such as water to encourage innovation and efficiency. A key point is that there is a range of perspectives about rural life and agriculture, some separate, some overlapping and many opposing each other. These perspectives include how farmers and communities should be supported, how resources should be used and how the social impact of policy changes should be factored into resource decision making. But it is not only perspectives that matter. McManus and Pritchard (2000, p. 219) note the 'multiple domains of action that influence the livelihoods of individuals and communities in rural and regional Australia'. These include decisions by financial institutions and multinational companies, policies developed by the three tiers of government, and trends in locations for retirement and investment. As the character of rural and regional Australia shifts, so do the different influences on the ebb and flow of people, products and wealth between cities, regional centres and rural areas.

Complexity and change

Lawrence and Gray (2000) in their discussion of the future importance of Australian agriculture note the difficulty in identifying patterns of change in agriculture because of the variety of farming systems. For example, an irrigated dairy farm is a different enterprise to a broadacre wheat farm, which in turn is unlike a mixed sheep and irrigated cropping farm. A trend in one industry is unlikely to be matched in another. But there are similarities in social structure. Family farms in different industries often rely on a combination of off-farm income, the labour of family members and a strong attachment to the land to survive economic downturns and climatic variability. Community is an important aspect of farming life. The declining population of some country towns has an impact on the social well-being and mental health of those left behind. Who bears the cost of rural restructuring is an enduring question: people in remote rural areas have to travel far to access what city people might consider to be basic services (Tonts 2000). A hidden cost of government restructuring is the loss of a 'holistic' perspective on the part of government agencies to be able to appreciate the 'cumulative collective effects of their behaviour' (Gerritsen 2000, p. 129). What may be a rational response by an individual agency may have negative consequences for a local community if the overall impacts of multiple changes are not considered. Another problem is the loss of local knowledge by centralised agencies that have become remote from their constituencies. According to Gerritsen (2000, p. 131) this 'regional decline created as a collective if unforeseen consequence of each agency's pursuit of rationality will add to the problems of all governments, ultimately negating the aims of each agency's original efficiency improvement'.

Where to next for rural Australia?

There has been a long-term debate about many aspects of rural and regional development including the role of government in setting agendas, creating programmes and funding different aspects of development such as irrigation infrastructure (see for example, Davidson 1969; Beer *et al.* 2003; Crase 2008; Connell and Grafton 2011). Concerns about the impact of mining on agricultural land reflect one aspect of this debate, with several states and the nation prospering from the mining boom. Brett (2011b, p. 140) discusses fears about the impact on agriculture and food production from mining and foreign-owned agricultural companies: 'land is still basic to people's sense of national sovereignty, and at base this is about governments protecting the material basis of life'. She concludes,

> Over the past few centuries, we in the affluent industrialised West have come to take food for granted. City folk may well question agrarianism's faith in the virtue of agricultural life, but they cannot deny its basic premise: that we all need to eat.
>
> (Brett 2011b, p. 140)

Brett calls for a debate about the future of Australian agriculture and food production (Brett 2011a; 2011b). She argues that the city should take a look at what benefits it receives from the country and outlines several ways in which rural Australia benefits the nation as a whole: food production, tourism, pleasure and recreation, the occupation of the land and its significance for national sovereignty. The people of the country, Indigenous Australians, farmers and pastoralists, not only inhabit the land but, in their different ways, they look after the land. Rather than looking at the *issues* facing country Australia, Brett suggests that Australians should look at the *strengths* of the country and its potential for the nation as the basis for a new country-city compact (Brett 2011a).

Responses to Brett's essay show the complexity of the debate about the future of rural Australia and the tensions between country and city. These include the underlying lack of equality between different areas and sections of society and the need for the long-term interests of the community to be a primary consideration (Knight 2011; Altman 2011). Botterill (2011, p. 130) describes her first-hand experience of what she sees as an attitude of 'benign indifference' towards rural people. She comments on the 'apparent lack of respect for rural Australians in general, and for farmers in particular' in community consultation meetings that she attended (Botterill 2011, p. 131). These meetings, organised to discuss water reforms with communities, instead seemed to show a 'lack of sensitivity for the profound impact the plan was likely to have on communities and how it appeared to be a fundamental attack on rural development and a repudiation of previous government support for nation-building irrigation schemes' (Botterill 2011, p. 131).

These experiences of community-government interactions form the context and backdrop of the voices of rural people presented in the next section. This context includes the way policy reforms are implemented and how they are received by those affected.

Voices and perspectives from rural communities

This section provides an overview of differing perspectives held by people living in rural communities. It is organised in three thematic areas: people's experience and views on their interactions with government agencies; how relationships and decision-making processes could be improved; and ideas about a vision for rural Australia.

Interactions: communities and government agencies

The struggle over water reform in the Murray–Darling Basin

An irrigation farmer talked about what she saw as a long-standing lack of foresight about the impact of water reform. She had grown up in an irrigation family listening to conversations about potential problems with water reform that had separated water from the land to encourage water trade. In her opinion the impacts of water reform had resulted in many people in the area becoming 'disenfranchised' with little say in decision making. At the root of the problem she saw 'patch protection' where people were protecting the decisions that they had made instead of getting people together to 'own the whole problem'. She had decided to become involved in 'doing something about it' and had become a member of a local grassroots community group called the Murray Valley Food and Fibre Association. This group had come together as a result of 'absolute frustration' with not having a representative group voice in the water reform debate for a broad range of commodity growers and communities, the 'end-users'. In her opinion farmers were 'fiercely independent' but in this case realised that they needed to become involved with decision making on water reform and to have a 'seat at the table' with the decision-makers in order for the community voice to be heard. She recounted one person saying 'if you're not sitting at the table you're probably on the menu'.

This farmer believed that there was a major gap in water reform in terms of agency information and advice to end-users as to how the reform was going to work 'on the ground' and how the end-users were going to make it work. In her opinion, 'most of the time they have absolutely no idea, none'. In her opinion the Murray–Darling Basin Authority and the Federal Government had not provided adequate answers to the local community to questions that they had posed. While she agreed with the goals of water reform she thought that unless it can be explained how it is going to work on the ground it becomes 'meaningless'.

Another irrigation farmer who had been involved in government-farmer interactions for many years talked about how frustrating he found it that people in government departments have to be 're-educated' about the use of water in agriculture in general, which he found a 'waste of time'. In his opinion the tendency of government departments to have meetings about water issues lasting several days were not a good use of his time because they invariably turned into a 'gabfest'. He preferred to talk in person to senior government agency people and liked to host people on his farm to show them directly what he meant. He thought that this was a better way of gaining an understanding of both sides. However, he was still unsure whether people really did understand his perspective saying 'we'll see with the outcome'. He talked about how practical knowledge in government departments has been 'whittled away' by the loss of people in government agencies from rural areas to cities and larger regional centres. He also commented on the loss of an 'independent voice' on the part of research agencies such as CSIRO which have become too corporatised. In his view there needs to be an 'attitude transplant' in some government agencies, such as the Murray–Darling Basin Authority where some people wanted to prove their theories were right, rather than listening to people who had practical knowledge of how things work.

A business owner in a town at the centre of a major irrigation area was concerned that people in government agencies do not take the time to understand the impact of policies on rural communities as a whole. He felt that the water reforms and the consultation processes around the release of the *Guide to the proposed Basin Plan* had been detrimental to his town and community overall because it had pitted one part of the community against another. He described how some irrigation farmers wanted to sell their water to the government as part of the buy-back scheme, but this would damage the community overall as water was sold out of the district. This had created some conflict. He was critical of the way in which consultation processes had been conducted, for example, with the Murray–Darling Basin Authority holding strictly controlled forums in which there was little meaningful interaction. He felt that the community had been treated badly and had not been given the information that they had requested.

An irrigator living in the same area gave a different perspective on the water reform outcomes, arguing that the local business community in the region should have 'pulled together' in some sort of trade-off in which those who wanted to exit the irrigation industry could do so. He was critical of business people in the local community for wanting to impose their ideas on individual irrigators. For him it was essential that people who wanted to sell their water could do so and he believed that the remaining irrigators would become more viable as a result of this rationalisation of the industry. Another irrigation farmer expressed her frustration with the government consultation process, suggesting that people give up: 'What's the point in trying?' In her opinion, the agricultural industry was a low priority for governments in general. She thought that governments had not listened or understood the fear held by communities about their future. She was convinced that her local township would 'die' if the proposed water cutbacks were implemented under the new Basin Plan. She also thought that the country would lose its farmers and that younger people would not stay on the land.

An ecologist who had considerable involvement in the inter-workings of government agencies and communities held the perspective that the debate around water reform was adversarial and that 'you can't get away from it' because 'it's the nature of it'. He pointed out that irrigators had been doing much more with water than in earlier days and that, for example, the rice industry should be recognised for their effectiveness in increasing water efficiency. He thought that there were few people in the irrigation industry who were really 'open-minded' and he held a personal distrust of many in leadership positions. He felt that many communities within irrigation areas were not 'collegial' with each other, for example upstream and downstream. From an environmental perspective, he thought that much progress had been made in recent years, and that many achievements had not been fully recognised. One aspect of government-community relations is the lack of clear communication between the groups. Where there is such lack of clarity then distress can be caused if people do not understand the impact on them. He thought that a big problem was the very complex nature of water and that it was very difficult for one person to fully inform themselves of the differing perspectives and facts. Regarding the Murray–Darling Basin Authority, he thought that there was some arrogance in their earlier approach.

Stakeholders and agencies: information flow, interactions and attitudes

A farmer who ran a mixed dryland-irrigation enterprise in the Murrumbidgee Irrigation Area was concerned that there were very few 'feedback loops' between a range of institutions including government agencies, irrigation companies, academic institutions and farmers. This farmer had previous experience of the way government agencies ran and was critical of the way that government agencies had been scaled back, and believed that interactions were now conducted within an atmosphere of 'disclaimers and liability' that got in the way of free-flowing information. She felt that too much risk was being pushed on to the customers or end-users and that this was not only affecting person-to-person interactions but also had a negative effect on water delivery and water quality for irrigators. In addition she found that people who are prepared to innovate or question current practices are not encouraged as part of an open exchange of information. Rather these types of people were seen as 'villains or pariahs'.

Along similar lines a grazier was highly critical of the Catchment Management Authority (CMA) in her area. This criticism derived from a specific incident in which work was being carried out on a neighbour's property to build a 'leaky weir' to conserve water upstream. She had not been given any notice of this by the CMA and was disappointed with the lack of communication from the CMA. This was during a time of peak drought and the project would have likely diminished the flow of water onto her property. This farmer criticised the CMA in general for its lack of proactive communication. For example, there were no newsletters about CMA activities and 'we don't even know what they are doing ... we have the worst CMA in the country'. She thought that this came down to people and personalities, with some being on a mission to 'save the environment' whereas others are more prepared to work with farmers: 'you have to get the right person on the right day'.

Interestingly, a biodynamic farmer and leader in agriculture had a very different experience with the same CMA. He had set up a floodplain and creek restoration project with the CMA on an experimental basis. He saw this as a great success and the CMA as being very supportive and broadminded about the unusual restoration techniques used within the project. He attributed the success to the 'organisational system' and process used to develop the project: 'it's not just the physical work that is done ... there is no point in doing the work if you don't bring the stakeholders together'. In this case stakeholders included the CMA, the Landcare group, the Federal Government, the landowner and the academic research institution which monitored the project. However, he described how the project had been made more complicated by the 'disenabling' nature of the law and regulations made many years ago. He used the example of a river being defined as an 'incised channel' which is a misnomer and 'not fair or just to the lore of the nation', because a river system is much more than the actual river channel. Rather, laws needed to be changed to reflect the connectivity of a river with its associated floodplains and wetlands.

Insights into the operation of a CMA were given by a catchment officer who focused on sustainable land use. The CMA that he worked in operated under considerable constraints and he described it as a 'lean and mean' organisation that was dependent on the NSW government for basic organisational services such as human resources, finance and information technology. He described the changing plans and principles under which the CMA operated: that it was moving from management based on themes such as land, water, biodiversity to a resilience-based way of planning with 'local people leading the way'. There were many aspects of running a CMA with tensions inherent in its activities: for example, the equity implications of deciding who is funded for what project, how to get the best environmental outcome for each dollar invested and how to include stakeholders from all areas.

The changing nature of community

Community was a recurring topic. Many commented on the dynamic and changing structure of community in their local area and the consequent problems and opportunities that arose. This was particularly evident in the Australian Capital Region where people talked about changing land use due to subdivision and purchase of smaller blocks by city people. One grazier talked about the impact on his farming operation in which domestic dogs from subdivisions had worried his sheep to the extent that he no longer grazed any stock on that property. Another wool-grower and fire volunteer in the Cooma area south of Canberra talked about a variety of tensions between rural areas and townships. The trend to subdivide had reduced the number of actively managed farms. Canberra people who had bought subdivisions were more likely to run one or two horses instead of cattle or sheep on their land. The issue of land management, particularly concerning weed control, was a concern and he wanted to see this new type of landowner from the city take more responsibility and understand more about the land and how to look after it. This disparity typically created tensions between neighbours if one was diligent about weed control and the other was not. He was critical of the local shire Council in terms of the way it distributed funds for projects, which in his opinion were mainly directed towards the towns and not rural areas. However, he also reflected on the positive aspects of changing communities and described how city people could bring different dimensions to country areas and had a lot to offer in the way of experience if people in different communities could get together and talk to each other. The Shire Council had failed in this area of community development with their 'once a year' meetings followed by 'nothing happening'. This results in cynicism about local government and 'the one councillor who is doing a good job is disillusioned and will not stand for re-election'.

A biodynamic vegetable grower in the same area also commented on the changing nature of community and food production in the vicinity of Canberra. She pointed out that Canberra used to be surrounded by food growers and much of the food was sourced from the local area. There were dairies and market gardens in the area. Now people had become disassociated from food production and were reliant on overly processed food manufactured elsewhere. She saw this as a problem, not only for the health of people, but also for the health of the environment.

A wool-grower and educator considered the relationship between communities, individuals and values. He asked the question 'what do we mean by community?' He suggested that a community of hobby farmers may not really be a genuine community and asked if the idea of community was now a waste of time. The changing face of rural Australia had changed the nature of community and putting people 'in boxes' as for example a 'wool-grower' wasn't particularly helpful because it ignores individuals and their values: 'we need to be valued as individuals'.

Improving engagement, relationships and community

Many people had ideas as to how they would like to be involved with government agencies and decision-makers. One irrigation farmer, when talking about the Basin Plan was highly critical of the Murray–Darling Basin Authority (MDBA) attitude, as well as previous government agency attitudes. His main criticism revolved around the approach of the agencies: 'we are sick and tired of people telling us they want something from us – stop turning up just to take something [like water]'. He would much prefer an approach along the lines of 'we want your help in how to achieve this, and how we can solve problems together to improve the situation'. He would rather be advised of the overall goals and what the authority was trying to achieve and then be involved in the process of how to get there. He recounted how meetings which purported to be 'open shed meetings' in which there was a discussion had instead degenerated into the typical 'slide show' with 'we'll take that on board' responses to suggestions. He felt that people from the MDBA tended to 'hide behind' computer models when asked to discuss the practical issues. Another farmer suggested that the MDBA appears to be working on some false assumptions including that they can 'manage nature' and that the 'rivers are dying'. They seem to be working on getting a volume of water and then working out how to use it, or in other words, 'they don't know what they want'. She believed that this is a result of poor policymaking stemming from the *Water Act*, and that it was conceited to believe that a bureaucracy can be the 'arbiter and protector of nature'.

Another point of contention was the way the senior officials of the MDBA talked about 'their plan' or even 'my plan', meaning the plan was completely owned by the MDBA. This was seen to be divisive, and that it would be much better to work together with the communities to try to share the problem and then share the solution. Using terms that give ownership of a plan to one side was seen to exacerbate the differences, rather than enhancing a working relationship. The way in which the MDBA engaged with people in communities was also criticised. One farmer had been to a meeting in which the Chair of the MDBA was present and was struck by the number of times he talked about 'I' and 'my' rather than 'we' and 'us'. Another farmer thought that 'a major mindset change' is required in order to work collaboratively with much greater interaction required between government agencies, leading scientists, farmers and agricultural students to transfer knowledge and experience. Others talked about how meetings between communities and government agencies need to be improved to quieten down the 'rowdy' voices and allow multiple voices to be heard.

A catchment officer described changes in the Catchment Management Authority which would improve community engagement. The Catchment Action Plan was based on a Natural Resource Commission framework in which resilience thinking and community engagement were major themes. This person described the Catchment Management Authority as a 'partnership broker' in bringing agencies and community together to develop new skills and new knowledge. For example in the NSW coastal area oyster growers and dairy farmers were successfully working together to improve water quality.

A biodynamic vegetable grower described how important community is in growing food and how she had tried to convince the local council to allow 'community title' of the farm to facilitate community involvement so that the land did not have to be subdivided. She attributed the failure of this initiative to a variety of factors including lack of understanding by local government: 'they don't have the protocols for understanding different aspects of farming' such as between biodynamic processes and conventional farming. But she also reflected that it was their responsibility to 'put in more legwork' to fully explain how community title would work and present it in a more professional way. Thus responsibility for change is a combination of local authorities' willingness to be open-minded as well as those individuals wanting to make the changes to take the responsibility to do the research. To enhance engagement within a community the farmer described how a 'common cause' needs to be developed, such as sustainable farming, under which individuals, communities and government agencies can unite and work together. However, this is difficult to achieve and individual experiences and starting points get in the way of finding common ground. One solution is to have mediators and 'elders' help devise processes and plans to facilitate community involvement.

Two leaders in agriculture described their perspectives for decision-making which would improve decision-making processes, engagement with communities, and the ultimate outcomes. Both perspectives were grounded in practical experience of projects on their farming operations and their own interactions with other people. The first farmer (described above with the successful Catchment Management Authority collaboration project) suggested that his project could be used as a model for similar landscape regeneration projects. He regularly hosted visits from interested groups: 'We try not to tell people what they should do … the best thing for us is to *do* what we do and show people the results … we get more traction this way'. He also suggested that people who have a clear vision and people who are good at 'the day-to-day stuff' need to be brought together to show others what can be done. The second farmer talked about the importance of holistic decision-making in which 'every decision needs to be financially, socially and environmentally sound'. Instead of 'someone else setting the agenda', people themselves need to ask what they should do, how they want to live, what sort of quality of life is envisioned, and how they want to be perceived. In terms of community engagement the people 'below' need to be confident about the people 'above' making their decisions. Thus a framework for decision-making is required in which the worst outcomes as well as the best outcomes of a proposed policy can be discussed within the framework.

Two other people in the Australian Capital Region, with long-standing involvement in community associations, suggested that city and country people could get together to learn from each other and respect each other's knowledge. One recounted how it is easy to criticise and much harder to communicate when people come from different backgrounds. A grazier said: 'we make them welcome … you might not agree with what they're doing, but we all need one another'.

Ideas about a vision for rural Australia

Several people talked about agricultural production as the basis of their vision for rural Australia. This was to grow food for consumption as well as to create wealth for the country. Agricultural production provides employment and is a basis for taxation, so farmers should be able to make a profit from their work. Some emphasised farming as a business whereas others were more concerned about long-term land management, stewardship of the land and sustainable food growing. Concerns over the future of family farms and the ability of farmers to make a profit were recurring themes. One farmer talked about the duopoly of the two large supermarkets in Australia, Coles and Woolworths, who she felt were hindering the ability of farmers to make a fair profit from their efforts. One farmer talked about family farms being the basis for rural production in preference to corporate enterprises. This is because families have a 'real' interest in continuity and stewardship of the land for the long-term, compared with organisations such as managed investment schemes which focus on financial gain. Keeping younger people on the land should be part of the vision. Many thought that children of family farmers were unlikely to take over from their parents due to several areas of uncertainty, such as water reform and climate variability. As young people migrate to regional centres and cities there is a loss of local knowledge being passed down from generation to generation and a loss of agricultural expertise. Thus a vision for rural Australia involves the continuity and stability of family farming based on thriving local cultural and agricultural activities. One commercial business-owner talked about the importance of rural townships as centres for social cohesion and a sense of community and place. The loss of vibrant main streets over the last few decades and the growth of peripheral enclosed shopping malls were contributing to the loss of culture and community spirit in many country towns.

Several people talked about the importance of rural Australia to the nation in terms of food production, food security and protection of agricultural land from urbanisation and mining. One citrus grower suggested that the vision should include a 'food security plan for Australia' and that this plan should recognise the trade-offs that need to be made concerning the use of water for food production and water for the environment. He also suggested that the vision for rural Australia will depend on what happens in the rest of the world, as Australia depends to some degree on changing global conditions and global markets. As part of a food security plan this farmer argued that it would be better to have fewer more efficient farmers and irrigators, allowing those less efficient farmers to exit the industry, and allowing those left to make a profit from their crops. This was in the context of some crops, such as citrus, which at the time was not yielding sufficient profit to be viable. In such cases farmers rely on other sources of income, including off-farm employment.

One grazier was critical of the government not taking action to protect agricultural land from 'urbanisation of the Food Bowl and mining of the Food Bowl' and in her opinion they lack the 'political balls to do anything about the miners because the miners bring in so much money'. She thought that most people in rural communities are supportive of protecting the environment but are 'picking up the pieces from earlier policies' that have resulted in environmental degradation such as loss of topsoil and invasion of weeds. She pointed out that 'the boot is on the government's foot and they should interact and mean it' and that we need 'people to come and talk to us'. Several people were concerned about companies or overseas purchasers buying up farms and land as well as the government increasingly opening up markets to food imports. One thought that the government should 'look after your own backyard and look after your own people ... treat people right and listen to them more'.

Two biodynamic food producers were concerned about sustainable food production, the health of ecosystems, and human health. One proposed a regional approach to food production. He suggested that rather than basing agriculture on production based on units per area, which does not take into account transport and other energy use, it should rather be based on the needs of the region and 'supplying the region you are in with local food grown locally'. This would entail less pressure on the environment and more community involvement: 'if food is so important to us why are we not involved in growing our own food?' This would improve the well-being of livestock through the use of local abattoirs as well as the health of people living in the area through active involvement in food growing. He thought that the drive for agricultural exports was too much about gross national product and not enough about decisions based on sound land management. Another biodynamic farmer articulated his vision as 'regeneration of growing food in a sustainable way without breaking the rules of nature'. He was optimistic that this would happen. He thought that there was a big future for small-scale farming and the connection of people with the land. He also thought that gardens were high producing areas and lessons could be learned from food production in places like Russia where 80 per cent of food is grown in gardens, and Europe and the UK where there is a long tradition of the population feeding themselves in emergencies.

Another area of vision proposed by several people involved the lack of understanding between city and country people, particularly where decision-making was concerned. One farmer in the Murrumbidgee Irrigation Area suggested that the vision for rural Australia includes 'fixing the rural–urban divide'. He argued that regions cannot be run from cities because people with a city outlook lack understanding and do not take a longer-term view in developing policy. Rather, policymakers take 'snapshots' and enact policy in response to short-term perspectives. Within this aspect of the vision, the general political nature of rural and agricultural policy should be recognised, in which 'votes' for politicians figure in policymaking. Another farmer in the Australian Capital Region had the same opinion about senior decision-makers: 'every major decision to do with what happens on the land in Australia is made by someone who lives in the city ... they've got no idea what it's like to be a farmer'. In his opinion what was critical for the future of Australia is 'the management of the land ... we regard ourselves as stewards of the land'. The fact that major decision-makers lack that deep understanding of stewardship and land management is a major issue. In answer to what can be done about it: 'they should be intelligent enough to at least listen and take some advice from the people that do understand ... the lead farmers ... the people out there doing things on the land'.

Another grazier suggested that people need to 'spend time in other people's existence to understand them'. He had been an innovator in his stock-grazing management and had now become an educator. He outlined the importance of developing holistic goals within a decision-making framework in which people could work out for themselves the options within a particular policy and how to feel confident about making decisions. In his opinion a vision for rural Australia should target 'how we want life in Australia to be'. It should include social, economic and ecological health; fairness and justice in society; acceptance and respect for different cultures; infrastructure investment in the rural sector which is the 'heart of the nation for social, economic and ecological wealth'; and opportunities for individuals to achieve a sense of 'belonging and pride in their local communities'.

Another issue raised was the separation between people working for agencies and institutions and those working on the land: that people in agencies and institutions should become more 'customer' focused in their interactions, rather than treating them as the 'end-user' with no 'say'. This farmer was referring to the lack of feedback loops between end-users and institutions and the lack of formal mechanisms to facilitate greater understanding. She also thought that institutions should recognise that the 'status quo' may not be the best option, and that people who are innovators should be respected for their ability to question the dominant mindset. She also thought that 'mentoring' is a good technique in which innovators can pass on thinking and knowledge to the next generation of farmers, in addition to the normal process of passing down knowledge through successive generations in families.

The Catchment Management Authority employee described what he would like to see for the future as 'fundamental ecological processes and structures within the landscape that buffer it from shock, creating refuges for wildlife ... [and] building resilience into farm models and management practices'. He used the example of riparian vegetation to separate stock from river banks so that the landscape can retain its function, such as withstanding massive storm events as well as creating a refuge for wildlife. An ecologist wanted to see practical solutions that would benefit the environment included in a vision. This should include more investment in infrastructure that would increase water efficiency in irrigation areas and more investment in the management of environmental water. He used the example of more connectivity being required between wetland areas. This could be achieved by lowering connection areas between channels and wetland areas. A farmer thought that there should be more encouragement for people on the land to 'work much more with nature', for example, using integrated pest management techniques in crop growing. Some thought that farmers should be recognised (for the large part) as being good environmental citizens and that they do generally recognise the importance of a healthy environment. Thus they should be encouraged as part of the overall vision for rural Australia to increase their innovations in adopting practices that are beneficial to the environment.

Developing a vision for rural Australia

People's aspirations: present and future

It is clear from these narratives that people think of a vision for rural Australia in terms of problems that need fixing as well as ideas for the future. Thoughts about the future have roots in people's experiences of past and current issues. Thus vision and current issues are interconnected. Proposals and thoughts about vision emerge in a number of areas: in the desire for agriculture to be seen as a source of production and to be respected for its contribution to the wealth and tax base of the nation; in the need for a coherent food security plan for Australia; in the need for a sustainable and resilient land management vision for Australia; in the need to balance community interests with individual farmer interests, for example, when water is sold out of a region; in the need to bridge the rural-urban divide; in the need for decision-makers to understand more about farming and land management; in the need for people in institutions and communities to work better together; and in the need for knowledge and experience to be shared and passed on. Vision for the future of agriculture also emerged out of current-day concerns about the future of the family farm, the rise of corporate agriculture and the ability of rural townships to maintain their sense of community culture and longevity. Vision included the need for investment in water-saving infrastructure and practical ways to use environmental water. It included a call for a more regional approach to food production in which communities were involved in growing food. It also included a call for farmers to be recognised for their ability to be good environmental stewards and for more to be done so that farmers can work closely with natural processes in their farming techniques.

People's thoughts about vision include many elements ranging from practical proposals to general ideas; from fears about the future to lack of understanding about the present; from short-term to long-term perspectives; from the city to the country; from food production to environmental protection; from community cohesion to individual choice; and from maintaining continuity to advocating substantial attitude change.

Ideas for a vision include environmental stewardship, maintaining family and community culture, engagement and working well together between city-based agencies and people in rural areas, decision-making based on transparency, trust and a real understanding of the issues, and future security in terms of community well-being and recognition of the importance of food production for Australia. Vision is viewed as absent from current debates in addition to being a future aspiration: it is a remedy for the present as well as an idea for the future.

A critical implication from this holistic view of vision is that decision-makers can gain a greater understanding of what people would like in a vision if they take time to understand present-day concerns as well as stated desires for the future. Current-day concerns are invariably rooted in past events: consideration of these is vital if people's desires for the future are to be understood. The voices and perspectives from rural communities in this chapter have shown that the rural-urban divide does exist but also that there are ways and techniques of fixing it. The divide is multidimensional. It embodies a lack of recognition that country people should be included in finding solutions; it is a lack of appreciation or valuing of food producers; it is a lack of respect for their environmental understanding; it is a lack of respect for long-standing knowledge and arrangements about how resources (such as water) are used; it is a lack of involvement of community in food production; and it is a lack of government capability to understand and engage with different sections of community to seek buy-in to difficult reforms (Gross 2011).

A holistic vision for rural Australia: implications for policymakers

There are several implications for policymakers and decision-makers. The first is to develop a holistic vision for rural Australia. This includes land stewardship, building resilience in rural societies, protecting fundamental ecological processes, and valuing rural communities as food producers and for their role of maintaining food security. Development of a vision needs broad engagement from people in rural and regional Australia. It should be well-articulated so that Australians appreciate the realities of growing food in Australia and the need for sustainable land management. Education about land management and food production is an important aspect of a vision. It includes a contextual history to help understand decision-making about what food is grown where and why. This would improve understanding about the choice of crops and use of water for irrigated agriculture. In this way people can enter the debate from a more informed position about how scarce resources such as water should be used.

A second implication is that a vision for rural Australia needs to include how people in country areas should be engaged in policymaking and decision-making. This is where fairness is vital. Fair decision-making processes include treating people with respect (starting with recognition that they should be involved); giving people an opportunity to be involved and to have a voice and a say in how the process is conducted; giving people the opportunity to receive the right level of information and to have their questions and issues discussed and answered; giving people time to be fully engaged in the process and a seat at the table. It has been shown that fair decision-making processes and treating people with respect leads to better outcomes and greater acceptance of outcomes (Syme and Nancarrow 2005; Gross 2007, 2014).

A third implication is that greater investment is required in creating an environment for the long-term in which knowledge and understanding can be shared between government agencies and country people. The availability of people on the ground and in government agencies who understand different aspects of agriculture and country life is critical if farming and resource use practices are to be understood, different perspectives are to be respected and understood, debate is to be encouraged and good policies are to be made. As Brett (2011b, p. 138) describes the problem:

> The lack here is not of information, nor of expert knowledge, but of professionally trained people able to communicate effectively with people in rural communities. This experiential gap in understanding seems greater now than it was 50 years ago.

This lack of shared understanding is an aspect of the rural-urban divide. The importance of long-term continuity in knowledge about how things work in the country, and how arrangements have been developed over many years, is under-appreciated in government agencies where people frequently move between roles. People from government agencies need to be able to talk comfortably with country people and community groups. It is in this area that the loss of government offices and facilities in regional and rural areas has had an impact (Mather 2011).

This chapter has shown that people in country areas have well-developed and strong views about their vision for rural Australia. At the heart of their vision rural communities seek security for their livelihoods and for their social well-being. Vision is not only about *what* should be done, but also about *how* it should be done and what people hold important in the way they live their lives. In other words, vision is not just about what should be done in the future: it is also about the 'here and now'. Vision is about how people communicate; it is about inclusion in decision-making processes, and it is about fairness and respect. Vision includes social, economic and environmental dimensions of rural life. Rural policies need to be holistic in recognising these dimensions, and policymakers must heed the importance of gaining social acceptance of policies. Security of livelihood, fair and respectful treatment, and being included in the conversation are all part of a vision for rural Australia.

References

Adams, P 2011, *Rural-urban divide in Australia? Late Night Live*, Australian Broadcasting Commission (ABC).

Altman, J 2011, 'Fair Share: Correspondence', *Quarterly Essay*, no. 43, pp. 127–128.

Beer, A, Maude, A and Pritchard, B 2003, *Developing Australia's Regions: theory and practice*, UNSW Press, Sydney.

Botterill, LC 2011, 'Fair Share: Correspondence', *Quarterly Essay*, vol. 43, pp. 129–131.

Boully, L and Maywald, K 2011, 'Basin Bookends, the Community Perspective', in Connell, D and Grafton, RQ (eds), *Basin Futures: Water reform in the Murray–Darling Basin*, ANU E Press, Canberra.

Brett, J 2011a, 'Fair Share: Country and City in Australia', *Quarterly Essay*, no. 42, pp. 1–67.

Brett, J 2011b, 'Fair Share: Response to Correspondence', *Quarterly Essay*, no. 43, pp. 137–140.

Connell, D and Grafton, RQ (eds) 2011, *Basin Futures: Water Reform in the Murray–Darling Basin*, ANU E Press, Canberra.

Crase, L (ed.) 2008, *Water Policy in Australia: the Impact of Change and Uncertainty*, Resources for the Future, Washington DC.

Davidson, BR 1969, *Australia Wet or Dry? The Physical and Economic Limits to the Expansion of Irrigation*, Melbourne University Press, Melbourne.

Gerritsen, R 2000, 'The management of government and its consequences for service delivery in regional Australia', in Pritchard, B and McManus, P (eds), *Land of Discontent: The dynamics of change in rural and regional Australia*, UNSW Press, Sydney.

Gross, C 2007, 'Community perspectives of wind energy in Australia: The application of a justice and community fairness framework to increase social acceptance', *Energy Policy*, vol. 35, no. 5, pp. 2727–2736.

Gross, C 2011, 'Why justice is important', in Connell, D and Grafton, RQ (eds), *Basin Futures: Water reform in the Murray–Darling Basin*, ANU E Press, Canberra.

Gross, C 2014, *Water under the Bridge: Fairness and Justice in Environmental Decision Making*, Routledge, Abingdon.

Knight, E 2011, 'Fair Share: Correspondence', *Quarterly Essay*, no. 43, pp. 124–126.

Lawrence, G 1987, *Capitalism and the Countryside: The Rural Crisis in Australia*, Pluto, Sydney.

Lawrence, G 1992, 'Farm structural adjustment', *Rural Society*, vol. 2, pp. 5–7.

Lawrence, G and Gray, I 2000, The myths of modern agriculture: Australian rural production in the 21st century, in Pritchard, B and McManus, P (eds), *Land of Discontent: The dynamics of change in rural and regional Australia*, UNSW Press, Sydney.

Lockie, S 2000, 'Crisis and conflict: shifting discourses of rural and regional Australia', in Pritchard, B and McManus, P (eds), *Land of Discontent: The dynamics of change in rural and regional Australia*, UNSW Press, Sydney.

Mather, T 2011, 'Fair Share: Correspondence', *Quarterly Essay*, no. 43, pp. 132–134.

McManus, P and Pritchard, B 2000, 'Concluding thoughts', in Pritchard, B and McManus, P (eds), *Land of Discontent: The dynamics of change in rural and regional Australia*, UNSW Press, Sydney.

Pritchard, B and McManus, P 2000, 'Introduction', in Pritchard, B and McManus, P (eds), *Land of Discontent: The dynamics of change in rural and regional Australia*, UNSW Press, Sydney.

Rural Women's Netword 2007, *Rural/Urban Divide Information and Statistics Report*, NSW Government Department of Primary Industries, NSW.

Salt, B 2011, 'Fair Share: Correspondence', *Quarterly Essay*, no. 43, pp. 135–136.

Syme, G and Nancarrow, B 2005, 'Creating Community Consent through Fairness Judgements', in Cryle, D and Hillier, J (eds), *Consent and Consensus: Politics, Media and Governance In Twentieth Century Australia*, API Network, Perth.

Thompson, F 2012, 'Singleton votes against coal seam gas industry', *The Newcastle Herald*, Newcastle.

Tonts, M 2000, 'The restructuring of Australia's rural communities', in Pritchard, B and McManus, P (eds), *Land of Discontent: The dynamics of change in rural and regional Australia*, UNSW Press, Sydney.

Wahlquist, A 2003, 'Media representations and public perceptions of drought', in Botterill, LC and Fisher, M (eds), *Beyond Drought: People, Policy and Perspectives*, CSIRO, Collingwood, Victoria.

Part IV

Moving forward

Visioning a future for rural and regional Australia

18 Country futures

Framing a policy agenda for rural and regional Australia

Anthony Hogan and Michelle Young

> Public policy is what public officials within government, and by extension the citizens they represent, choose to do or not to do about public problems. Public problems refer to conditions the public widely perceives to be unacceptable and therefore require intervention.
>
> (Kraft and Furlong 2012[1])

> Government is the right disposition of things, so as to lead to a convenient end.
>
> (La Perriere 1567, cited in Foucault 1991, p. 94)

Introduction

The material presented in this book makes it evident that people living in rural and regional Australia have undergone substantive social change over the past 40 years. This change has occurred within the agricultural industry, within the natural environment and at a social level. Productive processes have been intensified, and greater recognition has been given to developing ways of creating environmentally as well as economically sustainable productive processes. Yet progress on the economic and environmental fronts has not come without a social cost to family farmers and the villages and towns that originally emerged in the Australian landscape, to service the needs of these newly forming industries.

Within rural and regional Australia there is widespread discontent with the socio-economic outcomes resulting from national policy. People are questioning why these policy settings are necessary and in whose interests are they being pursued? While recent policy discourse has adopted the phrase *rural and regional Australia*, much of the discontent is arising within rural or, what was once referred to as country Australia. The adoption of the new phrase in many ways signals the direction in which policy settings are headed, that the rural be now understood as being part of a broader regional setting which in itself provides the basis for livelihoods. This is an important development and one which we will return to in the closing section of this chapter. But before doing so, we wish to bring together the issues that this book brings forward for what people understand to be country Australia. In framing the issues in this way we state that we do not necessarily agree with some of the positions being put forward. The purpose of this endeavour, as we noted in the introduction, is to provide new policymakers with a perspective on the issues arising in rural and regional Australia and to create a space wherein policymakers can more readily engage with the community around these issues.

From within the material presented in this book we have identified four distinct themes around which policymakers and the country community may engage in addressing a future policy agenda for country Australia:

- *Acknowledging the impacts of policy change*: the policy settings of the last 40 years have negatively impacted on the lives of many country people.
- *Engaging with the vision*: there is a vision for living in country Australia, a vision which builds on earlier policy settings – country Australians want to participate in the design of policy as they are invested in the outcomes.
- *Commonwealth responsibility*: there is strong evidence to support the view that the Commonwealth Government has a policy responsibility in country Australia; and
- *Governance structure*: the Commonwealth Government needs to put in place a governance structure which facilitates a strategic, harmonised, multi-level approach to governance of country Australia.

Acknowledging policy impacts in country Australia

Central to the discontent which exists in country Australia is the proposition that 40 years of significant policy change has failed to deliver on its promise of more prosperous, vibrant rural communities (following Smith and Pritchard, this volume). Country Australia calls on the Commonwealth Government to recognise and truthfully acknowledge the impact those 40 years of free market economics has had on the people living there. Country people argue that the consequences of change have fallen heavily on small family farmers with cascading effects on the livelihoods of people living in smaller country towns, evidenced in the loss of services and businesses, both large and small. While structural adjustment processes have been accessed by some parts of the agricultural industry, similar adjustment packages have not been available to the local industries and communities whose livelihoods relied on agriculture. Communities have been left to wither on the vine.

In consequence, people living in country Australia have come to feel forgotten (Lockie 2000) and 'abandoned and betrayed' (Brett 2011, p. 51) by urban governments and city folk. Along with the demise of the relative economic importance of agriculture came a similar demise in the importance of family farmers, who for so long held a special and privileged place at the policy table. People living in country areas frequently feel that their perspectives and interests are now neither understood nor valued by central policymakers or decision-makers. People fear for the future viability of their livelihoods, farms and the communities in which they live (Hogan *et al.* 2008; Boully and Maywald 2011).

A perception exists that there is some sort of gap between people living in cities and those living in country areas, manifest in a sense of a country-urban divide. Just what the country-urban divide is, and how it manifests itself, has been discussed widely in different public arenas including academia, community associations and the media (Rural Women's Network 2007; Adams 2011; Brett 2011a; Salt 2011). This country-urban divide can be attributed to a range of tangible and intangible factors, such as declining populations in some country areas (Rural Women's Network 2007), differing levels of access to health and transport services (Adams 2011), and a perceived lack of knowledge and understanding of country Australia on the part of city folk (Wahlquist 2003). Indeed, Judith Brett (2011) has written comprehensively about the past and current relationship between country and urban Australia and the demise of the city-country compact. The social fabric of country communities is seen to be undermined by the 'restructuring' of agricultural industries and the subsequent impact this has had on employment, education, health services and the general well-being of communities – changes that are not only keenly felt, but also visible in the rapidly changing high street of country communities (Tonts 2000; Brett 2011).

Yet the sense of disenfranchisement is about much more than just these things. This sense of disenfranchisement is about the failure of the policy promise to deliver prosperous outcomes for those most affected by the changes. It is about the social repositioning of the agriculture sector from hero to villain. This sense of disenfranchisement is about the fact that not only have policymakers not publicly recognised the impacts of their policies on country Australia, they have sought to construct the problem as being one where producers have failed to manage their risks. Policy took the view that producers' production practices were inefficient, and positioned producers as rent-seeking on the Australian taxpayers. From the rural perspective, policymakers are seen as having let the diswelfares (the compensable social and economic costs arising for specific sub-sectors of the community as a result of a policy strategy that is developed to benefit a nation as a whole) of policy change 'to lie where they fall' (Titmuss 2006, p. 44).

There has been little, if any, discussion about the fact that the challenges facing country Australia had their origins in deliberate policy decisions, rather than in the poor choices of individual farmers. There has been little, if any, acknowledgement that the assumptions which underpinned key policy decisions (e.g. that Australia has an abundance of water) may have been wrong. This sense of disenfranchisement is about the perception of policymakers to embrace free trade policies when many countries participating in the market have not also adopted either free trade or comparable ethical approaches to worker wages and working conditions, the use of chemicals, or commitment to ensuring specific environmental outcomes. It is about the fact that under the efficiency mantra, a race to the bottom has commenced with regard to the working conditions of Australians as compared with workers in developing countries, with the latter markets being constructed as more competitive rather than less just, safe or equitable. Similarly support is no longer there to enable Australian producers to compete in a world market. Overall, policymakers are not seen to have taken sufficient account of the historical settings which constructed the Australian industry in the way that it did.

This sense of disenfranchisement is about the application of the principles of neoliberal economics to social policy which has resulted in a change in the role of government. Australian agriculture (and in consequence many rural communities) was founded on a paradigm of state-supported industry and community (Smith and Pritchard, this volume). However, under neoliberalism, market outcomes must be left to take their course (Foucault 1991). Government is now neither the partner to economic development nor the rescuer of rural communities in times of strife. Rather individuals, producers and communities must now be economically and socially self-sufficient. From the perspective of family farmers in particular and country Australians more generally, this shift in policy, at its most fundamental level, represents a breach in the social contract which has existed between the country and the city for over a century. The breach appears to be exacerbated by government preparedness to heavily intervene to support industry development, but not to address the resulting transactional costs of economic policy on country communities (Cockfield, this volume).

Engaging with a vision for country Australia

It is evident from the research conducted in association with this book and the literature that country Australia has a vision for its future. In this section we bring together insights as to what this vision is about.

Within this vision, country townships are considered to be centres of social cohesion and provide a sense of community and place. Country settlements contribute to the quality of family and social life, community culture and diversity, social inclusion and well-being. As such, country communities are a vital part of Australian society. Country communities contribute to the iconic cultures that make up the Australian identity and make a valuable contribution to the nation's economic well-being. People living in country communities value themselves, including the places in which they live, as well as the people with whom they share their lives within a given place at a given time. Together 'we' make community, even when that community is a community of interest as much as a community of place, identity or culture. The interrelationship between society, economy and the environment is integral to the sustainability of our country communities. As such, the long-term sustainability of diverse country communities remains central to the nation's identity and future well-being.

Within this vision, future developmental policy strategy would bring about the realisation of the 'full potential' of regions, wherein full potential can be understood with regards to economic growth, regional prosperity and 'liveable people friendly communities' (Kinnear *et al.* 2013, p. xvi; see also Kinnear and Ogden 2013, p. 131). Such development would add to the diversity of industries which already exist in country Australia. Constraints to economic growth would be removed, particularly through the development of national infrastructure (namely transport, energy, communications and water), and the development of extensive soft infrastructure would enable the necessary and extensive planning coordination processes which are central to the success of such developments, to occur. Where national economic interests compete with local economic interests, the diswelfares of national policy will be offset at the local level, such that the sustainability of a given community is not threatened. Economic and social goals would be progressed within a context centred on sustainability, where sustainability is understood as 'development that meets the needs of the present without compromising the ability of future generations to meet their own needs' (Quinn and Kirby 2013, p. 42, citing the United Nations Brundtland Commission report 1987). Policy pathways would focus on the end-point of creating bottom-up, locally focused, innovation-oriented approaches that resulted in 'sustainable economic outcomes' (Perrem 2013, pp. 26ff.). Innovation would come about as a result of people and businesses within regions being both internally linked while being well connected to 'national and global innovation systems' (Perrem 2013, p. 37). Situated localism would be enacted as policy. Such a policy would give due recognition to the environmental and socio-economic factors that are in the control of local communities, with national policy taking responsibility for factors outside the control of a given community. Population policy would 'ensure that future population change is compatible with the economic, environmental and social well-being of Australia', ensuring that 'we have in place the necessary policy settings and governance arrangements which will deliver improvements in our wellbeing, at the local, regional and national levels into the future' (Quinn and Kirby 2013, p. 52).

Now it is well and good that country communities can articulate a vision for their future. What is more important is to identify the extent to which there is a case to make that the Commonwealth Government needs to play a more active role, to take greater responsibility with regards to the socio-economic sustainability of rural communities? And if so, what form should that responsibility take and which issues need to be addressed as a priority? It is to these questions that we now turn.

Perceptions of Commonwealth Government responsibilities

Based on the material reported in this book, there are strong justifications for the Commonwealth Government to take greater responsibility in country social policy. From the outset, the Commonwealth Government has demonstrated a strong and persistent history of involvement in rural Australia for over a century. Similarly, a series of High Court decisions (decisions that the Commonwealth Government itself sought from the Court) have made it evident that the Commonwealth Government has responsibilities which engage it directly (in terms of resourcing and policy coordination) in rural matters. Most specifically, the Commonwealth Government has initiated substantial changes to long-term policy settings; changes which have directly disrupted the lives of those whose livelihoods find their origins in early policy settings. From the country perspective, the Commonwealth Government has a responsibility to develop and implement policy which secures the basis of their livelihoods. And the basis of these livelihoods is agriculture, particularly family farming and the services and businesses that support the agricultural industry.

People in country Australia are looking for a new form of governance through which they can participate in the co-design of policy which impacts on their lives. In an ideal world, one could envisage substantial constitutional change which would reduce the complexity of existing governmental processes. At issue is not just the constitutional recognition of local government or the capacity for local communities to raise the resources they need to address the many social and infrastructure problems impacting on their communities. At issue is the fact that in addition to having three tiers of government, there are multiple non-governmental decision-making processes, including over 150 such organisations (see Kinnear *et al.* 2013, p. 5 for a detailed list) and peak bodies seeking to shape outcomes in the sector. A governance structure is required which can facilitate the vertical as well as horizontal coordination of policy. While we do not necessarily disagree with the question of the need for constitutional reform (for example, the devolution of the states and the rise of mega-councils, or the proposed new governance structure such as those suggested by Murray (2012) discussed below), we have also taken into consideration the nation's historical reluctance to pursue such kinds of reform. We have taken the view that while desirable, constitutional reform is perhaps not the first step to be taken to initially improve governmental arrangements, and as such we sought to identify options that policymakers may be able to consider as practical ways for moving forward towards longer-term and sustainable change.

Governance structure

Bringing together the insights developed by Paul Collits (this volume) and also work undertaken by Botterill (2009), Hogan *et al.* (this volume) proposed the establishment of an Office of the Commissioner for Country Australia as a statutory entity. This Office, made up of representatives of the jurisdictions and key stakeholder bodies (e.g. local councils and regional councils), supported by funded secretariats, would function in a similar manner to the way Safework Australia (and its predecessors such as WorkSafe Australia) have worked. Such an Office would have the capacity to develop a national strategic plan for country Australia which would coordinate the efforts of the jurisdictions as well as major stakeholders. In a participative and consultative fashion, the Office would develop priority policy targets to guide infrastructure and other forms of social expenditure (therein reducing duplication of effort) in order to coordinate and harmonise policy across and within jurisdictions (for further detail see Hogan and Young 2012). The insights arising from within this book suggest that key priority areas requiring coordinated national attention include natural resource management (including the rangelands), trans-regional aspects of localism, regional development and the question of the sustainability of country towns and villages, and rural social inclusion. The proposed governance structure would also provide a more appropriate mechanism for managing shorter-term reactive demands which arise from time to time for government. It provides a capacity to progress inter-regional issues in a strategic fashion. Such a body has the potential to address the many issues of multi-level governance arising in this space without having to secure constitutional change to progress it.

Other benefits may also be associated with the development of a new governance structure. It creates the capacity for an institutional memory to develop in this complex policy space. It can enable a breaking down of siloed approaches to governance, which to date have meant that policy learnings on specific issues or in specific spaces are not translated to new issues. A more coherent and stable governmental structure would also provide interested public servants with a viable career structure, and the benefit of creating a critical mass of expertise in this space. The idea of a council differs to Murray's (2012) idea of a governance process being centred upon the Council of Australian Governments (COAG). Not discounting Murray's proposal, we envisage a new kind of structure that provides resources for the kind of bureaucratic support that can be developed to support an Office focused on country Australia in its own right, and that supports the capacity of key stakeholders to participate in what would essentially be a public process.

The development of such an Office, however, is premised on the fact that policymakers actually want to join up the various policy approaches to country Australia (Jordan and Halpin 2006). But what if it is the case that overall policymakers are happy with the direction in which things are going and that they periodically put in place small yet insignificant programmes to address points of friction which may arise in the process from time to time (what Jordan and Halpin (2006) referred to as policy as a by-product of the main game; a main game which in this context is concerned with allowing markets to resolve issues of population and livelihoods in country Australia)? In proposing an Office of the Commissioner for Country Australia we take the view that all social problems cannot be left to markets to solve. La Perriere (1567) offered the important insight that government is about the right disposition of things, leading the community, as it were, to a convenient end. Such a process cannot be left to markets because markets are accountable to (often international) shareholders, and not to the Australian people. Markets are interested in profit optimisation where such optimisation is based upon minimising the cost of inputs and maximising the sale of outputs. They are not concerned with the welfare of individuals or their communities. What is required then is a governance structure whose focus is on addressing the policy outcomes which the community seeks.

Foucault compared the process of governance with the governance of a ship:

> It means clearly to take charge of the sailors, but also of the boat and its cargo; to take care of a ship means also to reckon with winds, rocks and storms; and it consists in that activity of establishing a relation between the

> sailors who are to be taken care of and the ship which is to be taken care of, and the cargo which is to be brought safely to port and all those eventualities like wind, rocks, storms and so on; this is what characterizes the government of a ship.
>
> (1991, p. 93)

Foucault's analogy of governance in terms of the steering of a ship can be extended to the governance of country Australia, the outcomes of which have already been described within this book. Country people are asking who is at the helm of this ship and in what direction is the ship being sailed? The storms and torrents of globalised economic life have rained down on rural and regional Australia (albeit factors which are not all in the control of policymakers), with members of these communities pointing out the evident risks and consequences of free market policy to the community, leaving them asking how will their communities be steered through such risks to safer harbours? For Foucault, laissez-faire economic policy is concerned with governments not impeding 'the flow of things'. But is not such a philosophy a strange underpinning for the governance of a society? Extending Foucault's analogy of the ship, it has to be asked whether or not one would simply let the *community* ship run aground or onto rocks, simply because that is where the wind blew or the currents led?

Central to the question of governance is the balancing of individual and collective needs. Insightfully, Foucault points out that the state doesn't sacrifice itself for individuals in the pursuit of the common good. Rather it is the other way around. But at issue here is exactly what is that common good (Gordon 1991), and how would we know it if we saw it? One thing is evident from this research – that there are boundaries to be placed around laissez-faire economics. A society that finds itself in the embrace of such a philosophy needs to be clear as to where those boundaries should lie. Moreover, it needs to be clear about the kinds of outcomes its governmental arrangements are facilitating and whether, as a society, these are the kinds of outcomes sought by the populace (Gordon 1991). This is a view that is echoed in the literature on governance. As Gordon remarks, policy is important because it 'determines citizens' rights and the conditions under which they will live and work' and by extension, the absence of policy is also policy because 'its non-agenda also by default, sets an agenda' (1991, pp. 28–29). Similarly, Gordon points out that governance structures which primarily focus 'on sectors and individuals distracts from the broader agenda of government which is its responsibility' (1991, p. 20).

Concluding remarks

Setting aside the aspirations and concerns of country Australia noted above, an issue that goes to the heart of this book is the sustainability of rural livelihoods. There is no getting away from the fact that today the family farm is limited in its capacity to support livelihoods compared with the way it used to. In the 1960s, for example, a family dairy farm in Tasmania may have carried 65 cows. Within

30 years that same farm carried over 250 cows, albeit that the farm was now larger in size while employing fewer people. At a national level, compared with other industries, agriculture is a minor employer and a comparatively small exporter. It adds the least value to the products it produces, and invests the least in industry research and development (Department of Innovation 2013). If at a national level policymakers are responsible for ensuring the well-being of citizens, there are compelling economic arguments that comparatively little focus be given to agriculture. Moreover, if the future of the industry lies within its capacity to further increase its international competitiveness, such competitiveness has to come from technological and mechanical innovation; innovations which in the past have resulted in fewer jobs in the agricultural sector.

However, we must not generalise the particular. Agriculture is just one part of country Australia. Country towns continue to provide significant infrastructure and services to other industries such as mining, transport and services – industries which are at the heart of the nation's contribution to gross domestic product. What is problematic in this setting though is the decoupling of the economic benefits of industry from the local communities (Hogan and Lockie 2013). Industries as such draw on the infrastructure provided by our key country towns, but may contribute little to maintaining their local economies whose resources they consume by the nature of their very existence. Local government budgets alone can be consumed by the impacts of heavy transport on their roads, particularly after periods of poor weather. While policymakers may well be justified, at an economic level, to provide less support to agriculture, it would be at the peril of Australia's push to improve its productivity to fail to provide the necessary infrastructure for ensuring that the country continues to provide its people with livelihoods. The relationship remains symbiotic. Industry inherently relies on the infrastructure provided by country people, while many country peoples' livelihoods also rely on the infrastructure. Similarly, if the promises of the digital economy are realised, one can envision new ways of living in country Australia. As our cities are increasingly congested, country living underpinned by jobs which provide livelihoods, offers a positive and healthy alternative to city living.

Australia has not developed a vision for country Australia since the post-war period. Since the late 1970s its policies have primarily focused on industry and economic development, and have used gross domestic product as the primary indicator of success. This focus has distracted policymakers away from the bigger issues for which they are constitutionally responsible. As Foucault suggests, 'government has as its purpose not the act of government itself, but the welfare of the population, the improvement of its condition, the increase of its wealth, longevity, health, etc…' (1991, p. 100). If one accepts that these are the ends to which government must work, then there are issues to be reconciled in country Australia. Notably there is a strong case for policymakers and citizens to work together towards the co-development of national policy that is designed to address the goals sought by the electorate. Importantly, there is a need for the development of policy specifically for country Australia. Within a constantly changing world, it is not realistic to expect that policy would be static over a long period of time. However, in steering policy through the storms and tempests which beset a nation, there needs to be a clear and coherent policy strategy which frames overall decision-making processes; one which has regard to the kinds of lives people living in country Australia wish to live.

The more recent policy language which frames the debate in terms of rural and regional Australia is formative, if not constructive. If only as a result of the development of the motor car, the nature of living in country Australia has changed. It may well be the case that the sun has set on the initial chapters of living in country Australia. It may well be that the future of living in country Australia must be understood at a regional level and that some form of hub and spoke or cluster model will be applied to the governance of country lives. Taking into account globalism, agribusiness, climate change and the internet, there may either be a further separation, or possibly a reunification, of country place and livelihood. Only time will tell. But the outcome is not really the point. What is at issue is that going into the future, governments at all levels need to engage with communities in the co-development of policy in a manner which is realistic, honest and collaborative.

Such a process assumes however that country people constitute a 'coherent public', that they can present a unified agenda to government, that such an agenda sits within the core policy programme being driven by the administration, and that such a policy programme is centred on an approach which seeks to link-up the various competing issues on the country and agricultural agendas (Jordan and Halpin 2006). The material presented in this book makes it evident that there is a core policy agenda at play in rural and regional Australia, an agenda which is about agricultural productivism, focused on the world stage, and that is based on the efficiency mantra. If it is the case then that the policy vision for country Australia is one centred on the ever-increasing productive efficiency of industries based in the rural or the regional, the socio-economic viability of many country settlements has to be at risk because such efficiencies are most readily gained by reducing input costs, particularly human labour. The push then for optimally efficient rural industries comes at the cost of rural jobs and the continued loss of jobs means an ever-decreasing capacity for the rural or the regional to provide livelihoods for the people who live there. As such, a policy programme centred on ensuring optimally efficient rural industries is unlikely, at the same time, to result in more vibrant, prosperous rural communities.

If it is the case that the sun has set on this initial phase of populating inland Australia, it is difficult to imagine a future for many country towns. Everywhere one travels across non-urban Australia, one encounters communities trying to identify some distinctive feature of their local community which may give them some advantage over others; an advantage that might throw them a socio-economic lifeline. At best, communities grapple to find a new industry which might provide jobs, hope that ageing city people in search of cheaper retirement living will settle in their community or hope that more people might want to visit their area on their lap around Australia. However, in the absence of substantive strategic change – the kind of change which can provide for livelihoods – one has to wonder what the future will hold for many communities in country Australia.

Note

1 Book accessed via Kindle; quote found at Chapter 1, location 678.

References

Adams, P 2011, 'Rural-urban divide in Australia?', *Late Night Live*, ABC.

Botterill, L 2009, 'Rural Policy Challenges', *Future of Farming Forum*, CEDA, South Australia, 18 September.

Botterill, LC 2011, 'Fair Share: Correspondence', *Quarterly Essay*, no. 43, pp. 129–131.

Boully, L and Maywald, K 2011, 'Basin Bookends, the Community Perspective', in Connell, D and Grafton, RQ (eds), *Basin Futures: Water reform in the Murray–Darling Basin*, ANU E Press, Canberra.

Brett, J 2011, 'Fair Share. Country and City in Australia', *Quarterly Essay*, no. 42, pp. 1–67.

Collits, P 2015, *Regional Policy in Australia Since World War II*, this volume.

Connell, D and Grafton, RQ (eds) 2011, *Basin Futures: Water Reform in the Murray–Darling Basin*, ANU E Press, Canberra.

Cockfield, G 2015, 'From state direction to community self-efficacy: The devolution of responsibility for regional development in Australia', this volume.

Collits, P 2015, 'Regional Policy in Australia Since World War II', this volume.

Department of Innovation 2013, 'Key Facts: Australian Industry 2011–2013'. Available at: www.innovation.gov.au/Industry/ReportsandStudies/Documents/KeyFactsAustralianIndustry.pdf. Accessed: 23 July 2013.

Edwards, G 2013, 'Regions and innovation: a reflection', in Kinnear, S, Charters, K and Vitartas, P (eds), *Regional advantage and innovation – achieving Australia's national outcomes*, Springer Verlag, Heidelberg, pp. 151–170.

Foucault, M 1991, 'Questions of method', in Burchell, G, Gordon, C and Miller, P (eds), *The Foucault effect – Studies in Governmentality*, Harvester Wheatsheaf, London, pp. 73–86.

Gordon, C 1991, 'Governmental rationality: An introduction', in Burchell, G, Gordon, C and Miller, P (eds), *The Foucault effect – Studies in Governmentality*, Harvester Wheatsheaf, London, pp. 1–52.

Hogan, A, Hanslip, M, Kancans, R, Russell, J and Maguire, B 2008, 'Social wellbeing of Australians – a comparative analysis of people working on farms in drought affected areas versus the Australian population using the Deakin Well-being Index', in *It's about people – changing perspectives on dryness. A report to Government by an expert social panel*, Bureau of Rural Sciences, Canberra. Available at: www.daff.gov.au/__data/assets/pdf_file/0007/836206/drought-pol-rep-app.9–11.pdf. Accessed: 21 March 2013.

Hogan, A and Young, M 2012, *Visioning a future for rural and regional Australia*, The National Institute for Rural and Regional Australia, The Australian National University, Canberra. Available at: http://nirra.anu.edu.au/news/scoping-vision-future-rural-regional-australia-discussion-paper-released. Accessed: 21 March 2013.

Houghton, K 2011, 'Characteristics of economic sustainability in regional Australia', unpublished discussion paper prepared for the HC Coombs Policy Forum, Australian National University.

Jordan, G and Halpin, D 2006, 'The political costs of policy coherence: constructing a rural policy for Scotland', *Journal of Public Policy*, vol. 26, no. 1, pp. 21–41.

Kraft, ME and Furlong, SR 2012, *Public policy: Politics, analysis and alternatives*, Sage Publications Ltd (CQ Press), London.

Kinnear, S, Charters, K and Vitartas, P (eds) 2013, *Regional advantage and innovation – achieving Australia's national outcomes*, Springer Verlag, Heidelberg.

Kinnear, S and Ogden, I 2013, 'Integrating innovation, sustainability and regional development goals: delivering national policy through "regional collaboratives"', in Kinnear, S, Charters, K and Vitartas, P (eds), *Regional advantage and innovation – achieving Australia's national outcomes*, Springer Verlag, Heidelberg, pp. 99–136.

La Perriere (1567) cited in Foucault, M 1991, 'Questions of method', in Burchell, G, Gordon, C and Miller, P (eds), *The Foucault effect – Studies in Governmentality*, Harvester Wheatsheaf, London, pp. 73–86.

Lockie, S 2000, 'Crisis and conflict: shifting discourses of country Australia', in Pritchard, B and McManus, P (eds), *Land of Discontent: The dynamics of change in Country Australia*, UNSW Press, Sydney.

Perrem, K 2013, 'Innovation in regional Australia: Effective, lagging and under-utilised', in Kinnear, S, Charters, K and Vitartas, P (eds), *Regional advantage and innovation – achieving Australia's national outcomes*, Springer Verlag, Heidelberg, pp. 21–40.

Quinn, J and Kirby, S 2013, 'The challenges of delivering a "sustainable Australia"', in Kinnear, S, Charters, K and Vitartas, P (eds) 2013, *Regional advantage and innovation – achieving Australia's national outcomes*, Springer Verlag, Heidelberg, pp. 41–72.

Rural Women's Network 2007, *Rural/Urban Divide Information and Statistics Report*, New South Wales Department of Primary Industry. Available at: www.dpi.nsw.gov.au/rwn/resources/rwn-state-advisory-committee-ruralurban-divide-statistics-project. Accessed: 3 June 2014.

Salt, B 2011, 'Fair Share: Correspondence', *Quarterly Essay*, no. 43, pp. 135–136.

Titmuss, R 2006, 'Universalism versus selection' in Pierson, C and Castle, FG (eds), *The Welfare State Reader*, Polity Press, Manchester, Great Britain, pp. 40–48.

Tonts, M 2000, 'The restructuring of Australia's rural communities', in Pritchard, B and McManus, P (eds), *Land of Discontent: The dynamics of change in Country Australia*, UNSW Press, Sydney.

Wahlquist, A 2003, 'Media representations and public perceptions of drought', in Botterill, LC and Fisher, M (eds), *Beyond Drought: People, Policy and Perspectives*, CSIRO, Collingwood, Victoria.

19 Reclaiming livelihoods

Initial steps to re-institute a viable socio-economic base for living in country settings

Anthony Hogan, Bruce Wilson, Douglas Baker, Lorelle Burton, Laurie Buys and Michael Cuthill

Introduction

A key feature of this text is that it unpacks the way neoliberal or free trade policies have been applied to agriculture and, in turn, living in country Australia over the past 40 years. Chapter 18 contains an overview of these changes and initiatives. This book sets out not just to lay before the reader the many impacts of this change process, but also to open up a new way forward. This process started in Chapter 18, which explores the issues of a governmental approach to change. This chapter focuses on responses that can be initiated from a community perspective. But before outlining the capacity for progress on these issues we must first identify the heart of the problem – our concern with the intensification of globalised free trade and what this means for the continued viability of country living. At the heart of this concern is that the changing way in which globalising enterprises operate increasingly constrains, at a local level, opportunities for everyday families and small businesses to maintain their livelihoods and communities. Much of the angst underpinning change in country settings centres on the extent to which cultures and community can be maintained. For Chris Hedges (2010; noting the work of Polyani) – unfettered capitalism results in the death of society. And so, this question of balancing the interface of economy and society is at the heart of this project. We revisit the question of what is the purpose of economy, if it is not to support peoples' livelihoods? This is the issue that we need to unpack somewhat before proceeding with the remainder of this closing chapter.

Free trade policies were designed to optimise the capacity for industry to maximise their return on investment, based on the philosophy of 'buy low, sell high', within a context of increasing globalised markets (Carr and Kefalas 2009). With the gradual removal of tariffs, producers who could conduct their businesses on a global scale were positioned to benefit. They were able to shift productive processes to places where they could cheaply access the factors of production (land, labour and capital), while being able to sell their products back into western markets at or near the usual price. Patel's (2007) study of coffee sales is a case in point. Yet as Carr and Kefalas have made evident, these kinds of policies were always going to be socially problematic, particularly for small family producers. They set in play a whole new agrarian revolution, on a global scale, displacing many family based producers and their families, while impoverishing many others. Central to this change process has been the disembedding of localised labour relations from the economic base and the subsequent decoupling of established communities from the local, and in turn global, economy (Bligh 2006). A new form of social relations resulted – a set of relations that conflates community identity and well-being with the success of global markets.

This new form of social relations has installed the price mechanism as the primary policy instrument for organising the economy. This is serving to restructure the nature of relations between business, labour and the state (Bligh 2006) with the enterprise becoming the true subject of government (Foucault 2008). Crudely installing price as the organising principle of the market, to the benefit of the enterprising subject, has also resulted in the social body and its governance being increasingly organised 'according to the rules of the economy' (Foucault 2008, p. 242). The emergence of free markets, the privileging of the globally oriented enterprising subject, and the devolution of both the means for community livelihoods and social protections, have had significant effects. It is not only country communities and regions that find themselves in a vulnerable position – whole aspects of our economies are increasingly constrained in their capacity to progress their economic development (Markusen 2007). The demise of manufacturing in westernised countries is a case in point. Australia has recently witnessed the loss of iconic producers of cars and white goods to so-called cheaper overseas countries, along with aircraft maintenance for our national carrier, all in the name of greater efficiency. The self-evident rationality of the logic of efficiency is put forward as though there were no local down sides to globalising processes. Developments in transport, information and communications technologies further accelerate these processes of change. These latter developments create radically different conceptions of the relationship between space and time, further weakening the link between locality, economy and community.

The issue here is not that one means of production has yielded to another. Some would argue that this is part of the natural progression for a society. The scale and social impact of this change process is the issue here, considering that not only agriculture but also manufacturing, business services, banking and increasingly medical services, are all following the same path. While automatic telling and online access did not mean the end of employment in banking, it certainly changed the nature of banking and the size of banks. Mechanising farming has not resulted in the end of food production, or consumption. However, changes in banking, education, governance, health care and agriculture are all central to the demise of rural living, as they underpin the basics of localised economies (Hogan *et al.* 2013). The combined impact of such change manifests itself in the loss of jobs and subsequent loss of local spending, resulting in many inland settlements, in their current form, being no longer socio-economically viable. Unlike cities, the play of the economic hand is quite manifest in country centres – one's expenditure is literally the other person's income. In the country setting one can more readily see the broader social consequences of spending patterns, whereas in cities, they are masked in anonymity. In the city, if a shop closes, another trader soon seems to take its place. In the country, a shop closes and it tends to stay empty. However, unlike many urban settings, in country settings it is most likely that you personally know the people affected.

At the same time, communities have witnessed the concurrent devolution of the role of the state to dispersed individual actors. Notions of localism proliferate. Workers, who would have once turned to the state for support and the protection of their livelihoods, are dislocated from the market (Bligh 2006). In the era of localised self-sufficiency, the state is increasingly shifting the responsibility for well-being onto individuals (Hogan and Lockie 2013). Writers such as Hedges (2010) foresee the death of the middle classes. New forms of social dominance will replace the benefits of several hundred years of enlightenment and the devolution of slavery, serfdom, classes and monarchical rule. But, in this case, the increasingly powerful but relatively small ruling classes have no responsibility for those who are unable to provide for themselves.

Just as the last agrarian revolution was closely associated with significant social, environmental, industrial and economic change, so too is this one. The last such change process was associated with significant transactional costs to those that it marginalised. There are significant socio-economic transactional costs associated with this change process; the global phenomenon of farmer suicide is just one (Hogan *et al.* 2012). One can question whether society is any better at managing processes of change now than we were several hundred years ago. Namely, that the costs of change are allowed to lay where they fall (Titmuss 2006) and that the process of change is set up to benefit the few at the cost of the many. In its initial stages this process was evident in the increasing differences between the very rich and the very poor, while the middle and upper middle across the world enjoyed increasing living standards. Notwithstanding that this is an issue in itself, concerns continue to be expressed that it is not just rural communities but also the middle classes that are now being hollowed out of the social equation. Our analysis of 40 years of rural and regional policy makes it evident that there is a long term policy in place, irrespective of whether it has been declared or not (Stoker 2012), and this is a policy that in its implementation provides for the depopulating of the rural or country space. The key issue on the table then is this – country people wish to continue to live in country places (see Chapter 18). The question in response to this demand within a democratic context, is what can be done to enable such a vision for living to be realised? There are a range of policy strategies at play that may ensure the viability of country settlements. We are going to look at these settings and consider why we cannot deploy such strategies simplistically, particularly when considering the issue of spatiality. We need to do this because we constantly see advocates taking up specific policy agendas without thinking through the consequences they may have for the situation of interest. We will then move on from being grumbly sociologists to identifying other ways of progressing the socio-economic viability of country settlements.

Localism as a response to globalisation

Among some policymakers, rural decline is not necessarily a problem. Their perspective is that those early forms of country living have served their purpose and it is now time to progress. Others believe many inland parts of Australia should never have been populated. Hindsight, informed by globalism and climate change, can provide a certain clarity in perspective. For many, decline, consolidation and the restructuring of the rural sector are nothing more than the realisation of the inevitable, the maturation of the neoliberalist strategy – there is no alternative. At the same time, local people are looking for ways to arrest decline and have embraced notions of localism as a way to solve their challenges. Localism has remerged across OECD countries as a policy strategy to provide local people with the capacity to take decisions which impact on the viability of their livelihoods (for a recent review of localism see Evans 2013). Hogan *et al.* (2013) point out that the strength of localism as a policy is that it situates place, rather than sector, at the centre of questions about the sustainability of inland communities in Australia. It identifies both a strategy and a national resource stream to fund development and change.

However, this text highlights that significant negatives offset such benefits. First, Collits (2013) observed that the social as well as economic issues impacting on the viability of in-land settlements may be beyond the control of local communities. For example, this includes the historic highs which the Australian dollar recorded over recent years and the dumping of agricultural products from a variety of sources into the Australian market. Similarly, factors such as increasing climate variability, and emergent climate change and globalisation, cannot be addressed at a local level. Second, the resources allocated to the process fell well short of what was required. Hogan *et al.* (2013) suggested that addressing the adaptive needs of Australia's regional development bodies would require a funding allocation of $55 billion. Even that, they argue, could not ensure the sustainability of such communities.

While regional policy continues to focus on the question of the sustainability of rural communities, Hogan and Lockie (2013) point out that at its centre, Australia's form of localism is centred on a principle of economic Darwinism. That is, under the current global economic settings, only some communities have access to the diversity of economic, natural and social resources required to be sustainable. Other communities, at best, will survive as dormitory townships in relation to these, or will wither on the vine (Hogan and Young 2013b). This outcome is in stark contrast to the policy rhetoric many of the nation's political leaders put forward. It seems unlikely under the existing policy settings that Australia's deserts will bloom again, if they ever did (Gross 2013). Yet, policymakers enthusiastically look to develop agriculture in areas such as Northern Australia (which is sparsely populated, has few available workers or accommodation, has a variety of climate patterns and challenging growing conditions, consists of rangelands and poor soils, and is isolated from markets) using a model that is not based upon family farming but on large, increasingly, globalised agribusiness. If agriculture is deemed to be uneconomic in places such as Tasmania (great soils, good rainfall, available workforce, good climate prospects but also geographically isolated) and parts of the Murray–Darling Basin (currently producing large proportions of Australian agricultural product), why would Northern Australia suddenly offer a viable alternative – unless of course there was a way to step around Australia's labour, wages and health and safety laws. But we digress. The question remains as to the extent to which economic policy adequately enables us to realise a vision for a populated, vibrant, and equitable rural and regional Australia (Smith and Pritchard 2013). This question takes on particular salience as change will continue to impact on country Australia.

Ongoing change

In country Australia in the 1930s, children would commonly walk or ride a horse to school. When Max Hogan (the first author's father) was a boy living in the Central West of New South Wales, he took 30 minutes to ride a horse 8 km to school. On Sundays his family drove the sulky 12 km to church, taking 45 minutes to get there. Both the school and the church are now closed. Those living in this area must now access school and church services by driving 30 minutes to the regional centre, which is 59 km away. Country people now commonly drive up to an hour to use the facilities available in regional shopping centres. They justify such journeys on the basis that regional centres offer cheaper prices (such as being able to purchase a $5 imported tee-shirt) without regard to the longer-term consequences of globally driven cannibalising market strategies designed to eliminate local competition.

Transport has been increasingly mechanised and streamlined. Agriculture is now also increasingly being mechanised while other labour intensive tasks are being designed out of existence through genetic modification (such as cotton). Producers can now single-handedly run large properties, using machinery (which can weed, cull and harvest a crop) and irrigation systems that are operated remotely. A similar situation exists with various machinery used in the mining sector. Mines are now staffed by fly in, fly out workers who are housed in dongas on the edge of townships. This living situation draws little if any of their needs from the local economy.

It is difficult to imagine that people would be prepared to give up the motorcar for the horse and sulky. It is readily imaginable that increased efforts will be made to improve links between farming regions and their markets so that products can be transported faster and cheaper. This further reduces the time distance between centres, opening up a greater choice of jobs and shopping experiences to residents in some smaller towns and villages. It is also readily imaginable that better broadband systems will allow many services currently provided in country towns to be accessed online (see Hogan and Young 2013b), placing further downward pressure on the viability of existing country services.

It is difficult to imagine that effective steps will be taken in the coming decade to prevent substantive global warming and thus climate change. In fact, country communities may face greater climate variability as well as shifts in weather and rainfall patterns. Similarly, one can expect that globalised agri-interests will continue to pursue greater productive efficiencies by continuing to mechanise their productive processes, while it is quite likely that there will be continued downward pressures on wages and conditions in westernised markets.

Recognising the issue of spatiality

The spatial and historical development of regions defines the socio-cultural and economic base that underlies most of Australia's country areas, yet there is little research that develops spatial theories unique to Australia. While regional decline is evident across most OECD (2006) communities, there are only a few member countries (e.g. the United States, Canada, Mexico and Spain, as well as Australia) where issues of rural place and space interface with policy in a profound and consequential manner. In many European countries, for example, there would be few rural settlements more than two hours' drive from a major regional centre or city. In any event, the European Union Common Agricultural Policy (CAP) has existed for many years to support farming families and sectors to adapt steadily to increasing global competition, and their incorporation into the European Union. Not so in countries such as Australia, particularly the outback, where the size of cattle stations can readily exceed 500,000 ha and where the drive to the nearest major metropolitan centre can be counted in days rather than hours. Where government support for transition has been available, it has been segmented and limited to arguably a specific individual's interests rather than to the collective needs of country communities and towns. Concerns exist that a more sophisticated form of pork-barrelling is at play, but there is little evidence to support such an assertion.

Relative proximity to a major metropolitan centre can mean that people living in a given place can continue to live within a rural setting and commute to employment elsewhere, if or when the economic base underpinning their livelihoods undergoes a significant shift. However, living more than two hours' drive from a major metropolitan or regional centre limits their capacity to adapt readily. Even where the nearest regional centre is within commuting distance, in Australia few of these have a population of more than 30,000 to 40,000 people. The problem is that settlements of this size have limited employment opportunities and tend to remain static, in population terms, over the longer term. The population of the city of Goulburn (inland New South Wales) has grown by barely 10 per cent in the past 40 years, with an increasing proportion of that population migrating out of the city to work in places such as Canberra.

Australia does have some notably large regional centres in its physically largest states (e.g. Queensland, New South Wales and Western Australia); however such regional centres tend to be situated on the coastal fringe. Other than Canberra, Albury-Wodonga, Wagga or Toowoomba, there are very few large inland centres in these states. This in turn means that when the traditional economic base that underpins such settlements declines (for example, the nineteenth century gold rush and pastoralism centred on farming families), there are few ready alternatives for local employment and thus reduced opportunities to support livelihoods and population. Victoria is interesting in that it has a number of large regional centres, most of which are also within a two-hour commuting distance of the city of Melbourne. In some ways, however, this has exacerbated the same trend in the decline of small towns; while some regional centres might be strengthening, it is still at the expense of communities that are 50–100 km distant.

Finally, Australian Government policy has not conceived its rural and regional space to be little more than places from which natural resources can be extracted and exported elsewhere. By and large, extraction from the rural and regional space has structured the development of rural and regional communities. The presence of these products (these staples) in conjunction with the capacity to efficiently extract and transport these staples out of the region to market, shapes a region in regard to it its place in the economy (Bunker 1989).

Space and time (to remove the resource) are significant elements in how a region develops, coupled with strong transport infrastructure. Bunker further argues that in such regions, 'the greater direct dependency on natural or environmental factors on the one hand and on external markets on the other constrains extractive economies in ways quite alien to analysts whose frame of reference is derived from industrial experiences…' (p. 592). Thus, the difference between industrial production economies in urban centres and the external regional economy that remains extractive, produces an 'unbalanced relationship' (p. 608) that is spatially, culturally and economically defined. Within this context the regional economies are tied to the export of the staple and the evolving economies are unable to diversify (see McCann and Gunn 1998; Filion 2010).

There are definite similarities between the Australian and Canadian experiences. The staples thesis underscores many of the issues facing country Australia and that are central to debates about the viability of industries in Tasmania (and that will confront the Northern Australia experiment as it seeks to expands its primary productive capacity while competing with access to export opportunities in the face of mineral and ore extraction). More broadly, the staples extracted from particular regions have determined the growth and decline of many country settlements. As the nature of markets and productive processes change, the capacity for a given area of industry to support employment, infrastructure needs and social networks, will also change.

Recent planning developments, such as those occurring in regional Queensland, underscore regional dependency on staples. After a decade of agonising over the role of regional planning in Queensland, and several iterations of regional plans, the most recent approach launched in 2013, reduces regional planning to support economic development in agriculture, mining and extractive resources, development and construction, and tourism (State Planning Policy Draft for Consultation). Planning, it seems, privileges industry and exports over any existing environmental or social concerns (Matthews 2013).

In these circumstances, it is hardly surprising that many have lost confidence in the state's capacity to service the interests of country people. On the one hand, government policy helped populate rural Australia in the first instance (see for example Henderson 2013 and Gross 2013). Policymakers wanted productive agricultural and mining industries and they wanted people to live in rural settings and work in such industries. Settler policies were put in place, which allocated farming blocks to returning soldiers and other settlers, even if at times such blocks were not suitable for sustained farming (Alston 2013). Some towns, such as Coleambally in inland New South Wales, were specifically established as part of policy initiatives in irrigated agriculture. Now, with the changes to the economic base, coupled with a changing environment, the wisdom of these earlier policy decisions is being called into question (see for example Murray–Darling Basin Authority 2010).

So the state has established a set of expectations and interests that have taken root, literally, over several generations, but has then adopted policy that undermines those expectations fundamentally, in support of a new set of interests. And herein lies the problem. Two distinct shifts in governance have occurred. The role of governance is now increasingly concerned with managing the interests of the financially vested on the one hand while seeking to disqualify itself from social action on the other (Foucault 2008). Industry seeks government support for the infrastructure it requires, or requests bail-outs to support its ailing enterprises. Similarly essential to their success, is disabling the governance processes that put such infrastructure in place – mechanisms that were also put in place to protect the interests of people. These public interests are manifested in and around the equitable distribution of income, social wages, public goods and regulatory processes which ensure a form of economic growth centred on the livelihoods of the people (Foucault 2008).

We have questioned the purpose of economy in relation to society. We must also question the role of formal government in relation to its people. If we reject the price mechanism as the principle upon which social and governance relations are organised, what 'should be the organising principle of governmental practice' (Foucault 2008, p. 29)? Cuthill (2004) has argued that community well-being is the ultimate goal of democratic governance. If the answer to this question, at least in part, is the well-being of its people and their capacity to provide for their own livelihoods, then the first thing that must happen is that price can no longer be the sole criteria or value that informs policy.

Price and the market system have to be tempered by other values. Until such values are brought forward and validated, it is difficult to see how the interests and well-being of regional Australians can be more broadly progressed. As Aarons (2009, p. 205) observes,

> ...effective policies have to be created through the power of ideas in contest: governments adequate for tackling present challenges can only come about by complex political and other processes which involve building a majority opinion for effective concrete policies expressing a wide social philosophy.

Central to this task is recognising that the issues impacting on country people, in western societies, are not that different from those impacting on urban dwellers.

Embracing the need for a value other than price as a principle for organising society

The 40-year sequence of institutional change in specific westernised country communities has disrupted well-institutionalised practices centred on productive family-based enterprises. This has put in train a process of rural transition. The focus on price as the organising principle and the subsequent focus on scaleable profit margins furthered a transition towards the optimal mechanisation and technological innovation around production. This subsequently made the capacity for scale and the elimination of labour critical factors in underpinning the organisation of markets. In short, neoliberalism put in place a set of economic relations, which could only benefit large players over smaller ones (Carr and Kefalas 2009) and issued a death warrant for small, localised producers.

This text focuses on country-based forms of production. We could tell a similar story about manufacturing, and soon about numerous other industries such as accounting, banking, information technology, health, education and food services. In short, any industries that can eliminate, reduce or outsource the inputs of labour are up for grabs. This strategy has efficiency, not people's livelihoods, as its central agenda and causes a situation which Bligh (2006, p. 9) refers to as 'Knightian uncertainty' wherein agents became 'unsure as to what their interests actually are. Let alone how to realize them'. How likely would it be, for example, that by further embracing market principles country people would be able to realise their social or economic interests? If they could, how would they do so in the context of processes which disembed local labour and subsequently contribute to the decoupling of their economy from their community?

Or, is it time, as De Sousa Santos (2008) suggests, for communities to consider alternate ways of organising production that provide for livelihoods at a local level? Communities could pursue a 'market economy on the non-capitalist principles of cooperation and mutuality', and develop an economic practice based on the values of 'autonomy, participatory democracy, equality, equity and solidarity' (Birchall 1997, cited in De Sousa Santos and Rodriguez-Garavito 2008, p. xxvii). Increasingly, country communities have to recognise that the globalising impacts of neoliberalism have left them in a developmental status, economically, such that they must re-envision economy and society through a new lens.

Re-envisioning the basis for the socio-economic viability of living in country settings

While country disruption and the need for change might stem from economic restructuring, Bligh suggests that communities can create new sequences and social processes which result in new institutional arrangements. In the context of

Knightian uncertainty, it is evident that there is not one strategy that will fix all ills (Bligh 2006). The adage must be applied, that if you have seen one country town, you have seen *one* country town. While globalised and generic performance indicators might serve to paint a homogenous picture of country people, any inquiry into the dynamics of a given area draws specific attention to the fact that the drivers, barriers and challenges to socio-economic viability vary from place to place. This means that all options are on the table and that the socio-economic viability of a given community may result from a variety of contributing factors. Inherently communities might seek to attract a new, big producer to town (what Carr and Kefalas refer to as elephant hunting). For the shorter term, such strategies can buy the community time. However, communities with which we have worked find themselves experiencing future shock (Toffler 1990) as they battle with the impacts of winning and losing a series of such industries over time.

To begin with, communities seeking to sustain or transform themselves have to start by first accepting that they are in a state of Knightian uncertainty – that it is hard to know what is in their best interests for the future. As Latour (2004) has observed, it is necessary to recognise that one has been affected, in this case, by the structural factors that are at play, and this realisation itself has to result from a sensitisation process (Hogan *et al.* 2012). This process of sensitisation involves methods that help enable communities to understand the process of change that they have been through, and to gain insight into the options available to them through which they might reimagine their futures (Taylor, 2004; Friere 1973). These insights are carefully and sensitively gained through methods such as those of the Sustainable Communities project (Hogan and Phillips 2013).

Central to the success of such processes is the organisation and development of localised governance structures, which give communities enough control over their infrastructure development and economic processes so that they can make the changes they need. This requires a rethinking of values, a reconsideration as to the extent to which organic social bonds exist and can be redeveloped centred on the notion of place and shared living experiences. It is a new form of *gemeinschaften* (Tonnies 1971), less the limitations of more traditional forms of patriarchal, kin-based community relations. While communities may not return to a family-based value system, they may rediscover the extent to which a shared social and economic structuring of their livelihoods is central to their survival and well-being.

At the same time, it may also be important to revisit the fact that country communities operate differently, in a social sense, to urbanised communities. Urban conceptions of the social should not be imposed on the country. In these contexts, public infrastructure funding must help generate sustainable local economic flows, which support local livelihoods. Community banks, competitive within the finance sector, can generate profits which support the development of critical local initiatives that can in turn reinvest in projects that generate livelihoods. To realise localism, then local people must own the means of production and the proceeds of such endeavours must stay in the local communities.

To achieve this, we must develop and use the wealth of expertise held by retiring baby boomers, many of whom wish to contribute something meaningful and significant to local communities, on a voluntary basis. It also means developing a genuinely civil economy – an economy whose primary purpose is to support the livelihoods of local people. Last, it needs new, locally-organised governance processes that can work with the community to develop its local vision, from a sound evidence base (Hogan and Phillips 2013) and in turn establish the institutional processes needed to create new forms of locally oriented productive activity. At the same time, we need to be realistic. A given geographic area may be limited in the extent to which it can provide livelihoods for a given community. To sustain itself, such a community may have to understand its socio-economic base in relation to a broader regional centre.

Houghton (2013) has identified up to 15 critical economic enabling factors that country communities can draw upon to sustain their livelihoods. These include a matrix of opportunities which may be realised from production to service industries, with the mix of economy being distinct to the local area and its asset base. The European Union's emphasis on 'smart specialisation strategies', as an integral component of their Regional Policy for 2014–2020, takes this approach a stage further. It emphasises regional stakeholders developing detailed analyses of their local assets, human and natural, and exploring new opportunities to build economic value from these assets in global value chains (see European Union 2013). This approach starts to realistically link local livelihoods and the global market in a sustainable manner.

Three other immediate options are evident. First, various forms of economic gardening (Barrios and Barrios 2004) offer communities ways to develop a more sustainable local economy, developed from within. Economic gardening is based on developing a series of smaller projects, rather than trying to secure one key enterprise. Separately, these projects cannot support a whole community, but coupled together they can underpin success. Such a strategy requires an increasing willingness, certainly in Australia, for governments to decentralise their activities to regional centres. The presence of gaols, government agencies and institutions in a specific centre can create a flow-on effect. These cases must consider the delivery of the service at a reasonable rather than optimal cost. This again requires a rethinking of values. The health and social benefits of socialising the cost of running a system that is somewhat less efficient than optimal, but which also addresses broader social goals, needs to be considered. Price, as we noted, can no longer be the sole determinant structuring our society.

The second possibility arises from problems that have occurred in many of the communities that we have studied, where unemployment has resulted because a business entity, often with a multinational focus, decided that better margins could be made elsewhere. It did not necessarily mean that the enterprise itself was not viable, particularly when part of the focus was on providing livelihoods from a basis of a positive rather than ever-increasing or optimal return. A 'good-enough' return may well be sufficient to cover the costs of financing and regeneration while at the same time generating important localised economic flows.

Third, there is a ground-swell of interest around the idea of consumption-based economies. Markusen (2007), for example, using cases of small towns in Minnesota, argues that a consumption-based theory of development provides a strong antithesis to export-based theories. Investment in consumption-based activities such as health care facilities, retirement communities, and cultural centres helps recycle income back into the community and support local jobs and business. Little research has focused on consumption-based strategies as an alternative to industry-focused economic development. However, it is evident that many country communities are positioning themselves as, for example, country retirement hubs, where baby boomers can move from cities to a more affordable lifestyle in the country while still being able to access the services that they need.

This may create a domino effect, with younger families moving there and generating further demand for health, education and other services, thus pushing a town towards a critical and sustainable mass of population over time. Hub and spoke options are again possible within such scenarios. The city of Orange, in country New South Wales is a case in point. It is surrounded by a number of smaller villages, which in themselves are not able to provide a wide range of livelihoods. But they can prosper as people move to the area to take up work, not simply in agriculture or mining, but in a wider range of occupations, while enjoying the health and social benefits of country living.

Fourth, the hub and spoke model can be extended to other models of regional development. In country Australia at present, there is a lot of enthusiasm for developing tourism as an option for economic sustainability. On the one hand, there is only so much capacity for tourism in an area or in a region (or total tourism numbers in Australia – not enough to go around). There is, however, capacity for towns within the same region to team up to create a coherent overall tourism experience rather than one that seeks to cannibalise the other. The development of wine trails and regional tourist experiences (e.g. a programme of outdoor holiday experiences across a region) would be a case in point. Similarly, if resources are used strategically, with a view to an equity of outcomes, towns do not have to grow at the expense of others. In situations where several towns exist close by (e.g. Harden, Young and Boorowa in New South Wales), they can avoid community cannibalism by agreeing to each progress with a unique part of the regional infrastructure, such that the region grows as a whole. Those who have lived in small country areas know that the viability and diversity of enterprises can only occur if the community as a whole chooses to spread their business around. Else, a given business goes under.

Fifth, using the internet as a job-generating tool has not been readily deployed in countries such as Australia. Generally, Australian country towns have not systematically embraced the networked economy, despite the fact that the rolling-out of the nation's new broadband internet system was prioritised to country towns. As an enterprise development tool, we are seeing isolated examples of specific entrepreneurs using the internet to establish global businesses from country towns (e.g. florists, clothing manufacturers, spare parts businesses, editors). The capacity of businesses to secure niche positions within local and international markets via the internet is just one example of how a community, seemingly isolated from global opportunities, can create sustainable opportunities for local livelihoods. Similarly, there are numerous examples of individuals using the internet as a basis for working from country and sea-side locations, even on a part-time basis. To the extent that such individuals have distinct skills and business networks that enable them to pursue such work, their presence in country towns contributes to local economic flows. It would be naive though, not to consider that the internet can as much take local jobs as it might generate them.

By extending the development of community driven brokerage models, such as the *make-it-work* brokerage system in Narrabri (New South Wales), local communities have an additional model for sustained country employment. In Narrabri, community entrepreneurs recognised that there were a variety of employment opportunities in the cotton industry, mining industry and local council road works. Individually, there was not enough work in any individual opportunity to justify maintaining a permanent workforce in each industry. But collectively, there were year-round employment opportunities for a number of workers, provided that they could have access to some form of job security. The local council undertook to employ the workers and brokered them out to the respective industries. This ensured the workers had continuity of employment and hence economic security, which meant that they could continue to live in the area. Local governments can develop a similar service base to support the networked economy where the initial start-up risks can be socialised. Participating in the networked economy is concerned with providing internet-based services to overseas countries such that while they are sleeping, we are working. It means that the data that they need analysed quickly can be processed overnight and reported back to the business by the time they return to work the next day. By developing a capacity for working in the networked economy, country towns develop the capacity to attract professional staff to their areas with flow-on effects to social capital and service utilisation.

Sixth, the issue of mobile workforces, in this sense 'drive out, drive home', is also emerging as a basis upon which workers can live in country settings and be away at work for intensive periods. Embracing such models of employment requires a rethinking not just of what it means to go to work, but also in terms of what it means to be a part of a community and a family. It is readily viable as a short-term strategy, but it is far from apparent that it is a viable employment option for the bulk of a community.

These suggestions are just some ways we can apply innovative thinking to sustaining country communities. We must also address the readiness of local residents to make room for change and for new people. Across many of the towns in which we have worked, specific individuals have often tried to thwart change. Central to the Sustainable Communities methodology is garnering the extent to which the community as a whole supports specific changes. By taking a community-wide approach you can confidentially determine the extent to which naysayers represent community views.

There is a smorgasbord of methods for developing localised economic options. However, achieving sustained outcomes requires some reworking of how a community operates. Compromises will be necessary and public resources may be required to back specific entrepreneurs. Securing a viable lifestyle in country areas, where higher incomes are harder to come by, does raise the question of how much is enough. That is, pursuing a non-urban lifestyle, particularly, may mean letting go of some of the excesses of a consumer society.

Conclusion

Clearly, specific challenges confront country communities seeking to explore and advance viable and sustainable socio-economic alternatives at the localised level. Nonetheless, there is a wellspring of community, industry and government support for sustaining country communities, many of which face an unavoidable transition. Decision-makers at all levels are looking for ideas, skills and tools that will enable them to work through this process of socio-economic change towards a more prosperous future. This book has detailed how we have reached our present situation and what has caused current troubles. We have also sought to open up thinking and discussion on how to secure a preferred future. Working towards the sustainability of localised communities requires an openness and commitment to the rediscovery of community, of collective interest and of long-term collective action.

The crisis that neoliberalism constitutes for country living is such that a rethinking of values, priorities and ways of making a living is needed for many communities to move forward. It is a question, as the adage goes, of having the capacity to win both the hearts and minds of the community, as well as being able to coalesce such commitment into sustained and unified action. If anyone can do this, it is certainly country people! This book aims to make clear that the decline of rural areas is not the result of individuals making poor choices. Rather it has occurred as a result of broader societal and economic decisions. And similarly, new decisions can be made that help build new futures for regional Australian communities.

Country people value country living. The country is not simply a basis for generating livelihoods. Country living is about connectivity, manifested within a strong social and cultural life, often situated within a beautiful environment. Country spaces are much more than just places where agricultural production has occurred, or where untapped opportunities exist for future economic gain. Place is about the lived experience – of home, family, identity, country, culture and well-being (Tuan 1977). Similarly, country decline involves a far greater range of issues than simply the changing face of productive processes. It centres on the loss of country identity and culture. Thus in considering the importance of socio-economic change, it is important to distinguish carefully between the baby and the bathwater. What is the point, people may well ask, of giving up the country lifestyle to pursue the intergenerational accumulation of wealth development via ever more efficient processes, if the end point of such wealth is to try and find a different, quiet place in the country or by the sea with a quality of life no longer possible in one's existing country community.[1] At the end of the day one is faced with the question of what is the purpose of the economy in relation to society? For some the economy will have no relationship to society other than as a means of accumulating wealth. But for many, many others, the purpose of the economy is forever Maslowian; it is about meeting the needs of people to live and to enjoy a comparatively good quality of life. And for the majority of the people on this planet today, this is simply not the case.

Note

1 With apologies to the Buddhist story this analogy is drawn from.

References

Aarons, E 2009, *Hayek versus Marx*, Routledge Frontiers of Political Economy, London.

Bligh, M 2006, *Great transformations – economic ideas and institutional change in the twentieth century*, Cambridge University Press, New York.

Barrios, S and Barrios, D 2004, 'Reconsidering economic development: The prospects for economic gardening', *Public Administration Quarterly*, vol. 28, no. 1, pp. 70–101.

Bunker, S 1989, 'Staples, Links, and Poles in the Construction of Regional Development Theories', *Sociological Forum*, vol. 4, no. 4, pp. 589–610.

Carr, PJ and Kefalas, MJ, 2009, *Hollowing out the middle: The rural brain drain and what it means for America*, Beacon Press, Boston.

Cuthill, M 2004, 'Community well-being: The ultimate goal of democratic governance', *Queensland Planner*, vol. 44, no. 2, pp. 8–11.

De Sousa Santos, B (ed.) 2007, *Another production is possible – beyond the capitalist canon. Reinventing social emancipations: Towards new manifestos*, vol. 2, Verso, New York.

De Sousa Santos, B and Rodriguez-Garavito, CA 2007, 'Introduction: expanding the economic canon and searching for alternatives to neoliberal globalisation' in De Sousa Santos, B (2007) *Another production is possible – beyond the capitalist canon. Reinventing social emancipations: Towards new manifestos*, vol. 2, Verso, New York, pp. xvii–lxii.

Evans, M, Marsh, D and Stoker, G 2013, 'Understanding localism', *Policy Studies*, vol. 43, no. 4, pp. 401–407.

Filion, P 2010, 'Growth and Decline in the Canadian Urban System: The Impact of Emerging Economic, Policy and Demographic Trends', *GeoJournal*, vol. 75, pp. 517–538.

Foucault, M 2008, *The birth of bio-politics – lectures at the College de France 1978–1979*, Picador (Palgrave-Macmillan), New York.

Friere, P 1973, *Education for Critical Consciousness*, A Continuum Book, The Seabury Press, New York.

Hedges, C 2010, *Death of the liberal class*, Nation Books, New York.

Hogan, A, Scarr, E, Lockie, S, Chant, B and Alston, S 2012, 'Ruptured identity of male farmers: Subjective crisis and the risk of suicide', *Journal of Rural Social Sciences*, vol. 27, no. 3, pp. 118–140.

Hogan, A and Lockie, S 2013, 'The coupling of rural communities with their economic base: agriculture, localism, and the discourse of self-sufficiency', *Policy Studies*, vol. 43, no. 4, pp. 441–455.

Hogan, A and Young, M 2013, 'Visioning a future for rural and regional Australia', *Cambridge Journal of Regions, Economy and Society*, vol. 6, pp. 319–330.

Hogan, A and Phillips, R (in press), *Sustainable rural communities*, Rural Industries Research and Development Corporation, Canberra.

Latour, B 2004, 'How to talk about the body – The normative dimension of science studies', *Body Society*, vol. 10, no. 2–3, pp. 205–229.

Markusen, A 2007, 'A Consumption Base Theory of Development: An Application to the Rural Cultural Economy', *Agricultural and Resource Economics Review*, vol. 36, no. 1, pp. 9–23.

Matthews, A 2013, 'Institutional perspectives on operationalising climate adaptation through planning', *Planning Theory and Practice*, vol. 14, no. 2, pp. 198–210.

McCann, L and Gunn, A 1998, *Heartland-hinterland: A regional geography of Canada*, Prentice Hall, Toronto.

Murray–Darling Basin Authority 2010, *The Basin Plan – Forward.* Available at: www.mdba.gov.au/basin_plan. Accessed: 18 June 2010.

Patel, R 2007, *Stuffed and starved – markets, power and the hidden battle for the world food system*, Portobello Books Ltd, Great Britain.

Queensland Government 2013, *State Planning Policy Draft for Consultation*, Department of State Development, Infrastructure and Planning.

Taylor, C 2004, *Modern social imaginaries*, Public Planet Books, Duke University Press, London.

Toffler, A 1990, *Future shock*, Random House, LLC.

Tonnies, F 1971, 'On Gemeinschaft and Gesellschaft' in Trussi, M (ed.), *Sociology: The classic statements*, Random House, New York, pp. 145–154.

Tuan, YF 1977, *Space and place – the perspective of experience*, University of Minnesota Press, Minneapolis.

Index

Page numbers in *italics* denote tables, those in **bold** denote figures.

www.ingramcontent.com/pod-product-compliance
Lightning Source LLC
LaVergne TN
LVHW011108300926
849160LV00008B/313
* 9 7 8 1 1 3 8 3 7 9 2 6 8 *